ENGAGING MUSIC

ENGAGING MUSIC

Essays in Music Analysis

EDITED BY

DEBORAH STEIN
New England Conservatory of Music

New York   Oxford

OXFORD UNIVERSITY PRESS

2005

Oxford University Press

Oxford   New York
Auckland   Bangkok   Buenos Aires   Cape Town   Chennai
Dar es Salaam   Delhi   Hong Kong   Istanbul   Karachi   Kolkata
Kuala Lumpur   Madrid   Melbourne   Mexico City   Mumbai   Nairobi
São Paulo   Shanghai   Taipei   Tokyo   Toronto

Published by Oxford University Press, Inc.
198 Madison Avenue, New York, New York 10016
www.oup.com

Oxford is a registered trademark of Oxford University Press

Library of Congress Cataloging-in-Publication Data
Engaging music : essays in music analysis / edited by Deborah Stein.
      p. cm.
   Includes bibliographical references (p.) and index.
   ISBN 0-19-517010-5
      1. Musical analysis. I. Stein, Deborah J. (Deborah Jane)
MT90.E64 2004
780—dc22   2004043494

Printing number: 9 8 7 6 5 4 3 2 1

Printed in the United States of America
on acid-free paper

CONTENTS

Preface   ix

Introduction to Writing Analytical Essays, *William Marvin*   xi

PART I.   Introduction to Analytical Topics and Techniques

Rhythm, Meter, and Phrase

1. The Phrase Rhythm of Chopin's A-flat Mazurka, Op. 59, No. 2, *Charles Burkhart*   3
2. Hypermeter and Hypermetric Irregularity in the Songs of Josephine Lang, *Harald Krebs*   13

Pitch

*3. Schenker's Conception of Musical Structure, *Allen Forte*   30
4. "Learn to Draw Bob Hope!" Mort Drucker, Arnold Schoenberg, and Twelve-Tone Music, *Andrew Mead*   36

Form

5. Analyzing the Unity within Contrast: Chick Corea's "Starlight," *Ramon Satyendra*   50
6. Form in Rock Music: A Primer, *John Covach*   65

Musical Ambiguity

7. Introduction to Musical Ambiguity, *Deborah Stein*   77
*8. Attacking a Brahms Puzzle, *Edward T. Cone*   89

PART II.   Model Essays: Text and Music

*9. Figaro's Mistakes, *David B. Lewin*   99
*10. Motive and Text in Four Schubert Songs, *Carl Schachter*   110
11. Isolde's Transfiguration in Words and Music, *Patrick McCreless*   122

*This chapter contains material published previously. See p. 341 for original publishing information.

12. Meaning in a Popular Song: The Representation of Masochistic Desire in Sarah McLachlan's "Ice," *Lori Burns* **136**
13. In Search of Purcell's Dido, *Janet Schmalfeldt* **149**

PART III. Model Essays: Instrumental

Performance and Analysis

14. The *Presto* from Bach's G-Minor Sonata for Violin Solo: Style, Rhythm, and Form in a Baroque *Moto Perpetuo, Joel Lester* **167**
15. Dramatic Progression in Haydn, Sonata No. 46 in A-flat, *Adagio, Marion A. Guck* **180**

Form

16. Formal and Expressive Intensification in Shostakovich's String Quartet No. 8, Second Movement, *Roger Graybill* **191**
17. Playing with Forms: Mozart's Rondo in D Major, K. 485, *William Rothstein* **202**

Pitch

*18. Two Post-tonal Analyses, Webern, "Wie bin ich froh!" from *Three Songs*, Op. 25; Schoenberg, "Nacht," from *Pierrot Lunaire*, Op. 21, *Joseph N. Straus* **215**
19. "This music crept by me upon the waters": Introverted Motives in Beethoven's "Tempest" Sonata, *Richard Cohn* **226**
20. "Rounding Up the Usual Suspects?": The Enigmatic Narrative of Chopin's C-sharp Minor Prelude, *Charles J. Smith* **236**

Texture

21. Texture and Timbre in Barbara Kolb's *Millefoglie* for Chamber Orchestra and Computer-Generated Tape, *Judith Lochhead* **253**

Scores **273**
Glossary **327**
Selected Bibliography **333**
Index **343**

PREFACE

The idea for this book emerged one year when I taught a lively class of music majors; when assigned analysis papers, they requested analytical readings by music theorists to use as guides. I could only come up with a few suggestions that didn't presume more knowledge than the students already had. Thus *Engaging Music*—a book of essays about analysis by music theorists—was born.

As the project began, every theorist I asked to contribute expressed wholehearted enthusiasm. While some could not participate due to other obligations, many agreed to write an essay. All too soon the volume was full and many, many potential authors could not be included.

The result is this remarkable collection of essays. The topics range from introductions to specific analytical approaches to a wide variety of essays that model different analytical techniques. The composers examined range from Purcell and Bach to the classical (Haydn, Mozart, Beethoven) and nineteenth-century masters (Schubert, Schumann, Brahms, Chopin, and Wagner). The music of the twentieth century includes early repertoire of Bartók, Schoenberg, and Webern, as well as a recent work by Barbara Kolb. Three essays examine popular music, and three treat the music of women composers.

Five authors (Edward T. Cone, Allen Forte, David B. Lewin, Carl Schachter, and Joseph N. Straus) graciously allowed us to include previously written essays. The other contributors wrote new essays or tailored previous material for our intended audience of upper-level music students. The task was not easy: the authors had to provide essays that were free of technical language from sophisticated analytical systems and didn't require explanation of numerous unfamiliar terms and concepts. Authors also had to contend with constraints of length and a limited number of musical examples.

In addition to a wealth of readings on a variety of topics and analytic approaches, this volume offers a glimpse into the lively discipline of music theory. In 2003, the Society of Music Theory celebrated its twenty-fifth anniversary; some of the approaches offered here were part of the beginnings of the new music theory discipline, Schenkerian analysis, set theory, and twelve-tone theory, as well as history of theory. As these analytic methodologies continued to develop, new approaches emerged, including the development of computer programs for music theory and analysis and the application of interdisciplinary models, such as feminism, linguistics, philosophy, aesthetics, semiotics, narratology, and mathematics. The field of psychology, especially of cognition, has been of enduring interest, while literary criticism has been a more recent influence. The pioneering work of Carl Schachter in the 1980s led to an important investigation of tonal rhythm and meter. And a broadening of the canon has led to increased study of women's music, world music, and popular music. To this day, many new techniques are being invented to address the diverse music composed throughout the twentieth century.

Ultimately, this book is about love of music, love that is nurtured through careful study and exploration. The authors have demonstrated their love of music with enthusiasm and respect for the art of music. We open the door and bid our readers to enter and share in what we do and what we cherish in our work. Do come on in and stay awhile!

ACKNOWLEDGMENTS

I first want to thank my fellow contributors, whose help and support extended far beyond submitting essays. In our group deliberations of definitions for the glossary, items for the selected bibliography, even the book's ultimate title, this wonderful group of theorists gave generously of their time and their ideas. Our discussions were stimulating and fascinating; the authors in this book are a talented, thoughtful, inventive group of teachers, performers, composers, and scholars!

I also want to thank several people for special contributions to the book: Cynthia Gonzales, for her generous assistance during the beginning stages of this project; John Roeder and Charles J. Smith, for help with computer software issues, especially the many fonts used for musical notation. Thanks, too, to New England Conservatory librarians Jean Morrow and Richard Vallone, for cheerful assistance in finding many needed resources. A special thanks is due to my friend and colleague Roger Graybill, who offered assistance in many ways: reading drafts of my writing; providing a sounding board for much rumination about difficult issues; giving support and encouragement, especially in the final few months; and helping me laugh during times of incredible stress.

I received two generous grants for this book. I thank the Society for Music Theory for a subvention grant and the New England Conservatory for a faculty development grant. This financial support made it possible to pay for many preparatory aspects of the book, including setting the musical examples into Finale.

Four students made important contributions to this project. At the early stage, Joelle Welling, then at the University of Texas at Austin, helped secure reprint permissions and assisted in many other important ways. At the final stage of the project, three students from the New England Conservatory provided critical help as well. Composers Marcin Bela and Derek Jacoby put over one hundred musical examples into Finale, all done with grace and good humor; tubist David Liquori read many of the essays in draft and offered superb editorial suggestions; and singer/pianist Bernard Lee provided diligent proofreading of Finale examples as well as many other important contributions. It is a tremendous pleasure to thank these wonderful students for helping to bring this project to fruition. I also thank them for their enthusiasm and their patience as we moved through a lengthy and arduous process.

I wish to offer deep gratitude to Oxford University Press editors Jan Beatty and Talia Krohn for having faith in the project and for providing much guidance in the final stages. Thanks too, to Leslie Anglin, who graciously shepardled the volume through production, and to Jimmée Greco for superb editing. They were a pleasure to work with.

I am grateful, too, for hundreds of students over the years who have inspired me in my teaching and my research, and whose curiosity and love of music inspired this volume.

INTRODUCTION TO WRITING ANALYTICAL ESSAYS

William Marvin

William Marvin has taught at Oberlin College and has recently returned to the Eastman School of Music, where he earned his doctorate. While a graduate student at Eastman he received two teaching awards: the Outstanding Graduate Teaching Prize (1990) and the Edward Peck Curtis Award for Excellence in Teaching by a Graduate Student (1992). He is especially active in developing aural skills training for undergraduates.

Marvin's research has involved a Schenkerian approach to tonality and form in operas by Wagner and Mozart. He has also focused attention on aural training in tonal and post-tonal music and the quodlibet as a contrapuntal device in Broadway musicals. He has published in Music Theory Online, the electronic journal of the Society for Music Theory, and the Journal of Musicology.

In this essay, Marvin's love of teaching and learning comes forth as he combines essential elements about writing prose with a deep regard for music's power and complexity to both the performer and the analyst.

Writing about music is comparable to performing music in that both require many hours of behind-the-scenes work. Just as the rehearsals, coachings, and extended practice sessions are largely invisible to audiences when a performer takes the stage, so are the hours of brainstorming, analysis, and revision invisible to readers of the final version of an essay. All of the essays in this volume are written by professional music theorists with years, even decades, of experience in crafting analytic prose. Yet each essay was drafted, edited, rewritten, and revised again before it was ready for print.

Music students frequently question the relevance of writing essays. Writing about music helps to clarify your understanding of a piece. It also helps to organize your thoughts in a deeper, more meaningful way. Analytic essays, like oral presentations, exist for the simple purpose of persuading others of your ideas on how music can be heard. Oral presentations are like improvisations, whereas written analyses can be viewed as compositions. While a transcendent performance can also accomplish the goal of informing or persuading others, prose can reach a wider audience than is possible with a single ephemeral performance. Further, an analysis can be comparative in ways that a single performance never can: two interpretations cannot exist simultaneously in performance, but the possibility of two or more feasible interpretations lies at the heart of musical analysis. Clear thought about music and clear writing about music are related—if you have difficulty articulating your thoughts on paper, chances are that the thoughts themselves are unclear. The clarity of thought you seek will then reinform your approach to performance; after committing your ideas to paper, new performance interpretations open up. In addition, given that performers in the twenty-first century are expected to include some form of communication with their audience, whether verbally or in the form of program notes, analytic prose is one form of communication that is indispensable.

Writing, like musical technique and artistry, requires practice. The limited space here precludes a discussion of how to select a topic for analysis. Once the piece, pieces, or analytic problem(s) have been chosen, however, the following steps will guide your creativity and help you develop an essay that communicates your insights most effectively.

STEP ONE: LEARN THE PIECE

This may seem obvious, but successful communication presumes that you have made the composition(s) your own. This means hours of immersion in the score, recordings, live performances, and practicing. Think about what interests you in the piece. What puzzles you about it? What does the piece seem to convey to you? You will need to approach the piece as a performer as well as from aural and visual study. Regardless of your own performance skills, a physical relationship to the piece through singing, playing, or both as well as multiple listenings is an essential prerequisite to being articulate about its formal and expressive features.

STEP TWO: BEGIN TO ANALYZE

There is no single approach for every piece, and most pieces can be understood by numerous analytic methods. However, you should consider the following questions about virtually any composition you choose:

1. What is the form of the piece, or how do you describe its parts and their relationships to each other?

2. What is the melodic and harmonic language of the piece, and what tools best describe these? (Roman numerals? Pitch-class set theory? Scalar/modal analysis? Contrapuntal relationships? Motivic/thematic development?)

3. What is the temporal organization of the piece, from the smallest level of pulses and subdivisions to the larger motions of phrase and hypermeter?

4. What is extraordinary, strange, unusual, or anomalous about the piece? Or, what feature of the work drew you to examine this piece closely?

Keep in mind that analysis involves detours and dead ends, just like your practicing can, and also that your final essay should not contain everything that you have learned, just as your various performance interpretations can never all be projected simultaneously; in other words, you must make choices. Perhaps most important: analysis is more than merely slapping labels on a piece of music. Analysis should articulate your most profound insights about the music's organization and meaning through your interpretation of the facts.

STEP THREE: RESEARCH (WHEN POSSIBLE)

Find out what else has been written about your chosen topic. This is part of your continual personal growth as a musician. Everything you read and hear contributes to this and can then be brought to bear on your own analysis and writing.

STEP FOUR: FORM A THESIS

Nothing is less interesting to read (or write) than a chronological description of what happens within a piece. After you have analyzed extensively, you will have a better idea about what is normative (i.e., aspects of the piece that are common to many other pieces) and what is unusual and special about the work(s) under consideration. Your knowledge of music theory and your experience of other repertoire play a central role here. For example, the bass line C–G–C–G–C in a C-major piece will be ignored as a completely standard cadential pattern, but an extended passage in E♭ minor in the same piece will stand out to you as significant and worth discussing. Insights on what such an unusual tonal area might mean are the types of ideas that will provide a conceptual framework for your essay. Such ideas, when developed as the organizing thesis in your paper, will draw the reader toward the most interesting and compelling musical features. Frequently, these issues are also the problematic elements of interpretation: an aspect of the piece that is puzzling to you will often lead you to an ideal topic for discussion, and such issues tend to be difficult in performance (because they are not clear).

STEP FIVE: WRITE

This is actually a misnomer; rather, this step involves organizing and presenting your findings. Successful presentation involves more than just writing coherent prose. Consider how diagrams, charts, or annotated musical examples can communicate your analysis more effectively and efficiently than prose, and then use words to highlight and augment what is already presented in graphic form. Technical terms are important for good writing; they can simplify the prose and keep your points succinct. Even so, it is important to know your audience: some terminology will be fine for a given reader or listener (such as your teacher!) but inappropriate for others (as at a talk to a lay audience).[1]

Organize and outline the essay before you start presenting your findings—this will prevent your analysis from turning into a meaningless hodgepodge of facts about the piece. Finally, cite the work of other scholars when appropriate. Just as you would not submit as your own an audition tape played by someone else, you may not quote or paraphrase other authors without acknowledging the ideas as belonging to them.[2]

STEP SIX: REVISE, REVISE, REVISE!

A musical performance does not spring fully formed from the head, voice, or fingers of a performer, and neither does an analytic essay jump directly onto the page in its final form. Reread your essay slowly, and *aloud.* You will hear problems in your writing that may not be as obvious when you see words on the page. Just like practicing, analysis and writing can sometimes feel unrewarding; all three activities are often best approached in short, intense sessions, because epiphanies or insights can and will occur when you least expect them. Further, try to read your prose objectively, putting yourself in the role of reader. As you read, make sure that every sentence is coherent and that it accurately expresses your ideas. Also determine whether the ideas follow one another logically. Revi-

---

1. Throughout this book, technical terms are presented in **bold.** Such terms are explained as they occur in essays and are defined again in the glossary.—Ed.

2. Inappropriate use of the work of others is called plagiarism. A more detailed discussion of this can be found in Richard J. Wingell, *Writing about Music,* 55–57 (see full citation cr. p. xiv).—Ed.

sion may mean correcting factual mistakes, changing the placement of sentences or paragraphs within your essay, adding material to clarify the logical steps of your argument, eliminating redundancies or statements that simply do not advance your ideas, or many other sorts of changes. Revisions will always be necessary in order to guarantee that you are presenting your best ideas most efficiently.

Ultimately, writing essays will help you understand how a given piece works and, if you are to perform it, how your understanding affects your performance. Just as ongoing performance preparation creates a deeper bond between you and the music, so writing about music helps forge a deeper connection as well.

FURTHER READING

Irvine, Demar. *Irvine's Writing about Music*. 3d ed. Revised and edited by Mark A. Radice. Portland: Amadeus Press, 1999. (This includes a valuable bibliography of other resources about writing.)

Wingell, Richard J. *Writing about Music: An Introductory Guide*. 3d ed. Upper Saddle River, N.J.: Prentice Hall, 2002.

ENGAGING MUSIC

PART I

INTRODUCTION TO ANALYTICAL TOPICS AND TECHNIQUES

~ 1 ~

THE PHRASE RHYTHM OF CHOPIN'S A-FLAT MAJOR MAZURKA, OP. 59, NO. 2

Charles Burkhart

Charles Burkhart (CUNY/Graduate Center and Queens College) is a well-known Schenkerian scholar who has written numerous articles on both tonal and twentieth-century music, including the classic 1978 essay "Schenker's 'Motivic Parallelisms.' " More recently he has explored various aspects of tonal rhythm.

The present essay focuses on what Burkhart calls "the very musicianly topic of the phrase—how a phrase is identified, how small phrases form larger ones, and how composers make phrases more flexible and expressive by means of 'extra' measures." The essay demonstrates the relatively new theory of tonal phrase structure as developed by two other authors in this volume, Carl Schachter (chapter 10) and William Rothstein (chapter 17). (Harald Krebs offers an introduction to this theory in chapter 2.) A pianist, Burkhart illustrates the "phrase rhythm" of Chopin's Mazurka in A-flat, op. 59, no. 2, with the sensitivity of one who has long been concerned with how analysis informs performance.

INTRODUCTION[1]

Before setting out to analyze a piece or to read an analysis of it, one must fully experience the piece as music. So, if you have not already done so, play or listen to this wonderful piece many times. Make it your own. Best of all, memorize it. Of course, as you

---

Some reminders: (1) all words in **bold** are defined in the glossary; (2) full citations for incomplete references are found in the selected bibliography; (3) the authors use their preferred notational system (e.g., Roman numeral, form label, and register notation). Most of the essays denote register by middle C as C^4.—Ed.

1. An introduction might appropriately begin by placing the work to be discussed in its cultural context, but for the sake of space I shall leave that to others. From a vast bibliography see, for example, Jim Samson, *The Music of Chopin* (New York: Oxford University Press, 1985), especially chap. 6, on the Polish spirit in Chopin's music, with extensive comment on the mazurkas, including brief consideration of op. 59 as a set. Jean-Jacques Eigeldinger's *Chopin: pianist and teacher—as seen by his pupils* (*Chopin vu par ses élèves*), translated by Naomi Shohet with Krysia Osostowicz and Roy Howat (Cambridge and New York: Cambridge University Press, 1986) is a mine of information on many topics pertaining to Chopin performance; on page 145 ff., he discusses the three folk dance types—*kujawiak, mazur,* and *oberek*—that underlie Chopin's artful creations called by the generic name "mazurkas."

form - section
(strongest ending)

phrases
(stronger endings)

subphrases
(weak endings)

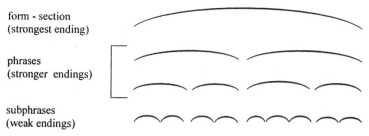

Example 1.1. Hierarchy of phrase structure

do so, you cannot help trying to make some kind of sense of the piece, and cannot help forming some mental image of it. (So you are already analyzing, whether you call it that or not.) And that image will inevitably be of a single entity—one unit—made up of a succession of shorter units. It is to certain of these shorter units that I draw your attention. I refer to the phrases.

Every musician is expected to recognize phrases and articulate them effectively. But what is a phrase? Some think it is the group of notes comprised under a slur. Such slurs, which indicate legato performance, are often loosely referred to as the "phrasing," but the notes they cover are usually not the same thing as what is meant by "phrase." I will define "phrase" as any group of measures (including a group of one, or possibly even a fraction of one) that has some degree of *structural completeness*. What counts is the sense of completeness we hear in the pitches, not the notation on the page. To be "complete" such a group must have an ending of some kind. The strongest ending is the *full*, or *authentic*, *cadence*, but there are many other ways to end—ways that shade off from strong to weak.

Imagine two phrases in succession. If the first is defined by a weak ending and the second by a strong, the total effect will be something greater than simply two phrases: the second ending, because it is stronger than the first, will create the effect of a *single* large phrase comprising the two shorter ones. (We will call such short phrases making up one longer one "subphrases.") In other words, phrases not only exist one after the other, but also form a hierarchy in which the shorter ones are subsumed by ever larger ones, with the largest constituting a section of the work's form. All this is pictured in example 1.1, which should be read from the bottom up.

Phrases are delineated by the tonal functions of pitch. They are not created by slurs or by legato performance. A phrase can just as well be composed of staccato notes or punctuated by interior rests without losing its essential unity. (Think of all the interior rests within the phrases—better, subphrases—of "Doe, a Deer." Where is the first really strong ending?) Sometimes a composer will even contradict a cadence by writing a slur over it as though trying to obscure it, but the pitch relationships will make it perceivable nevertheless. (This will occur, with charming effect, in the mazurka under study here.)

A phrase is not pitches only but also has a rhythmic dimension, and further, each phrase in a work contributes to the work's large rhythmic organization. "Phrase rhythm" is a general term denoting all the rhythmic aspects of phrase construction as well as the relationships between all the phrases in a given piece.[2] It is not at all a cut-and-dried affair, but the very lifeblood of music and capable of infinite variety. Discovering a work's phrase rhythm is a gateway to its understanding and to effective performance. I will be

---

2. The term "phrase rhythm" has received wide currency, thanks in large part to Rothstein, *Phrase Rhythm in Tonal Music*, in which phrase analysis is not only raised to a new level of precision but also applied to the study of historical styles. I will use here several of this book's categories, e.g., overlap, lead-in, expansion, reinterpretation—all of which the book fully explains and illustrates.

illustrating below some of the most common techniques of phrase rhythm. But for now—even if you are a beginner at all this—make a stab at the phrase rhythm of our mazurka. Writing on a copy of the score, mark off with slurs (as in example 1.1) the subphrases and phrases, identifying cadences by name and noting anything else you may observe. Only then read the rest of this essay.

Reading an analytic essay about a piece of music can be a cumbersome, time-consuming task. The author, who in a lecture might well communicate his or her conceptions directly by simply singing or playing them, must express them in the nonmusical medium of words. And the reader must then translate the words back into music to follow the argument. So, to reduce excessive verbiage I have devised a musical picture (of a type sometimes called a "sketch" or "graph") that represents the entire piece I am discussing and that directly communicates my essential points. Since my sketch offers a view that might be called panoramic, I will refer to it hereafter as PAN. PAN pretty much says it all (though not quite all).

Take a good look at PAN (with Chopin's mazurka now firmly in mind). Begin with the upper of the two systems, which accounts for every measure of the piece. Not only are all the phrases shown here, but also certain passages are further identified as "extensions" or "expansions." Therefore I will call this view of the piece EP, for Elaborated Phrases—that is, phrases elaborated via **extensions** and **expansions**. Now, such elaborations are a very important part of the art of music (and will bulk large in this essay). However, if we are calling them "elaborations," there must be something more basic that is being elaborated. That more basic something is shown in the lower system of PAN. Here all extensions and expansions are removed, leaving only the Basic Phrases, or BP. Though BP is a more abstract conception of the piece, it also is understood to represent the complete piece, or more precisely, its basic phrase structure.[3]

It is obvious that both EP and BP are the result of considerable pitch "reduction." That is, they show, in the manner of a **Schenker analysis,** two levels of the mazurka's basic voice leading and harmony. They also show much *rhythmic* reduction, again in the manner of Schenker's **foreground** graphs. Though the writing of such reductions takes much practice to do well, readers with little or no training in Schenker can, through careful comparison of the sketches with the score, grasp much of their meaning.[4]

THE A[1] SECTION[5]

The typical mazurka rhythm in bars 1–2 requires mention of the well-known tradition of performing mazurkas with a lengthening of certain notes beyond their written value, a complex performance-practice issue that can only be touched on here. Suffice it to say

---

3. Having stressed the point that the slurs in a score generally do not denote phrases, I should add that the slurs in PAN, as in ex. 1.1, do denote phrases. They are *analytic* slurs, not performance slurs. At the same time it is true that many of the phrases that my slurs point out would indeed be performed legato. Chopin's slurs are, of course, purely performance slurs. I leave to the reader the very practical question of why Chopin began and ended each of his slurs where he did.

4. PAN follows a style of notation employed in William Rothstein's "Rhythm and the Theory of Structural Levels" (PhD diss., Yale University, 1980) and Carl Schachter's "Durational Reduction," *The Music Forum* 5 (1980): 197–232 (reprinted in Carl Schachter, *Unfoldings*, 54–78), both of which demonstrate the rhythmic reduction of entire pieces.

5. While the conventional labeling for an opening section is simply "A", Burkhart here uses Schenker's practice of labeling the opening section "A[1]".—Ed.

PAN

PAN—*continued*

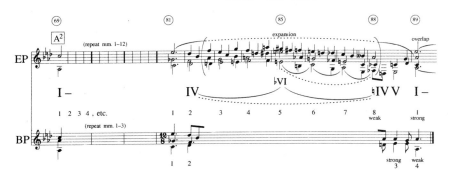

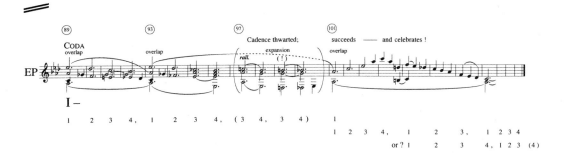

that the most common case is that of a quarter or dotted quarter note falling on the second beat. (Often such notes are also marked with an accent.) As for op. 59, no. 2, I feel that an exaggerated **rubato** would be out of place, but I like to play bar 2 (and rhythmically similar bars) with a slight hastening over the two eighths, playing "into" the second-beat quarter, which is thus slightly lengthened but not necessarily louder.[6]

The four-bar measure-groups throughout this mazurka are obvious. Though all of them could be called phrases, notice that generally it takes two of them (4 + 4) to reach a strong cadence. Therefore we will call them subphrases that together form an eight-bar phrase. Now it happens that the very first such phrase (bars 1–8) ends on a semicadence (V) that is composed in a most unusual way: in spite of the cadence, the melodic line willfully presses on into bar 9—and Chopin's performance slur from 5 into 9 clearly shows he wants it to be played that way. The result has a capricious, playful quality whose unexpectedness makes us smile. What is going on? In my view, as shown in PAN, the phrase basically ends on the B♭¹ of bar 8, but that note is treated to a tiny "extension" that endures until bar 9, beat 1. For a fuller picture we must go back to bar 4's high A♭, which, though the last note of the subphrase, is actually a kind of elaborative note because it is approached by a chordal skip and therefore is not part of the essential (stepwise) voice leading. (That is why it is omitted from BP.) Notice that bar 8 begins with a rhythmic foreshortening of bar 4, then hurries on to invade bar 9, which it can readily do because bar 9 begins with a rest. A lesser composer might have written the insipid version shown in example 1.2.

---

6. The many accounts of Chopin's rubato transmitted by his students and other listeners have received much attention by modern scholars. An invaluable source with many examples (including mazurkas) is Eigeldinger, *Chopin*, 49–52 and 118–23. See also Richard Hudson's *Stolen Time: The History of Tempo Rubato* (New York: Oxford University Press, 1994), chap. 7 ("Alteration of Note Values in the Mazurkas"), esp. p. 184.

A lesser composer might have written:

but Chopin wrote:

Example 1.2. Hypothetical and actual versions of bar 8

Chopin's version has the effect of whimsically obscuring the semicadence. In performing it, what might the pianist do to maximize its effect? (Articulations like these—that will-fully contradict the expected—are one of the great charms of Chopin's music, and other examples, though more modest, occur elsewhere in this piece. Be on the lookout for them.)[7]

The next eight-bar phrase is defined at bar 16 by a perfect authentic cadence in C minor, the key of III. But here again there is something unexpected: the leap up to high G (bar 16, 2d beat) thwarts a sense of full close. Twice more the phrase tries to end, and it finally succeeds on the third attempt (bar 20) when the high C confirms the tonic. Thus the phrase has been extended beyond its basic length. Note well how this has been rep-resented in PAN (bars 9–20): BP shows just the basic eight-bar length; EP shows the ba-sic length *plus the extension*. The analytic assumption here is that, in a sense, the piece could have done without the extension—that the phrase could have been concluded on the first beat of bar 16, then immediately continued as at bar 23. But in a piece by Chopin there must surely be a reason for the extension. What might it be? What artistic end does it serve? I'm not sure I can give a really persuasive answer. Is it just that the extension breaks the monotony of the four-bar groups and tantalizes by delaying the end? Perhaps these are reasons enough. Or is there more to it? Look back again at bar 4's high A♭. Shall this note just be left hanging there? Or could there be a long-range connection from bar 4's A♭ to bar 16's high G (supported by the two most important chords so far—the tonic of A♭ and the tonic of C minor)? Then this high G subverts the strong cadence needed to finish the A section, so the phrase *has to be lengthened* to allow the G to be replaced by a high C (bar 20). Is this plausible? Audible? In any event, this extension (bars 17–20) is surely trying to "tell a story" of some kind—not a literal story, of course, but a psycho-logical experience expressible only in tones. We can only use words in our attempt to suggest it. What might they be? More important, what strategies might the performer em-ploy to convey this "story" dramatically?

Bar 20's high C finally ends the extension. Or does it? What about 21–22? I hear these two bars as an extension of the extension. If BP represents the basic, or "primary," length of the phrase, and the extension in 17–20 is therefore a "secondary" order of time, measures 21–22 are "tertiary." They stretch out bar 20 itself for still another two bars. It

---

7. Chopin's propensity to write articulations that go counter to the norms of the tonal system was noted by Schenker, who points out and comments on examples of them in his *Free Composition (Der freie Satz)*, ed. and trans. E. Oster (1935; New York: Schirmer Books, 1979), par. 273, fig. 128, 2b and c. More recently Roth-stein's *Phrase Rhythm* (chap. 7) has picked up on this idea and extensively developed it. For another mazurka with highly capricious slurring throughout, see the C-sharp Minor, op. 30, no. 4.

seems to me wrong to call them an "extended upbeat" to the next phrase. Rather, they are an example of what is called a "lead-in"—a small group of tones that link one phrase with the next but are not essential to either, and are therefore omitted in a reduction such as BP. As for this lead-in, try playing from bar 13 leaving the lead-in out—just skip from 20 to 23. I leave the reader to ponder why Chopin put it in—what artistic mission it accomplishes.[8]

Bars 23–44 are structurally identical to the first twenty-two bars. What do they contribute to the piece that is new?

THE B SECTION

Have another look at PAN, especially at how the B section is represented. Recall that the A^1 section ended on a C-minor (III) harmony, and note how smoothly this connects with the B section's II^6_5. This basic harmony endures all the way to just before bar 60, where it moves to a C-major chord. The basic "top" voice here comes from the C^2 in bar 16, moves to $B\flat^1$ at 45, and returns to C^2 at 60. However, as EP shows, these basic pitches are frequently composed in higher and lower registers: C^2 is lifted up to C^3 at 20 (42), then brought down by the arpeggio of 43–44 to middle C in 44, from where it moves to the grace note $B\flat$ at 45 (not in PAN; see the score), then expressed as $B\flat^1$ through bars 46–58, lifted up at 59 to $B\flat^2$, from where it resolves to C^3 at 60!

As for the phrase rhythm, the four-bar grouping established in A^1 continues. We expect a cadence at the eighth bar, and indeed there is a V^7–I at 51–52. However, in my view this progression does not qualify as a cadence in the fullest sense, not because it is imperfect, but because it sounds merely "passing" within the more comprehensive II harmony that surrounds it. Compare its effect with that of the genuine V^7–I cadence at the turn of bars 88/89.

If, then, there is no real cadence at 51–52, the entire B section consists basically of one big sixteen-bar phrase (45–60) that cadences at bar 60 with the arrival of III♮.[9] This harmony is now prolonged from 60 to the first beat of 68 (note the bass C in every bar). In short, we have here another phrase extension—and one that leads back to the return of

---

8. Lead-ins are very common. A textbook example is Mozart, B-flat Major Piano Sonata, K. 333, movement 3, bar 4, last 3 eighth notes. Lead-ins usually occur within the last measure of a phrase, but Chopin's lead-in here is, unusually, extended for an extra two measures. If it were not so extended, it might go (awkwardly!) something like this:

9. Some may not be familiar with this chromatic chord, since it is often omitted in harmony courses. Properly called III♯, as would be E–G♯–B in C major, it is frequently mistaken for a V of VI. This is no quibble over terminology, for III♯ has its own particular function that deserves identifying by name. To call it V of VI would be to place the emphasis on VI (F minor), and that is not what happens here. For a useful discussion of important usages of III♯, see Edward Aldwell and Carl Schachter, *Harmony and Voice Leading*, 3d ed., 399. This chord, which occurs in the music of many composers, is frequently used at the end of the B section of a ternary form, as here, and, similarly, at the end of the development section of a major-mode sonata (see David Beach, "A Recurring Pattern in Mozart's Music," *Journal of Music Theory* 18 [1974]: 274–306). Chopin was very fond of the III♯. Other pieces of his that use it prominently are the G-flat Major Etude, op. 10, no. 5 ("Black Key"), bar 8; A-flat, Major Mazurka, op. 24, no. 3, bars 32–36; *Trois Nouvelles Etudes*, no. 2, in A-flat Major, bars 37–40; and the A Major Polonaise, op. 40, no. 1 ("Military"), bar 6.

the A section at 69. An extension that functions in this manner within the form, that is, which leads back to a returning form-section, is traditionally called a **retransition**, though most retransitions are harmonically based on V rather than on III, as here.

Something more is going on with the phrase rhythm at bar 60. Listen again to the B section, with special attention to the four-bar groups. Counting one beat per bar, one inevitably feels the 1-2-3-4 as strong-weak, strong-weak, just as in a single measure of 4/4. Arriving at 60, one first perceives that bar as metrically weak, but then, since it is also clearly felt as the *first* bar of the retransition, one immediately reinterprets it as strong. To test this assertion, just conduct from bar 45—down on all odd-numbered bars, up on even. What happens at 60? Schenker called this metrical phenomenon *Umdeutung*, or reinterpretation. A commoner name for it is **"elision,"** but "reinterpretation," despite its ungainly length, seems to me better because it focuses on the listener's reaction. (Note, by the way, how this is pictured in EP—how bar 60 shows "4" crossed out and replaced with "1.")

Again we may ask: why is an extension needed here? Why not just end the phrase with the cadence at 60, as in BP? Notice that the situation at 60 is rather like that at 20: after some expenditure of effort, the phrase starting at 45 reaches a cadence on C^3. And again like 21–22, the retransition (60–68) not only restores the basic register (C^2), but also celebrates the conclusion reached at 60. Here the celebration—a rather acerbic and intense one—lasts until 68, which metrically is an additional weak bar (see EP). And on the last beat of that bar Chopin writes a passing V_3^4, which smoothly ushers in the tonic with its concomitant **reprise**.

THE A² SECTION

The reprise begins with yet another "orchestration" of the mazurka's opening phrases. But more significantly, at bar 81 we are surprised that instead of one more four-bar group, Chopin now writes a phrase that takes *nine* bars (metrically felt as 8 + 1 or 4 + 4 + 1) to reach its end. Here is another phrase stretched out beyond its normal length—but with an important difference. In the two lengthened phrases we saw earlier, the extra bars occurred *after* the cadence, forming what I have called an extension. But here (81–89), the extra bars are in the interior of the phrase—*before* the cadence—puffing the phrase out in the middle. This I shall call an *expansion*.[10] In EP, the expansion is clearly marked by parentheses. And, as usual, BP shows the phrase's basic form—what it would be without the expansion.

Even more unusual than this phrase's unexpected length is its astonishing eruption of chromaticism. Indeed, the chromaticism is so extreme that it almost threatens the stylistic consistency of the piece, which has been fairly diatonic up to this point. I suggest that Chopin could get away with such a seeming inconsistency only because he placed it in an expansion—that is, in what we sense to be "nonessential" measures—outside the norm. Had he used such chromaticism in measures that were essential, it would have been *de trop*—too much.[11]

This highly unusual passage invites analysis in its own right. Notice how the constant repetition of the rhythm eighth-eighth-quarter-quarter sets off the extra bars, helping to define them as extra. As to pitch, the passage is composed of two chordal sequences,

---

10. Chapter 3 ("Phrase Expansion") of Rothstein's *Phrase Rhythm* is the primary presentation of this rich subject. But note that Rothstein does not use the term "extension." Instead he uses "expansion" to cover all cases, calling postcadential cases *external* expansions and precadential ones *internal* expansions.

11. Chopin liked to do such things. For an even more unusual eruption of chromaticism in an otherwise quite diatonic piece, see the expanded phrase (bars 129–32) near the end of the C-sharp Minor Mazurka, op. 30, no. 4.

a rising one through 84, then a falling one in 85–88. The falling one is particularly note-worthy for the way it traverses an entire octave from the E-major chord in 85 down in thirds—E♮–C–A♭—to the F♭ in 88. As I try to show in EP, I understand the E♮ as equiv-alent to the F♭, and these four bars as a whole as a prolongation (that is, an *elaboration*) of ♭VI, and this large ♭VI as contained within a still-larger prolonged IV stretching from the D♭ of 82 to the D♮—or ♮IV°⁷—at 88, 2d eighth note.[12] That is, the large IV is pro-longed via a move up to its third, F (chromatically altered to F♭), which is expressed as the root of ♭VI (85–88), then back down to its very brief, chromatically altered root. In sum, we find Chopin's harmonic daring not only on the surface—from one chord to the next—but also in the underlying structure![13]

One more technique of phrase rhythm—one not yet encountered—is illustrated at 89, where A²'s final phrase ends: notice here that the *next* phrase begins in the same bar—89. (Do not be misled by the fact that this next phrase, like so many previous ones, be-gins on beat 2. Its first *bar* is still 89.) When two successive phrases do this—begin and end in the same bar—they are said to "overlap." The bar in which they do so (here 89) is said to contain a "phrase overlap," or simply an "overlap."

Now something similar to this did indeed occur at bar 60, where one phrase ended as the next began. What occurred there was also a phrase overlap but of a more drastic type: there the flow of four-bar measure-groups was disturbed—with a clearly perceiv-able bump—when bar 4 had to be reinterpreted as the next group's bar 1. But at 89 no such reinterpretation occurs. See in EP the measure-group numbers (1 2 3 4, etc.) under-lying the A² section. Note at 89 how they simply flow on undisturbed, resulting in a gen-tler kind of overlap—no bump.[14]

THE CODA

Our mazurka has so far produced a quite clear ABA form, which firmly concludes with the full cadence in the tonic at 88–89—the first in the piece. Yet there is still one more section to come. One might logically call this section "C" because its thematic material is new, but this would be to overlook the form-defining power of tonal structure. Because the tonal structure of ABA is, broadly, *tonic–digression therefrom–return thereto*, it man-ifests a built-in completeness. If one more section follows, it too must be founded on the tonic and therefore must prolong the goal already reached. Such a prolongation is very common, and theory has long called it a "**coda**"—a tail trailing off from the main body.

Yet codas often seem so necessary. What is it about them that makes them, if not "struc-turally" essential, so aesthetically satisfying? I suggest that the answer lies in what happens

---

12. The Roman numeral ♮IV°⁷ follows Schenker's convention, which is not found in many textbooks.—Ed.

13. This view of the structure of bars 82–88 stems from an unpublished partial analysis by Ernst Oster. I give a fuller account of this unusual passage in "Chopin's 'Concluding Expansions,'" in *Nineteenth-Century Piano Music: Essays in Performance and Analysis*, ed. David Witten (New York: Garland, 1997), 99–102.

14. Throughout this essay I have used the term "measure-group" (sometimes just "group") as a synonym for the less-readily understood term "**hypermeasure**." It is important to remember that "hypermeasure" (and "measure-group," as here used) denotes, just like the term "measure," a purely metrical phenomenon. It refers to the realm of time only, not pitch. The term "phrase" refers to *both* pitch and time. A phrase is music, a hyper-measure just time. Many phrases are commensurate with hypermeasures, but many others, such as a phrase that overlaps the next, are not. As to what happens at our mazurka's bars 60 and 89, many writers and teachers would apply the term "**elision**" to both. This is not wrong, but since I think it important to differentiate between the two types of situation, I prefer not to use "elision" at all, but rather "overlap" (as at 89) and "reinterpreta-tion" (as at 60), understanding that a reinterpretation is a special kind of overlap because here *the hypermea-sures also overlap*. [Chapter 2, by Harald Krebs, in this volume introduces hypermeter in greater detail.—Ed.]

just before the coda—that the coda is a kind of dramatic response to the events of the main body. Many pieces, in the course of working an idea through to its structural conclusion, have, just before the close of their main body, a particularly effortful passage. Such a passage often reaches a climax of some kind and often involves an expanded phrase. I suggest that it is such a phrase that particularly arouses the need for a coda. The main body, having expended all that extra energy, cannot just suddenly stop at the cadence. Too much momentum has been built up. The listener needs more time to take it all in. The coda lets us down easy, as it were, and restores a sense of balance. A coda "looks back" on the main body, as though contemplating or commenting upon it. And of course a coda is another species of extension—an extension to the entire main body. So, as in the phrase extensions we have seen, a coda can also celebrate a successful conclusion, now of the main body, even to the extent of being more emphatic, perhaps faster, louder, or higher.[15]

In our mazurka, since the coda is an extension, it too does not exist in BP. Having no "extra" measures, BP needs no coda. Notice that, as a result, BP ends in the fourth, and therefore weak, measure of a four-bar measure-group. Now compare the actual final phrase (bars 81–89) together with its representation in EP: in the *expanded* phrase, the number of bars now causes the cadential tonic chord to fall on a *first* measure, which, because it is strong, serves as a springboard for the ensuing coda. This entire procedure— approaching the coda via an expanded phrase plus overlap—is a frequent technique of phrase rhythm in classic and romantic music and occurs quite often in Chopin.[16]

Our coda, having started with phrase overlap, now continues to use it. Also, it brings one more expanded phrase, as shown in EP. This expansion has a particularly charming feature: notice how the Cb in bar 95 is a kind of intensification of the C♮ of 91; since 97 brings back C♮, one expects that 99 will perhaps bring Cb again. But instead Chopin writes at 99 a still more intense, because so unexpected, G-major $\frac{6}{4}$ chord, which necessitates B♮ instead of Cb. This is not just a notational convenience, but also a genuine enharmonic change. Yet at the same time it is obviously the same pitch as Cb. (Accounts of Chopin's life tell us he was a gifted mimic who kept his friends in stitches with imitations of their acquaintances. This B♮ is mimicking Cb—a kind of musical pun.) Observe how Chopin has marked off these bars with his "rall . . . . . ." Could he have spelled out any more clearly that these are special bars within the phrase, that they keep us in suspense, holding our breath, until the phrase is finally permitted to end at 101?

Having made it through the uncertainties of the expansion, the piece now dispels all tension with a brilliant nine-bar flourish. As I show in EP (by the numbers under the staff), I can hear the metrics of this flourish in two different ways. How do you hear them? Could Chopin's pedaling influence how one hears them?

Finally, we know from the manuscript sources of op. 59, no. 2, that Chopin had difficulty finding an ending that satisfied him.[17] He rewrote the last bars several times before arriving at the idea of the curious repeated chords in the last two measures. What is one to make of them?

---

15. I must add that there are two very distinct types of coda, and that my remarks apply only to the older, more traditional type. In the second type, the climax and most definitive close occur *in the coda;* therefore the coda is part of the essential structure of the piece. Such a coda occurring in a sonata form constitutes a fourth form-section, a section on a par with each of the earlier three—exposition, development, and recapitulation. Beethoven invented this type of coda, and his works afford numerous examples, e.g., the first movements of the *Eroica* Symphony and the *Appassionata* Sonata.

16. See Burkhart, "Chopin's 'Concluding Expansions' " for numerous examples.

17. For locations see Krystyna Kobylanska, *Thematisch-bibliographisches Werkverzeichnis* (Munich: Henle, 1979).

~2~

HYPERMETER AND HYPERMETRIC IRREGULARITY IN THE SONGS OF JOSEPHINE LANG

Harald Krebs

For two decades, Harald Krebs (University of Victoria) has studied tonality in nineteenth- and early-twentieth-century music, with emphasis on the *Lied* genre. Recently he has turned his attention to various aspects of rhythm and meter: his book *Fantasy Pieces: Metrical Dissonance in the Music of Robert Schumann* won the Society for Music Theory's Wallace Berry Award in 2003. In the present essay, Krebs brings together his interests in song and rhythmic/metric structure. He focuses on one of the most important concepts of recent rhythmic theory, namely large-scale meter, or "hypermeter." Edward T. Cone first introduced the latter term in 1968 (in *Musical Form and Musical Performance*), and Carl Schachter, William Rothstein, Richard Cohn, and Charles Burkhart (see chapter 1) have further developed the idea. Krebs summarizes the theory of hypermeter and analyzes hypermetric structure in the songs of Josephine Lang.

Josephine Lang (1815–80) composed contemporaneously with the Schumanns, Brahms, and Wolf. While many other nineteenth-century women composers received little encouragement in their day, Lang's compositional work was supported by such renowned figures as Felix Mendelssohn (1809–47) and the composer and conductor Ferdinand Hiller (1811–85), with the result that she attained some prominence. Recent research has confirmed that her lieder offer a wealth of fine music for performers and scholars to study and savor.[1]

Some reminders: (1) all words in **bold** are defined in the glossary; (2) full citations for incomplete references are found in the selected bibliography; (3) the authors use their preferred notational system (e.g., Roman numeral, form label, and register notation). Most of the essays denote register by middle C as C^4.—Ed.

1. Josephine Lang was one of the most prolific female composers of lieder in the nineteenth century. She was born in Munich in 1815, where she attained some fame for her song compositions and for her performances of them. In 1842 she married the poet and law professor Reinhold Koestlin, whom she joined in Tübingen, where he held a university position. When he died in 1856, she supported their six children by teaching voice and piano and by composing. She died in 1880. For additional information about Josephine Lang, see Ferdinand Hiller, "Josephine Lang, die Lieder-Componistin," in *Aus dem Tonleben unserer Zeit* (Leipzig: H. Mendelssohn, 1868), 2:116–36; Heinrich Adolf Köstlin, "Josefine Lang: Lebensabriß," in *Sammlung musikalischer Vorträge* (Leipzig: Breitkopf und Härtel, 1881), 51–103; Roberta C. Werner, "The Songs of Josephine Caroline Lang: The Expression of a Life" (PhD diss., University of Minnesota, 1992); Harald Krebs, "Josephine Lang," in *Women Composers through the Ages*, vol. 7, ed. Martha Schleifer and Sylvia Glickman (New Haven: G. K. Hall, 2003), 113–142.

Example 2.1. Opening of Josephine Lang's "An den See," op. 14, no. 4 (1840)

AN INTRODUCTION TO HYPERMETER

Most musical scores contain conventional signs that to some extent reveal the composer's intentions regarding the meter of the given work—intentions that performers are to communicate to listeners. In the work shown in example 2.1, for instance, the composer Josephine Lang provides a 2/4 time signature and a series of bar lines, which indicate that the quarter-note beats are to be grouped into pairs consisting of alternating strong and weak beats. As we perform the work, we realize that Lang's time signature and bar lines comfortably "fit" the music; these notational devices accurately represent one level of the song's meter. We also realize, however, that Lang's metric notation does not tell the whole story. As we listen, we become aware that the song contains metric groupings larger than the pairs of quarter-note beats indicated by the time signature and bar lines. At the melodic high point in m. 3, a grouping of four quarter notes, or two bars, begins to become apparent; we perceive the accent resulting from this high point as initiating a new musical segment. The two-bar grouping is maintained by the changes of harmony that occur at the beginnings of subsequent odd-numbered measures and is further reinforced by the fact that some harmonies last precisely two bars (see mm. 9–10, 11–12, 13–14, etc.). An even larger metric grouping—one of eight quarter notes, or four bars—becomes apparent when the harmony changes for the first time in m. 5, with the result that we perceive the four bars preceding that change as a unit. The following four-bar segments are not as obviously delineated by harmony, but significant harmonic changes do occur at their beginnings (see mm. 9, 13, and 17), and two of the four-bar segments—mm. 13–16 and mm. 17–20—contain almost identical harmonic progressions. The fact that the four-bar segments are all characterized by similar melodic rhythms further reinforces this subdivision of the passage.

There is no doubt that the music of example 2.1 divides into two- and four-bar segments—but in what sense are these segments "metric groupings"? Their metric status is not determined solely by their equivalent duration (although such regularity is one important aspect of musical meter). They qualify as metric units—as large-scale measures—also because, like the notated measures of the song, they are perceived as consisting of alternate strong and weak beats. In example 2.1, I have indicated this characteristic of the four-bar units by placing numbers above the staves, which assign to each notated bar the function of a strong or weak beat within a large-scale measure. The strong beats are those marked "1" or "3"; the weak beats, those marked "2" or "4." Counting or even conducting according to these numbers will verify the validity of this large-scale metric analysis; nothing in the music contradicts this way of counting the passage, and many musical features support it—particularly the changes of harmony at strong beats.

Meter at a level higher than that shown by time signatures and bar lines is most easily perceived in quick pieces in 2/4 or 3/4 time; it can, however, be present in tonal compositions written in any meter. Example 2.2a reproduces a work in common time in which the existence of large-scale meter is somewhat less obvious—Josephine Lang's song "Mignons Klage." Numbers above the vocal staves again indicate how the notated bars function as strong or weak beats within larger metric units (two- and four-bar units). The manner in which the bars of the song act as beats would become more clearly apparent if the song were performed at a higher speed. Example 2.2b simulates such a performance of the opening measures by rewriting them in smaller note values; each notated bar is represented in example 2.2b by a half-note value.[2] The bar lines and brackets in the renotated example show the large-scale metric groupings that emerge at this "higher speed." The bar lines, which group the half notes into twos, represent a two-bar grouping in the score, and the brackets, which group the half notes into fours, represent a four-bar grouping in the score.

A careful listening to examples 2.2a and 2.2b demonstrates that the given analysis of large-scale meter makes aural sense; it "fits" the music, specifically the harmony. Boundaries of the song's two-bar and four-bar units are coordinated with harmonic changes, just as the metric boundaries—the bar lines—are notated in the score. The harmony also supports the designation of large-scale beats as weak or strong. The beginnings of bars marked "1" or "3" in example 2.2a are associated with motions to particularly significant harmonies—to the overall tonic on the downbeat of m. 3, and to the new temporary tonic of D major on the downbeat of m. 5. Weaker large-scale beats (those marked "2" or "4") are generally associated with less-stable harmonies than the surrounding strong beats (the D-major tonic in m. 8 being an obvious exception). The large-scale metric analysis of the passage, then, is not something that has been arbitrarily imposed upon it; it corresponds to features built into the music.

It is noteworthy that all of the large-scale measures shown in examples 2.1 and 2.2 comprise two or four bars. This circumstance raises two questions: (1) Do large-scale measures always contain an even number of bars? And (2) Could the large-scale metric hierarchy illustrated in the examples—beats, single bars, groups of two bars, groups of four bars—be expanded upward to encompass even larger units? Nonduple large-scale measures can and do occur; we shall encounter a few examples later in this essay. Duple

---

2. Renotations of this type for the purpose of facilitating high-level metric analysis are called "durational reductions." Good examples can be found in Carl Schachter, "Rhythm and Linear Analysis: Aspects of Meter," 10–11 and 20–21, and William Rothstein, *Phrase Rhythm in Tonal Music,* 8 and 10. Some of these durational reductions combine metric analysis with Schenkerian analysis of pitch structure.

Example 2.2a. Josephine Lang, "Mignons Klage," op. 10, no. 2 (1835)

units, however, are much more common in tonal music, for reasons that have never been satisfactorily explained.[3] And theoretically, the duple hierarchies in the two examples could indeed be expanded upward to encompass even larger measurelike units. It is ques-

---

3. Eighteenth-century theorists already pointed out the prevalence of duple grouping; see, for example, Johann Philipp Kirnberger, *The Art of Strict Musical Composition*, trans. David Beach and Jurgen Thym (New Haven and London: Yale University Press, 1982), 408–16. Kirnberger does discuss the possibility of nonduple struc-

Example 2.2a. (*Continued*)

tionable, however, whether units more than four bars in length can be perceived as genuinely metric in nature. Even if we could apprehend the durational equivalence of, say, eight-bar "measures," we would probably not be able to classify such large units as strong

tures; see also Rothstein, *Phrase Rhythm*, 33–40. Rothstein briefly summarizes various attempts to explain the predominance of duple organization on pp. 33–34. For Heinrich Schenker's explanation, based on physiological grounds, see *Free Composition*, trans. and ed. Ernst Oster (New York and London: Longman, 1979), 119.

"Mignon's Lament"

Only those familiar with longing
Know what I suffer.
Alone and cut off
From all joy,
I gaze at the firmament,
In all directions.
Oh, he who loves and knows me
Is far away!
I am dizzy, my innards burn.
Only those familiar with longing
Know what I suffer.

—Goethe

Example 2.2a. (*Continued*)

or weak beats within even larger measures (except, perhaps, in very quickly moving works). In this essay, I shall not pursue metric hierarchies beyond the level of four-bar units.[4]

The terms "large-scale measure" and "large-scale meter" are rather cumbersome; fortunately, more compact and elegant terms are available. In 1968 Edward Cone referred to large-scale measures as "hypermeasures."[5] Later writers adopted his term and created the related terms "**hypermeter**" and "**hyperbeat**."[6] The above brief discussions of hypermeter at the openings of two songs have already suggested the meanings of these terms; however, the following definitions might nevertheless be helpful. A **hypermeasure** (a large-scale, or high-level measure) is a segment of music that is larger than a notated bar, is perceived as a unit, is composed of some pattern of strong and weak hyperbeats (large-scale beats), and joins with similar adjacent units to create a sense of hypermeter (large-scale meter).

Example 2.2b. Durational reduction of "Mignons Klage," mm. 1–8

4. For discussions of the upper limits of large-scale meter, see Fred Lerdahl and Ray Jackendoff, *A Generative Theory of Tonal Music*, 21–25, and Joel Lester, *The Rhythms of Tonal Music*, 161–63.

5. *Musical Form and Musical Performance* (New York: W. W. Norton, 1968), 79.

6. See, for example, Jonathan Kramer, *The Time of Music: New Meanings, New Temporalities, New Listening Strategies*, as well as the works by Rothstein and Schachter cited above.

TABLE 2.1 The Distinction between Hypermeasures and Phrases

Hypermeasures (metric units)	Phrases (formal units)
• Equality of duration	• No requirement for equality of duration
• Organized into strong and weak beats	• Contain beats, but beats are not elements of the phrases themselves
• Must begin with a strong beat and end with a weak beat	• May begin and end with either a strong or a weak beat
• Generally begin with a significant new harmony (which contributes to their initial accentuation), but otherwise no requirements for harmonic path	• Traverse a particular harmonic path and end with a sense of harmonic **closure**

Since some textbooks define phrases as four-bar units, and since many hypermeasures encompass four bars, it is easy to confuse the two types of units; it might appear, in fact, that "hypermeasure" is merely a more erudite term for a phrase. The two concepts are, however, by no means equivalent. The difference between them can be summarized by stating that hypermeasures are metric units, whereas phrases are units of musical form. To qualify as hypermeasures, given segments of music must fulfill the requirements for metric units, namely equality or at least similarity of duration with respect to surrounding units and organization into strong and weak beats (with a strong beat at the beginning and a weak beat at the end). These conditions do not apply to phrases. The phrases of a given work need not be equal or even similar in length; whereas phrases often exhibit some regularity, even the substantial deviation of an individual unit from an established norm would not preclude that unit from being a phrase. Furthermore, organization into strong and weak beats does not specifically appertain to phrases. Although any phrase contains strong and weak beats, we do not consult these beats in order to determine whether a given unit is a phrase, and we do not expect a phrase to exhibit any particular organization of beats. Whereas hypermeasures *must* begin with a strong beat and end with a weak beat (because such organization is part of the nature of any type of measure), phrases may begin and end with either strong or weak beats.

The most significant difference between hypermeasures and phrases lies in the harmonic domain; harmonic characteristics are much more central to the identity of a phrase than to that of a hypermeasure. In order to qualify as a phrase, a unit must traverse a particular harmonic path; as William Rothstein puts it, a phrase is a "directed motion in time from one tonal entity to another."[7] We expect a phrase to depart from a particular harmony, to make its way toward some harmonic goal, and to end by establishing that goal with a harmonic progression that expresses harmonic closure (a cadence). Although hypermeasures generally begin with a significant "tonal entity" (such a beginning contributes to the sensation of an initial strong beat), there are no additional requirements for the harmonic path that they traverse or for the harmonies with which they conclude. Table 2.1 summarizes the differences between phrases and hypermeasures.

A glance at an actual musical context further clarifies the distinction between the two types of units. In example 2.2a, the four-bar units within mm. 1–8 do not fulfill the harmonic requirements for phrases. The unit in mm. 1 to 4 begins with the tonic and initiates a motion to a different tonal entity, but that entity is not yet reached at the end of m.

---

7. Rothstein, *Phrase Rhythm,* 5.

4; the harmony is quite unstable at that point. The unit comprising mm. 5–8 could more readily be perceived as a phrase; it begins with a weak statement (a first inversion) of D-major harmony and leads to a strong cadence on the root position of that harmony. In context, however, bar 5 sounds *too* weak to be considered the beginning of a phrase; the bar sounds more like the middle of a tonal motion than the beginning. These four-bar units, then, are hypermeasures (because of the metric properties discussed earlier), but they are not phrases. The first complete phrase in the song actually encompasses the first eight measures; only at m. 8 does one have the sense that the music has traversed a harmonic path and attained a harmonic goal—albeit a temporary one.

The first four bars of example 2.1 and bars 24–27 of example 2.2a offer additional demonstrations of the nonequivalence of hypermeasure and phrase. The individual bars within these four-measure units clearly alternate between strong and weak; the first and third bars are more strongly accented than the second and fourth. The conditions for hypermeasures, then, are fulfilled. The units are, however, not phrases, as they involve no tonal motion; they are harmonically static, prolonging a single harmony.

Since they are different classes of units, phrases and hypermeasures can and frequently do "coexist in a state of creative tension."[8] The third four-bar segment of example 2.2a (mm. 9–12), however, illustrates that these units can on occasion coincide. The segment conforms to the above definition of a phrase; it begins with the tonic of the newly established mediant key, then moves toward and ends on a different stable harmony, namely the dominant of the same key. Yet this four-bar segment also qualifies as a hypermeasure. Its constituent bars can be heard as alternating strong and weak beats—not because of the harmonic progression or other musical features, but because this pattern was securely established earlier, and because there is no obstacle to its continuation within mm. 9–12.[9]

HYPERMETRIC IRREGULARITY

We have so far discussed hypermeter as a succession of units of equivalent duration. But meter on any level is not a matter of absolute regularity. The notated measures of a work, for example, may be prolonged by a ritardando or a fermata without detriment to an overall sense of meter. The durational equality that I have ascribed to hypermeasures, too, must not be interpreted as precluding a stretching or a contraction of individual units.

"Mignons Klage" provides numerous illustrations of hypermetric irregularity. The first three four-bar hypermeasures of "Mignons Klage" exhibit perfect regularity; the hypermeasure beginning in m. 13, however, demonstrates **expansion** beyond the established four-bar length. This hypermeasure could have ended in m. 16, resulting in a four-bar unit like those that subdivide mm. 1–12. Measure 17, however, continues the dominant harmony of m. 16 and therefore fails to produce the impression of a strong hyperbeat and thus of the initiation of a hypermeasure; it is only when the resolving tonic appears in m. 18 that one hears a hypermetric downbeat. The hypermeasure initiated in m. 13 is thus five instead of four bars long—our first example of a hypermeasure composed of an odd number of bars. Notice that the metric numbers above the vocal staves reflect the expansion of the hypermeasure. Whereas in the earlier, hypermetrically regular passages, both on the two-bar and the four-bar level, one number was associated with each notated

---

8. Ibid., 28.

9. This passage illustrates an observation of Joel Lester's (made with respect to surface-level meter, but just as valid on the hypermetric level): "Once a metric hierarchy has been established, we, as listeners, will maintain that organization as long as minimal evidence is present" (*The Rhythms of Tonal Music*, 77).

bar, in mm. 16–17 the numbers extend across two bars, showing the stretching of a hyperbeat.[10]

When a hypermeasure within a context dominated by duple structure deviates from that structure, this hypermeasure can usually be interpreted as modifying a hypothetical duple unit. In mm. 13–17 of "Mignons Klage," the four-bar hypermeasure that one might expect after the "four-square" opening measures can be constructed by omitting m. 17; m. 17 is an "extra" bar of dominant harmony—"extra" in the sense that the passage would remain syntactically and stylistically correct without it (although it would be much less expressive). The hypermeasure in mm. 13–17, then, is expanded by stretching the dominant harmony. The next hypermeasure in the song is expanded in the same manner. Measures 18–23 reestablish the mediant key (D major), and its dominant arrives at m. 20 (in the form of a cadential $^6_4$ chord). Just one more bar of dominant would have completed a four-bar hypermeasure (at m. 21), and the resolution of the dominant to the tonic of D major could then have initiated the next hypermeasure (at m. 22). Instead, Lang prolongs the $^6_4$ chord of m. 20 in m. 21, inserts a poignant neighboring ii$^6_5$ chord in m. 22, then returns to the dominant in m. 23; the result is a total of four bars of dominant prolongation (mm. 20–23) instead of just two. To reduce the hypermeasure to a hypothetical four-bar duration, we could imagine mm. 18–20 being followed by m. 23. Notice again how much less expressive this regularized hypermeasure would be than the expanded hypermeasure that Lang wrote.

Yet another example of a hypermetric expansion involving an elongated dominant is found in mm. 28–33 of "Mignons Klage." The hypermeasure beginning in m. 28 could have consisted of two bars of ii^7 harmony (in the key of B minor), followed by two bars of dominant. Instead, Lang stretches the dominant harmony across four bars (mm. 30–33). The "extra" measures, mm. 30–31, are occupied by a cadenzalike "solo," which, with its expressive upper-neighboring motion, constitutes one of the most touching moments in the song.

We have seen several examples of hypermetric expansion by the elongation of a dominant harmony, but expansion could theoretically occur by the stretching of any harmony. Within the final vocal utterance of "Mignons Klage," a Neapolitan sixth harmony is implicated in hypermetric expansion. This harmony could have occupied only mm. 39 and 40 instead of mm. 39–42, and m. 40 could have been followed by the dominant-prolonging mm. 43–44. Bars 41 and 42, then, are "extra" measures, expanding the Neapolitan harmony.[11]

Lang's song "Nur den Abschied schnell genommen" (example 2.3) contains even more hypermetric irregularity than "Mignons Klage," some arising in ways not yet discussed. The first four bars fall into place as a four-bar hypermeasure, and we therefore expect m. 8 to be the end of a hypermeasure as well. The fact that the voice part of mm. 5–8 has the same rhythm as that of mm. 1–4 reinforces the impression that the second unit is a hypermeasure parallel to the first. The continuation, however, confounds this interpretation. Measure 11 contains a strong arrival on tonic harmony and therefore sounds like a hypermetric downbeat. But if m. 8 is the last beat of a hypermeasure, and m. 11

---

10. This method of using metric numbers to show expansion has been used by Heinrich Schenker and also by recent writers on hypermeter; see Heinrich Schenker, *Free Composition*, figures 146/5, 148/2, 148/3c and others, and Rothstein, *Phrase Rhythm*, 81 and 85–86. An obvious alternative to the numbering method used here would be to show m. 17 as the fifth bar of a hypermeasure; the method used in my examples, however, more precisely indicates how the passage deviates from an established hypermetric norm.

11. See Rothstein, *Phrase Rhythm*, 80–87, for further discussion and examples of the stretching of harmonies.

Example 2.3. Josephine Lang, "Nur den Abschied schnell genommen" (1838)

the first beat of another, what is the function of mm. 9 and 10? It is not convincing to re-gard these two measures by themselves as a mini-hypermeasure. They sound, rather, like a "retake" of mm. 7–8 (as is suggested by the bracketed numbers above the staves) and, therefore, like a continuation of the hypermeasure initiated in m. 5. The impression of a "retake" arises in part from melodic factors; m. 9 is melodically similar to m. 7. Harmonic factors, however, play an even larger role. As is shown by the small staff above m. 8, a

Example 2.3. (*Continued*)

perfect authentic cadence in Db major could have occurred here. Lang, however, deceptively resolves the dominant harmony to V of vi at the end of m. 8. In mm. 9–10 she returns to the dominant and takes another run at the expected authentic cadence. It is the
latter aspect of these measures that contributes the most to the impression that they are a
"retake" of mm. 7–8 and, hence, part of the same hypermeasure as those bars. The hypermeasure beginning in m. 5 thus turns out to be six instead of four bars in length (mm.

Example 2.3. (*Continued*)

5–10). The extra measures result from the deceptive resolution, and from the necessity of "correcting" this resolution.[12]

---

12. For a discussion of the deceptive cadence as a technique of expansion, see Rothstein, *Phrase Rhythm*, 78–80. This and other techniques of expansion mentioned here are often referred to as techniques of *phrase* expansion, which is by no means incorrect. When a phrase is expanded, one or more hypermeasures that impinge on that phrase will also be affected, and conversely, the expansion of a hypermeasure results in the expansion of the phrase within which it lies or with which it coincides.

Example 2.3. (*Continued*)

Measures 36–37 of "Nur den Abschied" demonstrate an entirely different type of hypermetric irregularity—a type not based on the expansion of hypermeasures. In context, m. 36 sounds like a hypermetric downbeat (as did mm. 28 and 32). The bars after m. 36, however, cannot convincingly be analyzed as the continuation of the hypermeasure initiated in m. 36. The dramatic change of harmony in m. 37 causes this bar to sound like a hypermetric downbeat rather than like a second beat. Furthermore, if m. 37 were treated as a second hyperbeat, m. 38 as a third, and so on, problems would arise at m. 41; this bar would then be beat 2 of a hypermeasure—but the significant harmonic resolution to

"Take farewell quickly"

Take farewell quickly,
Don't delay, don't complain;
Faster than the tears flow,
Tear yourself away undismayed.

Untwine yourself from the arms,
No matter how this may burn in your breast;
That which came together in this life
Is also separated in this life.

Should you bear, must you bear,
Bear it with a firm spirit!
Your sighs, your complaints
[Shall] blow away in the breezes.

If pain is not to conquer you,
Then conquer pain yourself,
And wilted blossoms shall twine themselves
Freshly around your wounded heart.

Example 2.3. (*Continued*)

the local tonic of E major implies that it is actually a hypermetric downbeat. Analyzing mm. 36 and 37 as "successive downbeats"—William Rothstein's term for this type of irregularity—avoids these problems.[13] One could regularize the passage by adding three more bars of A♭ harmony after m. 36 to complete a four-bar hypermeasure prolonging that harmony. This hypermeasure would be similar to the two preceding ones (mm. 28–31 and 32–35); this circumstance on the one hand indicates that the proposed regularization makes sense in the context but, on the other hand, suggests why Lang didn't actually write this hypothetical version. Yet another four-bar hypermeasure prolonging A♭ major would have been monotonous.

"Mignons Klage" (example 2.2a) offers another example of successive downbeats. We might expect an authentic cadence at mm. 37–38; the vocal portion of the song could theoretically end with an arrival at tonic harmony at m. 38. Such an ending would, however, result in a disproportionately brief final section—a problem that Lang avoids by writing a deceptive cadence instead of an authentic one. Measure 38, occupied by submediant harmony, sounds like a hypermetric downbeat, not only because it follows the fourth bar of a hypermeasure, but also because it contains a significant, albeit unexpected, resolving harmony. Measure 39, however, with its dramatic and dynamically accented new harmony—the Neapolitan sixth chord—gives an even stronger impression of being a downbeat, with the result that one hypermetric downbeat is immediately followed by another. Again, one could regularize this passage by adding three measures of G-major prolongation after m. 38. An alternate regularization is suggested in a later section of this essay.[14]

---

13. Rothstein, *Phrase Rhythm*, 58–63.

14. Numerous techniques other than those discussed here can create hypermetric irregularity, including elongation of a hypermetric upbeat (see Rothstein, *Phrase Rhythm*, 39 and 56–57); metrical reinterpretation—the double function of a hyperbeat (ibid., 52–56); repetition of a passage within a hypermeasure (ibid., 74–80); and interpolation of a parenthetical passage into a hypermeasure (Ibid., 87–91). For examples of some of these procedures in songs of Josephine Lang, see Harald Krebs, "Irrégularités hypermetriques dans les chansons de Josephine Lang," *Revue de Musique Classique et Romantique* (October 1999): 33 57.

Below, I discuss a regularization of the complete "Nur den Abschied," in order to summarize the hypermetric devices mentioned above and to lay the foundation for a subsequent discussion of the expressive function of hypermetric irregularity. My regularized recomposition of "Nur den Abschied" can be tracked by following the arrows and the added small vocal staves in example 2.3. This recomposition, containing just enough music to declaim the text at a uniform pace, could be regarded as the most obvious possible setting of the text (using Lang's musical ideas).

The recomposition demonstrates that the first stanza could have consisted of two four-bar hypermeasures, ending with a perfect authentic cadence in m. 8. As was mentioned, however, Lang extends the second hypermeasure by writing, then "correcting" a deceptive resolution of V. The second stanza, beginning at m. 16, could also have been set to two four-bar hypermeasures; the cadence to the dominant that ends the stanza at m. 28 could have occurred at m. 23, where it would have been prepared by the ii chord of m. 22. But Lang avoids the dominant at m. 23, inserts a parenthetical tonicization of ii, and then writes a renewed approach to the dominant harmony. The latter approach takes place in a very leisurely manner. The harmonies of mm. 24 to 28 could have occurred within just two measures; one could imagine mm. 24 and 25 moving twice as quickly and filling just one bar, and the prolonged dominant of mm. 26–28 occupying just one bar. Abbreviating the harmonies in this manner would result in a melodic and harmonic rhythm matching the rapid rhythms of the earlier portion of the song. The avoidance of the cadence to V in m. 23 and the elongations of harmonies in mm. 24–27 result in a second stanza that is five bars longer than the hypothetical eight-bar duration. In hypermetric terms, these expansion techniques result in the stretching of the second hypermeasure of the stanza, a potential four-bar hypermeasure (mm. 20–23), to a length of nine bars.[15]

The lingering pace of mm. 24–27 continues in the third stanza. Lang could have moved through this stanza just as quickly as through the first, as my recomposition demonstrates by removing the interludes and by cutting the voice's note values in half to create rhythms much like those found in Lang's song prior to m. 24.

The final stanza, similar to the first, begins in m. 62 with a four-bar hypermeasure, and we thus expect the second hypermeasure to be the same length; m. 69a shows how the second hypermeasure and the entire stanza could have ended. Lang, however, resolves V deceptively at precisely that point, as she did in the first stanza (cf. m. 8). The process of "correcting" the deceptive resolution now occupies not three measures, as at the end of the first stanza (mm. 9–11), but five (mm. 70–74).

The regularized version of "Nur den Abschied" shown within example 2.3 makes perfect musical sense and represents a viable setting of the text. Comparison of this version to Lang's actual composition, however, reveals that with the elimination of hypermetric irregularity the song would lose almost everything that makes it beautiful, interesting, and expressive.

---

15. The numbers above the staves in example 2.3 do not show this expansion. They show instead that four of the "extra" measures involved in this expansion themselves form a regular hypermeasure (mm. 24–27). This passage illustrates that hypermeter can operate simultaneously on different levels. The hypermeasure in mm. 24–27 belongs to the level that is closest to the musical surface, whereas the hypothetical four-bar hypermeasure that could end in m. 23 belongs to an underlying level. Measures 66–74 also illustrate the existence of two hypermetric levels—a succession of two four-bar surface-level hypermeasures (mm. 66–69 and 70–73) and a single underlying hypermeasure (mm. 66–69a). For more-detailed discussions of surface-level and underlying hypermeter, see Rothstein, *Phrase Rhythm*, 97–99 and 161–68.

Hypermetric Irregularity and Expression

The above discussion will already have suggested some answers to the question of why Lang, or any composer, would want to employ hypermetric irregularity. It is obvious, for example, that constant regularity would become monotonous in any substantial piece of music; the unpredictability associated with hypermetric irregularity is a significant source of interest in tonal music. The songs shown in Examples 2.2a and 2.3 also suggest some less obvious motivations for the introducing of irregularity. They show, for instance, that hypermetric irregularity can be involved in the creation of a sense of closure. In both "Mignons Klage" and "Nur den Abschied," many of the elongated hypermeasures serve to emphasize the final measures of phrases, subsections, or sections. In "Mignons Klage," the expanded hypermeasure at mm. 13–17, for instance, highlights the end of the sub-section comprising mm. 9–17. The more substantially expanded hypermeasure at mm. 28–33 similarly adds weight to an important formal boundary—the boundary between the central and the final sections. The same is true of the long final vocal phrase with its expanded Neapolitan harmony. In "Nur den Abschied," too, expanded hypermeasures emphasize the ends of musical sections and hence contribute to a feeling of closure.

The songs discussed in this essay suggest that a particularly important rationale for the use of hypermetric irregularity is its value as an expressive device.[16] The hypermetric irregularities in "Mignons Klage" undoubtedly arise in large part from Lang's effort to convey the poignant emotions in Goethe's poetic text. Many of the irregularities seem to have been inspired by her desire to emphasize particularly expressive words by repeating or elongating them. At mm. 20–23, it was surely her wish to stress the intense phrase "es brennt" ([my innards] burn) that inspired her to expand the cadential dominant. Similarly, the desire for an especially emphatic final statement of the lines "Nur wer die Sehnsucht kennt, weiss was ich leide" (Only those familiar with longing Know what I suffer) must have influenced Lang's decision to employ hypermetric irregularities in mm. 38 to 44. At the opening of the song, she moves quite quickly through this text. She begins the final section of the song with a similar statement of these lines but then balances the quick presentation with elongation; the opening line "Nur wer die Sehnsucht kennt" increases in duration within the final section from one bar (m. 34) to two (mm. 39–40).

Lang also progressively expands the word "leide" (suffer); from the curt two-beat statement of m. 35, she moves through a three-beat statement in mm. 37–38 to a final one more than two bars in length. The expansion of "leide" at m. 37 results in the successive downbeats in mm. 38 and 39. Had this word been declaimed within two beats, as it was in m. 35, the G-major harmony that occupies m. 38 could have occurred at the end of m. 37 to conclude a four-bar hypermeasure (mm. 34–37). Moreover, the Neapolitan harmony could have appeared at the beginning of m. 38 as the sole hypermetric downbeat in the vicinity.[17] The expressive expansion of the opening lines during the final vocal utterance—particularly the lingering presentation of "weiss"—results in the aforementioned elongation of the Neapolitan harmony and hence in a significantly enlarged hypermeasure.

---

16. The connection between hypermeter and expression has been explored by a number of authors, most frequently in the analysis of instrumental works. See, for example, Richard Cohn, "The Dramatization of Hypermetric Conflicts in the Scherzo of Beethoven's Ninth Symphony," *19th Century Music* 15, no. 3 (spring 1992): 188–206. For an example of the discussion of hypermeter and expression in the context of song, see Rothstein, "Beethoven with and without *Kunstgepräng*," in *Beethoven Forum IV*, ed. Christopher Reynolds, Lewis Lockwood, and James Webster. (Lincoln and London: University of Nebraska Press, 1995), 186–93.

17. The regularization of the passage proposed here is an alternative to that suggested earlier (namely, following m. 38 with three more bars of G-major harmony).

In "Nur den Abschied," the hypermetric irregularities are no less clearly linked to text expression.[18] Many of the words involved in hypermetric expansions are associated with pain and with its cause (namely separation). By stretching harmonies (and hence an underlying hypermeasure) at mm. 24–28, Lang gives the impression of meditating on the line "wird im Leben auch getrennt" (is separated in this life). She also lingers on the third stanza of the poem, in which the idea of bearing pain is emphasized. She begins the setting of this stanza ("Should you bear, must you bear"—m. 31) with rhythmic values twice as slow as those beginning any other stanza, and further draws out the first line of the stanza by placing interludes between text segments. The development of the poetic theme of bearing pain in mm. 41–45 and 49–56 ("Your sighs, your complaints") similarly involves rhythmic values slower than those of other stanzas. Particularly striking is the expansion of the word "Klagen" (complaints) near the end of the third stanza (mm. 52–53), which represents the culmination of a trend toward increasing elongation of words. Finally, note the elongation of the word "wundes" (sore or wounded) in mm. 72–73.

Lang's emphasis by hypermetric expansion on words denoting sorrow goes beyond the mere highlighting of significant words of the text; the prevalence of hypermetric expansions at just such points of the poem suggests a critical, questioning stance with respect to the poet's message. The message, apparently directed at the poet's beloved, can be summarized as follows: farewells are inevitable and should take place without delaying, and the resulting pain must be borne courageously. By consistently dwelling on words denoting pain, Lang subtly undermines this rather cocky and egotistical message; she responds to the call for quick farewells with musical suggestions of lingering, and to the exhortations *not* to yield to pain with an insistent, vivid evocation of present sorrow. It is possible that this response to the poem is an unconscious one—that Lang wished to subscribe to and reinforce its message (and did so with the generally confident, assertive, even noble tone of much of the music), but that contradictory feelings broke through in the form of the frequent hypermetric expansions.

Lang's artistic and subtle treatment of hypermeter would be effective even in the absence of text, but viewed in conjunction with the poetry, her hypermetric irregularities become all the more telling, sometimes reinforcing the meaning of a text, and sometimes counterpointing its meaning with quite a different one. Analysis of her music from a hypermetric standpoint illustrates that hypermeter, like surface-level meter, is more than a theoretical concept; in the hands of a fine composer, it can become a significant vehicle of musical expression.

---

18. According to the published score, the poem is by Lang's husband, Reinhold Köstlin. Sharon Krebs, who has looked at all of his poetry manuscripts in the German Literature Archive in Marbach, has not, however, been able to verify that it is indeed by him. Since Lang wrote the song before she met Köstlin, she would have had to come across it in a periodical; no such publication has yet been located.

~3~

SCHENKER'S CONCEPTION OF MUSICAL STRUCTURE

Allen Forte

When Allen Forte (Yale University) published this essay in 1959, Heinrich
Schenker's theory of tonal music was still relatively new to American composers and theorists. Since then, Schenker's work has become much discussed
and highly influential, but Forte's essay remains one of the most lucid and
succinct introductions to Schenker's analytical system. For those who wish
to learn more about Schenkerian theory, the following can be recommended:
Forte's own *Introduction to Schenkerian Analysis*, with coauthor Steven Gilbert,
and *Analysis of Tonal Music: A Schenkerian Approach*, by Allen Cadwallader
and David Gagné.

Forte has written on numerous topics, including atonal theory and the
music of Schoenberg, Webern, Stravinsky, and Messaien. His 1995 book *The
American Popular Ballad of the Golden Era, 1924–1950*, won the Society for
Music Theory's Wallace Berry Award.

Through the efforts of Forte and others, Schenkerian analysis is now regarded by many as a basic component of music theory. Among harmony texts
that reflect Schenker's ideas are Forte's *Tonal Harmony in Concept and Practice*, 1979, and Edward Aldwell and Carl Schachter's *Harmony and Voice Leading* (1978; rev. ed., 2003); new theories of tonal rhythm, some of which are
introduced in this volume (chapters 1 and 2), also derive from Schenker's
theories. The excerpt reprinted here offers a bird's-eye view of Schenkerian
theory. It is an early offering from one of the founding fathers of music theory doctoral studies in the United States.

I can think of no more satisfactory way to introduce Schenker's ideas, along with the terminology and visual means which express them, than to comment at some length upon
one of his analytic sketches. For this purpose I have selected from *Der freie Satz* a sketch
of a complete short work, the second song from Schumann's *Dichterliebe* (example 3.1).
I shall undertake to read and interpret this sketch, using, of course, English equivalents
for Schenker's terms.

Some reminders: (1) all words in **bold** are defined in the glossary; (2) full citations for incomplete references
are found in the selected bibliography; (3) the authors use their preferred notational system (e.g., Roman numeral, form label, and register notation). Most of the essays denote register by middle C as C^4.—Ed.

Schumann, "Aus meinen Tränen spriessen" (*Dichterliebe*, no.2)

Example 3.1. Schenkerian analysis of Schumann's "Aus meinen Thränen spriessen" (figure 22b from Anhang, *Free Composition*)

Here in visual form is Schenker's conception of musical structure: the total work is regarded as an interacting composite of three main levels. Each of these structural levels is represented on a separate staff in order that its unique content may be clearly shown. And to show how the three levels interact, Schenker has aligned corresponding elements vertically. I shall first make a quick survey of this analytic sketch and then give a more detailed explanation.

The lowest staff contains the major surface events, those elements that are usually most immediately perceptible. Accordingly, Schenker has designated this level as the *foreground*. In deriving his foreground sketch from the fully notated song, Schenker has not included all its actual note values. Those which he does include represent in some cases the actual durational values of the work; but more often they represent the relative structural weight which he has assigned to the particular tone or configuration. This sketch omits repeated tones and shows inner voices in mm. 8–12 only, indicating that there they have greater influence upon the voice leading.

On the middle staff Schenker has represented the structural events which lie immediately beyond the foreground level. These events, which do not necessarily occur in immediate succession in relation to the foreground, comprise the *middleground*. It should be evident now that the analytic procedure is one of reduction; details which are subordinate with respect to larger patterns are gradually eliminated—in accordance with criteria which I will explain further on.

Finally, on the upper staff, he has represented the fundamental structural level, or *background*, which controls the entire work.

Now let us consider the content of each level in some detail. This will provide an opportunity to examine other important aspects of Schenker's thought, all derived from his central concept.

A series of sketches such as this can be read in several directions. For the purpose of the present introductory explanation it would seem advantageous to begin with the level which contains the fewest elements and proceed from there to the level which contains the most—thus, reading from top to bottom or from background to foreground. By reading the sketches in this order we also gain a clear idea of Schenker's concept of *prolon-gation:* each subsequent level expands, or *prolongs,* the content of the previous level.

The background of this short song, and of all tonal works, whatever their length, is regarded as a temporal projection of the tonic triad. The upper voice projects the triad in the form of a descending linear succession which, in the present case, spans the lower tri-adic third. Schenker marks this succession, which he called the *Urlinie,* or fundamental line, in two ways: (1) with numerals (and carets) that designate the corresponding dia-tonic scale degrees, and (2) with the balken which connects the stemmed open notes (I shall explain the black noteheads shortly). The triad is also projected by the bass, which here outlines the triadic fifth, the tonality-defining interval. Schenker calls this funda-mental bass motion *Bassbrechung,* or bass arpeggiation. Like the fundamental line, it is represented in open noteheads. The fundamental line and the bass arpeggiation coordi-nate, forming a contrapuntal structure, the *Ursatz,* or fundamental structure, which con-stitutes a complete projection of the tonic triad. Thus, to Schenker, motion within tonal space is measured by the triad, not by the diatonic scale.

Observe that in this case the most direct form of the fundamental structure would be the three-interval succession in the outer voices:

fundamental line, $\hat{3}$–$\hat{2}$–$\hat{1}$
bass arpeggiation, I–V–I

The background sketch shows that this succession occurs consecutively only in the last part of the song. The song begins unambiguously with $\hat{3}\atop\hat{1}$; however, it does not progress immediately to $\hat{2}\atop V$ and from there on to $\hat{1}\atop 1$; instead, the first interval is *prolonged* as shown in the sketch: the upper voice C♯ first receives an embellishment, or diminution, in the form of the third-spanning motion, C♯–B–A (represented in black noteheads), and then moves over a larger span (shown by the beam) to B on the last eighth note of m. 8, where it is supported by the bass V. (This V is not to be equated with the final V (m. 5), which effects a closure of the fundamental line.) Schenker then shows how this initial prolon-gation is followed by a restatement of $\hat{3}\atop 1$ and the completion of the succession $\hat{3}$–$\hat{2}$–$\hat{1}\atop\text{I–V–I}$.

To recapitulate, there are two prolongational classes shown in this background sketch. The first includes diminutions, or prolongational tones of shorter span (represented by black noteheads); the second includes the larger prolongational motion from $\hat{3}$ to $\hat{2}$ (con-nected by the beam), which comprises the controlling melodic pattern of the first phrase. Schenker regards this larger prolongational motion as an *interruption* of the direct suc-cession, $\hat{3}$–$\hat{2}$–$\hat{1}$, and represents it by placing parallel vertical lines above the staff follow-ing $\hat{3}$–$\hat{2}\atop\text{I–V}$. The fundamental structure, which is in this case the uninterrupted succession $\hat{3}$–$\hat{2}$–$\hat{1}\atop\text{I–V–I}$, therefore may be considered as the essential content of the background. In reading Schenker's analytic sketches a distinction must often be drawn between the background level in *toto,* which sometimes includes prolongations of primary order as in the present case, and the essential content of that level, the fundamental structure. Thus *fundamental structure* designates a specific contrapuntal organization which assumes several possible forms, whereas *background* is a term which may include other events in addition to the fundamental structure, as in the present instance, where it includes two prolongations, each belonging to a different structural order. This distinction, not always clearly drawn by Schenker, is indispensable to the full understanding of his sketches and commentaries. In this connection I point out that within each of the three main structural levels several sublevels are possible, depending upon the unique characteristics of the particular composition.

The idea of the interrupted fundamental line provides the basis for Schenker's con-cept of form. For example, in the typical sonata-allegro form in the major mode, interruption of the fundamental linear progression at the close of the exposition normally gives rise in the development section to a prolongation which centers on V. Of course, the prolonged fundamental line component varies, depending upon which form of the fundamental structure is in operation and upon which specific prolongation motions occur at the background level.

Before explaining the middleground, I should like to direct attention again to the diminution which spans the third below C♯ (black noteheads). By means of the numerals 3, 2, 1, enclosed in parentheses, Schenker indicates that the motion duplicates the large descending third of the fundamental line. This is an instance of a special kind of repetition which Schenker called *Uebertragung der Ursatzformen* (transference of the forms of the fundamental structure). Throughout his writings he demonstrates again and again that tonal compositions abound in hidden repetitions of this kind, which he distinguishes from more obvious motivic repetitions at the foreground level.

We can interpret the content of the middleground most efficiently by relating it to the background just examined. The first new structural event shown at the middleground level is the expansion of the smaller prolongational third (black noteheads) by means of the upper adjacent tone D, which serves as a prefix. The sketch shows how this prolongational element is counterpointed by the bass in such a way as to modify the original (i.e., background) third. That is, the figured-bass numerals in parentheses indicate that the second C♯ (black notehead) is a dissonant passing tone and therefore is not to be equated with the initial C♯, which serves as the point of departure for the fundamental line. The adjacent tone D recurs in m. 14, where Schenker assigns more structural weight to it, as indicated by the stem. I reiterate that conventional durational values are used in the analytic sketches to indicate the relative position of a given component or configuration in the tonal hierarchy—the greater the durational value, the closer the element to the background.

In addition to the prolongation described in the preceding paragraph, the middleground contains the essentials of the prolongational middle section (mm. 10–12), which appears in more detail in the foreground sketch. Schenker regards this entire middle section as a prolongation of the background fifth formed by $\hat{2}$ over V. Its main feature is the inner voice which descends from G♯ To E, a middleground duplication of the fundamental line's third. The bass which counterpoints this inner voice arpeggiates the tonic triad, E–C♯–A. Schenker shows how the arpeggiation is partially filled in by the passing tone, D, and by slurring E to A he indicates that he considers that motion to be the controlling bass motion, within which the C♯ functions as a connective of primarily melodic significance. Here we have an example of the careful distinction which Schenker always draws between major bass components, or *Stufen,* which belong to the background level, and more transient, contrapuntal-melodic events at the foreground and middleground levels.

A brief consideration of three additional events will complete our examination of the middleground level. First, observe that the diatonic inner-voice descent in the middle section, G♯–E, is filled in by a chromatic passing tone, G. Schenker has enclosed this in parentheses to indicate that it belongs to a subsidiary level within the middleground. Second, observe that just before the inner-voice motion is completed on the downbeat of m. 12, the G♯, its point of departure, is restated by an additional voice which is introduced above it. Schenker has pointed out that in "free" compositions, particularly instrumental works, the possibility of more elaborate prolongation is greatly increased by introducing additional voices, as well as by abandoning voices already stated. The final event to observe here occurs in the middle section: the motion from B, the retained upper voice, to C♯ on the downbeat of m. 12. This direct connection does not actually occur at the foreground level, but Schenker, feeling that it is strongly implied by the voice-leading context, encloses the implied C♯ in parentheses and ties it to the actual C♯, thereby indicating that it is an anticipation.

In the foreground sketch Schenker represents for the first time the metrical organization of the song. As I have already mentioned, he shows there some of the actual durational values, in addition to using these as sketch symbols. This reveals the position assigned to meter and rhythm in his system: he considered them to be important structural determinants at the middleground and foreground levels but subsidiary to the fundamental tonal organization, which, he maintained, was arhythmic. I shall return to this further on when I consider the general problem of constructing a theory of rhythm for tonal music.

Let us now examine some of the relationships which Schenker has shown in his sketch of the foreground, this time beginning with the bass. In m. 3 he encloses the bass note A in parentheses and marks it with the abbreviation Kons. Dg. (*Konsonanter Durchgang*, or "consonant passing tone"). By this he indicates that the tenth which the bass A forms with the upper-voice C♯ transforms the latter, a dissonant passing tone at the middleground level, into a consonance at the foreground level. In this way he also intends to indicate the function of the chord at that point. Since it supports a passing tone in the upper voice it is a passing chord. In addition, it belongs only to the foreground and therefore is to be distinguished from the initial tonic chord, a background element. Two of Schenker's most important convictions underlie this treatment of detail: (1) that the study of strict counterpoint provides the indispensable basis for a thorough understanding of the details, as well as the larger patterns of a composed work, and (2) that the function of a chord depends upon its context, not upon its label. This can be seen in his notation of the chords in this sketch. Although he uses the conventional Roman numerals, he provides them with slurs, dashes, and parentheses to show their relative values in the tonal hierarchy. Thus, the long slur from I to I indicates that the IV and V chords lie within the control of that chord, while the abbreviation Vdg. (*Vordergrund*) shows that the succession belongs to the foreground. And in the middle section, mm. 8–12, the parentheses show that the chords between V and I are subsidiary chords. These arise as part of the prolongational complex at that point and stand in contrast to the stable background chords I and V.

Now let us turn to the melody. We can most efficiently examine its structure by first comparing each foreground prolongation (slurred) with the larger middleground prolongation immediately above it, and then by relating both the foreground and middleground to the background. In this way we see that the foreground prolongation of the first section spans a descending third twice, thus duplicating the successively larger thirds at the middleground and background levels. In the middle section the melody undergoes more elaborate development. There, by means of connecting beams, Schenker shows how the upper voice skips down to the inner voice and back again. The ascending skips comprise a sequence of two fourths, which are marked by brackets and emphasized by a typically Schenkerian exclamation point. This sequence lends support to his reading of the implied anticipation of C♯ in the upper voice of m. 12, mentioned earlier.

The foreground of the middle section provides a good example of Schenker's concept of "melody" (he avoided the term in his writings) as a self-contained polyphonic structure. This valuable aspect of his theory—an aspect absolutely indispensable to any kind of intelligent melodic analyses—is well substantiated by compositional practice. There are many passages in the literature where polyphonic melodies, implied at one point (often the beginning), are subsequently realized in full, for example in the first movement of Mozart's Sonata in A Minor, or in Brahms's Intermezzo in B-flat Major, op. 76, no. 4; and, of course, we find a special development of this concept in Bach's compositions for solo violin and for solo cello. Here, in the foreground sketch of the middle section, the diagonal beams show that the vocal melody shifts back and forth between two lines, the lower of which belongs to the accompaniment. It is evident that this section contains the most intricate upper-voice prolongation.

It also contains the most elaborate bass motion. The sketch shows how the bass provides counterpoint to the upper-voice (foreground) prolongation of B, bass and upper voice comprising the interval succession 5–10–5–10–5, which is enclosed within the middleground outer-voice succession, $\frac{B-C\sharp}{E-C\sharp}$. Observe that the upper voice alternates between an upper adjacent-tone prolongation of B (marked Nbn.) and the skips into the inner voice which were explained in the preceding paragraph. The lowest voice in this passage is subordinate to the voice which lies immediately above it, E–D–C$\sharp$, the latter succession being the actual bass line (cf. middleground sketch). Nor does its registral position above the foreground bass lessen its importance as the main motion-determinant in the lower voices. Therefore, the foreground bass which displaces or covers it registrally might be termed a "pseudo-bass."

One final aspect of the foreground sketch deserves mention: the form. Schenker indicates this with the customary letters and exponents. The foreground form therefore corresponds to the form-generating interruption at the middleground and background levels as follows:

Statement	Interruption	Restatement and Closure
A^1	B	A^2

It should be apparent that an analysis of this kind embraces all the information generally included under the heading "form and analysis" but that it goes far beyond to interpret the relationships to the background which are revealed during its initial phases, where the main concern is to achieve an accurate reading of foreground and middleground.

A summary of this analysis should properly include a classification of the chromatic chords in the middle section of the piece and a more precise explanation of the coordination of linear intervals at the foreground level, the descending thirds and fifths (which later take the form of diminished fifths and ascending fourths in the middle section). However, because of space limitations, I shall not undertake a summary here but instead shall go on to discuss other aspects of Schenker's work. If the preceding commentary has succeeded in demonstrating some of Schenker's more important ideas, as well as clarifying some of the vocabulary and visual devices which he employs to express those ideas, it has fulfilled its purpose.

~4~

"LEARN TO DRAW BOB HOPE!"
Mort Drucker, Arnold Schoenberg,
and Twelve-Tone Music

Andrew Mead

Andrew Mead (University of Michigan) is a composer and scholar of the sophisticated world of twelve-tone music and analysis. He has published on the
music of Milton Babbitt, Elliott Carter, and composers of the Second Viennese School. His introduction to twelve-tone music, using a minimum of technical language, was a remarkable challenge; the author introduces the key
concepts and terminology for analyzing atonal and twelve-tone music only
after spending time with the music first.

It's an old story: a student submits an analysis of a twelve-tone piece that consists solely
of an enumeration of the work's twelve-tone rows. A reviewer presents a garbled rehash
of some composer's off-hand remarks and dismisses a work on the grounds that such a
way of proceeding couldn't possibly make any musical sense. A young composition student is warned away from twelve-tone music and is left with the idea that trying to com-
pose that way will remove invention, spontaneity, inspiration. Twelve-tone music seems
to have drawn people's attention more because it is twelve-tone than because it is music,
and much of this attention has proven negative. So what is a student to do when faced
with trying to analyze a twelve-tone work? In the following I won't try to answer that directly, but I hope I can, with a few anecdotes and examples, suggest some ways that students can engage with the twelve-tone repertoire in a rewarding way.

One of the problems students face is that for the most part they receive their first impressions of twelve-tone music not from listening, but from some encounter with a description of its compositional technique. And often such descriptions sound pretty silly. I
once was present when a very able amateur musician and music lover described twelve-
tone composition, using the familiar sort of explanations of selecting a row, playing it forward and backward, upside down, and upside down and backward, and somehow making that music. He was baffled, and I had to agree that given such an explanation, the
technique would seem utterly arbitrary. He was simply repeating what he had encountered in popular writing about contemporary music. While such descriptions contain some
truth about what a twelve-tone composer does, it wasn't made clear to him why anyone
would possibly want to do those things in the first place. And the seeming sheer arbi-
trariness of the process, not to mention his understandable assumption that one was ex-

Some reminders: (1) all words in **bold** are defined in the glossary; (2) full citations for incomplete references
are found in the selected bibliography; (3) the authors use their preferred notational system (e.g., Roman numeral, form label, and register notation). Most of the essays denote register by middle C as C^4.—Ed.

pected to hear things forward and backward and upside down, foreclosed on his willingness to engage the music as he had freely listened to other music.

My own first encounters with twelve-tone music and twelve-tone theory show the problem from a slightly different angle. I was lucky enough to encounter the music of Schoenberg when I was in my teens, and I listened repeatedly to my LP of his violin and piano concertos, following along with the scores and trying to thump them out at the piano. I was falling in love with a lot of different kinds of music at that point, and so my engagement with Schoenberg didn't feel all that different from my attempts to get through a Bach fugue or a Beethoven sonata. When I first began to read a bit about twelve-tone composition (mostly descriptions along the lines mentioned above), I found myself not able to connect what I was reading with the music I was hearing, except in a superficial, factual way. I could indeed find the rows in a piece, but when I tried to follow the rules and write a piece of my own, it sounded absolutely terrible. However, since my initial investment (quite literally, $1.98 for the LP) was in listening to the music, I was more ready to throw away the descriptions as inadequate to the music than to dismiss the music as the result of a misbegotten compositional technique.

My sense of my predicament was summed up around the same time in a cartoon by Mort Drucker I saw in *Mad Magazine*. In it, Drucker, a gifted caricaturist, parodied the sorts of ads for art schools one used to find in the Sunday supplements. In four panels, he offered to teach the reader how to draw Bob Hope. Step one was an oval; steps two and three added dots for eyes and a dash for a mouth. Step four, however, was a perfect rendering of Hope's visage, down to the ski-slope nose, the twisted lip, and the supercilious eyebrows. For years I have been trying make the connection between the equivalent of steps three and four in twelve-tone music, both for myself, and for my students. But this is only possible if we can recognize that step four looks like Bob Hope, so to speak.

I believe it is possible to engage twelve-tone music in ways that are musically vivid and that take advantage of the theoretical apparatus that has grown up around it while avoiding a fixation on the issue of twelve-tone rows. Part of this involves seeing how much musically intelligible insight may be gleaned from a work *without* dealing with its row structure. Example 4.1 is the second movement of Anton Webern's *Variations for Piano,* op. 27.[1] What may we draw from sitting down at a piano for a time with this brief page of music?

It quickly becomes clear that virtually every gesture in the piece is based on one or more pairs of notes rhythmically spaced an eighth note apart and broken between the two hands. While these pairs are often separated from each other by rests, they are sometimes strung together continuously. These note pairs are sometimes elaborated by adding grace notes or by, in effect, "thickening" each note in a pair into a three-note nontonal chord (called a "**trichord**"). But most important to notice is how all of these features share in a game of symmetrical registral distribution. Whether we play these gestures as written or "cheat" by redistributing notes to avoid all the hand crossings, it quickly becomes clear by sheer feel that the upper and lower notes of each of these pairs fall symmetrically in register above and below the repeated As.[2]

---

1. This movement has been analyzed extensively by several musicians; a reasonably complete list may be found in Andrew Mead, "Webern, Tradition, and 'Composing with Twelve Tones,'" *Music Theory Spectrum* 15, no. 2 (1993): 173–204.

2. I am assuming little or no familiarity with set theory or twelve-tone theory on the part of the reader, and I beg the indulgence of those for whom these concepts are familiar. Excellent primers on this topic are John Rahn, *Basic Atonal Theory,* and Joseph N. Straus, *Introduction to Post-tonal Theory.*

Example 4.1. Webern, *Piano Variations,* op. 27, no. 2

One more point can be drawn out at this stage of the game. As we play through the opening of the movement, we will be struck in bar 6 by the E♭ octave (written E♭/D♯) produced between our left and right thumbs in the second occurrence of the grace note patterns. Stopping to think about this, we will realize that indeed if the upper and lower notes of all the note pairs we have been playing are symmetrically distributed around the repeated As, then E♭ (D♯) will of course have to appear both above and below A. (This is illustrated in 4.2a.) But that might make us reflect upon the remaining notes and wonder if they also change register. Up through bar 7 they don't, but with the downbeat of bar 8 we encounter such a move associated with the same kind of grace note pattern that first

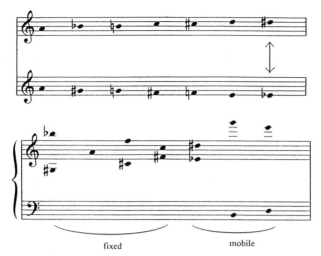

Example 4.2. Symmetrical distribution around A

drew our attention to the issue of octave shift. Furthermore, the notes that have moved, B, D, G, and E, first occur in the piece between bars 2 and 3, B and G in the first occurrence of grace notes. A quick run through the rest of the movement shows us that only those notes we have so far encountered moving between registers (E♭, B, D, G, and E) continue to do so: the remaining seven notes are always fixed in register. (This is illustrated in example 4.2b.) The issue of notes either fixed or changing register helps show us the need for a useful concept, based on our ability to recognize octaves. Theorists usually use the term "pitch" to refer to a particular frequency and "**pitch-class**" to refer to any or all of those notes related to a given pitch by octave or octaves. This is a concept already built into our language, exemplified by our use of only seven letter names (plus accidentals) to refer to notes in any register. We'll find this a useful concept in what follows.

At this point, we have enough information to start to make some sense of the overall shape of Webern's second movement. Its repertoire of materials is quite small, but what we might find interesting is how they are compounded with each other in the music's surface. I will not try to offer a comprehensive picture of the movement but will follow one strand of details that is readily recognizable. First, it is not hard to hear that the movement contains two halves that are repeated. (In fact, that's how it is notated in the score, complete with repeat marks, but I am emphasizing listening here.) Furthermore, it is not hard to hear that the beginnings and endings of the two halves are marked by the same pair of notes, B♭–G♯. What can give more shape to our hearing of these two halves involves that particular pair with what follows it in bars 1 and 2: the repeated As and the pair C♯–F. This same batch of notes (Bb–G♯, A–A, C♯–F) returns together at the end of the first half, with the initial pair "thickened" into three-note trichords. If we think of the initial passage as a "tune," then its varied return helps to round out the first half (this is marked on example 4.1).[3] But there's more: in the second half of the movement, starting in bar 18, this same tune recurs once more, embedded in a gesture that brings back several different features of the movement. This passage, rich in return, serves for the movement as a whole what the return of the tune served at the close of the first half.

---

3. David B. Lewin's "A Metrical Problem in Webern's Op. 27" (*Music Analysis* 12, no. 3 [1993]: 343–54) introduces the term "tune" to refer to this passage.

Many other lovely details of this work can be discerned by musing over it at the keyboard. I have said nothing about the subtle changes of touch and attack or the forced **rubato** occasioned by the need to shift hands swiftly from one register to another, and from one dynamic level to another. But what I hope to have suggested is that a close engagement with this as music *played* can alone draw us into some interesting analytical observations.

Once we have connected with the music, we can move to the question of the role of twelve-tone rows in a composition with a little more surety. But it is still helpful to put that question into a historical context. Too often in popular presentations of twelve-tone theory it would seem that Schoenberg's insight came from nowhere, as though it were an arbitrary decision made in a musical vacuum. But this was not the case. Far better to see the techniques of twelve-tone composition as a solution to a preexisting compositional challenge, one of perhaps many solutions to the challenge of composing in the total chromatic.

The problem of writing music in which the diatonic scale had been chromatically saturated was a challenge faced by virtually any European composer during the first decade of the twentieth century, and each dealt with the question in different ways. For many composers, certain habits and practices of tonal composition remained a guide, even as the features of musical structure that had originally led to those practices dissolved. Schoenberg's piano piece, op. 19, no. 2, is a particularly good example of an atonal work that still contains many features of tonal music. Examples of both local and long-range stepwise voice leading abound in this work, and the piece maintains a careful distinction in role between thirds of various types and seconds of various types, despite obliterating the very musical structure that establishes such differences, the diatonic scale.[4] But these habits did not remain with Schoenberg for long, and by the end of the second decade of the century he found himself at sea in the total chromatic.[5]

One way to navigate this space is to assemble motives with vivid elements or qualities (called "attributes"), abstract musical characteristics that will remain recognizable under certain kinds of musical change or variation. This is a practice, familiar from tonal music, that is sufficiently flexible to be adapted in a nontonal realm. Such attributes might occur in any musical dimension, but for our purposes here, let us think only about pitch. Tonal music invites us to recognize the notion of the triad as an abstraction in various interlocking ways, based both on pitch-class content and intervallic distribution. Think of a C-major triad: we can and do recognize that concept no matter what register it appears in, and no matter how its notes are distributed from treble to bass. By extension, we can recognize and remember strings of triads, to which we ascribe functions. Because of these abilities, we can recognize that the same tonal progression or sequence of triads can underlie two otherwise very different musical passages. A great deal of tonal understanding depends on just this sort of thing. Similarly, in the total chromatic we can recognize that two otherwise different passages might use the same repertoire of collections of pitch-classes, and so connect them either locally in a work or over longer time

4. A number of articles have been written about this piece: these include Elaine Barkin, "play it AS it lays," *Perspectives of New Music* 17, no. 2 (spring-summer 1979): 17–24; Marion Guck, "'Anoir—a mirroir': Past Senses/Reverses, Nests (A Priori?)," *In Theory Only* 2, no. 10 (January 1977): 29–34; Deborah Stein, "Schoenberg's Op. 19, No. 2: Voice-Leading and Overall Structure in an Atonal Work"; and Roy Travis, "Directed Motion in Schoenberg and Webern," *Perspectives of New Music* 4, no. 2 (spring-summer 1966): 85–89.

5. The term "total chromatic" is used to refer to the world of the twelve note equal tempered musical space that is the result of the total chromatic saturation of the diatonic scale. In this space, scale degrees cannot be differentiated, as all are related to each other in the same way.

spans.[6] The challenge for the composer is to find ways of creating such connections and then to weave them into some larger network of relationships.

Let's see what happens when we try to put together some fairly simple sets of connections. What follows will initially seem a little abstract, so let me set up the rules of the game. I'm going to take the twelve pitch-classes and distribute them into discrete batches. We can think of these batches as representing the pitch-classes of motives, chords, or figures in some musical passage. I'm not interested in anything more than what could be called the "pitch-class attributes" (pitch characteristics) of such passages, so the examples that follow might result in musical passages that otherwise could sound very different from each other, in terms of rhythm, gesture, dynamic, or shape.

Next, I'm going to do things to these distributions of our twelve pitch-classes (i.e., the sets of batches of pitch-classes mentioned above). I will limit myself to two *operations*. Both are fairly familiar, but I will give brief explanations. My first operation is **transposition**. This is a concept familiar from tonal practice, but we need to be careful to understand what this means when applied to pitch-*classes*, as opposed to actual pitches. A "quick and dirty" way to describe this operation would be to think of each pitch-class as an actual pitch (middle C, as opposed to any C), shift it up by a given number of half-steps, and then use the pitch-class of the resulting pitch. Thus, we can transpose pitch-class C by four half-steps, yielding pitch-class E. This, of course, will hold even when the particular C and E in question are arranged so that the E is eight half-steps below the C. We could write this as "transpose by four half-steps," but such a cumbersome notation can readily be abbreviated as "T4."

My other operation, perhaps less familiar from tonal music, is **inversion**. Once again, we need to be careful to understand its sense when applied to pitch-classes. I can use a similarly "quick and dirty" way to describe the results of inversion as I did for transposition. First, as before, imagine each pitch class as a particular pitch. Next, for each pitch, find the nearest C and figure out the interval between the two notes. Finally, find the pitch the same interval above or below the C, on the opposite side from the initial pitch. The pitch-class of this new note will represent the pitch-class inversion of the initial note. Since the operation inversion (which we will abbreviate as "I") always works around C, we can actually eliminate all of the above simply by remembering the following: C becomes C; C♯ becomes B (and conversely, B becomes C♯); Bb becomes D (and vice versa and so on); A becomes E♭; G♯ becomes E; G becomes F, and F♯ becomes F♯ (see example 4.3a). The results can then themselves be transposed, as we did above.[7]

For the purposes of our exercise, I'm going to apply my operations to distributions of pitch-classes in ways that will preserve or exchange the contents of my batches of pitch-classes. A quick familiar example: if I have two tonal triads, C major and F♯ major, I could transpose each of them by a tritone (six half-steps, or "T6" in our shorthand) to yield an F♯-major triad and a C-major triad (see example 4.3b). But now let's try this with a distribution of all twelve pitch-classes. Consider the following distribution, which yields

6. This, in part, is the purview of set theory. See Allen Forte, *The Structure of Atonal Music,* as well as Rahn, *Basic Atonal Theory,* and Straus, *Introduction to Post-tonal Theory.*

7. Once again, I am assuming little familiarity with terms on the part of the reader, but I have decided to use what has become the most widely familiar notation for Tranposition and Inversion, Tn/TnI notation. My accounts are largely heuristic; please refer to Rahn, *Basic Atonal Theory*, Straus, *Introduction to Post-tonal Theory,* and Morris, *Composition with Pitch-Classes,* for fuller and much more elegant accounts.

Example 4.3a. Inversional distribution around C

Example 4.3b. Pitch-class collection preserved under tritone transposition

three four-note collections, labeled a, b, and c. I'll call the distribution "Q," just to give it a name.

Q:	{A, B♭, C♯, D}	{C, E♭, E, F}	{F♯, G, A♭, B}
	a	b	c

This could represent the pitch-classes of three motives, three chords, or some combination thereof. My only concern is that these three batches of pitch-classes be somehow recognizable in a passage. Furthermore, I'm not concerned about the particular order of the pitch-classes within each batch, although I would want each batch to represent a recognizable feature of the musical surface. Now let's first invert Q, and then transpose it up eleven half-steps. We can abbreviate that as T11 of IQ, or T11IQ. (A simple way to read this is right to left: take Q, invert it, then transpose it as indicated.)

T11I Q:	{D, C♯, B♭, A}	{B, A♭, G, F♯}	{F, E, E♭, C}
	a	c	b

As you can see, and as is also illustrated in example 4.4, doing this to Q results in the preservation of the content of the first batch of pitch-classes and the exchange of the content of the second two. I've indicated the exchange of content by means of the letters a, b, and c, used above. If Q were a pitch-class attribute of one musical passage and T11 Q a pitch-class attribute of another, I think it would not be hard to recognize a connection between the two of them based on the fact that they employed the same repertoire of four-note collections. Since I am not concerned here with the internal order of the four-note collections, that would permit me a fair amount of difference between other attributes of the two passages, such as rhythm, dynamics, articulation, and so forth.

Now let's consider another distribution of the twelve pitch-classes, this time into three-note collections (labeled d, e, f, and g). I'll call this distribution "P." We'll also

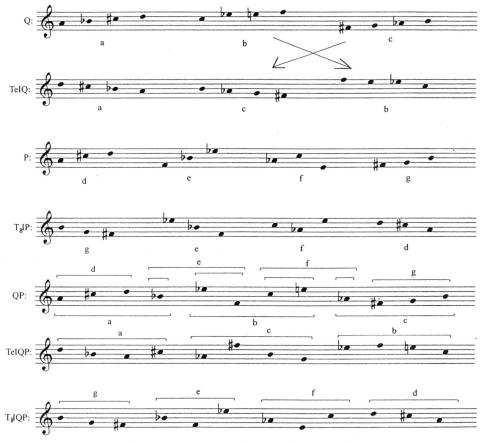

Example 4.4. Sample realizations of Q, P, and QP

look at what happens when we invert P and transpose the result up eight half-steps
(T8IP):

P:	{A, C♯, D}	{F, B♭, E♭}	{A♭, C, E}	{F♯, G, B}
	d	e	f	g
T8I P:	{B, G, F♯}	{E♭, B♭, F}	{C, A♭, E}	{D, C♯, A}
	g	e	f	d

Once again, I've set this up so that the contents of each batch is preserved or exchanged with another batch. As before, two passages having P and T8I P as pitch-class
attributes could readily be associated. And as before, this too leaves a lot of potential for
difference between the two passages, while giving us one way of connecting them. I want
to keep emphasizing that our particular interests are only on one aspect of our hearing
and should not be thought of as eclipsing the rest of our experience of the music. This is
illustrated in example 4.4.

The next step in our exercise is to see if the two sets of associations we have constructed can be combined. Let us constrain ourselves a bit here: let us insist that while we

are not concerned with the internal order of the three- or four-note collections, we do want to maintain the relative order of the collections in each case to each other. With a little shuffling of the internal order of Q's and P's batches of pitch-classes, we can come up with the following, which I will call QP:

	a	b	c
QP:	{A, C♯, D} {B♭}	{E♭, F} {C, E}	{A♭} {F♯, G, B}
	d └ e	└ f	g
T11I QP:	{D, B♭, A} {C♯}	{A♭, F♯} {B, G}	{E♭} {F, E, C}
	a	c	b
T8I QP:	{B, G, F♯}	{B♭} {F, E♭}	{A♭, E} {C} {D, C♯, A}
	g	e	f d

As you can see, and as is also illustrated in example 4.4, the appropriate operations will allow us to maintain the same sorts of connections between passages based on pitch-class attributes. But here is the interesting part: while the QP passage will relate to the T11I QP passage by maintaining the collections of our distribution Q, and will relate to the T8I QP passage by maintaining the collections of P, those two passages (the T11I QP passage and the T8I QP passage) will not relate to each other by the collections of either distribution Q or P. By these very limited standards, the QP passage becomes centrally referential among these three passages; in other words, it will be the one passage of the three that relates to both other passages.

We can superimpose additional attributes on QP. For example, we might notice that without any more specificity than we already have, we could Invert and then Transpose QP by still a different number of half-steps:

QP:	{A, C♯, D} {B♭} {E♭, F}	{C, E} {A♭} {F♯, G, B}
	h	i
T9I QP:	{C, A♭, G} {B} {F♯, E}	{A, F} {C♯} {E♭, D, B♭}
	i	h

While T9I QP does not preserve the batches of pitch-classes of either Q or P, it does give us a new distribution into two six-note collections (**hexachords**) that *are* preserved. Nor need we limit ourselves to pitch-classes that are next to each other: if we further specified the interior order of QP's first three notes and some of its last few notes, we could set up the following:

QP:	{D} {C♯} {A} {B♭} {E♭, F} {C, E} {A♭} {G} {F♯, B}
T6 QP:	{A♭} {G} {E♭} {E} {A, B} {F♯, B♭} {D} {C♯} {C, F}

These are illustrated in example 4.5.

What we have done here is to create several coexisting sets of pitch-class attributes for a passage from which we can create linkages with other passages that share one or more of these attributes. We can see by analogy that we could create additional linkages with still others and thereby could begin to create networks of relationships among passages in the total chromatic based solely on their shared pitch-class attributes. Doing so in the way we have just done gives us terrific leverage to start building musical structures

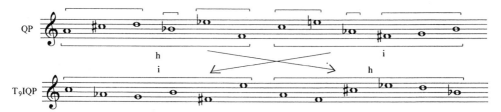

Example 4.5a. Six-note collections

Example 4.5b. Nonadjacent note pairs

in which many passages are related variously to one or more centrally referential passages, and so start to create hierarchies among passages in a work.[8]

Of course all this will seem arbitrary and abstract, if we cannot make a case that a given passage can manifest a variety of pitch-class attributes. Consider example 4.6.

This contains the opening bars of Arnold Schoenberg's Fourth String Quartet, and as you will quickly recognize, it partakes of the repertoire of pitch-class attributes we have been examining. In the melody in the first violin, we can readily hear our last example, in the long durations of D, C♯, Ab, and G. The melody's rhythm can lead us to hear the four-note collections of Q, and the way it is accompanied gives us the three-note collections of P. While the six-note collections we derived from QP are not as directly projected in the melody, they form the basis for its continuation and so are used as an immediate connection to what follows: the several successive phrases of the melody are all made of this pair of hexachords.[9] In the piece Schoenberg uses these four sets of attributes along with others to create local and long-range connections. For example, when this melody recurs in the middle of the first movement, it is transposed by T6, thus exchanging the locations of the dyads D, C♯ and Ab, G.

You will have noticed two things about the preceding. First, as we compounded our different sets of attributes, we found ourselves gradually imposing more and more constraints on how pitch-classes were ordered. Take this a few steps further, and we would have achieved a single ordering of the twelve pitch-classes. Second, for our exercise to make any sense we had to be sure that those attributes we were interested in could be

---

8. The various examples I have derived here are all familiar properties of the row of Arnold Schoenberg's Fourth Quartet. I am not claiming any originality for these insights but am merely taking us through how these interact as a pedagogical exercise. Many of these features are discussed in Milton Babbitt, *Words about Music,* ed. Stephen Dembski and Joseph N. Straus (Madison: University of Wisconsin Press, 1987). Some of the mathematical contingencies of combining attributes as we have done are explored in David B. Lewin, "A Theory of Segmental Association in Twelve-Tone Music," *Perspectives of New Music* 1, no. 1 (1962): 89–116. This work is also featured in Straus, *Introduction to Post-tonal Theory.*

9. In fact, as Milton Babbitt points out (*Words about Music*), the opening melody *does* articulate the hexachords, by placing the second hexachord as an actual *pitch* inversion of the first.

Example 4.6. Schoenberg, Fourth String Quartet

gleaned from hearing the musical surface. This is crucial to the understanding of twelve-tone music. Note, please, that I have tried, even when working backward from the abstract attributes to the heard musical surface, to emphasize that these pitch-class collections be understood as *attributes* of that musical surface, and not that the surface is just an embodiment of these collections. The surface has many other attributes, of pitch and rhythm, dynamics, and articulation, that are all part of our hearing.

We are finally in a position to think about twelve-tone rows and their role in a twelve-tone composition. In our previous exercise, we all but generated a twelve-tone row by combining desired sets of attributes. As these various desires were combined, we found ourselves with less and less wiggle room within our collections. We had come close to saturation: a few more steps and a row would have crystallized, so to speak. The previous exercise was also about creating connections between passages based on shared sets of pitch-class attributes, and we did so by using two simple pitch-class operations, trans-position and inversion. Put these two ideas together, and one arrives at the central con-cepts of twelve-tone composition. To wit, a "row" can be defined as a particular order-ing of the twelve pitch classes, from which one can generate a "row-class," being all rows equivalent to each other under a specified set of operations. In Schoenberg's practice, those operations are Transposition, Inversion, and Retrogression.[10]

Lest it seem as though I am leaping from an oval with two dots and a dash in it to a portrait of Bob Hope, let me quickly add that we must now apply the lessons learned from our exercises to these concepts. Our elaborated QP above was generated by combining a number of desired attributes that would remain recognizable in various ways under cer-tain operations. We can extend that idea by realizing that a given row will contain every possible pitch-class collection (potential attribute, in the terms we have been using) in some configuration. A row-*class* will offer a wide range of the sorts of associations we were looking at above, based on ways of preserving various sorts of attributes under the prescribed operations.

Several things fall out of this way of thinking about twelve-tone rows. First, a row-class offers a particular perspective on the possibilities available in the total chromatic. It effectively sorts those possibilities by their placement within its rows. Second, since any member of a row-class can be used to generate that row-class, no member of that row-class is inherently more significant than any other. It is useful to think of the rows as things that can be changed into each other by some combination of a row-class's pre-scribed operations.

But most important is that all of the sorts of relations among members of a row-class are only *potential:* it is the act of composition that can bring them to life. Think back to example 4.6. Had Schoenberg changed the rhythm or the register of that melody, or had he used some other accompanimental strategy, some or all of the attributes we were con-sidering would have disappeared! Others would have emerged, no doubt, but the poten-tial network of connections to other passages in the piece would have been different. To hear this, one need only listen to the third movement of the quartet. It opens with a melody whose sequence of pitch classes is the same as the opening of the first movement, trans-posed down a major second. However, their registral distribution and rhythmic articula-tion lead to very different consequences in the body of the movement.[11]

In this view of twelve-tone composition, the rows certainly do not "write the piece for you," nor do they force you to "write notes you don't want" any more (or less) than composing within tonality. What they do provide is sets of contingencies (possible con-sequences) and opportunities that one can take advantage of, just as happens in tonality. Decisions beget consequences: if I have decided to write a piece in C major, that deci-sion will have an impact on my desire to write an Ab in that piece. Not only will I know that it is not part of diatonic C major, but I will know just how it is not part thereof; I will even know that it will differ in behavior from G#, which in equal tuning will sound the same as Ab. Those are some serious and particular consequences of my desire to write

---

10. These are now generally referred to as the interval-preserving operations. It is, of course, possible to create row-classes with additional or even different sets of operations. For example, Schoenberg himself used "rota-tion" (shifting elements from the beginning to the end of a row) as an additional operation in his Wind Quin-tet, op. 26.

11. See Milton Babbitt, "Set Structure as a Compositional Determinant," *Journal of Music Theory* 5, no. 1 (1961): 72–94, reprinted in *Perspectives on Contemporary Music Theory,* ed. Benjamin Boretz and Edward T. Cone (New York: W. W. Norton, 1972), 129–47, as well as Bruce Samet, "Hearing Aggregates" (PhD diss., Princeton University, 1987) for an account of this movement.

an Ab. But there are also opportunities available: if I notice in my same piece that a dominant seventh chord built on that same Ab sounds an awful lot like a German augmented sixth, I can have all sorts of fun shifting between those two interpretations. Schubert certainly did!

Composers have taken advantage of the twelve-tone world's contingencies and opportunities in a wide variety of ways. For Schoenberg, this was an opportunity to invest music written in the total chromatic with the sorts of distinctions of here and there, arrival and departure, stability and instability that had been drowned out of tonality by the rising tide of chromaticism. His twelve-tone compositions reinvigorate many of the formal strategies of his tonal forebears in a radically different pitch context. However for Milton Babbitt, the implications of Schoenberg's work, along with that of Webern, suggested entirely new ways of unfolding the narrative of a composition.

The preceding is a very quick sketch and is far from complete; it is meant primarily as a guide to a useful orientation toward thinking about twelve-tone music. Obviously, there are many extensions I have left untouched. Furthermore, I have only begun to tell half of the story. For our purposes, I have restricted my notion of attributes in the pitch domain to recurrences of unordered pitch-class collections. But I could have taken another angle, looking for the preservation of intervallic configurations in changing pitch-class contexts. From this vantage, it is the interval patterns that are preserved, as opposed to the pitch-class collections. One of the reasons that twelve-tone composition has at its center the operations of Transposition, Inversion, and Retrogression is because these are the operations that (to within certain simply specified constraints) preserve intervals. A fuller examination of the consequences of twelve-tone composition would need to examine the interaction of these two perspectives; I have implicitly suggested this above in my mention of the return of the melody transposed by a tritone in the middle of the first movement of Schoenberg's quartet. My immediate interests were in the preserved pairs of notes, but I of course relied on my ability to recognize the return of the opening melody's sequence of intervals as key in alerting me to the dyad connection.

Lastly, twelve-tone composition even in its various ramifications is still but one solution to composing in the total chromatic. All sorts of different approaches have been creatively used by musicians since Schoenberg "emancipated the dissonance" at the beginning of the last century. But twelve-tone composition has much in common with many of these approaches, both in specifics and in a general desire to afford consequences to one's compositional actions.

So how might we use the preceding to help us in analyzing a twelve-tone piece? First, and I hope this has been loud and clear from the start, we must steep ourselves in it as *music,* as something we play and listen to. Our Webern example above was all about listening and playing, and doing so led us to recognizing certain recurring features in the music. The recurrence of what I called the tune is a prime example of this, and one of the features that allowed us to recognize it in its various guises was the fact that in all three instances it contained a particular pitch attribute, initially unadorned but still recognizable when combined with other pitch attributes.

The beginnings of the next steps would involve seeing how the pitch and pitch-class attributes (as well as the interval-pattern attributes) of those features that have drawn our attention interact with the underlying row structure. This would entail finding the rows in a piece and seeing what operations related them to each other. The danger here, of course, is imagining that doing a twelve-count of a piece is in itself especially useful. As I hope the foregoing makes clear, I certainly don't think it is sufficient to constitute an analysis, and it could be argued that it is perhaps not even necessary.

Finally, approaching twelve-tone music in this way should defuse the ever-present notion that we are supposed to hear "the row" in a twelve-tone piece, or that we are supposed to hear things backward or upside down. Certainly, we are hearing the *consequences* of a work's row-class, as realized through the compositional choices made by the composer, but I doubt it is necessary to come away from a twelve-tone composition knowing its row anymore than one comes away from a tonal composition marveling on the fact that in the diatonic collection each interval class is present a unique number of times.[12]

But the key to all of this is *listening*. When I found myself some years ago talking with that music lover who was baffled and annoyed with what it was he thought he was being asked to do to hear twelve-tone music, I asked him how he had developed his love of music in the first place. Not surprisingly, he replied that he had simply heard a lot of music, and played a lot of music and that over the years the exposure had let the pleasure of the experience grow on him. I suggested that perhaps a similar approach might lead to an enjoyment of twelve-tone music, setting aside his assumptions either of how it had been made or what he was supposed to hear. More recently I had occasion to talk with him again about certain twelve-tone pieces that he had been listening to, and he said, "You know, that stuff's *music.*" While we did not pursue the topic any further, we could at least agree that step four was a mighty good drawing of Bob Hope.

FURTHER READING

Babbitt, Milton. *Words about Music.* Edited by Stephen Dembski and Joseph N. Straus. Madison: University of Wisconsin Press, 1987.

Rahn, John. *Basic Atonal Theory.* New York: Longman, 1982.

Straus, Joseph N. *Introduction to Post-tonal Theory.* 3d ed.

---

12. Despite the fact that much that we cherish about tonal music is based on this fact: see Richmond Browne, "Tonal Implications of the Diatonic Set," *In Theory Only* 5, nos. 1 and 2 (1981): 3–21.

~ 5 ~

ANALYZING THE UNITY
WITHIN CONTRAST
Chick Corea's "Starlight"

Ramon Satyendra

Ramon Satyendra (University of Michigan) is a composer, performer, and scholar with a wide range of interests. As a composer, he writes music in classical idioms. As a performer, he plays Western classical music on the piano; jazz on the piano, B3 organ, and guitar; and Indian classical music on tablas. As a scholar his research includes nineteenth-century chromaticism, especially in the music of Liszt, Indian music, and jazz.

Keyboard virtuoso Chick Corea is a major jazz figure whose four-decade career has spanned many stylistic and compositional phases. He has worked extensively in traditional modern jazz (combo performances of standards and bop), Latin jazz, avant-garde jazz, jazz-rock fusion, jazz-classical fusion, and contemporary classical music. The author recommends the following recordings for an introduction to Chick Corea: *Now He Sings, Now He Sobs* (1968); *Bitches Brew* (1969); *Hymn of the Seventh Galaxy* (1973); *Remembering Bud Powell* (1997); and *Origin: A Week at the Blue Note* (1998). Satyendra played with Chick Corea's bandmate Gary Novak for several years; at that time he developed analytical interest in the music of Chick Corea's Elektric Band. The present essay illustrates some of the results of this study; it also provides an excellent guide to writing an analysis paper.

How are we to make sense of sharp contrasts within a composition? Since there is scarcely a piece of music that does not employ contrast, this question naturally arises when listening. This essay addresses the question of musical contrasts by presenting an important analytical principle that yields insights into musical technique and has also furnished the basis for many published musical analyses. This article is in three parts. I first present the analytical principle and sketch its historical and intellectual context. Second, I cover terms and concepts that will come into play in the analysis. The last part of the article analyzes "Starlight" by Chick Corea and John Patitucci and gives detailed suggestions on how to write up the findings as an analysis paper.

Some reminders: (1) all words in **bold** are defined in the glossary; (2) full citations for incomplete references are found in the selected bibliography; (3) the authors use their preferred notational system (e.g., Roman numeral, form label, and register notation). Most of the essays denote register by middle C as C^4.—Ed.

HISTORICAL AND INTELLECTUAL CONTEXT

I begin with an idea from aesthetics:

> A musical work is successful to the extent that its various ingredients are coherent and unified, that is, bound together through some sort of musical "logic."

The aesthetics of unity expressed above has had an enormous influence on the development of academic music theory and analysis.[1] According to this line of thought, a piece consisting of nothing but sharp contrasts would be incoherent and therefore unsuccessful. But what, then, would be a successful piece? A piece that presents a series of units that do not contrast with one another? Many music critics reject this other extreme as well.[2] According to them, overemphasizing coherence—whether in music, visual arts, or speech—produces an unduly repetitive and potentially boring presentation.[3] In between the extremes of excessive contrast and excessive unity lies a middle ground, expressed in the following qualified version of the aesthetics of unity as it might pertain to music:

> Musical composition involves striking a pleasing balance between the use of repetition to express unity of materials and the use of variation and contrast to provide a sense of development, change, transformation, and momentum.[4]

This leads directly to the analytical principle we are going to examine:

> If a musical contrast between two parts is to succeed, prominent elements in one part need to be present in the other in a latent form.

In other words, in a successful contrast there is always an element of concealed repetition. Hans Keller, perhaps more than anyone else, championed this principle. Before his analysis of Mozart's Piano Concerto in C Major, K. 503, Keller writes

> The analysis which here follows is based on the tenet that a great work can be *demonstrated* to grow from an all-embracing basic idea, and that the essential, if never-asked questions of why contrasting motifs and themes belong together, why a particular second subject necessarily belongs to a particular first, why a contrasting middle section belongs to its principle section, why a slow movement belongs to a first movement, and so forth, must be answered if an "analysis" is to deserve its name.[5]

I suspect that most of us have heard statements about the musical "logic" of Beethoven and Bach, though perhaps would be hard-pressed to say exactly of what that logic consists. Keller intended that his analytical theory would tell us what musical logic is. He

---

1. Some aesthetic positions do not assume that artworks need to be unified. See Jean-Francois Lyotard, *The Postmodern Condition: A Report on Knowledge*, trans. G. Bennington and B. Massumi (1979; Minneapolis: University of Minnesota Press, 1984).

2. The composers of the Second Viennese School were critical of excessive repetition. For a discussion of the dialectical tension between variation and repetition, see Alban Berg, "Why is Schoenberg's Music so Hard to Understand?" *The Music Review* 13 (1952): 187–96.

3. Many genres, such as ritual music designed to induce trance, employ unremitting repetition. Such music would call for a different kind of analysis than considered here.

4. Although this idea predates Arnold Schoenberg, his views about it were particularly influential on the development of music theory. See Arnold Schoenberg, *Fundamentals of Musical Composition*, ed. Gerald Strang and Leonard Stein (London: Faber and Faber, 1967).

5. Cited from Hans Keller, "K. 503: The Unity of Contrasting Themes and Movements, *Music Review* 17 (1956): 50. Keller's range as a writer on music was enormous. For more of his writings see Hans Keller, *Essays on Music,* ed. Christopher Wintle, with Bayan Northcott and Irene Samuel (New York: Cambridge University Press, 1994).

had harsh words for critics who appealed to a notion of musical logic without defining it adequately:

> The instrument of torture which the [music] critic here employs, without the remotest attempt at substantiation . . . are words which we use in order to describe conceptual, verbal sense-making and nonsense-making: "argument," "consistency," "validity," "logic," "well-reasoned," or "badly reasoned," "fallacy," "contradiction" are favorite metaphors of high criticism of musical composition. There certainly is such a thing as musical logic, but since no critic using the concept of logic has ever disclosed what it is, it must remain meaningless.[6]

Keller's belief that musical coherence stemmed from the unity within contrasts was not just a theorist's abstraction but something embraced by musicians. Arnold Schoenberg spoke of pursuing just this kind of analysis in his own music:

> After I had completed the work [Chamber Symphony] I worried very much about the apparent absence of any relationship between the two themes. Directed only by my sense of form and the stream of ideas, I had not asked such questions while composing; but, as usual with me, doubts arose as soon as I had finished. . . . About twenty years later I saw the true relationship. It is of such a complicated nature that I doubt whether any composer would have cared deliberately to construct a theme in this way; but our subconscious does it involuntarily.[7]

Keller's idea also had connections to intellectual culture outside of music. Keller was an expert in psychoanalytic theory, and it is probable that his method of musical analysis was influenced by Freud's ideas.[8] The notion of "latent content" (*latenter Inhalt*) appears in Freud's *The Interpretation of Dreams*, a book the author regarded as his greatest work. "Latent content" has been defined as

> groups of meanings revealed upon the completion of an analysis of a product of the unconscious—particularly in a dream. Once decoded, the dream no longer appears as a narrative in images but rather as an organization of thoughts, or a discourse, expressing one or more wishes.[9]

This psychoanalytical meaning for "latent" compares with Keller's musical meaning: Keller uses the same term, "latent," to describe subsurface elements within a work that need to be decoded by the musical analyst.[10]

---

6. Hans Keller, "Music Criticism," in *Criticism*, ed. Julian Hogg (1945; London: Faber and Faber, 1987), 114–15.

7. Arnold Schoenberg, "Composition with Twelve Tones," in *Style and Idea*, ed. Leonard Stein, trans. Leo Black, (Berkeley and Los Angeles: University of California Press, 1975), 222.

8. "After many years of patient and personal investigation—which, in the words of a psychoanalyst of the old guard, Willi Hoffer, produced an 'unequalled knowledge of the psychoanalytic literature'—I came to the definite conclusion that what, outside analysis, are known as the psychoanalytic dogmata, are in fact a single man's discoveries of world-shaking truths (shaking the mental world, that is): the dynamic unconscious, repression (Verdrängung) in the strictly analytic sense, infantile sexuality and its consequences, the Oedipus complex (at least in Western civilizations), and the validity of the free-association technique." Hans Keller, "Psycho-analytic Congress 1975," *Hans Keller 1975 [1984 minus 9]* (London: Dennis Dobson, 1977), 86–87.

9. This definition is taken from *The Language of Psycho-analysis*, by J. Laplanche and J. B. Pontalis, trans. Donald Nicholson-Smith (New York: W. W. Norton, 1973), 235.

10. It is important to keep in mind the larger intellectual context for ideas used by musicians today. In many instances, a musical idea used in analysis has its roots in the intellectual history of disciplines other than music. Generally speaking, the intellectual climate in Vienna at the turn of the century exerted a tremendous effect on the development of music theory and analysis. For more about this fascinating period of intellectual history, see Allan Janik and Stephen Toulman, *Wittgenstein's Vienna* (New York: Simon and Schuster, 1973).

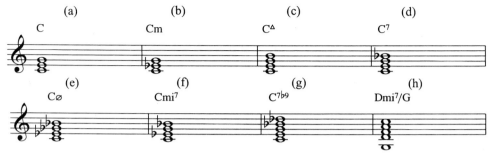

Figure 5.1. Chord nomenclature

BACKGROUND TERMS AND CONCEPTS

In addition to Keller's idea, the musical analysis in this article draws on ideas from jazz and other theory, which we shall now briefly review.

1. *Blues scale.* {C, Eb, F, F♯, G, Bb}. This scale (and its transpositions) is used in the melody of blues, as well as much jazz and popular music.[11]

2. *Blues pentatonic scale.* {C, Eb, F, G, Bb}, and its transpositions.

3. *Chord nomenclature.*[12] Chick Corea's use of chord symbols is summarized in figure 5.1.

As shown in figure 5.1, a–g, roots of chords appear in capital letters. The symbols in figure 5.1a–e are interpreted as follows: "△" = major seventh chord; "7" = dominant seventh chord; "mi" = minor; "ø7" = half-diminished seventh. The symbols can be combined (figure 5.1f). When added notes are desired, they are written after the main symbols in small type (figure 5.1g). The horizontal slash is used to describe a chord as a combination of a chord and bass tone (figure 5.1h).

4. *Equivalence.* In music theory, if a feature in one spot occurs later in the exact same form, the two occurrences are termed "equivalent." When analyzing, it is important to remember that any repeated musical event will involve both equivalence and nonequivalence. For instance, if a violin melody is repeated in the flute, the two occurrences of the melody are equivalent in pitch and rhythm but not equivalent in timbre.[13]

5. *Latent.* A musical feature is latent if it is present but not prominent and is masked by the simultaneous presence of prominent musical features.

6. *Degrees of melodic closure.* "Degrees of melodic closure" is an idea that addresses the sense of finality—closure—that can be imparted by a melodic tone by virtue of its position within a scale. Since it will play a central role in our analytical work, I consider it here in some detail.

---

11. Covering the complex history of the notion of a "blues scale" is beyond the scope of this paper. For more on blues-scale usage in jazz, see Mark Levine, *The Jazz Theory Book,* 235–36 [The curly brackets indicate that the pitches within are unordered; see the glossary.—Ed.]

12. A complete glossary of jazz-chord nomenclature and vocabulary is in Sher, Chuck, *The New Real Book: Jazz Classics, Choice Standards, Pop-fusion Classics: Created by Musicians—For Musicians* (Petaluma, CA: Sher Music Co., 1988), viii. Chick Corea provides a summary of his usage of chord nomenclature in *Light Years: Chick Corea Elektric Band* (Milwaukee: Hal Leonard Publishing, 1989), 7.

13. For more on equivalence relations in analyzing the features of a musical event, see Nicholas Cook, *A Guide to Musical Analysis,* 151–82.

Figure 5.2. Analysis of a melodic archetype in "Homesick and Lonesome Blues"

In the melody of "Starlight," the scalar frame of reference is the **blues scale**. Figure 5.2 presents an analysis of a melodic archetype that is based on the blues scale.[14] Figure 5.2a is a simplified transcription of the opening phrase of a traditional blues song, "Homesick and Lonesome Blues."[15] The music of figure 5.2a is repeated (with variation) in lines 1–4 of the song's six-line stanza, figure 5.2b shows the cadential motive of lines 5 and 6. Figure 5.2c analyzes the octave descent of the opening material; figure 5.2d interprets the cadential couplet as composed of two subphrases, the first of which dwells on $\hat{5}$, the second on $\hat{3}$, with a final close on $\hat{1}$. Taken together with the $\hat{1}$ of the initial phrase, the melody instantiates the blues melodic archetype, $\hat{8}$–$\hat{1}$–$\hat{5}$–$\hat{3}$–$\hat{1}$, as shown in figures 5.2c and 5.2d.

Figure 5.2 indicates degrees of closure as follows: $\hat{8}$ is least closed, with $\hat{5}$, $\hat{3}$ and $\hat{1}$ being increasingly more closed (the final $\hat{1}$ being full closure). These varying degrees of closure shape the musical process. When the melody moves between the high note $\hat{8}$ and $\hat{1}$ in the first half of the structure, the melody seems very active, and the expectation that the melody will fall and resolve will be strong. Scale degree $\hat{5}$ constitutes a secondary point of activity, still requiring movement to the lower tonic. Finally, $\hat{3}$ is a direct anticipation of the arrival of $\hat{1}$.[16]

7. *Microtonal inflection* (pitch bending). The idiom of "Starlight" liberally employs ornamental pitches other than those of the equal-tempered scale. In "Starlight," these expressive microtones appear as sliding glissandi before, after, and between principal tones.[17]

8. *Normative.* A musical trait is normative if it is the expected practice of an idiom. For example, it is customary for works in the tonal period to conclude on the tonic triad in root position. So a root-position tonic triad at the conclusion of a sonata would be a "normative" feature, and a non-tonic conclusion would be irregular.[18]

---

14. "Archetype" denotes a pattern that is characteristic of a particular idiom, in this case, traditional blues.

15. Blind Boy Fuller, *The Ultimate Encyclopedia of American Blues Classics*, CD1, track 7, RETRO R2CD 40-33, 1997. The transcriptions in figures 5.2a and 5.2b are by the author.

16. A theory for degrees of closure in jazz is set forth in Ramon Satyendra, "The Dual Structure of Blues-Influenced Jazz" (paper presented at the Seminar for Jazz and Popular Music, Yale University, spring 2001).

17. On synthesizers, the glissando feature is referred to as "pitch bending." The feature is activated by applying pressure on the key bed after a key is depressed or by manipulating a pitch wheel with one hand while playing the keyboard with the other.

18. For more on style analysis and norms, see Leonard Meyer, *Style and Music: Theory, History, and Ideology* (Philadelphia: University of Pennsylvania Press, 1989), 38–69 and 218–71

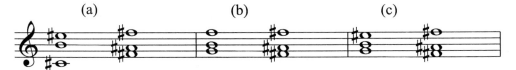

Figure 5.3. Tritone substitution

9. *Tritone substitution*. In jazz theory, a tritone substitution is the substitution of a dominant chord with a chord whose root is a half-octave distant from the dominant pitch. For example, the dominant-seventh chord in F♯ minor (and its normal resolution) is shown in figure 5.3a. In figure 5.3b the same progression is rewritten with a G chord substituting for the C♯ chord. Since the distance between G and C♯ is a "tritone," the G is regarded as a "tritone substitution" for the C♯ chord.[19] Although the chord in figure 5.3b is spelled as a dominant-seventh chord because of conventions in jazz theory, classical theorists would spell it as an augmented-sixth chord, as shown at in figure 5.3c. In classical theory, tritone substitution is taken up in the analysis of a German sixth as a substitute for V/V; the German sixth is enharmonically equivalent to a dominant seventh whose root is a half-octave distant from the root of a V/V.

AN ANALYSIS OF "STARLIGHT"

This section breaks the task of analyzing a musical contrast into seven steps. The piece for analysis, "Starlight," appears on the Elektric Band's second album, *Elektric City,* which was released in 1987. The instrumentation is keyboards, electric guitar, alto saxophone, electric bass, and drums. In 1988 Corea completed an edited version of the score for "Starlight" that uses "only the notes from the original score."[20] Example 5.1 shows Corea's score for "Starlight's" introduction. The only items I have added to Corea's score are the drum staff and the scale-degree carets above the staff. Example 5.2 sketches the main elements of the five-measure theme section that follows the introduction. After the sixteen-measure tune is stated, the keyboard plays an improvised solo over the chord changes of the theme section. The solo is transcribed in example 5.3.[21] After the solo, the introductory music (example 5.1) returns as a coda.

While the contrast between the introduction and theme is striking, the two sections seem to fit together well. If Keller's principle holds, the sense that they fit together indicates that there is a unity of materials between the sections. Our analytical task, then, is to show that elements that are latent in one section manifest themselves in another and vice versa. We can consider our analytical approach in seven steps. Each step is briefly described below and, where pertinent, is followed by an illustrative example of how it might be pursued in an analysis of "Starlight."

---

19. Strictly speaking, the term "tritone" denotes the interval spanned by three ascending "tones" (in medieval theory, a "tone" is the term for a step within the scale). So while the interval from B up to F is not a tritone because it involves four steps, the interval from B to E♯ is a tritone. Today, this distinction is usually ignored and writers call any half-octave interval a "tritone"—diminished fifths as well as augmented fourths.

20. Corea, *Light Years,* 5. The music of example 5.1 is directly taken from Chick Corea's score; the chord symbols are his.

21. The transcription is by the author.

Example 5.1. Annotated score for "Starlight," introduction, mm. 1–9

Become Familiar with the Work

For any analysis to proceed, it is vital to first gain a close familiarity with a work's musical ingredients—such as its style, texture, form, harmony, thematic layout, pitch and rhythmic elements, motives, and dynamic shape. Some scholars believe this identification of ingredients is the essence of music analysis. Ian Bent defines analysis as "the resolution of a musical structure into relatively simpler constituent elements, and the investigation of the functions of those elements within that structure."[22] As we become familiar with a work, connections between features naturally are noticed and identified, and we come to see how elements are recombined so as to fashion musical similarities and contrasts.

When I speak of a work's ingredients, I do not mean to imply that musical units can be objectively determined. Rather, identifying musical units is more a matter of judgment

---

22. Ian Bent, *Analysis,* 1.

Example 5.2. Reduced score and analysis of "Starlight," theme section, mm. 17–33

than of fact. Consequently, it is unlikely that any two persons will entirely agree upon how units in a work are to be identified or interpreted. However, in order to arrive at an analysis that will seem sensible to others, it is vital to know a work intimately so that analytical judgments have a basis in musical experience. A common pitfall is to begin an analysis too soon, before the sound of the music is internalized.

Identify Elements That Contribute to the Impression That Ideas Are Opposed
An analyst can take an inventory of first impressions before framing a thesis and developing an argument. First impressions of contrasts within "Starlight" might look like this:

The nine-measure introduction (example 5.1) contrasts strikingly with the subsequent five-measure theme section (example 5.2) in several ways.

a. *Rhythm.* The pulse in the introduction is the half note, whereas in the theme section it is a quarter note.

b. *Arrangement.* The arrangement in the introduction is more compositional than improvisational: as shown in the drum staff of example 5.1, drum "hits" match the accent pattern in the melody. The bass is a composed counterpoint to the melody. In contrast, the theme section is more improvisational. In the recording, the rhythm section plays straight "pocket" (idiomatic rhythmic and pitch elements that combine to create a steady, vigorous groove) as a backdrop to the composed melody.

Example 5.3. Transcription of the keyboard solo, "Starlight," mm. 34–66

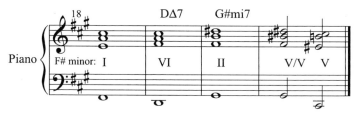

Figure 5.4. Harmony of the theme section, mm. 18–21.

The theme section's improvisational character is reflected in Corea's score, which switches from the introduction's note-for-note notation to a lead sheet format in the theme section.

c. *Idiom.* The introduction illustrates the fusion idiom for which Corea became well-known in the 1970s, an idiom that draws on classical and nonimprovisational big band elements. On the other hand, with its straightforward harmonic structure and ample space for improvised rhythm-section stylings, "Starlight's" theme dramatically contrasts with the introduction. The theme is in the distilled funk idiom of Corea's influential Elektric Band from the late 1980s.

Locate a Primary Opposition of Elements in the Piece

Any one of the above items could serve as a point of departure for our analysis. For our purpose, I will focus upon one item not yet mentioned: the harmonic contrast between "Starlight's" introduction and theme sections. An analyst's first impressions would probably include noticing that the harmony of the introduction is complex and unstable, whereas the harmony of the theme section is formulaic and stable (that is, cadential in F♯ minor).

To articulate this first impression analytically, we first note that the nine-measure introduction (example 5.1) is composed of two harmonic processes. The first is pedal-point harmony extending from mm. 1 to 4 centered on A, and the second is a descending fifths progression extending from mm. 5 to 9, traversing the bass tones F♯–B–E–A–D–G. The introduction is harmonically transitional and, accordingly, tonally ambiguous. The initial point of harmonic arrival is the A-major seventh chord that corresponds with the melodic arrival, E, at m. 4. While it may seem that the music is going to proceed from an A-major tonic, this expectation is undermined, for the roots of the subsequent descending-fifths progression are not taken from the key of A but from G major. The possibility of G major is itself then undermined. The harmony supported by G in the bass is not tonic but functions as a tritone-substitution dominant in F♯ minor, the key of the theme (compare with figure 5.3b).

In stark contrast with the introduction, the theme section has an unambiguous harmony that readily lends itself to conventional tonal analysis (figure 5.4).

As shown in figure 5.5, in the melody's second repetition beginning in mm. 22–25, Ebm7b5 substitutes for D-major seventh (VI) as a passing chord—Eb passing in the bass— and D-major seventh (VI) substitutes for G♯-minor seventh (ii). Neither of these adjustments changes the unambiguous character of the harmonization. The B section of the theme (mm. 26–29) is also tonally unambiguous. As shown in figure 5.6, D major is briefly tonicized (note Eb as a tritone-substitution dominant).

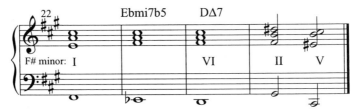

Figure 5.5. The harmonic variation in mm. 22–25

Identify Similarities, Both Explicit and Latent, Between the Opposed Ideas

We begin by observing that both introduction and theme sections (examples 5.1 and 5.2) contain melodic figures drawn from the blues scale. In the theme, the melody is mostly comprised of the notes F#–A–B–C–C#–E. (The foreign notes G# and A# in mm. 31 and 32 are neighbor notes that are directly absorbed into the blues-scale pitches A and B, respectively.) In the introduction, the presence of the blues scale is less obvious because of the complex harmonization, but we can interpret it as present nonetheless, as shown by the scale-degree carets in example 5.1, mm. 2–8.

Formulate a Hypothesis About the Piece That Encompasses and Organizes the Individual Analytical Observations Made Thus Far

As a rough hypothesis, let us say that the melody of the introduction and the melody of the theme share in common a blues idiom.

To justify this view will require some analytical explanation, since the blues idiom is not immediately apparent in the introduction's melody. From Keller's point of view, it is because the blues idiom is "latent" that it would merit analytical attention. In any Keller-influenced analysis, we can speak of a "masking strategy," that is, a strategy wherein a dominant feature camouflages a latent feature. In the introduction, the strategy masking the blues idiom comprises two elements. First, the harmonic support for the melody is irregular. The melody in mm. 2–8 would be a normative blues descent only if we imagine the keynote is E, from E minor. But the music is not in E minor here, so the melody does not have a normative harmonization. The normative context for the melody is shown by scale-degree carets in example 5.1, which analyzes B–A–G–E as a descending $\hat{5}$–$\hat{4}$–$\hat{3}$–$\hat{1}$ in a minor **pentatonic** scale rooted on E. In this normative context, the motive's arrival on $\hat{1}$ would be supported in a stable fashion, by a chord whose root is $\hat{1}$. In the introduction to "Starlight," however, a tonic chord does not support the arrival of $\hat{1}$ in m.4 (as reckoned from an E-minor tonic), but rather, the arrival is the fifth of an A chord.

Second, the augmented rhythmic values weaken the clear association of this motive with a blues idiom: in a normative blues context, the motive $\hat{5}$–$\hat{4}$–$\hat{3}$–$\hat{1}$ characteristically

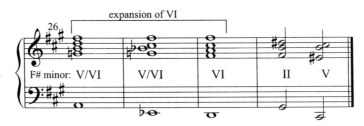

Figure 5.6. The harmony of the B section, mm. 26–29

spans only several beats rather than several measures. Because of these masking elements, we can regard the blues idiom of the introduction's melody as "latent."

To further pursue an analysis of a blues idiom in "Starlight," we need to examine degrees of melodic **closure** (as defined earlier).[23] As shown in the upper staff of example 5.2, "Starlight's" theme is itself in an ABA form, with the initial A section spanning the $\hat{1}$–$\hat{8}$ octave and with the B section pausing on $\hat{5}$. The final A section completes a $\hat{4}$–$\hat{3}$–$\hat{1}$ descent. This reading is shown with beams in example 5.2. The structure, ($\hat{1}$–$\hat{8}$) $\hat{5}$–$\hat{3}$–$\hat{1}$, is the same as that of our blues example (figure 5.2). We recall that figure 5.2 shows a blues melodic archetype: a first half that spans the $\hat{1}$–$\hat{8}$ octave and a melodic second half that takes points of repose on $\hat{5}$ and then $\hat{3}$ before closing on $\hat{1}$ in a cadential context. The presence of this archetype in "Starlight" further supports our view that a blues idiom underlies the work—including its contrasting sections.

To be sure, in "Starlight" the archetype ($\hat{1}$–$\hat{8}$) $\hat{5}$–$\hat{3}$–$\hat{1}$ occurs over a longer span than it does in the blues example of figure 5.2. Nonetheless, in "Starlight's" theme section, many tones in the surface motives are treated as one might expect in a blues idiom. The blues stylings are especially clear throughout the keyboard solo.

Also notable is the similarity of the solo's structure to the theme's—a similarity that is consistent with Keller's claim that overt contrasts depend upon a latent element of repetition. Some of the similarities between the theme's and solo's structure may be seen by comparing the scale-degree annotations on example 5.2 with those on example 5.3. The solo's opening phrase establishes the $\hat{1}$–$\hat{5}$ relationship found in the theme opening. Then the solo continues with phrases regularly ending on $\hat{5}$, just as medial phrases in the theme did. Particularly significant is the solo's climax (mm. 66–67), for it includes the introduction's descent, $\hat{5}$–$\hat{4}$–$\hat{3}$–$\hat{1}$, now in a *normative* cadential context, that is, terminating on $\hat{1}$ over tonic harmony. (See the brackets in example 5.3.) This descent is also normative in that it spans several beats (rather than measures as it did in the introduction) and incorporates idiomatic microtonal inflections. The end of the keyboard solo, then, makes explicit the latent blues character of the introductory melody by recasting the same melodic descent in a normative context, void of masking strategies.

We can refine our earlier rough hypothesis as follows: the introduction's structure (the descending $\hat{5}$–$\hat{4}$–$\hat{3}$–$\hat{1}$ of example 5.1) is equivalent to the theme's (example 5.2) and the solo's climax (example 5.3). In Keller's terms, this equivalence comprises a latent unity behind the contrast between the introduction and the theme section. Further, all three occurrences are unified by their common dependence upon a blues idiom, an idiom that is conveyed through various supporting traits including the structural use of the melodic archetype ($\hat{1}$–$\hat{8}$) $\hat{5}$–$\hat{3}$–$\hat{1}$ (example 5.2 and figure 5.2). The initially enigmatic relationship of the introduction to the other music becomes clear by the time the **coda** is reached because of all the associations set up in the course of the piece.

This reading brings to light a four-stage musical process encompassing the different treatments of the descending $\hat{5}$–$\hat{4}$–$\hat{3}$–$\hat{1}$ structure:

1. *Introduction.* The structure is present but in a latent form, masked by an unusual harmonization and augmented rhythmic values.

2. *Theme.* The structure is presented again, now at a subsurface level, spanning many measures.

---

23. In a larger paper, we could use the notion of "levels of melodic closure" to develop the argument that the melodic syntax of closure—as expressed by individual melodic pitches in a blues motive—still has force even when the motive is transplanted to a non-normative harmonic environment. This would strengthen our claim that the blues idiom is latent in the introduction. See Satyendra, "Dual Structure."

3. *Solo's climax.* The structure is finally revealed at the surface.

4. *Coda.* The listener associates the introduction's melody in the coda with the solo's climax; at this point the association of the introduction with the theme is at its most explicit.

An analysis paper would typically relate more details to the central point as strengthening evidence. Other categories of investigation that could develop more evidence for the claim of unity include (but are certainly not confined to)

1. absolute pitch associations, such as the appearance of B as a climax tone in both the introduction and theme sections;

2. metric features, such as the common initial ascent to an accented long tone in both the introduction and theme melodies; and

3. sonorities, for instance, the equivalence of the upper structure of the beat 1 chord at m. 7 in the introduction with the beat 1 chord in mm. 17 and 29 and the beat 3 chord at m. 21 in the theme.

The changes in the repetition of mm. 17–21 in mm. 30–33 that maintain the focus on $\hat{3}$ (established in mm. 24–29) are important details of craft that could be worked into the prose argument. The effect of these changes in articulating $\hat{3}$ within the melodic structure is visible in the upper staff of example 5.2.

Write Up Your Analysis, Not in the Order of Investigation, But in Good Expository Form
Avoid the impulse to write everything you have noticed in the order in which you noticed it. In the course of working on an analysis, one gets drawn into the details of a work and then identifies and considers an enormous number of elements. In an analysis paper, however, it is prudent to mention only those elements that directly bear on the paper's thesis. To include more information would potentially exhaust the reader in an excess of detail. While it might seem a shame not to be able to report in a paper everything one has discovered, it is heartening to note that the pleasures of analysis are not circumscribed by the content of a write-up but are much greater, encompassing the process of getting to know a piece of music—right down to its subtleties. I believe that this process of internalizing a piece of music is what makes music analysis such a rewarding discipline, one that can heighten our listening experience immensely.

POSTLUDE

In examining features beneath the surface, there is a danger of stressing relationships that are remote from anyone else's experience. To be sure, an analysis need not always address a listener's experience but can take something else as its object; this is particularly common in specialized research. But by and large, analysis (as represented by papers written in general music courses) seeks to communicate effectively and interestingly to another person who is using his or her own experience of a composition as a point of reference.[24] But going too far in the direction of emphasizing shared experience—by only describing features that are readily perceptible—produces an analysis that is uninformative, that presents information which can be directly noticed in a listening.

---

24. The question of what is represented in a musical analysis is taken up by Mark DeBellis in "The Paradox of Musical Analysis," *Journal of Music Theory* 43, no. 1 (1999): 83–100.

This problem of striking a balance between pointing out the obvious and pointing out the invisible is addressed by Edward Cone in an influential article titled "Analysis Today."[25] Cone claims that simple analytical tasks such as assigning Roman numeral labels to chords or order numbers to tones in a serial work does not constitute analysis, properly speaking, but rather are simple description. At the other extreme is what Cone calls "prescription": "the insistence upon the validity of relationships not supported by the text" (41). Cone's central point is that analysis "exists precariously between description and prescription, and it is a reason for concern that the latter two are not always easy to recognize" (41). According to Cone, analysis should probe beyond the surface of descriptive features but stop short of forcing a theory upon a piece that goes against what a reasonable listener might intuit.[26]

A shy approach to music analysis, which avoids developing a view of how listeners might organize musical experience, diminishes our scope to only the least adventurous of observations.[27] One of the challenges in music analysis is to increase the limits of our hearing and understanding with the goal of reaching for more within the works we love. Keller's strong thesis about the underlying unity of contrasting elements takes up this challenge. It urges us to go beyond the obvious and to hear and rehear music with engagement and creativity. Perhaps its capacity to inspire new insights is why Keller's principle remains ubiquitous in music analysis today.

FURTHER READING[28]

Berliner, Paul. *Thinking in Jazz*. Chicago: University of Chicago Press, 1994.

DeVeaux, Scott. *The Birth of the Bebop: A Social and Musical History*. Berkeley and Los Angeles: University of California Press, 1997.

Folio, Cynthia. "An Analysis of Polyrhythm in Selected Improvised Jazz Solos." In *Concert Music, Rock, and Jazz since 1945: Essays and Analytical Studies*, edited by Elizabeth Marvin and Richard Hermann, 103–34. Rochester, New York: University of Rochester Press, 1995.

Larson, Steve. "Schenkerian Analysis of Modern Jazz: Questions about Method." Music Theory Spectrum 20 (1998): 209–41.

Levine, Mark. *The Jazz Theory Book*. Petaluma, Calif.: Sher Music Company, 1995.

---

25. Edward T. Cone, "Analysis Today," in *Music: A View from Delft*, 39–54.

26. While Cone's dichotomy puts the issue of what Keller's principle can do for us into relief, we may not want to regard it as absolute. For a compelling critique of Cone's dichotomy, see Joseph Dubiel, "Analysis, Description, and What Really Happens," *Music Theory Online* 6, no. 3 (August 2000).

27. I borrow from the philosophy of mind in my description of the "shy" approach in speculative inquiry. See Owen Flanagan, *The Science of the Mind*, 2d ed. (Cambridge: MIT Press, 1991), 312.

28. For those interested in learning jazz theory, see Levine's comprehensive volume. Early important works in jazz theory are George Russell, *The Lydian Chromatic Concept of Tonal Organization* (New York: Concept Publishing Co., 1959) and John Mehegan, *Jazz Improvisation*. The analysis in this essay has implicitly suggested parallels in compositional technique between jazz and the kind of Western classical music that Keller had in mind when he developed his theory. Indeed, a number of jazz scholars have pursued motivic, structural, and harmonic analytical methods that are normally associated with Western classical music (Martin, Larson, Folio, Strunk). Other jazz scholars have focused upon the differences between jazz and Western classical music. Some examine the special role in jazz performance of improvisation and ensemble interaction (Sarath, Monson). Others study jazz's unique cultural and social context (DeVeaux, Berliner).

Martin, Henry. *Charlie Parker and Thematic Improvisation*. Lanham, Md.: Scarecrow Press, 1996.

Mehegan, John. *Jazz Improvisation: Rhythmic and Tonal Principles*. New York: Simon and Schuster, 1959.

Monson, Ingrid. *Saying Something: Jazz Improvisation and Interaction*. Chicago: University of Chicago Press, 1996.

Sarath, Ed. "A New Look at Improvisation." *Journal of Music Theory* 40 (1996): 1–38.

~ 6 ~

FORM IN ROCK MUSIC
A Primer

John Covach

John Covach (University of Rochester) began his career with a Fulbright to the University of Vienna for research in the areas of music aesthetics and philosophy. He also continued both performing and teaching classical and jazz guitar. In recent years, his research has shifted to the emerging field of popular music study by music theorists.

Covach's interest in form in rock music derives from fascination and pragmatism. Since many styles of popular music do not include music notation (except perhaps after the fact, in the form of a transcription), rock performers need to organize musical sections of any given song conceptually in order to keep the song and the arrangement fixed in memory. Thus, in the present essay, Covach provides a comprehensive introduction to various forms that rock musicians have used over the past five decades. Applying technical terms to familiar rock forms, Covach's survey details what forms are common to much rock music, as well as how formal structure articulates and distinguishes rock as a stylistic category.

INTRODUCTION

In its almost fifty-year history, rock music has presented its listeners with a wide variety of styles and approaches. From the swing-influenced early rock and roll of Bill Haley and the Comets through the bouncy two-minute singles of the early Beatles and the Supremes to the ambitious epics such as Pink Floyd's *The Wall*, rock music has encompassed both the simple and the complex, the serious and the frivolous, the emotionally direct and the technologically mediated. This essay will provide an introduction to the types of formal structures that can be found in rock music. Considering the wide range of music that could be classified as rock, this survey will provide only a glimpse of some typical structural features of the repertory. Despite such broad stylistic diversity, however, there are a number of formal types that return frequently in the repertory, crossing stylistic and historical boundaries in sometimes predictable—but also in sometimes surprising—ways. This essay will identify some of the most common formal schemes to be found in rock music.[1]

Some reminders: (1) all words in **bold** are defined in the glossary; (2) full citations for incomplete references are found in the selected bibliography; (3) the authors use their preferred notational system (e.g., Roman numeral, form label, and register notation). Most of the essays denote register by middle C as C^4.—Ed.

1. The analysis of rock music has received increasing attention among theorists in recent years. See, for instance, Allen Moore, *Rock: The Primary Text* (Buckingham: Open University Press, 1993); *Understanding Rock: Essays in Musical Analysis*; and *Expression in Pop-Rock Music: A Collection of Critical and Analytical Essays.*

Generally speaking, harmonic structure tends to be a primary factor in determining formal units at all levels of structure. Typically the analyst determines the meter of the song, analyzes the chord progressions, and charts the number of measures in a section, considering phrases within that section where applicable. These sections then add up to articulate the form of the song, which will often fall into one of the general types that will be explained below. In considering form in rock (as in many other types of song), it is also helpful to separate out harmonic concerns from those regarding the lyrics, at least provisionally. As will be shown, for instance, the pacing and repetition of harmonic materials need not always align with that of the lyrics: lyrics can be repeated over different sets of chord progressions, and the same progression can support different lyrics. It is thus helpful to remain mindful of the dialectical tension that can arise between these dimensions of the musical fabric, as such relationships can be useful in making important formal distinctions (as will be seen below). Organizational schemes in the melodic, timbral, textural, and rhythmic dimensions frequently reinforce those found in the harmonic and lyric dimensions of a song, though detailed analysis will often reveal distinct schemes that complement the overriding formal one. The common strategy of building up an arrangement by adding new layers to the texture as a song progresses, for instance, is one example of such a scheme. The form of a song is thus only one aspect of its structure.

For the purposes of this broad introductory survey, consideration will be limited to the twelve-bar blues as an organizational pattern and to several formal types: AABA, contrasting and simple verse-chorus, simple verse, and compound forms. A wide range formal variation in rock music can be understood in terms of these basic schemes, and while these schemes cannot account for all rock, they offer a solid foundation for the formal analysis of much rock music. This essay should be studied with the recordings of the songs discussed below readily at hand. The examples provided for discussion are well-known songs in the style—all of them are hit records that are likely to be both familiar and easily accessible to most readers who listen to rock music. In general, earlier songs have been chosen over later ones, though no claim is made that any of the songs is the first instance of a given formal type.

THE TWELVE-BAR BLUES

The influence of post–World War II rhythm and blues on rock and roll in the 1950s is obvious in many ways. In the great rush toward providing music for the craze created by this new youth-oriented musical style, many white acts re-recorded songs that had become hits for black artists on the rhythm and blues charts. These "cover" versions were in many cases hardly different from the originals, though frequently lyrics were changed to remove references that white middle-class listeners might find offensive. As these cover versions climbed the pop charts, original rhythm and blues recordings of other songs also charted, crossing over from the rhythm and blues charts to the pop ones. These crossovers and covers make up much of the original rock and roll of the mid 1950s.[2]

2. For a fuller account of cover versions and crossover hits in the 1950s, see Charles Hamm, *Yesterdays: Popular Song in America* (New York: W. W. Norton, 1983), 391–424; Steve Perry, "'Ain't No Mountain High Enough': The Politics of Crossover," in *Facing the Music*, ed. Simon Frith (New York: Pantheon, 1988), 51–87; David Brackett, "The Politics and Musical Practice of 'Crossover,'" in *Popular Music: Style and Identity, International Association for the Study of Popular Music Seventh International Conference on Popular Music Studies*, ed. Will Straw, Stacey Johnson, Rebecca Sullivan, and Paul Friedlander (Montreal: Centre for Research on Canadian Cultural Industries and Institutions, 1995), 23–31; and John Covach, "Jazz-Rock? Rock-Jazz? Stylistic Crossover in Late-1970s American Progressive Rock," in *Expression in Pop-Rock Music*, 113–34.

Measures (beats)	1 1234	2 1234	3 1234	4 1234		5	6	7	8		9	10	11	12
Chords	I	(IV)	I	I		IV	IV	I	I		V	IV	I	V
Phrases	Question ------------------|					Question again ------------|				Answer ------------------|			

Example 6.1. The twelve-bar blues (Muddy Waters, "Train Fare Blues" [1948])

In terms of organizational patterns, one clear model for much rock and roll—since the 1950s and up to the present day—is the twelve-bar blues. This pattern derives mostly from the kinds of blues played by blues and jazz bands in the years before the Second World War; while solo blues artists were sometimes much freer in terms of phrasing and meter, musicians playing together in a group setting were able to play easily by simply following this twelve-bar scheme. Good examples of this pattern may be found in tracks such as Muddy Waters's "Train Fare Blues" (1948), Howlin' Wolf's "Evil" (1954), and many others.[3]

The pattern is made up of three phases, each four measures in length (see example 6.1). The first phrase prolongs the tonic harmony. The second phrase moves to the subdominant for two measures and then returns to the tonic for two measures. The lyrics and melody from the first phrase are often (though not always) repeated in the second, making the second phrase a contrasting restatement of the first. The third phrase moves from dominant harmony through a passing subdominant harmony to tonic, while offering contrasting lyrics and melodic material. The musical effect of these three phrases can be understood as analogous to posing a question, reposing the same question, and then providing an answer, and this scheme serves to unify the three phrases into a single twelve-bar unit that then can be repeated as many times as the musicians see fit. Improvised solos tend to respect this question-question-answer scheme as well, frequently withholding the strongest melodically cadential material for the conclusion of the third phrase.

Big Joe Turner's "Shake, Rattle, and Roll" provides a nice example of the twelve-bar blues in a rock and roll context. In light of the discussion above, it is worth noting that this tune was a rhythm and blues hit for Turner in 1954 but became a pop hit when Bill Haley and the Comets covered it in 1955. A formal diagram of Turner's version of "Shake, Rattle, and Roll" can be found in example 6.2.[4] Note that after a four-measure introduction vamping on the tonic chord, the remainder of the tune consists of eight times through the twelve-bar blues in the key of Eb. This song follows the practice of repeating the lyrics to the first phrase in the second, with the third phrase offering the completion of the idea that began in the first two. The song differs somewhat from traditional blues by providing a **chorus** (the catchy "shake, rattle, and roll") in which the lyrics remain constant each time it sounds. This verse-chorus scheme based on the twelve-bar blues can be found in many other early rock and roll hits, including Bill Haley and the Comets' "Rock around the Clock" (1955) and Chuck Berry's "Johnny B. Goode," though these songs do not repeat the first-phrase lyrics of the **verse** in the second phrase. A suc-

---

3. See Dave Headlam, "Blues Transformations in the Music of Cream," *Understanding Rock*, 59–92; and "Does the Song Remain the Same? Questions of Authorship and Identification in the Music of Led Zeppelin," in *Concert Music, Rock, and Jazz since 1945: Essays and Analytical Studies*, ed. Elizabeth West Marvin and Richard Hermann (Rochester, N.Y.: University of Rochester Press, 1995), 313–63, for detailed consideration of how blues models make their way into British rock in the 1960s and 1970s.

4. The formal diagrams provided in this study provide both measure counts and CD timings. CD timings should be understood as approximate, since some deviations can occur between re-released versions of the same recording.

0:00-0:07	**Introduction**, 4 mm.
0:07-0:25	**Verse**, 12 mm.
0:25-0:43	**Verse**, 12 mm.
0:44-1:02	**Verse**, 12 mm.
1:02-1:21	**Chorus**, 12 mm.
1:21-1:40	**Verse** (instrumental), 12 mm., sax solo
1:40-1:58	**Verse**, 12 mm.
1:58-2:17	**Chorus**, 12 mm.
2:17-2:36	**Verse**, 12 mm.
2:36-3:00	**Chorus** with ending, 12 mm.

verse = twelve-bar blues in E♭, as shown above without optional harmonies in parenthesis

Example 6.2. Big Joe Turner, "Shake, Rattle, and Roll," words and music by Jesse Stone (Charles Calhoun), produced by Ahmet Ertegun and Jerry Wexler. Reached no. 1 on the Billboard Rhythm and Blues Chart in late 1954.

cession of twelve-bar verses without chorus can be found in Elvis Presley's "Hound Dog" (1956) and Little Richard's "Lucille" (1957), among many others. Discussion below will focus on larger formal issues concerning these songs. For present purposes, it is enough to point out that despite a certain amount of variation in the handling of the lyrics and melodic material, a formal scheme consisting of repetitions of the twelve-bar harmonic pattern made up of three four-bar phrases remains constant among all these tracks.

The twelve-bar pattern can itself be modified, leading to eight-bar and sixteen-bar schemes. Example 6.3 shows Elvis Presley's "Heartbreak Hotel," in which two four-bar phrases replace the three phrases discussed above. In this case, the first phrase is consistent with the twelve-bar version while the second is not. This second phrase can be seen as something of a conflation of the second and third phrases found from the twelve-bar arrangement, with mm. 5 and 6 matching the beginning of phrase 2 while mm. 7 and 8 do not strictly correspond to any pair of measures from the twelve-bar pattern. These last two measures serve to drive the eight-bar pattern to harmonic closure, and in this way can be seen to parallel—at least in function—the last four bars in the twelve-bar scheme. Example 6.4 shows a sixteen-bar scheme, and a comparison with the twelve-bar version in this instance reveals much clearer parallels. The first phrase of Elvis Presley's "Jailhouse Rock" expands the usual four measures to eight, while the remainder of the pattern duplicates the second and third phrases of the twelve-bar blues. While the harmonic schemes of these tunes have clear links to the twelve-bar pattern, both "Heartbreak Hotel" and "Jailhouse Rock" break with the question-question-answer lyric pattern of the traditional blues.

0:00-0:22	**Verse**, 8 mm.
0:22-0:42	**Verse**, 8 mm.
0:42-1:01	**Verse**, 8 mm.
1:01-1:21	**Verse**, 8 mm.
1:21-1:42	**Verse** (instrumental), 8 mm., 4 mm. guitar + 4 mm. of piano
1:42-2:05	**Verse** with ending, 9 mm.

verse = E: I | I | I | I | IV | IV | V | I ‖
          1   2   3   4   5   6   7   8

Example 6.3. Elvis Presley, "Heartbreak Hotel," words and music by Mae Boren, Tommy Durden, and Elvis Presley, produced by Steve Sholes. Reached no. 1 on the Billboard Pop and Country Charts in early 1956; reached no. 5 on the Billboard Rhythm and Blues Chart.

0:00-0:06   **Introduction**, 4 mm.

0:06-0:29   **Verse**, 16 mm.
0:29-0:52   **Verse**, 16 mm.
0:52-1:15   **Verse**, 16 mm.
1:15-1:26   **Partial Verse** (instrumental), 8 mm.
1:26-1:48   **Verse**, 16 mm.
1:48-2:11   **Verse**, 16 mm.
2:11-2:21   **Fade on Vamp**

verse = E♭: I | I | I | I | I | I | I | I | I | I | IV | IV | I | I | V | IV | I | I ‖
           1 2 3 4 5 6 7 8   9   10 11 12   13 14 15 16

Example 6.4. Elvis Presley, "Jailhouse Rock," words and music by Jerry Leiber and Mike Stoller, produced by Steve Sholes, Jerry Leiber, and Mike Stoller. Reached no. 1 on the Billboard Pop, Country, and Rhythm and Blues Charts in late 1957.

AABA FORM

While the twelve-bar blues addresses how a verse or chorus may be constructed, in terms of overall form, this scheme only requires that the twelve-bar (or eight- or sixteen-bar) pattern be repeated, determining little about the specific larger form of a song. Rock music does operate according to a number of larger formal designs, however, and one frequently employed formal scheme in rock music is the AABA pattern. While this form can be found in much music in the Western tradition, rock musicians have been influenced most by the use of the thirty-two-bar AABA scheme in American popular song during the first half of the twentieth century.[5] While other thirty-two-bar schemes can be found among Tin Pan Alley pop songs, the formal design shown in example 6.5 is one of the most common. After a four-measure introduction, the first verse of "Over the Rainbow" consists of eight bars, which are then repeated for the second verse. Note that the verses are harmonically closed, cadencing in the home key of Ab major. The eight-bar **bridge** presents contrasting material, and while it does not modulate in this instance, modulations during this section—often referred to as the "middle eight"—are common. The bridge is harmonically open, ending with a dominant sonority in the home key that pre-

0:00-0:11   **Introduction** (4 mm.), A♭: I | I | I | iv V^7 |

0:11-0:34   **Verse** (8 mm.)
0:34-0:55   **Verse** (8 mm.)
0:55-1:18   **Bridge** (8 mm.)
1:18-1:40   **Verse** (8 mm.)

1:40-2:01   **Verse** (8 mm.)
2:01-2:25   **Verse** (8 mm.)
2:25-2:46   **Partial Bridge** (4 mm.)

verse = A♭: I vi | iii V^7/IV | IV vii^{o7}/iii | iii V^7/ii | ii iv | I V^7/ii | ii V^7 | I (V) |
bridge= A♭: I | V7 | I | ii V | I | V7/iii | iii | ii V$^9_{\#5}$ |

Example 6.5. Judy Garland with Victor Young and his Orchestra, "Over the Rainbow," words by E. Y. Harbaugh, music by Harold Arlen. Reached no. 5 in the Billboard Pop Chart in fall 1939.

---

5. For a fuller analytical account of the music of Tin Pan Alley songs during this period, see Allen Forte, *The American Popular Ballad of the Golden Era, 1924–1950.*

0:00-0:08   **Introduction** (4 mm. prolongation of G: V drawn from *d*)

0:08-0:29   **Verse** (12 mm., 4*a* + 4*a* + 4*b*)
0:29-0:51   **Verse** (12 mm.)
0:51-1:11   **Bridge** (11 mm., 4*c* + 7*d*)
1:11-1:33   **Verse** (12 mm.)

1:34-1:54   **Bridge** (11 mm.)
1:54-2:22   **Verse** with tag (15 mm., 4*a* + 4*a* + 7*e*)

a = G: I | V | vi | iii |
b = G: IV V | I vi | IV V | I |
c = C: ii | V | I | vi |
d = C: ii | V | I
                 G: IV | V | V | V | V |
e = G: IV V | I vi | IV V | III | IV V | IV | I ||

Example 6.6. The Beatles, "I Want to Hold Your Hand," words and music by John Lennon and Paul McCartney, produced by George Martin. Reached no. 1 in UK charts in late 1963 and no. 1 on the Billboard Pop Chart in early 1964.

pares the return of the verse. The last verse returns after the bridge, rounding out a thirty-two bar scheme made up of four eight-bar phrases that can be labeled AABA overall.

It is important to note that Tin Pan Alley songs typically consist of two sections, often called the "verse" and the "**refrain**" but perhaps better labeled the "sectional verse" and "sectional refrain." The sectional verse is a kind of lead-in to the song, with lyrics that set up the sentiment expressed in the sectional refrain. The sectional verse tends not to be heard much in modern performances, and the sectional refrain is what most listeners would recognize as the song itself. Example 6.5 thus accounts only for the sectional refrain of "Over the Rainbow," and care must be taken not to confuse the term "verse" as it is used in this example from the other sense of the term, used to describe a larger section that is not under analytical consideration here. Singers and big bands frequently dispensed with the sectional verse, and recorded versions of Tin Pan Alley songs usually feature the complete thirty-two bar sectional refrain, which is then repeated within the time constraints of the 78 rpm record of the time. In the case of "Over the Rainbow," the full AABA scheme is followed by an abbreviated **reprise** featuring two verses and an ending crafted out of material drawn from the bridge.

Professional songwriters in the late 1950s and early-to-mid 1960s (especially those working out of the Manhattan's Brill Building) frequently employed modified versions of the thirty-two bar AABA form that was standard among the earlier Tin Pan Alley songwriters. Individual sections often deviated from the eight-bar model, with verses sometimes running to twelve or sixteen bars, and bridge sections may also have exceeded eight measures in length. Under the influence of these American songwriters, John Lennon and Paul McCartney also employed the AABA form with abbreviated reprise in many of their early British-invasion hits. Example 6.6 shows the formal design of "I Want to Hold Your Hand." Note that after a four-measure introduction, the verses are each twelve measures in length. Harmonic progressions are represented by italic lowercase letters (see the bottom of the example), and thus 4*a* + 4*a* + 4*b* in the first verse indicates that four measures of the *a* progression are repeated and followed by four measures of the *b* progression.[6] The bridge is modeled on the eight-bar scheme, with three measures added by extending the dominant sonority of m. 8 in mm. 9–11. The turn to the subdominant key

---

6. While this song would never be considered blues, it is interesting to note that the harmonic and melodic structure here matches the question-question-answer model described above.

area of C major here is strongly reminiscent of Tin Pan Alley practice. Note also that the verses are harmonically closed, while the bridge is open. The abbreviated reprise brings back only the bridge and verse, with the last articulation of the verse extended by three measures. These three measures employ a "tag," which in this case is the repetition of the IV–V–I cadential formula from the last two measures of *b*, here modified in m. 4 of *e* to land on a major mediant sonority, and in m. 6 on a subdominant sonority before the cadence on the tonic in m. 7.

Instances of the AABA form can be found in Jerry Lee Lewis's "Great Balls of Fire" (1957), The Everly Brothers' "All I Have to Do Is Dream" (1958), The Shirelles' "Will You Still Love Me" (1960), The Beach Boys' "Surfer Girl" (1963), and Beatles numbers from early ("From Me to You," 1963) to late ("Hey Jude," 1968), among many others. The AABA form is common in 1950s and 1960s rock, and its use generally marks the influence of the Tin Pan Alley professional songwriter pop tradition. As the 1960s progressed, however, there was a trend away from the AABA form as it occurs in these songs and toward versions of the verse-chorus form.

VERSE-CHORUS FORM

In an AABA song, the focus of the music is in the verse sections; the bridge exists simply to offer contrast, making the verse seem fresh on its reappearance. In a verse-chorus song, by contrast, the focus of the song is squarely on the chorus. In a way that parallels on a smaller scale the larger sectional verses and refrains of Tin Pan Alley songs, the verse serves primarily to prepare the return of the chorus. Thus the strategy of a verse-chorus song differs in a fundamental way from that of an AABA tune. The Ronettes' "Be My Baby" (see example 6.7) offers a clear example of this. After a four-measure Introduction, a sixteen-bar verse leads to the focus of the song, the eight-bar chorus. The second verse and the chorus that follows it bring back the same music. The variously repeated "be my baby" lyrics set to the conventional I–vi–V–V harmonic pattern combine to form the song's "hook"—that part of the song meant to catch the ear of the listener. Note that the third verse is played instrumentally but only contains the first eight bars of the previous verses, proceeding directly to the chorus; after an abbreviated return to the Introduction, the chorus then repeats twice more and fades. In the course of two and a half minutes of music, the chorus appears five times. Since each iteration of the chorus

0:00-0:08	**Introduction,** 4 mm. (2 mm. drums alone plus 2 mm. on E: I)
0:08-0:37	**Verse 1,** 16 mm., 4*a* + 4*a* + 8*b*
0:37-0:52	**Chorus,** 8 mm.
0:52-1:22	**Verse 2,** 16 mm.
1:22-1:37	**Chorus,** 8 mm.
1:37-1:52	**Partial verse** (instrumental), 8 mm., 4*a* + 4*a* only
1:52-2:07	**Chorus** (8 mm.) as before
2:07-2:10	**Reprise of intro** (2 mm.), drums only
2:10-2:36	**Chorus** (2 x 8 mm. chorus then fade)

a = E: I | I | ii | V |
b = E: V⁷/vi | | V⁷/ii | | V⁷/V | | V⁷ | | |
chorus = E: I | | vi | | IV | | V⁷ | | |

Example 6.7. The Ronettes, "Be My Baby," words and music by Phil Spector, Jeff Barry, and Ellie Greenwich, produced by Phil Spector. Reached no. 2 on the Billboard Pop Chart in late 1963.

0:00-0:14	**Verse 1**, 8mm., 8*a*
0:18-0:35	**Verse 2**, 8 mm., 8*b*
0:35-0:52	**Chorus**, 8 mm.
0:52-1:09	**Verse 3**, 8 mm., 8*a*
1:09-1:26	**Verse** (instrumental), 8 mm., 8*b*
1:26-1:42	**Chorus**, 8 mm.
1:42-1:59	**Verse 4**, 8 mm., 8*a*
1:59-2:16	**Verse 5**, 8 mm., 8*b*
2:16-2:33	**Chorus**, 8 mm.
2:33-2:58	**Chorus**, 9 mm., 8 mm. in B, with 1 m. added at end

a = B: I | ii V | I | | i | i/g# bass | ♭VI^7 | V$^{4\text{-}3}$ | V$^{4\text{-}3}$ |

b = B: I | ii V | I | | i | i/g# bass | ♭VI^7 | V$^{4\text{-}3}$ | IV |
A: V$^{4\text{-}3}$ |

chorus = A: I | I^6 | IV | | I | I^6 | IV | B: V |

Example 6.8. Beatles, "Penny Lane," words and music by John Lennon and Paul McCartney, produced by George Martin. Reached no. 2 in the U.K. charts and no. 1 on the Billboard Pop Chart in early 1967.

takes fifteen seconds, one minute and fifteen seconds—almost half the song—is devoted to this section.

Another instance of verse-chorus form can be found in the Beatles' "Penny Lane" (see example 6.8). Here two verses and a chorus are grouped together and sound three times overall, with the chorus repeated once more at the end. Both the verse and chorus sections are eight measures in length. While the verse and chorus in "Be My Baby" were in the same key (E major), the verse and chorus in "Penny Lane" are in contrasting keys: the verse is in B major while the chorus is in A major. Note that the appearance of the V sonority in A in the last measure of the verses using *b* material and the V of B in last measure of each chorus make the modulations between B and A go smoothly. When the dominant of B arrives in the penultimate chorus, it leads to a repetition of the chorus in the home key of B (instead of A), allowing the song to end in the same key in which it begins. Deep Purple's "Smoke on the Water" provides a representative example of the way verse-chorus forms are handled in the 1970s (see example 6.9). The scheme consists of four iterations of a verse-chorus pair, with the same distinctive guitar riff (marked "interlude") preceding each. The prominence of the guitar riff combined with a full verse-chorus guitar solo emphasize the increased focus on instrumental playing and virtuosity that characterizes much 1970s rock. It also exemplifies a general approach to form that tends to present some kind of contrasting material after the second verse-chorus section; in this instance it is the guitar solo, with the chorus altered slightly. As we will see in the discussion of example 6.11 below, this tendency can result in an entire contrasting section.

Despite their differences, "Be My Baby," "Penny Lane," and "Smoke on the Water" each use a scheme that employs different music for verse and chorus, and this formal type will be called "contrasting verse-chorus form." A large number of other songs are in contrasting verse-chorus form, including Buddy Holly's "That'll Be the Day" (1957), The Beach Boys' "California Girls" (1965), The Beatles' "All You Need Is Love" (1967), Jimi Hendrix's "Foxey Lady" (1967), and Bad Company's "Can't Get Enough" (1974).

Joe Turner's "Shake, Rattle, and Roll" (discussed above, see example 6.2) provides another instance of a verse-chorus form; in this case the chorus lyrics bring back the phrase "shake, rattle, and roll," while the verse lyrics change with each new verse. As was men-

0:00-0:51	**Introduction**, 24 mm., 4 + 4 + 4 + 4 + 4 + 4 using 4mm. guitar riff
0:51-1:25	**Verse 1**, 16 mm., 4*a* + 4a + 4*a* + 4*a*
1:25-1:38	**Chorus**, 6 mm., 4 + 2
1:38-1:55	**Interlude**, 8 mm., 4 + 4 using 4 mm. guitar riff
1:55-2:28	**Verse 2**, 16 mm.
2:28-2:41	**Chorus**, 6 mm.
2:41-2:58	**Interlude**, 8 mm.
2:58-3:31	**Verse** (instrumental), 16 mm.
3:31-3:39	**Chorus** (instrumental), 4 mm., based on chorus, g: IV ∣ IV ∣ ♭II ∣ ♭II ∣
3:39-3:56	**Interlude**, 8 mm.
3:56-4:29	**Verse 3**, 16 mm.
4:29-4:42	**Chorus**, 6 mm.
4:42-5:35	**Coda**, 16+ mm., 4 + 4 + 4 + 4 using 4 mm. guitar riff, then fade on vamp

a = g: i ∣   ∣ i ♭VII ∣ i ∣
chorus = g: IV ∣♭II ∣ i ∣   ∣ IV ∣♭II ∣

Example 6.9. Deep Purple, "Smoke on the Water," words and music by Ritchie Blackmore, Ian Gillian, Roger Glover, Jon Lord, and Ian Paice, produced by Deep Purple. Contained on the album *Machine Head*, which reached no. 1 in the U.K. and no. 7 on the Billboard Album Chart in mid 1972. Reached no. 4 on the Billboard Pop Chart when released as a single in mid-1973.

tioned above, this song is based entirely on the twelve-bar blues pattern; and thus, while the lyrics are structured according to a verse-chorus pattern, the harmonic scheme offers no contrast between these sections. Such a scheme will be termed a "simple verse-chorus form." While many songs use a blues scheme to structure the verse and chorus, it is also possible to employ a scheme not derived from blues practice, and The Kingsmen's "Louie Louie" (a 1963 cover version of a Richard Berry song written in imitation of Jamaican music) or Ritchie Valens's "La Bamba" (a 1959 hit based on a Mexican wedding celebration song) provide good examples.

Another formal pattern that can be clearly distinguished from both kinds of verse-chorus forms but that is similar in many respects to the noncontrasting verse-chorus form is the "simple verse form." Santana's "Evil Ways" provides a clear example in which music is repeated from verse to verse and no chorus is present (see example 6.10). The harmonic progression on which the song is based consists of a move from a tonic G-minor chord to a subdominant C major, suggesting the **dorian** mode. This one-measure progression—and variants of it—make up almost all of the music; the one exception oc-

0:00-0:18	**Introduction,** 8 mm., vamp on g: i IV ∣
0:18-0:47	**Verse 1,** 14 mm., 4 + 4 + 4 on vamp, plus 2 mm. on V
0:47-0:55	**Interlude,** 4 mm. on vamp
0:55-1:23	**Verse 2,** 14 mm.
1:23-2:25	**Instrumental solo** (organ), 30 mm., on vamp, in 2-bar phrases
2:25-2:53	**Verse 3,** 14 mm.
2:53-3:53	**Instrumental solo** (guitar), 30 mm., on vamp with fade

Example 6.10. Santana, "Evil Ways," words and music by Clarence Henry, produced by Brent Dangerfield and Santana. Contained on the album *Santana,* which reached no. 4 on the Billboard Album Chart in late 1969. Single reached no. 9 on the Billboard Pop Chart in early 1970.

curs at the end of each verse, where two measures of dominant set up a return to the two-chord progression. The introduction is based on this progression, as are the two instrumental solos. Songs in simple-verse form can sometimes feature an instrumental bridge that is contrasting, and this occurs in The Byrds' "Eight Miles High" (1966), The Beatles' "Tomorrow Never Knows" (1966), and Jimi Hendrix's "Purple Haze" (1967), among others. Traditional blues songs without chorus are often in simple verse form, and blues-influenced numbers such as "Heartbreak Hotel," "Jailhouse Rock," "Hound Dog," and "Lucille" (discussed above) are good examples.

COMPOUND FORMS

The formal types discussed thus far or features of them can be combined to create more complicated forms. Boston's "More Than a Feeling" (1976) serves as a representative example of such a formal type (see example 6.11). After a six-measure introduction, a verse-chorus pair appears once and is repeated. After the second chorus, a bridge section occurs that functions much like a bridge in an AABA form: it prepares the return of the third verse-chorus pair, which follows immediately. Thus the features of a contrasting verse-chorus form are combined with those of an AABA to form a "compound AABA form." Note that when compared to "Smoke on the Water" (discussed above, example 6.9), "More Than a Feeling" can be seen to solve the problem of providing contrast after the second chorus in a more ambitious manner; while "Smoke on the Water" employs an instrumental verse that provides contrast by focusing the listener's attention on the guitar solo, here the guitar solo is set to new music, creating a more independent contrasting section. Compound AABA form can be found in the Righteous Brothers' "You've Lost That Lovin' Feelin' " (1964), Led Zeppelin's "Whole Lotta Love" (1969), and Tom Petty's

0:00-0:18	**Introduction**, 6 mm., 2a + 2a + 2a (fade in)
0:18-0:42	**Verse 1**, 11 mm., 2a + 2a + 2a + 5b
0:42-1:17	**Chorus**, 16 mm., (2c + 2c) + 2c + 2c + 2c + 6d
1:17-1:51	**Verse 2**, 15 mm., (2a + 2a) + 2a + 2a + 2a + 5b
1:51-2:30	**Chorus**, 18 mm., (2c + 2c) + 2c + 2c + 2c + 8e
2:30-2:55	**Bridge**, 11 mm., 11f (harmony-guitar solo)
2:55-3:48	**Verse 3**, 24 mm., (2a + 2a) + 2a + 2a + 2a + 2a + 2a + 2a + 2a + 6b
3:48-4:41	**Chorus**, 20 mm., (2c + 2c) + 2c + 2c + 2c + 2c + 2c + 2c + 2c + 2c + fade

a = D: I | bVII IV |
b = D: I | bVII | IV |
　　　　　G: I | ii I | V | (to c)
c = G: I IV | vi V |
d = G: I IV | bVI | vi
　　　　　D: ii | V | IV | IV | I (elides to a)
e = G: I IV | bVI | vi
　　　　　D: ii | V | vi | IV | V⁴ | ³ |
f = D: I IV | I⁶ V | I IV | I⁶ V | I IV | vi V | I vi | ii V | IV | IV | I |

Note: parentheses in the notation of verses and choruses above indicates instances of the given pattern that do not feature singing

Example 6.11. Boston, "More Than a Feeling," words and music by Tom Scholz, produced by John Boylan and Tom Scholz. Reached no. 5 on the Billboard Pop Chart in September of 1976. Contained on the album *Boston*, which reached no. 11 on the U.K. charts and no. 3 on the Billboard Album Chart.

0:00-0:17	**Introduction (instrumental)**, 8 mm., *8a*
0:17-0:33	**Verse**, 8 mm., *8b*
0:33-0:49	**Verse**, 8 mm., *8a*
0:49-1:06	**Bridge 1**, 8 mm.
1:06-1:22	**Verse**, 8 mm., *8b*
1:22-1:43	**Bridge 2**, 10 mm.
1:43-1:59	**Verse**, 8 mm., *8b*
1:59-2:15	**Verse**, 8 mm., *8a*
2:15-2:32	**Bridge 1**, 8 mm.
2:32-3:01	**Verse (with extension)**, 14 mm., *8b* + last 4 mm. of *8b* + 2 mm. of vi
3:01-4:05	**Coda**, 28+ mm., *4c* + *4c* + *4c* + *4c* + *4c* + *4c* + fade

a = A♭: I | | vi | | IV | V | I | |
b = A♭: I | | vi | | IV | V | vi | |
bridge 1 = A♭: IV | | I | | V/V | | V | |
bridge 2 = A♭: ♭VI | | ♭VII | | ♭VI | | ♭VII | ♭VI | |
c = A♭: I | | vi | IV |

Example 6.12. The Police, "Every Breath You Take," words and music by Sting, produced by Hugh Padgham and the Police. Reached no. 1 on the both the U.K. charts and the Billboard Pop Chart in mid 1983.

"Refugee" (1979), among many others. It is perhaps surprising that as rock music in the mid-1960s tends to move away from AABA forms and toward verse-chorus forms, the music of the 1970s shows a strong tendency toward compound AABA forms.

Another instance of compound form can be found in The Police's "Every Breath You Take" (1983). Here a clear thirty-two-bar AABA form frames a central bridge section (marked "Bridge 2" in example 6.12), making the overall form a compound ABA. Perhaps the most interesting aspect of "Every Breath You Take" is the way in which the use of a thirty-two-bar AABA scheme constitutes a clear reference to earlier practice. The harmonic pattern of I–vi–IV–V harkens back to 1950s doo-wop ballads, which make such extensive use of it that any parody of the style is bound to include it. While The Police are not offering a parody in this instance, the combination of this harmonic pattern with the formal type most often employed with this earlier style of music makes the stylistic reference clear. This example indicates one way in which formal designs can be used to invoke other styles within rock music, allowing formal structure to participate in an interstylistic dialectic that may also include other dimensions of the music. This last point especially brings out an important aspect of the role of formal structure in rock music. While it is crucial to understand the formal design of any song under analytical consideration, often the most interesting features of a song involve the ways in which the form interacts with other dimensions of the music.

This survey of common formal types in rock music merely provides an overview of the patterns of structural organization that may be found in this music; much has had to be left out. Aspects of form in Motown songs, large-scale song structure in concept albums such as Jethro Tull's *A Passion Play*, and formal issues in highly improvised music, for instance, could each be topics of entire chapters.[7] Still, the formal types surveyed here will apply to much of the rock repertory, especially if handled flexibly. In many ways, form in rock music raises a number of interesting questions about form in music

---

7. See my "Progressive Rock, 'Close to the Edge,' and the Boundaries of Style," in *Understanding Rock*, 3–31, for an extended consideration of a twenty-minute track by Yes that turns out to be a version of the compound AABA form described above.

generally. For instance, the examples above are all based on recordings, not on printed scores. A second recorded version of the same song may well differ from the first—and this can happen even when both versions are by the same band or artist. The sections themselves will not be altered much in most cases; rather, the way in which sections are repeated or extended is likely to be the primary source of the differences. In rock music, like in most popular music, the precise formal arrangement often varies from version to version. Perhaps this ought to encourage analysts to think of form in more flexible terms when dealing with other music as well. Even this brief consideration of such concerns suggests the interesting issues that the careful study of rock music can present for music theorists and analysts.

FURTHER READING

Everett, Walter, ed. *Rock Music: Critical Essays on Composition, Performance, Analysis, and Reception.*

Covach, John, and Graham Boone, eds. *Understanding Rock: Essays in Musical Analysis.*

~7~

INTRODUCTION TO
MUSICAL AMBIGUITY

—————— *Deborah Stein* ——————

Deborah Stein (New England Conservatory) has focused her research on the German lied: how *Lied* composers created not just text depiction, but also a musical version of the poetic text. This approach has led to examining remarkable and innovative musical designs, such as songs beginning and ending in different keys (called directional tonality) and songs using unusual degrees of ambiguity. Stein's *Hugo Wolf's Lieder and Extensions of Tonality* (1985) explored the musical innovations of a mid- to late-nineteenth-century *lied* composer; her book *Poetry into Song: Performance and Analysis of Lieder* was named Outstanding Academic Book of 1996 by Choice.

The present essay introduces various ways to analyze musical ambiguity; other essays in the volume that explore ambiguity are by Cone (chapter 8) and Lester (chapter 14).

Analyzing a piece of music is an act of faith. We pose questions we assume we can answer; we use techniques that should result in finding what we seek. There are times, however, when what we expect does not occur, when our efforts to find specific musical norms (predictable forms, key schemes, symmetrical phrase structure, etc.) are frustrated.[1] In such times, we may want to consider whether the lack of clarity might be purposeful, whether the composer is using musical ambiguity as part of a compositional design.[2]

Some reminders: (1) all words in **bold** are defined in the glossary; (2) full citations for incomplete references are found in the selected bibliography; (3) the authors use their preferred notational system (e.g., Roman numeral, form label, and register notation). Most of the essays denote register by middle C as C^4.—Ed.

1. In a study that remains a classic, Leonard B. Meyer explored the concepts of expectation and perception in *Emotion and Meaning in Music* (Chicago: University of Chicago Press, 1956). In another classic, Suzanne K. Langer examined "the significance of music" in *Philosophy in a New Key* (1942; Cambridge: Harvard University Press, 1957) and "the symbol of feeling" and "Expressiveness" in *Feeling and Form* (New York: Charles Scribner's Sons, 1953). More recent studies include Peter Kivy, *The Corded Shell: Reflections on Musical Expression* (Princeton: Princeton University Press, 1980), reprinted in *Sound Sentiment: An Essay on the Musical Emotions* (Philadelphia: Temple University Press, 1989), and Anthony Newcomb, "Sound and Feeling," *Critical Inquiry* 19 (1984): 514–43.

2. Acknowledgment of the musical power of ambiguity was cited as early as 1976 by Leonard Bernstein, who lectured on "Delights and Dangers of Ambiguity," in *The Unanswered Question: Six Talks at Harvard* (Cambridge MA: Harvard University Press), and in 1979 by David Epstein, who wrote an entire chapter, "Ambiguity as Premise," in *Beyond Orpheus: Studies in Musical Structure* (Cambridge: MIT Press). Wallace Berry discusses ambiguity as a unique compositional element in *Structural Functions in Music* (Englewood Cliffs, N.J.:

Composers embrace musical ambiguity in every domain of musical structure and for all sorts of reasons. Sometimes a non-musical element such as a poetic text (in an art song) or a drama (in an opera or ballet) suggests a need to express conflict or ambivalence or some sort of struggle or confusion. Other times, in music not associated with any external element (what is called "absolute" music), a composer wants to create tension and drama for its own sake: for heightened expressivity and musical intensity.[3]

Two examples of nineteenth-century tonal ambiguity will demonstrate. Example 7.1 shows the score of Robert Schumann's famous setting of Heinrich Heine's poem "Im wunderschönen Monat Mai" from the cycle *Dichterliebe* (1840). The text in example 7.1 presents a statement about May's promise of love as ironically experienced by a poet yearning for a once-happy love in the past.

The opening piano prelude suggests the song to be in F♯ minor, with the opening progressions iv^6–V^7 of F♯ minor intensified by suspensions and other nonchord tones. But there is no authentic cadence in F♯ minor, just half-cadences, with V^7. The authentic cadences that do occur in the song (mm. 6, 8, 17, and 19) are in A major, the relative major. Is the song's tonic F♯ minor or A major? Schumann uses tonal ambiguity or duality to express the twofold sense of time: (1) remembering a past time of fulfilling love in May in A major during (2) a present time of feeling the pain of lost love in May in F♯ minor. The song begins and ends in the painful present, and the poet's ultimate lack of fulfillment is musically depicted when the song ends on an unresolving V^7 of F♯ minor. Listen to the song's tentative opening, the strong arrival on A major followed by the return to V^7 of F♯ minor and then the repetition of the whole cycle for the song's second half. The song concludes ambiguously: we, like the poet, remain suspended in irresolution.[4]

Example 7.2 shows an opening tonal ambiguity in Brahms's *Intermezzo*, op. 76, no. 2. The key signature is two flats, and the piece seems to begin on an F^7 chord, or V^7 in B♭ major. Is B♭ major the tonic? As the work proceeds, there is no resolution to I in B♭; rather, the first authentic cadence is in the relative, G minor, mm. 12–13. Is G minor the tonic? After what appears to be a close in G minor in m. 19, the opening section ends on a first inversion E♭-minor chord functioning as iv^6 going to V^7 of B♭ again for the repeat![5] The second half (not shown here) begins again in B♭ (on an E♭-minor mixture chord), and by mm. 32 ff, we are back on V^7 of B♭. By the work's conclusion, the ambiguity finally is resolved: G minor never returns, and the piece ends on the *first* clear B♭ tonic of the

---

Prentice Hall, 1976), and a decade later I coined the term "The Ambiguity Principle" in *Hugo Wolf's Lieder and Extensions of Tonality* (Ann Arbor, Mich.: UMI Research Press, 1985). Numerous analyses have explored musical ambiguity in the past thirty years. See, for example, Robert Bailey, "Analytical Study," in *Prelude and Transfiguration from "Tristan und Isolde"* (New York: W. W. Norton, 1985), 116–146. Fred Lerdahl and Ray Jackendoff, *A Generative Theory of Tonal Music;* William Rothstein, "Beethoven's with and without Kunstgepräng: Metrical Ambiguity Reconsidered," *Beethoven Forum 4*, edited by Christopher Reynolds, Lewis Lockwood and James Webster (Lincoln: University of Nebraska Press, 1995), 165–93; Edward T. Cone, "Ambiguity and Reinterpretation in Chopin," in *Chopin Studies 2*, ed. John Rink and Jim Samson (Cambridge: Cambridge University Press, 1994), 140–60; and Janet M. Levy, "Beginning—Ending Ambiguity: Consequences of Performance Choices," in *The Practice of Performance: Studies in Musical Interpretation*, edited by John Rink (Cambridge: Cambridge University Press, 1995), 150–69.

3. Eminent musicologist Carl Dahlhaus presents a powerful study of the topic in *The Idea of Absolute Music*, trans. Roger Lustig (Chicago: University of Chicago Press, 1989) (originally *Die Idee der absoluten Musik*, 1978).

4. Charles Rosen offers provocative insight into this work in *The Romantic Generation*, 41–48.

5. The complex tonal relations between the relative major and minor scales have been discussed by many. See, for example, Bailey, "Analytical Study," where he considers tonal ambiguity between the relative major/minor scales as a foundation for much later nineteenth-century tonal expansion, and Rosen, *Romantic Generation*, who believes the relative major/minor pair functions as a single tonality.

Dichterliebe, Op. 48

Example 7.1. Tonal ambiguity in Schumann, "Im wunderschönen Monat Mai"

whole work. However, the fact that we conclude in B♭ does not take away the opening ambiguity; rather, the final B♭ resolves *at the work's conclusion* the ambiguity of the opening half. That is, we experience the ambiguity over time, and the concluding resolution cannot change the temporal experience.

Tonal ambiguity is but one of many forms of musical ambiguity, which may occur in any aspect of a work, including harmony, rhythm, meter, phrase structure, and form.

"Im wunderschönen Monat Mai"

In the wondrous month of May,
When all buds burst open,
Then it was my heart
Filled with love.

In the wondrous month of May,
When all the birds sang,
Then I confessed to her
My longing and desire.

—*Heinrich Heine* (my translation)

Example 7.1. (*Continued*)

Musical ambiguity may occur at a work's opening, at its closing, or in between. It may occur in a specific section of a work or it may recur throughout.

While it is not possible to discuss this topic here in great scope or detail, I introduce an approach to analyzing musical ambiguity: how to recognize the ambiguity and how to trace its use throughout an entire work. For this introduction, I use an atonal piano work: Bartok's "Boating" from his piano series *Mikrokosmos*. The titles for Bartok's famous progressive piano studies offer uncommon insight into his compositional approach; in this artful little piece, Bartok conveys the unique tension of a boat floating upon the water. This musical depiction utilizes several types of ambiguity; we will examine two: use of pitch and of rhythm and meter.[6]

6. Composer and theorist Peter Child offers an insightful analysis of this work in "Structural Unities in a Work of Bartok: 'Boating' from *Mikrokosmos, Vol. 5,*" *College Music Symposium* 30, no. 1 (spring 1990): 103–14. His focus is on three interconnecting "musical systems": "phrase structure and grouping, pitch-class set structure, and pitch function." (p. 103)

Intermezzo

Example 7.2. Tonal ambiguity in Brahms, *Intermezzo*, op. 76, no. 2

Musical ambiguity often occurs at the outset of a work, where an initial ambiguity poses a compositional issue or problem that is worked out over the rest of the piece.[7] This was the case in the tonal ambiguity explored above, and it also occurs in Bartok's "Boating." As we listen to the opening section, mm. 1–14, we hear a two-voice texture that in-

---

7. Schoenberg called this process of presenting an initial idea for development a "Grundgestalt"; see "Linear Counterpoint," in *Style and Idea,* ed. Leonard Stein, trans. Leo Black (Berkeley and Los Angeles: University

volves continuous eighth-note motion. We'll examine the pitch structure first, then the use of rhythm and meter.

PITCH AMBIGUITY

In tonal music, pitch ambiguity can involve ambiguity of harmonic function or, as already shown, of tonal design. We expect harmonies to function in specific ways and we listen for the stabilizing anchor of a tonic. In an atonal work such as Bartok's "Boating,"[8] we anticipate that pitches will relate to one another in some sort of organized way, and that one pitch may function like a "tonic" in what is called an **atonal pitch center**.[9]

In tonal music, the pitch organization is the inherent hierarchy of all pitches relating to a specific tonic. In atonal music, on the other hand, a variety of nontonal materials may be used instead with little or no inherent pitch hierarchy beyond a contextually defined "pitch center": church modes (scales with specific characteristics borrowed from pretonal music, such as **Dorian, Mixolydian**, etc.), scales such as the **pentatonic**, or scales of limited transposition (scales with specific arrangements of whole and half-steps, such as **wholetone, octatonic**, etc.).[10]

As soon as we hear "Boating" (see Ex. 7.4) we know the pitch resources are complex; we observe that (1) we hear two lines, a wandering melody in the treble (piano right hand, RH) accompanied by a repeated pattern, called an **ostinato**, in the piano bass (or left hand, LH); (2) the melody uses only the black notes of the piano and the LH ostinato uses only white notes (thus there are no common pitches); (3) the melody seems to float, without a clear pitch center, while the ostinato seems to be anchored on the G, the lowest note that recurs on the downbeat of each bar. (Note that the G is embellished by the neighbor A in the same low register.)

We thus hear two different pitch systems working simultaneously in a melody-accompaniment texture. Example 7.3 shows what happens if we put each collection into scalar form: the melody is pentatonic and the ostinato is a mode lacking a third and having a lowered scale degree 7 (either G Mixolydian with B♮ or G Dorian with B♭).[11] So rather

---

of California Press, 1975). Many composers, both tonal and nontonal, use this compositional practice, and several studies over the past two decades have examined this concept in great detail: David Epstein, *"Ambiguity As Premise"*; Patricia Carpenter, "Grundgestalt as Tonal Function," *Music Theory Spectrum* 5 (1983): 15–39; Severine Neff, "Aspects of Grundgestalt in Schoenberg's First String Quartet, Op. 7," *Theory and Practice* 9, nos. 1–2 (1984): 7–56; Walter Frisch, *The Early Works of Arnold Schoenberg* (Berkeley and Los Angeles: University of California Press, 1993); and Hali Fieldman, "The Grundgestalt and Schubert's Sonata Forms" (PhD diss., University of Michigan, 1996).

8. The term "pitch centricity" was coined by Arthur Berger in "Problems of Pitch Organization in Stravinsky," *Perspectives of New Music* 2, no. 1 (fall–winter 1963): 11–42, reprinted *Perspectives on Schoenberg and Stravinsky*, rev. ed., edited by Edward T. Cone and Benjamin Boretz (1968; New York: W. W. Norton, 1972), 123–54.

9. Some might hear the pitch focus as a tonal "tonic" in an enlarged concept of the tonality that includes modes and nontonal scales as well as the major/minor system of common practice tonality.

10. Many textbooks explain the modes and scales used in late-nineteenth and early-twentieth century music. See, for example, more recent texts by Robert Gauldin, *Harmonic Practice in Tonal Music;* Stefan Kostka and Dorothy Payne, *Tonal Harmony*, chap. 28; and Stefan Kostka, *Materials and Techniques of Twentieth-Century Music*, chap. 2.

11. A pentatonic scale is best understood as a symmetrical structure around a central pitch. In "Boating," for example, the central pitch would be A♭. Move out from A♭ in both directions a M2d and then a m3d and you get five pitches: E♭–G♭–A♭–B♭–D♭. These pitches can be shown in a different format, for example G♭–A♭–B♭–D♭–E♭, where the M2nds are more prominent. It is easy to remember the pentatonic collection as all the black notes on the piano; however, the collection can occur in twelve unique forms.

Pentatonic

G mixolydian?

G dorian?

Example 7.3. Scale representations of pitch material

than having one pitch system, Bartok presents us with two. And he underscores this duality by having different dynamics for each hand: the LH is p, sempre legato, and the RH is mf. The juxtaposition of two pitch collections can be called "**bimodal**,"[12] and the resultant tension between the two modes is analogous to the two tonalities cited in our opening examples of tonal ambiguity. More important, we have two different kinds of modal ambiguity here: (1) the conflict between the RH pentatonic and a different LH mode, and (2) the possibility of two different modes being used for the ostinato. Each ambiguity serves a different musical function: the first (LH versus RH) seems to depict the unique tension of a boat (LH) floating upon water (RH), while the second (which of the two possible modes in the ostinato) captures the vivid image of water's gentle, floating suspension.

Once we've noted the opening modal ambiguities, we need to determine whether they continue throughout the piece and whether the dualities ever resolve into one governing pitch system or one single pitch center. But first we'll examine the role of rhythm and meter in the first fourteen bars.

RHYTHMIC-METRIC AMBIGUITY

Again we listen first. What meter do we hear? Even though Bartok notated the piece in 3/4, we tend to *hear* it in 6/8: the LH ostinato **groupings** suggest two groups of three: (1–2–3) + (4–5–6).[13] Such three-groupings of notes are called **trichords**: three notes that are grouped together but are not tonal triads. These trichords result from **contour**, or melodic shape.[14] The two perfect fourths (P4s) group together into a single upward sweep, and the next gesture is also an upward sweep of P4 + M2.[15] The ostinato, then, is heard in 6/8.

---

12. Terms such as "bimodal" or "bitonal" convey the juxtaposition of two modes or keys. "Polytonal," then, refers to the simultaneous use of more than two keys at the same time. The music of Charles Ives offers vivid examples of polytonality.

13. Grouping occurs when notes are perceived as a unit because of contour, rhythm, accent, and other characteristics. According to Lerdahl and Jackendoff: "the process of grouping is common to many areas of human cognition. If confronted with a series of elements or a sequence of events, a person spontaneously segments or 'chunks' the elements or events into groups of some kind" (*Generative Theory*, 13).

14. Contour refers to the shape of a line, whether it rises, falls, or some combination of the two. The contour of lines is very audible and plays an important role in motivic development, closure, and expressivity.

15. Chords built of juxtaposed fourths rather than thirds are sometimes called quartal. (See the textbooks in the selected bibliography.)

The RH melody does not clarify the metric confusion. The opening trichord in eighths suggests a pickup or **anacrusis** to the sustained B♭, which overshadows, through **agogic accent,**[16] the written downbeat of m. 4. Measures 6–10 seem more in sync with the LH downbeats in 6/8, but is the melody in 6/8 or 3/4? The last phrase begins (m. 11) with the same ascending fourth anacrusis and concludes with a similar sustained tone, this time A♭, but what is the meter?

Example 7.4 shows the score with perceived meters indicated for LH and RH. For the first fourteen bars, the LH clearly begins in a 6/8 grouping. The RH can be played in 3/4, but a 3/4 metric downbeat is constantly undermined by other kinds of accents where beats 2 and 3 have more emphasis than the written downbeat. Accents on normally weak beats are called **phenomenal accents** and are used in both tonal and nontonal music to undermine or cloud a given meter.[17] Thus, any possible sense of 3/4 in the melody is weakened by conflicting musical accents; only mm. 6 and 8 have a clear sense of down-beat in 3/4. Or is it all in 6/8?

Within this first section, one measure of the melody can be played in either of the two possible meters: m. 8 has, for the first time, only eighth notes, and thus the group-ings can create either 6/8 (two groups of three) or 3/4 (three groups of two). Performers can try both ways and determine what works best; in either case, the phrase goal, A♭, is embellished by neighbors G♭ and B♭.

The metric ambiguity is thus twofold: (1) for the performer, the LH 6/8 opposes the written 3/4 meter, and (2) for both performer and listener, the two hands play in two dif-ferent meters. The tension thus is not so much about "which meter" as about both meters operating simultaneously, or what is called **polymeter.**[18] Does this metric ambiguity con-tinue? And is the metric ambiguity clarified by the work's end? Let's find out.

Having noted the ambiguities of pitch and rhythm-meter at the outset, we then proceed to trace them throughout the rest of the work. The work subdivides into four large sections:

mm. 1–14 = Section I (opening material);

mm. 15–23 = Section II (contrasting material);

mm. 24–34 = Section III (development and climax);

mm. 35–end = Section IV (return to opening material and closure).

Do the opening ambiguities continue in Section II? In terms of pitch, the pentatonic melody is replaced by descending scalar modal fragments, and the G pedal (from the os-tinato) is replaced by a descending chromatic bass. The RH melodic fragments (using only white notes now!) oppose the LH chromatic descent (using both black and white notes), and the pitch duality continues, albeit in a different way.[19]

---

16. An "agogic accent" occurs when a usually weak beat is accented by long duration.

17. The term "phenomenal accent" was coined by Fred Lerdahl and Ray Jackendoff in *Generative Theory*, 17 ff. Joel Lester presents the clearest, most thorough explanation of the concept in *The Rhythms of Tonal Music* (Carbondale: Southern Illinois University Press, 1986), chap. 2.

18. The use of multiple meters simultaneously is called either "bimeter" or, more often, "polymeter." The term refers to a variety of kinds of double or more meters and is explained in the several textbooks to twentieth-century music listed in the selected bibliography.

19. While the pitches change and the bass descends, the two trichords of the ostinato continue in this section: the juxtaposed P4s followed by the P4 + M2. Thus a section that in many ways contrasts with the opening Sec-tion 1 also develops intervallic material from mm. 1–14.

Example 7.4. Metric ambiguity in Bartok, "Boating"

The opening metric tension between 3/4 and 6/8 also continues. The 6/8 trichord groupings of the LH continue until m. 21. The melody, with its repeated notes and rests, can be heard in either 6/8 or 3/4, the lack of a distinct rhythmic character tending to draw the performer into 6/8 because of the LH. As the section begins to come to a close, two significant metric changes occur. First, the RH melody goes into a clear 6/8 in m. 20, and second, the LH ostinato breaks, putting the bass temporarily into 3/4. The closing two

Example 7.4. (*Continued*)

bars seem to be in 3/4 for both hands, a moment of relative metric clarity that accentu-ates the closure of this section.

Section III begins with the 6/8 LH ostinato (now in the right hand) and develops the RH opening pentatonic melody in the left hand by presenting the first four notes (a four-note group is called a **tetrachord**) as a short melodic fragment that represents the whole melody. Such an abbreviated melodic idea is often called a "**head motive**" or "**motto**"; the head motive recurs in an imitative fashion in various registers. The opening imitation yields to a transposed repetition of the motto tetrachord (m. 28) that creates **acceleration** toward the climax in m. 31. The approach to the climax intensifies through a change in meter that results in shorter measures (2/4) that speed up the motion.

The pitch material in Section III thus begins with the bimodality of Section I and achieves the climax through a more complicated combination of pitch material. Example 7.4 identifies the pitches from the ostinato (LH) or melody (RH) throughout mm. 28–34. The climax occurs on two notes from the ostinato: the A–E outer pitches of the second trichord. This high point is accented by metric stress (occurring on a downbeat!), a notated accent over the E, and a series of rising contours in m. 30.

The **dénouement** from the climax prepares for the return of the opening material in Section IV.[20] The sustained A in the LH creates a neighbor pedal (similar to the V pedal **retransition** in sonata form) that will descend to the G in m. 35. In the melody, meanwhile, pentatonic pitches are stressed: the D♯ (E♭) in m. 32 and the A♯ (B♭) in m. 33.

The metric ambiguity continues in this section. Wherever the ostinato appears, the trichord subdivision continues in 6/8. But as shown in Example 7.4, the tetrachord motto in the LH can be heard in 3/4. In addition, several factors undermine these meters. The 2/4 of m. 29 breaks the 6/8, and the grouping of the RH in mm. 30–32 strongly suggests 6/8. The arrival on bass A is again agogic and undermines the downbeat accent on the melodic E, m. 31. The 3/4 meter might continue in the RH over the A pedal, mm. 31–34; however, even there, the contours and accents (notated and agogic) either preserve 6/8 or simply preclude 3/4. Despite the brief but strong emergence of 3/4, then, the metric tension continues.

Our final section brings back the ostinato in its original register and the opening melody an octave higher. This abbreviated **reprise** leads to the work's closing section (mm. 38–47), where the pitch and metric ambiguities continue. The melody concludes on B♭ from the pentatonic collection. The LH, meanwhile, concludes in the white-note collection but significantly on B♮. The LH ending on B♮ resolves the ambiguity of the LH mode: it is G mixolydian rather than G dorian. However, the opposition of the B♮ with the B♭, emphasized by a dynamic swell and metric placement, brings the work to an end with the same modal juxtaposition heard from the beginning. The pitch duality thus remains unresolved.

The reprise brings back the initial metric conflicts as well. Closure begins in m. 38, with the interruption of the ostinato; but the 6/8 continues in the ostinato fragments, and a new lack of metric clarity occurs within the ensuing section of imitation, mm. 40–42. A change then occurs in m. 43. As the counterpoint concludes, both hands begin homorhythmic fragments. The use of fragments, or **fragmentation**,[21] is a common technique of closure, especially for Bartok, and he utilizes rests on written downbeats and puts melodic goals on beat 3 to give these final gestures a tentative, even more ambiguous quality. The three gestures of mm. 43–end thus create a small amount of metric tension prior to the work's conclusion in 3/4! But there is a final glitch. The three eighths in m. 45 can be heard in 6/8 as well as in 3/4: Is the 3/4 "resolution" thus illusory? Or does this moment of 6/8 simply recall the earlier metric tensions at the work's end?

---

20. The French term "dénouement" describes the gradual decrease in tension following a climax in theater. The term works well when applied to the decrease in tension following a climax in music as well.

21. The technique of fragmentation, the division of a musical idea (gesture, motive, theme, etc.) into segments or fragments, is common in both tonal and nontonal music. Fragmentation is commonly used in development sections and sections of closure. Another term for fragmentation used by Arnold Schoenberg is "liquidation"; the two terms are explored by William Caplin in *Classical Form: A Theory of Formal Functions,* 10–11.

Bartok's "Boating" has shown a pervasive use of pitch and metric ambiguity from the work's opening to its conclusion. The ongoing tensions resulted from, on the one hand, dualities—opposing pitch collections and meters—and, on the other hand, localized ambiguities in both domains. In the area of pitch, the two systems combine into a bimodal clash that remains at the work's conclusion. In addition, while the LH ostinato seems grounded on G, the pentatonic melody had no such anchor, and the final B♭ seems suspended, not a pitch of resolution. In the metric domain, the opposition of 3/4 versus 6/8 was ever-present except for selected moments where either the two parts played in the same meter (mm. 15, 20, 43–47) or a given part might be played in either meter (mm. 8, 15–19, 21, 40).

Both of these forms of ambiguity are common to Bartok, where juxtaposition and opposition contribute to his rich, dynamic language. In this particular work, the ambiguities create a vivid musical depiction of a boat floating upon a buoyant surface, of two elements juxtaposed and yet connected in a dance of irresolution.

FURTHER READING

Antokoletz, Elliott. *The Music of Béla Bartók: A Study of Tonality and Progression in Twentieth-Century Music*. Cambridge and Berkeley: University of California Press, 1984.

Dunsby, Jonathan. *Structural Ambiguity in Brahms: Analytical Approaches to Four Works*. Ann Arbor, Mich.: UMI Research Press, 1981.

Stevens, Halsey. *The Life and Music of Béla Bartók*. 3d edition. Edited by M. Gillies. Oxford, U.K.: Clarendon Press, 1993.

~ 8 ~

ATTACKING A BRAHMS PUZZ

———————— *Edward T. Cone* ————————

Edward T. Cone (Princeton University) has long been one of the most accessible and enlightening analysts in either musicology or theory. Robert P. Morgan, editor of the collection of essays by Cone, *Music: A View from Delft,* states it thus: "During the past few decades Edward T. Cone has written some of the most perceptive commentary on music that has appeared in our time. . . . Cone has viewed the field from an unusually comprehensive perspective, writing in a style notable for its literacy and clarity" (vii).

Indeed, Cone's writings have been read and reread by students and music professionals for decades. The present essay, published in 1995, shows Cone's analytical approach to a Brahms piano piece that is characterized by pervasive ambiguity of form and thematic design and of harmonic and tonal structure. Cone's analysis is highly influenced by his personal experiences as a composer and a pianist. He is deeply concerned with how analysis relates to performance, and many of his writings, especially his two books (see Selected Bibliography), warrant multiple readings.

Ambiguity is a word that recurs frequently in discussions of Brahms. "Ambiguity in Brahms's music," says David Epstein, "played more than a specific role in particular pieces. Its presence was pervasive throughout his works; it became virtually a part of this style."[1] Jonathan Dunsby entitles a book *Structural Ambiguity in Brahms.* As he explains his purpose,

> The concern running through all the studies is musical ambiguity. Brahms's music is characterized by an avoidance of straightforward relationships. There may often be a simple aesthetic framework for his ideas, for example, in periodic phrasing. . . . At some level of the structure, however, Brahms usually creates a functional ambiguity, giving his music its typically elaborate and complex character.[2]

Today, as we know, ambiguity in art is considered a praiseworthy characteristic. The two cited authors had no intention of denigrating Brahms—quite the contrary. Nevertheless, ambiguity, to be artistically effective, must be bounded. Not all instances of ambiguity admit of resolution, but the most successful are delimited by a context of relative

---

Some reminders: (1) all words in **bold** are defined in the glossary; (2) full citations for incomplete references are found in the selected bibliography; (3) the authors use their preferred notational system (e.g., Roman numeral, form label, and register notation). Most of the essays denote register by middle C as C^4.—Ed.

1. David Epstein, *Beyond Orpheus,* 179.

2. Jonathan Dunsby, *Structural Ambiguity in Brahms* (Ann Arbor, Mich.: 1981), 1.

directness and clarity. That is why Henry James stressed the importance of a "lucid re-flector" in the telling of his stories, and that is perhaps why *The Turn of the Screw,* for all its fascination, remains for many of us something less than a first-rate work of art. Un-bounded ambiguity results in what we call vagueness; ambiguity resolved or successfully delimited is described as subtle. Typically, Brahms's tonal and harmonic ambiguities are eventually resolved; his rhythmic ambiguities are heard against a steady, if not always immediately perceptible metrical background; his formal ambiguities are projected upon a recognizable, sometimes even conventional, schematic pattern.

For this reason it is unsettling to encounter, among the short piano pieces of the mas-ter's last period, one whose formal articulation seems to resist every attempt at clarifica-tion. Indeed, during an earlier phase of my own struggle with the Intermezzo, op. 116, no. 4, I was tempted to surrender by describing it as a *durchkomponiertes Lied ohne Worte*—the transcription, as it were, of a song based on an imagined but unstated poem whose nature might be implied by the original title of the piece, "Nocturne." Dunsby him-self, in an essay demonstrating the overall unity of the *Fantasien,* op. 116, seems at a loss. He points out convincing connections between no. 4 and other members of the opus, but confesses that this singular formal centre of the *Fantasien . . .* seems to offer an example of lack of wholeness or of excessive implication."[3] While granting that "some future anal-ysis may show the harmonic and tonal continuity in this piece," he nevertheless warns against "the casuistry this would involve."[4] In effect, he suggests that no. 4, unlike the other members of the opus, is not to be construed as a self-contained unit, but must be heard in its position at the centre of a complex "multi-piece."

Casuistry, according to the first definition in *Webster's Seventh New Collegiate Dic-tionary,* is "a method or doctrine dealing with cases of conscience and the resolution of questions of right and wrong in conduct." I assume, however, that Dunsby is relying on Webster's second meaning: "sophistical, equivocal, or specious reasoning." That is a heavy accusation against one trying to make sense of a short piano piece, but I shall have to risk it. I shall leave it to the reader to decide whether or not I am guilty—and whether I have shown no. 4 to be subtle or simply vague.

What difficulties confront the would-be analyst of this piece? On the largest scale, both the harmonic-tonal shape and the thematic design are puzzling. The most likely can-didate for a final structural cadence occurs in bars 66–67, where the melodic line comes to rest on the tonic; but the requisite dominant harmony is apparently subverted by the tonic pedal that has persisted since bar 55. On the other hand, the last (indeed the only) previous authentic cadence in E, that of bars 54–55, supports no cadential melody.

Example 8.1 indicates what is heard superficially as the basic harmonic movement signaled by phrase-openings and cadential progressions. In addition to the problem of the final cadence, other peculiarities to be noted are the unusual expansion of the mediant, and the failure to consummate the strongly implied turn toward the subdominant. (A sub-script after a bar-number means a specific beat in the bar. The line marked "Pedals" des-ignates the bar-lengths and the precise limits of the tonic pedals in the bass.)

Also outlined in example 8.1 is the obvious thematic pattern. The opening material is designated as MA in order to distinguish between the introductory motif (M) and the lyrical phrase that answers it (A). In that way the motif can be singled out later on when it is extended (as indicated by Mx). In point of fact, M overlaps A. Brahms's insistence on the use of the right hand for the low E, together with the absence of a rest at that point in the upper staff, implies that the low E really initiates the melody continued by the right

---

3. Jonathan Dunsby, "The Multipiece in Brahms: *Fantasien,* Op. 116," in *Brahms: Biographical, Documentary and Analytical Studies,* ed. Robert Pascall (Cambridge, Cambridge University Press, 1983), 176–77.

4. Ibid., 178.

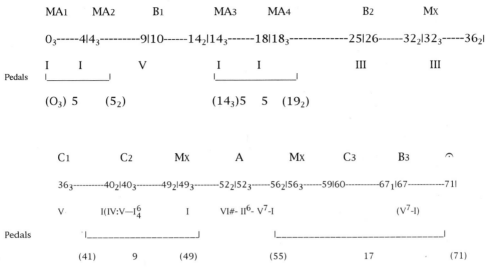

Example 8.1. Brahms, op. 116, no. 4: harmonic movement and thematic design

hand in the treble clef (example 8.2a). Twice—in bars 32–36 and 49–52—the right-hand bass develops a line of its own; but the original connection is reinstated when the descending fifth in bars 51–52, G♯–C♯, is immediately echoed by the soprano continuation (example 8.2b).

What is the overall design? The initial section presents no problem. There are four statements of MA, presented two by two. In each pair the antecedents remain in the tonic; the consequents move to V and III respectively. The pairs are irregularly but convincingly balanced: 4–5, 4–7. The cadential chord of each consequent is elaborated by an extension (B_1, B_2) that turns into a transition. In the first case, five bars return to a modification of the original antecedent (MA_3); in the second, seven bars lead to an expansion of M. It is noteworthy that each transition is the same length as the consequent that engenders it— the first of a number of such correspondences that, far from being coincidental, appear rather to govern the proportions of the piece.

So far, then, the pattern of the material presented conforms in a free way to that of many opening sections of short compositions: it is essentially a double period—and could be played as a simple one by omitting the transitional sections. The most surprising event

Example 8.2. Introductory motive (M) overlaps lyrical phrase (A)

is the concluding expansion of what has heretofore been heard as an introductory motif, which now flowers into a cadential passage (bars 32_3–36), a complete four-bar phrase confirming III. (It does so by developing the tonal ambiguity inherent in the chromaticism of the opening motif.) By its finality, the passage tries to persuade us that what we have heard so far is the opening section of a presumably three-part design.

What follows is indeed a contrasting section (C). It begins conventionally enough with what appears to promise two balancing four-bar phrases; the first, over a pedal on V, overlaps the second, over a pedal on V/IV. But instead of the expected resolution to IV, we are given a five-bar dissolution of the consequent, uneasily alternating between V/IV and IV$^6_4$, and coming to rest on the latter (bars 48–49). At the same time, chromatic motion insinuated between the soprano C♯s and Bs recalls the opening motif M. As if emboldened by this suggestion, M returns forthrightly, with a new expansion into a three-bar cadence on VI♯—yet another exploitation of M's tonal ambiguity that aborts any chance of further development of the contrasting theme C. Instead, we seem to be prematurely launched upon the reprise; for, despite the cadential form of M, it is followed by a version of A that pushes toward its own cadential goal. Its underlying harmony, as revealed by the bass, is II^6–V^7–I; but the tonic is represented by an unresolved diminished seventh unfurled over a tonic pedal. So when M undergoes yet one more extension (bars 56_3–59), we are ready for a final statement that will resolve A both melodically and harmonically. But what actually happens? Theme C returns in full force, utilizing to its advantage the chromatic motion that interrupted it before. This time the chromaticism helps the phrase to continue its downward motion to a melodically satisfactory resolution on E (bar 67). Thus Theme C has replaced the expected conclusion of Theme A with one of its own; but apparently Theme B is not disturbed. Indifferent to the fact that it is now attached to the upstart C instead of its own parent A, it extends the final tonic to create a coda.

Partially as a consequence of these peculiarities of thematic design, what might be called the rhetorical form of the Intermezzo is unclear. The encroachment of the reprise on the central section, together with that section's revenge by insisting on its own reprise, results in a work of unusual proportions. The opening section, instead of representing the normal fraction—say one-quarter to two-fifths—of the full tripartite extend, occupies almost exactly one-half—36 out of 71 bars. Furthermore, if the demands of Theme A are so urgent as to justify its unexpected reprise, why is a dynamic culmination thwarted? Even without obvious thematic completion, the *crescendo* of bars 54–56, leading to the only *forte* in this section, presages something more assertive than the *pianissimo, una corda, diminuendo* conclusion that takes over in the very next bar. What has happened?

In an attempt to make sense of these anomalies, let us begin at one unmistakable point: the cadence on III midway through the piece. Its position is so unusual, and so nearly exact, as to tempt one to try further subdivisions. So, ignoring for the time being the thematic structure, let us examine each half. We find a striking correlation. The move toward the mediant so firmly established at bar 36 is initiated at the midpoint of the first half by the phrase beginning in bar 19 (or, more precisely, in bar 18_3). That is the first progression away from the I–V–I of the opening. (There is an interesting symmetry within the opening section, too, as a result of the phrase-division already noted: a four-bar phrase in I plus a five-bar phrase moving to V, exactly balanced by a five-bar phrase prolonging V plus a four-bar phrase in I.)

At bar 37 an extended dominant inaugurates the second half of the composition; and at bar 54, its midpoint, that dominant bids us farewell. The ensuing seventeen bars retain a tonic pedal throughout. If we allow the closing fermata to represent an eighteenth bar, the result is a quadripartite division of strict exactitude: eighteen bars each of I, III, V, I.

We should not be seduced into accepting this account too easily, however. It is only one way of hearing the tonal structure, and not necessarily the most compelling. For there is an important harmonic element that seeks to impose its own pattern, sometimes supportive of the one just outlined, sometimes at odds with it. I refer to the recurring pedals that so persistently establish a tonic bass. By their length, as indicated in example 8.1, they seem to govern much of the harmonic structure. (Note that I have not included bar 6, which only apparently continues the opening pedal. True, the E is retained, but in bar 6 it has a new meaning as the bass of V^2/V. Compare the corresponding point in bar 20, where a different bass-note performs an analogous function.) The resulting ratios, 5:5:9:17 bars (lo: again 36!) can be construed as a modification of 4:4:8:16, which of course is simply 1:1:2:4. I think we are encouraged to hear the proportions in this way. The first two pedals basically govern four-bar phrases, the pedal being extended in each case to initiate the following phrase. As for the nine-bar pedal, it gains its final bar by a written-out *ritardando* or fermata. And the extra bar in the concluding pedal—58—constitutes an interpolation, which I shall try to explain later.

The harmonic structure suggested by the pedals is most obviously at odds with that determined by the bisections when the third pedal produces, within the presumably dominant section (bars 37–54), a disproportionately long stretch governed by the tonic—exactly half the section. But such control is not necessarily to be construed as absolute. Is E major in fact that prevailing harmony of those bars? If it is, then A major, even though tonicized by the persistent D♯s of bars 40–43, is a neighbouring IV$^6_4$ resolved in bars 45, 47, and at the end of bar 49. But perhaps the extended IV$^6_4$ itself takes over as the principal harmony. Now the E major triads of bars 45 and 47 are the neighbours, that of 49$_3$ functioning as an upbeat to the following phrase. Even though discriminating performance could enable us to hear the passage in either way, the latter interpretation is the one encouraged by the low register of 49$_3$. How, then, should we hear the relation between tonic bass and subdominant superstructure?

In answer, I refer to what I once wrote of Mahler: that it is possible to hear "tension between the harmony implied by the motionless bass and those outlined by the moving voices and chords above it." in which case "the functional role of the bass is called into question."[5] In the present instance, the subdominant's claim to a functionality independent of the bass is supported by the careful distinction between *legato* and *portamento* in bar 48. Like the similar distinctions already indicated in bars 9 and 25, this one implies at the least a special rhythmic articulation. But it permits a harmonic articulation as well by calling attention to a root-position IV embedded within the $^6_4$. The result is a simple version of the harmonic tension described above; for, against the tonic bass, IV can be heard as functional, eventually leading through its relatives, VI♯ (bars 50–52) and II^6 (bar 53), to the brief restatement of V in bar 54. Obviously, then, the damper pedal required for bar 48 must not be so pervasive as to obscure the indicated phrasing—just as later on, the pedal specified in bars 67–68 must not cover the left-hand rests.

We must now attempt a clarification of the thematic pattern. The first step is to uncover the basic kinship among the elements I have labeled A, B, and C. Example 8.3 points out the most obvious correspondences; the vertical alignment shows how subsequent thematic material arises from simple variations of A. A more complex relationship is exhibited by two passages (bars 44–48 and 64–66) that insinuate into C the original rhythm and contour of A against references to M and its retrograde (example 8.4). I emphasize these relationships, not in a spirit of Réti-like tune detecting, but as evidence that in this piece there are not strict boundaries, that themes spill over into one another, and that some passages may perform more than one task.

In the light of that interpretation, consider bar 58. By the exchange of hands, Brahms has identified it as an interpolation within the expansion of Motif M. Clearly it refers to

---

5. Edward T. Cone, "Analysis Today," in *Music: A View from Delft*, 48–49.

Example 8.3. Correspondences between themes A, B, and C

Example 8.4. Combination of A, M, and C

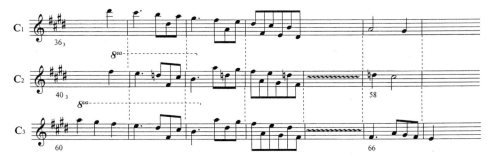

Example 8.5. Phrases in theme C

Theme C, connecting its last appearance, the dissolution of bars 48–49, with its return in bar 60. The *una corda* specification, recalling the one in bar 36, which introduced Theme C, clinches the identification. The interpolated bar, however, is more than a bridge between the two statements. I believe that it represents a feminine cadence missing from C_2, one expected as a parallel to bar 40 but postponed by the references to M and A. Its model, however, bar 40, included not only the feminine cadence of C_1 but the upbeat to C_2 as well. In the present case, the corresponding upbeat to C_3 has been expanded so as to encompass all of bar 60. Theme C thus consists of three successive but dislocated phrases. With the references earlier material omitted, its outline emerges as in example 8.5: bars 36_3–40, 40_3–43 with 58, and 60–63 with 66–67.

In somewhat similar fashion Theme A, left dangling in bar 56, can be completed. A's earlier statements, we remember, were paired. What is now missing is an A_6 to balance A_5. We are certainly led to expect that by the version of M that immediately succeeds A_5. Like those that followed A_1 and A_3, this one (although slightly expanded) should herald an answering form of A. Is it possible, then, to read bars 60–67 in a different sense—not as C_3 embedding a reference to A, but rather as A_6 expanded by a reference to C? Example 8.6 shows that it is. Taking bar 60 again as anacrustic, this time we consider bars 61–63 as parenthetical and 64–67_1 as thematic. The resulting phrase brings to a satisfactory conclusion another tripartite design: MA_1–MA_2, MA_3–MA_4, MxA_5–MxA_6.

To be sure, although we can *read* the phrase of bars 60–67 either as C_3 with an interpolated A, or as A_6 within an interpolated C, both those readings are analytical abstractions from what we actually *hear* as a unified peroration interlocking the two themes in a single melodic-harmonic line. For that reason, an even more satisfactory outcome results from our acceptance of one more dislocation: the postponement of the effective tonic from bar 67 to bars 70–71. There all elements of the composite line, in every register, achieve resolution.

That postponement results from the reappearance of theme B in bar 67. It is no mere reminiscence, for some form of B has previously succeeded each paired statement of MA. This version not only complements MxA_5–MxA_6 but completes one more triple: B_1, B_2, B_3. It performs another task as well: it prepares for the delayed fulfilment of motif M. For M has been striving to achieve thematic status of its own, as Mx. Not surprisingly, that development too is governed by the ubiquitous triple phrasing. Each of the first two

Example 8.6. A_6 expanded C

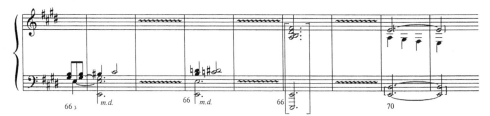

Example 8.7. Third statement of M

statements is continuous: bars 32_3s–36_2 and 49_3–52_2. But the third is broken: bars 56_3–57, 59, and now 70–71—a scattered phrase to which bar 66 may also contribute (example 8.7). Thus, connected to the preceding by register and pianistic spacing, the final two bars can again be heard as resolving a harmonic and melodic progression previously left hanging. Only a pedant would complain that the final cadence does not retain the *m.d.* bass.

This extraordinary composition thus exhibits not one form but a multiplicity of forms. If op. 116 as a whole comprises what Dunsby called a multi-piece, it is appropriate that it should exhibit as its central component what, in a different sense, might be called a multi-piece on its own. Most remarkable, however, it not that center's multiplicity but its unity: in the final fifteen bars all strands coalesce and achieve resolution. Why, then, does the rhetoric seem to falter here? Why, as the dénouement approaches, does Brahms call again for the *una corda* of bar 38 and the *pianissimo* of bar 48—an instrumentation appropriate for a dreamy interlude but oddly out of place for a final summation?

The trouble arises, I am convinced, from a misunderstanding of the marking in bar 58. Although no further dynamic sign appears until the *diminuendo* of bar 68, the *pianissimo una corda* must apply to bar 58 alone—and quite properly so, for that interpolation refers to the earlier locus of the same dynamic level. What follows it, however, returns to the line and the pianistic layout of bar 57, which, completing a *crescendo*, has arrived at a *forte*. Does the return in bar 59 not require a similar or an even higher level? That supposition is further supported by the full right-hand chords of bar 60, which produce startling dissonances against the left-hand arpeggio. The pianistic brilliance persists, contrasting C_3 with its calm predecessors C_1 and C_2. Moreover, the coalescence of C_3 and A_6, as they make for a common goal, demands a *piena voce* rendering. Finally, the *diminuendi* of bar 68 makes sense only if granted a strong (*forte*) point of departure, after which it can signal a welcome détente.

The restriction of a dynamic marking to a delimited passage, without any sign of cancellation, may be unconventional; but Brahms depended on it elsewhere, and in this very opus. In no. 2, a *pianissimo* is used consistently to emphasise an echo—in bars 9, 18, 74, and 85. In each case the context makes it clear that the marking applies to the echo only, even when it is not explicitly cancelled for the next phrase. And as for the *una corda,* Brahms often expected the pianist to gauge its extent, as in op. 118, nos. 3 and 6.

The test of the foregoing analysis lies, of course in performance. To a certain extent that is true of any analysis, but it is especially true of one that, in trying to make sense of a problematic work, implies specific recommendations about interpretation. In the present instance what is actually required is a series of performances, for no single rendition can do justice to the complementary interpretations suggested here. That does not mean that one must necessarily play the piece oneself. One can read it silently, rehearsing it mentally. Or one can listen critically to another pianist. In each case, one encourages performance and analysis to criticize each other, as it were. In so far as the dialogue proves to be interesting and fruitful, the analysis will have been a success.

PART II

MODEL ESSAYS: TEXT AND MUSIC

The setting of words or drama to music has been a rich human enterprise for as long as we have recorded history. As early as 3000 BC, religious and secular texts were set to music in Mesopotamia and Egypt, and in the fifth-century, classical Greek music rhythms were related to poetic rhythms. Indeed, the very language we use today for music came from ancient Greece: words such as tone, *melos,* rhythm, and harmony. Medieval and Renaissance composers brought text setting to a new level of artistic achievement, and settings of both sacred and secular texts and dramas have poured forth in glorious music throughout the centuries that followed—all the way to the present day.[1]

The essays in this unit investigate the magical relationship of music to text and drama in a dazzling array of topics and approaches. Each of the essays illustrate an important text-music genre of the given century, from Purcell's seventeenth-century operatic setting of the famous Greek drama *Dido and Aeneas* to Mozart's eighteenth-century comic opera of love, deception, and class struggles to the two primary text-music genres of the nineteenth century: Schubert's intimate miniature settings of German romantic verse and Wagner's operatic transformation of text, music, and drama, and finally, a twentieth-century setting within a newer genre of popular song (here by Sarah McLachlan).

The challenge of transforming a text or drama into musical form resulted in tremendous musical innovation as composers sought new ways to express emotions and depict dramatic events. Innovations in form, language, rhythm, and meter, virtually every aspect of musical expression, have emerged from textual or dramatic inspiration: Mozart,

Verdi, and Strauss developed complex tonal relations for their operas; Schubert, Schumann, and Brahms extended tonal relations and norms of rhythm and meter in the new lied genre; Beethoven and Mahler altered the symphonic form with texted movements; Stravinsky created a new atonal world in his ballet scores; Schoenberg invented *Sprechstimme*; and American composers such as Ives and Berio transformed the art song into expressions of daring and complexity.

This modest analysis sampling shows the remarkable depth and breadth of the interpenetration of text/drama and music, the wonderous impact of the text upon the composer's creativity and the powerful impact of music upon the written word.

FURTHER READING

The following readings offer a range of discourse about this fascinating topic.

Bonds, Mark Evan. *Wordless Rhetoric: Musical Form and the Metaphor of the Oration.* Cambridge: Harvard University Press, 1991.

Carter, Tim. "Artusi, Monteverdi, and the Poetics of Modern Music." In *Musical Humanism and Its Legacy: Essays in Honor of Claude V. Palisca,* edited by N. K. Baker and B. R. Hanning, 171–94. Stuyvesant, N.Y.: Pendragon Press, 1992.

Cone, Edward T. *The Composer's Voice.* Berkeley and Los Angeles: University of California Press, 1974.

———. "Words into Music: The Composer's Approach to the Text." In *Music: A View from Delft* (see the selected bibliography for full citation).

Hoffmann, E. T. A. *E. T. A. Hoffmann's Musical Writings: "Kreisleriana," "The Poet and the Composer," and Music Criticism.* Edited by David Charlton, translated by Martyn Clark. Cambridge: Cambridge University Press, 1989.

Kerman, Joseph. *Opera As Drama.* Rev. ed. Berkeley 1956; and Los Angeles: University of California Press, 1988.

Kivy, Peter. *Sound Sentiment: An Essay on the Musical Emotions* [including *The Corded Shell*]. Philadelphia: Temple University Press, 1989.

Kramer, Lawrence. *Music and Poetry: The Nineteenth Century and After.* Berkeley and Los Angeles: University of California Press, 1984.

Robinson, Paul A. "The Self and Nature: Franz Schubert's *Die schöne Müllerin* and *Winterreise*." In *Opera and Ideas: From Mozart to Strauss.* New York: Harper and Row, 1985.

Scher, Steven Paul, ed. *Music and text: critical inquiries.* Cambridge: Cambridge University Press, 1992.

Thompson, Virgil. *Music with Words: A Composer's View.* New Haven: Yale University Press, 1989.

Wagner, Richard. *On Music and Drama.* Translated by H. Ashton Ellis. London: Gollancz, 1964; Lincoln: University of Nebraska Press, 1992.

Winn, James. *Unsuspected Eloquence: A History of the Relations between Poetry and Music.* New Haven: Yale University Press, 1981.

~9~

FIGARO'S MISTAKES

David B. Lewin

David Lewin (Harvard University) has written extensively on a wide variety of topics, including history of theory, tonal and twentieth-century analysis, twelve-tone theory, text and music, and phenomenology. His training as a pianist, composer, and mathematician has led to unique analytical insights. In the last two decades, Lewin combined music and mathematics to create a revolutionary general model of musical relationships—harmonic, melodic, and rhythmic—called "transformational networks." By 1987 his ground-breaking book *Generalized Musical Intervals and Transformations* (or *GMIT*) began a new direction for music theory that continues today. His subsequent book *Musical Form and Transformation*, which earned him the Deems Taylor Award in 1994, extended his theory into aspects of large-scale form.

The present essay, written in 1995, combines several of Lewin's favorite topics: text depiction, mathematics, pitch analysis, and rhythmic analysis of tonal music. It also shows his love of theater and humor.

AUTHOR'S NOTE I was invited to lecture on a topic of my choice by the Mur-
ial Gardiner Program in Psychoanalysis and the Humanities, of New Haven, Con-
necticut. I delivered the following lecture on January 28, 1993. I repeated it for
the Symposium on Music and Psychoanalysis at Harvard University on October
16, 1993. The lecture was directed primarily at psychoanalysts educated in the tra-
ditional musical canon. I had in mind as well a number of literary academics who
attended the New Haven lecture. I was concerned not to bore a number of musi-
cians who attended each lecture, but I was not thinking of them primarily when I
prepared the material.

Freud, in the second of his *Introductory Lectures,* catalogs some common forms of erro-neous performance, such as misspeaking, misreading, mishearing, and mislaying.[1] In that

---

Some reminders: (1) all words in **bold** are defined in the glossary; (2) full citations for incomplete references are found in the selected bibliography; (3) the authors use their preferred notational system (e.g., Roman nu-meral, form label, and register notation). Most of the essays denote register by middle C as C^4.—Ed.

1. Sigmund Freud, *Vorlesungen zur Einführung in die Psychoanalyse* (Berlin: Gustav Kiepenheuer Verlag, 1955), 18–34. "Erroneous performances" translates *Fehlleistungen*; "misspeaking," "misreading," "mishearing," and "mislaying" translate *das Versprechen, das Verlesen, das Verhören, and das Verliegen*, respectively (18–19).

Camera quasi smobiliata.	A half-furnished room.
Figaro prende la misura d'un	Figaro is measuring a bed;
letto; Susanna prova il suo	Susanna is trying on her
cappello di nozze.	wedding hat.

Figaro: Cinque—dieci—venti—trenta—	F: Five—ten—twenty—thirty—
trenta sei—quarantatre.	thirty-six—forty-three.
Susanna: Ora sì, ch'io son contenta,	S: Yes, now I'm happy.
Sembra fatto in ver per me.	It really seems made for me.

F: Cinque—	F: Five—
S: Guarda un po', mio caro Figaro!	S: Just look, Figaro dear!
F: Dieci—	F: Ten—
S: Guarda un po', mio caro Figaro!	S: Just look, Figaro dear!
F: Venti—	F: Twenty—
S: Guarda un po',	S: Just look,
F: Trenta—	F: Thirty—
S: Guarda un po', guarda adesso	S: Just look, look at my
il mio cappello,	hat now,
F: Trenta sei—	F: Thirty-six—
S: Guarda adesso il mio capello!	S: Look at my hat now!
F: Quaranta tre.	F: Forty-three.
S: Guarda un po' mio caro Figaro,	S: Just look, Figaro dear,
guarda adesso il mio capello,	look at my hat now,
il mio cappello, il mio cappello!	my hat, my hat!

F: Sì, mio core, or è più bello,	F: Yes, my love, it's prettier now,
sembra fatto in ver per te,	it really seems made for you;
sembra fatto in ver per te.	it really seems made for you.

S: Guarda un po'!	S: Just look!
F: Sì, mio core.	F: Yes, my love.
S: Guarda un po'!	S: Just look!
F: Or è più bello.	F: It's prettier now.
S: Ora sì, ch'io son contenta,	S: Yes, now I'm happy,
Ora sì, ch'io son contenta,	Yes, now I'm happy!
sembra fatto in ver per me,	it really seems made for me,
per me, per me!	for me, for me!
F: Sì, mio core, or è più bello,	F: Yes, my love, it's prettier now;
sembra fatto in ver per te,	it really seems made for you,
per te, per te!	for you, for you!

F&S: Ah! il mattino alle nozze	F&S: Ah! with our wedding day so
vicino, quant'è dolce al tuo	near, how sweet for your
(mio) tenero sposo, questo bel	(my) tender tender fiancé is this
cappellino vezzoso, che Susanna	pretty, charming little hat, that
ella stessa si fé.	Suzanna herself has made.

Figure 9.1. Mozart/Da Ponte, *The Marriage of Figaro*, Act I, opening duet[2]

connection he analyzes various theatrical passages.[3] Today I propose to continue those lines of thought, analyzing the opening duet from Mozart's *The Marriage of Figaro*. There, as we shall see and hear, the musical aspect of the theater work lends special interest to Figaro's miscounting and mis-singing.

---

2. Robert Pack and Marjorie Lelash, *Three Mozart Libretti: Complete in Italian and English* (New York: Dover, 1993); my translation.

3. Freud, *Vorlesungen*, 18–34. Freud discusses passages from Schiller and Shakespeare on 32–34. In the third lecture Freud also mentions a passage from Shaw (51). It is curious that all three playwrights' names begin with the same phoneme. I have been unable to make a Freudian analysis of that, but I am sure that Freud himself would have found one, had we been able to ask him for free associations.

F: Dix-neuf pieds sur vingt-six.	F: Nineteen by twenty-six.
S: Tiens, Figaro, voilà mon petit chapeau: le trouves-tu mieux ainsi?	S: Well, Figaro, there's my little hat; do you like it better this way?
F: (lui prend les mains) Sans comparaison, ma charmante. Oh! que ce joli bouquet virginal, élevé sur la tête d'une belle fille, est doux le matin des noces, à l'oeil amoureux d'un époux!	F: (taking her hands) Incomparably, my charmer. Oh! how sweet, on the wedding morning, is this pretty bridal bouquet crowning the head of a beautiful girl to the amorous eye of a fiancé!

Figure 9.2. Beaumarchais, *Le marriage de Figaro*[4]

I shall first play the number. The text, with my translation, appears as figure 9.1. Before listening, you should know that Figaro and Susanna, about to marry, are servants in the employ of Count Almaviva, that the count has been making harassing advances toward Susanna, that Figaro does not yet know of those advances, and that the bedroom that the count is providing for the couple lies close to his own quarters. [Here I played a recording.]

One immediately notices tension and conflict in the opening of the scene. Susanna, anxious about the marriage and confronting a serious problem with the count, is looking to Figaro for affection and support. Figaro is compulsively evading Susanna's appeals; he is clearly terrified by the bed he is measuring, in which he will have to measure up to what he imagines as Susanna's sexual expectations. Using the magic of his phallic measuring instrument, he is trying to avoid confronting such menacing female symbols as the bed and the flowery hat, not to mention the woman herself, and the imminent marriage. "Don't distract me," he is saying in effect, "I am trying to do serious and difficult male business." The tensions are particularly clear if one compares the opening of our scene to the opening of the Beaumarchais play (figure 9.2).

The French Figaro is not compulsively measuring and remeasuring; he has just finished measuring. He has measured the room, not the bed. Furthermore, when Susanna asks him for concern and reassurance, he is right there, understanding her emotion even though he is not yet aware of her problem with the count; his flowery response immediately gives her everything she wants. Going back to the Italian libretto of figure 9.1, we can see that the drama of the operatic scene is constructed around Susanna's gradually winning Figaro's attention, allaying his anxieties sufficiently for him to allay hers. That process, as we shall see, is essentially musical rather than textual.

Before proceeding to the music, though, let us review the numerical series 5, 10, 20, 30, 36, 43, provided by Mozart's librettist Da Ponte. Figure 9.3 will help us out. The idea, I think, is this. Figaro begins measuring 5, 10, 20, 30, and we infer that his measuring instrument is ruled in groups of five units. The measurement 36, 6 more than 30, then makes sense only as an estimated final measurement. But then the whole structure collapses with 43, which is 7 more than 36. The joke is one of the *lazzi* associated with stage business

5 10 20 30	36	43
Multiples of 5; ruler or tape presumed so grouped	6 more; estimated final measurement?	7 more; nonsense.

Figure 9.3. Mozart/Da Ponte, *Marriage of Figaro*, 1, opening duet, numerical series

4. Pierre Augustin Caron de Beaumarchais, *Le mariage de Figaro*, 19th ed., ed. Pierre Richard (Paris: Classiques Larousse, 1934), 45.

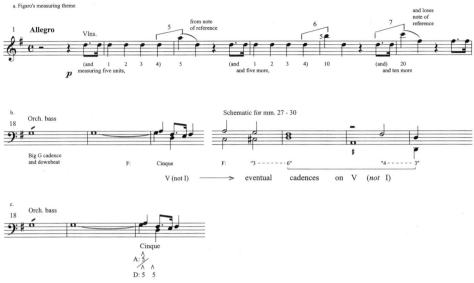

Example 9.1. Mozart, *The Marriage of Figaro*, I, opening duet

in the commedia dell'arte tradition; one imagines Figaro holding up his measuring tape or rod to the audience after each announcement. [I acted this doing so, while speaking the pertinent numbers.] The business is very thematic for the opera, which throughout contrasts the obsessive calculations of its men—calculations that always go haywire—with the appeals for recognition and love from its women.

Example 9.1a shows aspects of Mozart's response to Da Ponte's joke. The music is the version of Figaro's measuring theme played by the violins in measures 1–6. Beneath the music is some commentary showing how the rhythm suggests measuring in groups of five units; this is a strong mimetic cue for the actor measuring the bed. [Here I sang the violin theme and acted measuring "1, 2, 3, 4, 'Cinque'" in rhythm.] More commentary appears above the music; it shows how the theme first measures off the bracketed interval of a *fifth* from the melodic note of reference [here I played the bracketed fifth], then the interval of a *sixth* [simile], and then the interval of a *seventh* [simile], after which the note of reference is lost. The numerical scheme correlates perfectly with figure 9.3: An interval of 5 becomes an interval of 6, which becomes an interval of 7, after which the structure breaks down. In both text and music, the idea of the expanding intervals, followed by a deflating collapse, is suggestive in connection with the phallic aspect of Figaro's compulsive and unsuccessful measuring.[5]

Example 9.1b shows another "five-ish" aspect of Figaro's theme, now in the sung version. Measure 18, the cadence of the orchestral introduction, provides a big tonic downbeat in G major [I played into the cadence and remarked, "that's what I mean by 'tonic downbeat'"]; two measures later, when Figaro first sings, his vocal motive changes the harmony from tonic to dominant, that is, to the harmony on the *fifth* degree of the key. [I played I–V in G, then relevant G and D harmonies from the passage.] Harmonically, Figaro's entrance thus asserts both not-tonic and dominant. The theme as a whole ca-

5. The discussion around figure 9.3 and example 9.1a uses some materials from my earlier article "Some Musical Jokes in Mozart's *Le nozze di Figaro*," in *Studies in Music History: Essays for Oliver Strunk*, edited by Harold Powers (Princeton: Princeton University Press, 1968), 443–47.

dences on a strong dominant, expanding this gesture. The right side of example 9.1b schematically shows the cadence. Note that there are actually two dominant cadences here: first, the music cadences on the dominant at the sung number 36, following the model of the orchestral introduction. [I played the cadence, singing "trenda sei."] The number 36 is the estimated final measurement. But Figaro still has the "mistake" number 43 to sing; in order to get it in, he **extends** the music two more measures, to provide a new and confirming cadence on D. [I played the cadence, singing "quaranta tre."] The idea of *extending* the Figaro theme thus arises from the superfluous and ill-fitting mistaken measurement of 43.

Example 9.1c focuses in on the way in which "Cinque" changes the tonic harmony to dominant. Figaro's first sung note, the A of "Cin—," turns the tonic G into a suspension dissonance [I played the pertinent music, singing "Cin—"; then I sang "Cin—" while playing G]' the dissonant G then resolves into the dominant harmony, with the sung D of "—que" as its bass. [I did appropriate singing and playing here.] The fifth of "Cinque," A to D, is not $\hat{5}$ to $\hat{1}$ in G [playing D–G], but rather $\hat{5}$-of-$\hat{5}$ to $\hat{5}$ [playing A–D]. Figaro, that is, characteristically moves *to* the dominant, even elaborating it with its own dominant. The move from A to D will later expand into a large-scale tonal progression, when Figaro first sings Susanna's theme [I played and sang the beginning of "Sì, mio core"]; as sung at that time, in Figaro's key of D, the theme moves from A harmony to D harmony. [I played quickly through the "Sì, mio core" theme, emphasizing the A and D harmonies at its beginning and end. Then I played A–D, saying "Cinque."]

G as tonic key and harmony, of course, represents the proper state of affairs. Susanna's theme, as originally presented, moves from D to G, from dominant to tonic [I played its beginning and end in G]. Later on in the opera, the wedding ceremony begins in G major [I played its opening]; G major is also the key in which the final reconciliation of the count with the countess will occur [I played "Contessa, perdono!"]. Figaro's emphatic rejection of G harmony and G key, in examples 9.1b and 9.1c, can thereby be associated with his compulsive evasion of Susanna's emotional appeals, at the opening of the scene.

The top sections of figure 9.4 summarize some features we have observed anent the metaphorical interplay of music and drama. Pass 0 (the orchestral introduction) and Pass 1 both present the Figaro theme as rejecting tonic and moving to dominant, rejecting G and moving to D, rejecting the real state of affairs and moving into his erroneous computing fantasy. Pass 0 and Pass 1 both present the Susanna theme as moving from Figaro's dominant back to tonic, moving from Figaro's D back to G, attempting to pull Figaro back from his fantasy to the exigencies of the dramatic reality. Pass 1 extends the Figaro theme, as already noted, to fit in the superfluous and mistaken number 43.

Example 9.2 shows how Figaro makes a crucial mis-singing mistake at the beginning of Pass 2. The G-major tonic downbeat that begins the music is now provided not by a purely orchestral introduction, but by the cadence of Susanna's actual sung theme, on the word "me!," Figaro is so distracted by her audible person that he starts his theme wrong when he tries it again. He starts singing a measure and a half too soon. In the previous versions of the Figaro theme, the "Cinque" motive came in exactly two measures after the tonic G downbeat, in a relatively strong metric position. [I played the pertinent music, emphasizing the downbeat.] But now the motive appears only a half-measure after the big G downbeat, in a very weak metric position. [I played the pertinent music, emphasizing the downbeat.]

Furthermore, Figaro mis-sings the characteristic fifth of "Cinque" [playing it], singing instead a fourth [playing it], so distracted is he by Susanna. Instead of contradicting the tonic note G, making it dissonant by singing A as in example 9.1c [playing it], he now

Introduction:

Pass 0:
Figaro's theme: rejects G, goes to D;
rejects tonic, goes to dominant.
Susanna's theme: from D to G, from
dominant to tonic.
(Codetta: subdominant and cadence.)
Pass 1:

F: Cinque—dieci-venti—trenta—
  trenta sei—quarantatre
S: Ora sì, ch'io son contenta,
  Sembra fatto in ver per me

Figaro's theme: rejects G, goes to D
rejects tonic, goes to dominant.
Susanna's theme: from D to G
from dominant to tonic.
Pass 2:

F: Cinque—
S: Guarda un po', mio caro Figaro!
F: Dieci—
S: Guarda un po', mio caro Figaro!
F: Venti—
S: Guarda un po',
F: Trenta—
S: Guarda un po', guarda adesso
  il mio cappello,
F: Trenta sei—
S: Guarda adesso il mio capello!
F: Quaranta tre.
S: Guarda un po' mio caro Figaro,
  guarda adesso il mio cappello,
  il mio capello, il mio capello!
F: Sì, mio core, or è più bello,
  sembra fatto in ver per te,
  sembra fatto in ver per te

Figaro's theme: because of Figaro's big
mistake, Susanna can take control of his
theme.

After the first D cadence (36), she leads
the theme's extension for "43" to an A
cadence, and extends that extension,
prolonging A harmony.

Susanna's theme, sung by Figaro!: He can sing
it because he is on A, the dominant of D.
The theme goes from dominant to tonic,
but now in D, so that he can move to D.
Pass 3:

S: Guarda un po'!
F: Sì, mio core.
S: Guarda un po'!
F: Or è più bello.
S: Ora sì, ch'io son contenta,
  Ora sì, ch'io son contenta,
  sembra fatto in ver per me,
  per me, per me!
F: Sì, mio core, or è più bello,
  sembra fatto in ver per te,
  per te, per te!

After four measures confirming the local
D tonic, Susanna leads Figaro through
rising notes of the D harmony, (somewhat
in the manner of *Figaro's theme*). Introducing C♮, she changes the D from a
local tonic back to a global dominant
(seventh).

And Figaro follows along.

F&S: Ah! il mattino alle nozze vincino,
  quant'è dolce al tuo (mio) tenero
  sposo, questo bel cappellino vezzoso,
  che Susanna ella stessa si fè!

Now it is time to sing *Susanna's theme;*
Figaro obliges, singing together with
her, *supporting her* as she goes from
D to G, and from dominant to tonic.

Figure 9.4. Mozart, *Marriage of Figaro*, I, opening duet

accepts, sings, and reverberates the tonic note G upon which he has just heard Susanna cadence [playing Susanna's G and Figaro's subsequent "Cinque"]. We can imagine him thinking at Susanna, "Now look what you've made me do! I'll never get this measuring done properly if you keep disturbing me."

Example 9.2 shows Susanna's response to Figaro's blunder. She takes Figaro's mistaken sung G and moves it to the correct note A at the correct time, two measures after the G downbeat. [I played the music from Susanna's "me!" through her "Figaro!," putting a strong accent on the latter.] We may imagine the subtext sketched on example 9.2: "Oh dear, let me help. You meant to sing on A at this moment, didn't you, Figaro dear?" And Figaro echoes her "correction" a half-measure later, with his "dieci" on A. [I played the A–D while singing "dieci."] The pitches are now correct, a half-measure late, but the num-

Example 9.2. Mozart, *The Marriage of Figaro*, I, opening duet, mm. 36–40

ber is now wrong, "dieci" instead of "cinque" on the sung fifth. Figaro continues echo-
ing the note Susanna gives him, as he did two measures earlier with her G. This state of
affairs continues through the theme; example 9.2 shows the next stage, where Susanna
leads Figaro by the nose to the note B at the right time, and Figaro echoes her "correct"
pitch a half-measure later, using the number that belongs a measure and a half later, all
of this in relatively weak metric positions. [I played and sang the pertinent music].

One must admire the dramatic complexity of Susanna's musical behavior here; it is at
once hypocritically helpful, manipulative, and truly helpful. It is hypocritically helpful because Susanna has no desire to help Figaro with his maniacal miscalculations, as her tune
might suggest to him. In that sense she is being manipulative, seizing control of his theme
and of the dramatic flow. There is indeed a Strindberg drama just under the surface of the
opera, and it is important to recognize the Punch-and-Judy aspects of the farce. Peter Sellars's recent production showed how effective that directorial approach can be (though he
did not apply it to this scene). The problem with the Sellars production, I feel, is not that
the approach is false, but rather that it brings the Strindberg drama right up to the surface,
as secondary elaboration, rather than leaving it lurking under the surface, as primary process. And that distorts other aspects of the classical comedy. Finally, Susanna is being really helpful here, because her manipulations are directed toward a loving and therapeutic
end, to get Figaro back on track with reality, and with their relationship. As we shall see,
she will allow him considerable space to work out his psychic problems on his own terms.

Example 9.3 shows that Susanna, in leading Figaro through his Pass 2 theme, finally
gets him together with the correct number "36" at the correct time for the usual D cadence
that has always set the text "36" (the estimated final measurement). [I played and sang the

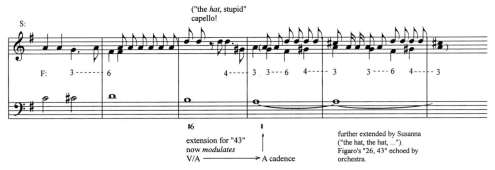

Example 9.3. Mozart, *Marriage of Figaro*, I, opening duet

beginning of example 9.3.] We shall explore later just how she does this. As before, the theme must now be extended so that Figaro may sing the superfluous number "43." Susanna continues to lead; now she controls the extension so that the music, instead of making another D cadence as before, modulates to A major, the dominant of D, and cadences there, followed by an extra extension prolonging A major. [I played and sang the pertinent music.] In modulating to A, Susanna actually lands on the dominant of A [playing the harmony at "capello!"], that is, the dominant of the dominant of the dominant in the main key. [I played E–A–D–G harmonies as I said "dominant," etc.] In presenting Figaro with a heap of piled-up dominants in this way, Susanna is further solicitously making amends for having caused him to sing her tonic harmony at the beginning of example 9.2. Figaro, as we have heard, likes dominants; they are a way of manifesting his obsession with fives. When Susanna, on example 9.3, presents him with the dominant of A, he is all too happy to sing "43," believing that he is now in control of the situation, in a very dominant position.

Among the other nice things about the A harmony, for Figaro, is that it can serve as the dominant of his favorite key, D. We noticed that on a small scale in example 9.1c; there the fifth of his first sung music, the fifth of his original "Cinque," was A to D [playing it]. Now that Figaro is on a big A harmony at the end of example 9.3, he can proceed to his favorite key, D, via a big tonal **expansion** of the A–to–D motif.

And a theme lies conveniently at hand that will enable him to carry out that idea. It is Susanna's theme, which leads a local dominant to its local tonic. Accordingly, Figaro sings Susanna's theme in the key of D. [I played the pertinent phrase.] In doing so, he must proceed from local dominant to local tonic, something he has not done before. On the other hand, by treating D as the local tonic, he can satisfy his urge to sing music that aims for D harmony, being consistent with his earlier behavior. Susanna's modulation to A has thus provided Figaro with an occasion to exult in his favorite harmony of D; he has only to acknowledge her presence by singing her theme. In this way, both characters give some to get some. As before, Susanna's behavior is at once hypocritically helpful, manipulative, and truly helpful. In particular, the helpful transaction between the couple, each giving and getting, could not have taken place without her initiative. (Figure 9.4 summarily logs the musical analysis we have been making to the right of the text for Pass 2.)

At the end of Pass 2, Figaro believes himself satisfied. He has established D major as tonic, and Susanna has recognized his desire to do so, temporarily abandoning her distracting G major, even helping him by providing the occasion for him to establish the key. Susanna, however, is not yet satisfied. Figaro has noticed her hat, the ostensible subject of her nagging, but he has not yet acknowledged her real concerns, of which the hat is only a symbol—that is, her anxiety over the forthcoming wedding and her uncertainty over the extent to which he will support her in future complications involving the Count. D major is the key of Figaro's calculating, not the key of their love.

Accordingly, Susanna has yet to establish G major, to get Figaro to agree to G major, and to win from him the emotional acknowledgment she needs. These ideas are sketched on figure 9.4, to the right of the text for Pass 3. During this pass, as the commentary explains, Susanna leads Figaro though rising notes of the D harmony, somewhat in the manner of the Figaro theme [playing pertinent music]. Then she introduces C♮, the seventh of the D harmony [playing it]. (This is the interval "7" of example 9.1a [playing it], the interval where the Figaro theme and the calculating numbers have always broken down before.) The seventh of the harmony changes D from a local tonic, back to a global dominant. Figaro is happy to follow Susanna along, since she has already obliged him by her earlier leading behavior, which allowed him to attain his favorite key. And after they linger on the dominant-seventh harmony [playing the "lingering" music], he is happy to accompany her as she sings her theme in G, from dominant to tonic, from D harmony to G harmony. [I played quickly through that music.] She has already given him what he wanted; now he rec-

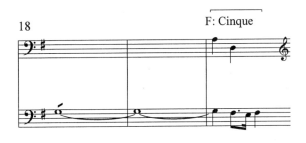

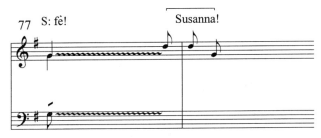

Example 9.4. Mozart, *Marriage of Figaro*, I, opening duet

iprocates in kind. He is not just singing along with her, he is *supporting her* in counterpoint as she sings her theme. Her machinations-cum-therapy, that is, have served their purpose.

There follows a **coda**, prolonging G major with various cadences. Particularly amusing is the motive Susanna sings right after the big downbeat that begins the coda (shown on the right side of example 9.4).

Here, Susanna's falling fifth, D to G, on her text "Susanna!" [playing it] is the G-major answer to Figaro's D-major falling fifth, A to D, on his opening "Cinque" [playing it]. Susanna's fifth is the "right" fifth for the tonality, and as the final text says, "Susanna herself made it."

Example 9.5 studies in further detail the vicissitudes of the Figaro theme in passes 0, 1, and 2, where Susanna takes control of it. The three versions are aligned by their bass lines. That is a significant formatting, since alignment by consecutive barlines would give quite a different picture; so would alignment by the numbers of the series 5, 10, and so forth. In the formatting of example 9.5, the beginnings of the three versions all align at the big G downbeats, and the D cadences at the number 36 all align.

Pass 0 is completely orchestral, so the numbers under the violin part on the example are bracketed; they correlate with the numbers Figaro sings in Pass 1. It takes two measures to get from the G downbeat to the number 5, two more measures to get from there to the number 10. Then Figaro's rate of measuring increases: it takes only one musical measure to get from 10 to 20, and only one measure to get from 20 to 30. After that Figaro's measuring calms down again, taking two measures again to get from 30 to the estimated final measurement, 36. The theme cadences there, and there is no music for the erroneous number 43 in this first version of the theme.

In the pass 1 version, Figaro is singing, calling out the numbers, and not just silently measuring. Very audible from the example is the way in which he squares off the rhythm of the Pass 0 version. The numbers are called off at a regular rate, a number every two measures. [While acting the measuring, I tapped off the quarter-note beats with my foot, calling out the numbers at regular temporal intervals.] The calm and steady rate of Figaro's pronouncements makes a hilarious cognitive dissonance against the nonsense of his number series. We see at the end of the Pass 1 version how the embarrassing extra number 43 neces-

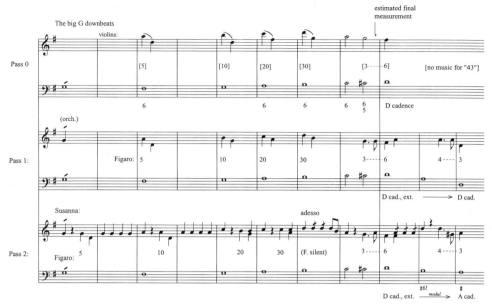

Example 9.5. Mozart, *Marriage of Figaro*, I, opening duet passes 0–2

sitates extending the theme beyond the Pass 0 version; here, as observed earlier, the thematic extension confirms the D cadence, thereby preserving Figaro's dignity to a certain extent.

In Pass 2, the measures underlie the measures of Pass 0 perfectly, up to the D-major cadence at the number 36. One hears thereby how Figaro's anxiety surfaces again, disturbing his "rational" every-two-measures rhythm of Pass 1. As discussed earlier, the number 5 of Pass 2 comes one and a half measures too early, compared to Pass 1, and its pitches are wrong. Alternatively, we could say that the pitches A–D of Pass 2 come a half-measure too late, with the wrong number. This state of affairs continues up to the measure marked "adesso"; that is, where the word (meaning "now") first appears in the text. According to the pattern established so far, Figaro ought to sing "36" at the point marked "now." But Susanna activates her singing rhythm into eighth notes just here, to distract Figaro from that idea [playing her line]. She pauses only a measure later, enabling Figaro to get himself into phase with the tune so that he can sing "36" at just the proper moment, the D cadence [playing it yet once more]. In this way Susanna helps Figaro get back on track, after his initial blunder.

Example 9.5 beautifully illustrates Mozart's virtuosity in projecting large-scale rhythmic complexities. There are three different time-systems on the example. In one system, we count the passing of time by the progress of the bass line; this is the system that controls the underlay format of the example. A second, different, system marks the passage of time by the Newtonian or Kantian time-flow of the measures; in this system, Passes 0 and 2 contract the longer time-flow of Pass 1, presumably reflecting Figaro's anxiety. A third and yet different time-system marks the passage of time by the numbers 5, 10, and so forth of Figaro's measuring series; this is the time-system in which Figaro's "Cinque" of Pass 2 is judged as one and a half measures too soon, rather than a half-measure too late. Mozart's compositional virtuosity here is much subtler than that in the notorious passage from *Don Giovanni,* where three different bands are playing three different dances at the same time, in different rhythms.

Example 9.6 is a Schenkerian analysis of the number, up to the end of Pass 3, omitting the coda. [I said that the best way for nonmusicians to get a sense of the symbols was to listen to a performance that projected them. Then I played example 9.6, using sus-

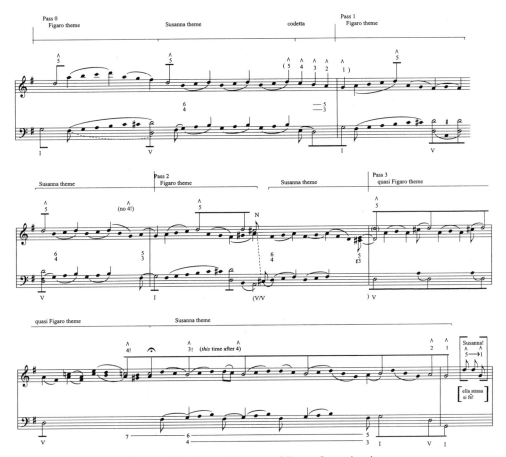

Example 9.6. Mozart, *Marriage of Figaro*, I, opening duet

taining, accenting, phrasing, and pedaling to project the assertions of the sketch.] The beamed tones with open noteheads on the treble clef constitute a Schenkerian *Urlinie;* they build a structural line which is supported by a bass using notes of the G harmony to form an *Ursatz.* The *Urlinie* descends from $\hat{5}$ of the G-major scale, stepwise down through $\hat{4}$, $\hat{3}$, $\hat{2}$, and $\hat{1}$. The descent from $\hat{5}$ to $\hat{1}$, step by step, is delightfully thematic here as a "Cinque." A lower-level structural descent from $\hat{5}$ to $\hat{1}$ in the melody takes place at the end of Pass 0, to foreshadow the larger structure.

Up until the beginning of Pass 3 the melodic D, the $\hat{5}$ of the *Urlinie,* is in force. In particular, Susanna's theme in Passes 0 and 1 puts structural weight on its D [playing the opening of the theme with weight on the D], rather than its B [playing the music with weight on the B]. It is only with Susanna's C♮ of Pass 3, marked with a $\hat{4}$ and an exclamation point on the example, that the structural line can begin to descend from $\hat{5}$. In particular, after that $\hat{4}$, the line descends to $\hat{3}$ (with exclamation point), when Susanna's theme begins for the last time. The structural weight of the theme thus shifts here, to fall on the B [playing] rather than the D [playing]. At the end of the example, one hears how the little Susanna motif in the coda [playing it] summarizes the overall descent of the *Urlinie* [playing it].

Figaro's mistakes, as we have just seen, eventually lead him to reaffirm his commitment to Susanna, thanks to her insightful management of the situation. Figaro, in German, *verspricht sich* first in one sense (making slips of the tongue) and then in the other sense (promising himself to Susanna in marriage). Freud, I think, would have been pleased.

~10~

MOTIVE AND TEXT IN FOUR
SCHUBERT SONGS

Carl Schachter

Carl Schachter began playing the piano at five and entered the Mannes College of Music as a conducting major. He was introduced to Schenkerian analysis at Mannes by Felix Salzer, one of Schenker's pupils, and thus began a lifelong dedication to the study of Schenker's theories and analytical method. Schachter began teaching at Mannes, where he also served as Dean for several years; he later joined the faculty at Queens College and the CUNY Graduate Center, where he is now Distinguished Professor Emeritus. He continues to teach at Mannes and the Juilliard School.

Schachter has long been one of the most important Schenkerian scholars. As William Rothstein states on the cover of Schachter's collected essays (*Unfoldings: Essays in Schenkerian Theory and Analysis,* edited by Joseph N. Straus): "Carl Schachter is one of the preeminent music theorists, or music analysts, in the English-speaking world, and he is the world's leading practitioner of Heinrich Schenker's analytical method." Schachter has also been a pioneer in the application of Schenkerian theory to the study of rhythm in tonal music. His seminal work in this area has led to remarkable developments in rhythmic theory by three other authors in this volume: Charles Burkhart (chapter 1), Harald Krebs (chapter 2), and William Rothstein (chapter 17). Schachter has long been involved in linking analysis to performance, and he is currently writing a book on the topic.

Schachter uses Schenker's method not for its own sake but, rather, to uncover layers of meaning that even expert listeners may have only dimly perceived. In the current essay, written in 1983, Schachter demonstrates some of the deep interconnections that exist between poetry and music in the lieder of Franz Schubert—specifically, the elegant way in which motivic repetition, both on the surface of the music and at a deeper level of structure, can reflect the meaning of a poetic text.[1]

Some reminders: (1) all words in **bold** are defined in the glossary; (2) full citations for incomplete references are found in the selected bibliography; (3) the authors use their preferred notational system (e.g., Roman numeral, form label, and register notation). Most of the essays denote register by middle C as C^4.—Ed.

1. The author uses the Schenkerian uppercase Roman numerals rather than upper- and lowercase.

Music set to words can reflect them in many different ways. Perhaps the most fascinating and greatest settings are those where the tonal and rhythmic structure, the form, and the motivic design embody equivalents for salient features of the text: grammar and syntax, rhyme schemes and other patterns of sound, imagery, and so forth. Structural connections between words and music occur frequently in the art-song repertory—above all, in the songs of Schubert. Yet they seem to have attracted less attention, at least in the published literature, than prosody, tone painting, and affect.[2] In this paper I shall concentrate on one type of connection—that between the imagery of the poem and the motivic design of the music. The examples come from four Schubert songs: (1) *Der Jüngling an der Quelle* (D. 300), (2) *Dass sie hier gewesen,* op. 59, no. 2 (D. 775), (3) *Der Tod und das Mädchen,* op. 7, no. 3 (D. 531), and (4) *Nacht und Träume,* op. 43, no. 2 (D. 827).

DER JÜNGLING AN DER QUELLE

Our simplest example comes from the **coda** of this early song.[3] The poem is by the Swiss writer Johann von Salis-Seewis; since I am going to discuss only one detail, I shall not quote the whole text, but only the last two lines. The words are those of a boy, unhappy in love, who tries to forget his coy friend in the beauties of nature. But they bring renewed desire rather than consolation; the poplar leaves and the brook seem to sigh her name, Luise. The final lines, as Schubert set them,[4] go as follows:

ach, und Blätter und Bach	ah, and leaves and brook
seufzen: Luise! dir nach.	sign, Luise, for you.

The song is pervaded by a typically murmuring accompaniment pattern, which imitates the sound of the leaves and brook. Example 10.1, which quotes the beginning of the introduction, illustrates. Note that the right-hand part centers on the broken third $C\#^2–E^2$.

The introductory material returns in bars 23–26 to become the main part of the coda. Rather unusually, this coda is not a simple postlude for the piano; the singer joins in, repeating the name "Luise" (example 10.2). His exclamations are set to the very pitches—$C\#^2$ and E^2—that have pervaded the accompaniment. There is even a return to the $C\#^2$, which recalls the oscillating piano figuration (see the brackets in example 10.2). Like the boy in the poem, the listener hears an indistinct pattern transformed into a clear one; the sounds of nature become the girl's name, and the murmuring accompaniment becomes a melodic figure of definite shape. Schubert creates his musical image out of a structural

2. A notable exception occurs in Anhang A of Oswald Jonas, *Einführung in die Lehre Heinrich Schenkers,* rev. ed. (Vienna: Universal, 1972). Jonas was the first to discuss in a systematic way the implications of Schenker's ideas for the analysis of music composed to a text; his treatment of the subject contains many remarkable insights. A splendid study of a Brahms song is to be found in Edward Laufer, "Brahms: 'Wie Melodien zieht es mir,' op. 105/1," *Journal of Music Theory* 15 (1971): 34–57, reprinted in Maury Yeston, ed., *Readings in Schenker Anlaysis and Other Approaches* (New Haven: Yale University Press, 1977), 254–72. In my opinion, the most profound insights into the relation of music and words—especially in Schubert songs—were achieved by the late Ernst Oster. It is a great misfortune that he published none of his work in this area.

3. The date of composition is unknown; according to the revised Deutsch catalog, it was probably written in 1816 or 1817. See Otto Erich Deutsch, *Franz Schubert: Thematisches Verzeichnis seiner Werke in chronologischer Folge,* ed. Werner Aderhold, Walther Dürr, Arnold Feil, and Christa Landon (Kassel: Bärenreiter, 1978), 183–84.

4. Schubert made a slight change in the words either inadvertently or to produce a rhyming couplet at the end (the original is unrhymed). Salis had written "mir zu" (to me) and not "dir nach" (for you). But either way, the leaves and brook speak her name.

Etwas langsam

Example 10.1. Der Jüngling an der Quelle, 1–3

connection between accompaniment and melody: both center on the prominent pitches $C\sharp^2$ and E^2. This connection is underlined during the last three bars, in which the piano continues alone with only $C\sharp^2$–E^2 in the right-hand part; the murmuring dies away into a final block chord, which, rather unusually, has the fifth, E^2, on top.

Artless as it is, the musical image that Schubert creates in *Der Jüngling an der Quelle* has points of similarity with some of his subtler and more complex settings of words. As a consequence, the passage is a good introductory example of his practice. The following features deserve mention:

Example 10.2. Der Jüngling an der Quelle, 23–29

1. The transformation of the accompaniment into a melodic idea has nothing to do with "tone painting," although the accompaniment itself, of course, is intended to summon up the sound of leaves and water. Nor does it convey a "mood," although few listeners, I suspect, would complain that Schubert had failed to match the emotional tone of the words.

2. By associating accompaniment and vocal line Schubert creates a musical analogy to the sequence of ideas in the poem; the accompaniment is to the melodic figure derived from it as the indistinct sounds of nature are to the specific name that they evoke. Without the words, any extramusical association would disappear, but the connection between accompaniment and melody would remain perfectly comprehensible as a musical relationship. This is typical of Schubert's method, which sustains a remarkable equilibrium between sensitivity to the text and compositional integrity.

   Yet it would probably be going too far to maintain that *Der Jüngling an der Quelle,* played as an instrumental piece, would sound completely natural. This is because the pervasive $C\sharp^2$–E^2 is too neutral a figure and is treated with too little emphasis to justify its very conspicuous transformation into a melodic idea at the end of the piece. It is the words, which begin by invoking the murmuring spring and whispering poplars, that draw the listener's attention to the accompaniment and thus supply the necessary emphasis.

3. In creating his musical image Schubert reaches a far higher level of artistry than Salis-Seewis, for the poem, charming as it is, merely asserts that the leaves and brook sigh the girl's name. Of course the name itself—"Luise"—sounds more like whispering leaves and water than, say, "Katinka" would. But this is the easiest kind of onomatopoetic effect, with little inner connection to the poem as a whole. In Schubert's song, on the other hand, the musical image *is*, in symbolic form, what the words talk about; it grows out of the earlier part of the song with wonderful naturalness.

DASS SIE HIER GEWESEN

This song is set to a beautiful poem by Rückert. Schubert probably wrote it in 1823; it was published in 1826.[5] I am going to discuss the first stanza, composed to the following text:

Dass der Ostwind Düfte	That the east wind
Hauchet in die Lüfte	Breathes fragrance into the air
Dadurch tut er kund	In that way he makes it known
Dass du hier gewesen.	That you have been here.

The musical style of *Dass sie hier gewesen* could hardly be more different from that of *Der Jüngling an der Quelle.* The tonal ambiguity of the opening bars is such that a listener hearing them without knowing where they come from could easily date them from the 1890s rather than the 1820s.[6] No tonic triad appears until bar 14; indeed, the listener receives not even a clue that the piece is in C major for six bars at a very slow tempo (example 10.3). The very first sound is doubtful. It turns out to be a diminished seventh chord

---

5. Revised Deutsch catalog, 466.

6. Richard Capell finds the opening similar to Wolf's "Herr, was trägt der Boden"—a similarity that seems rather external to me. See Richard Capell, *Schubert's Songs* (London: Ernest Benn, 1928), 200.

Sehr langsam

Example 10.3. Dass sie hier gewesen, 1–16

with an appoggiatura, F³, in the top voice, but for a bar or so the listener might hear the chord as G–B♭–D♭–F rather than the G–B♭–C♯–E sonority that in fact it is. After we have our bearings about the diminished seventh, we remain in the dark as to the function of the D-minor chord to which it resolves; a listener might easily take it for a tonic. The attraction of C as center begins to be felt only in bars 7–8 and is not evident beyond a doubt until the authentic cadence of bars 13–14. Comparing Schubert's music with the words, we can see how marvelously it embodies the semantic and syntactic structure of this involuted sentence, whose import becomes clear only with the key predicate clause—"that you have been here"— the clause to which Schubert sets the clinching authentic cadence of bars 13–14.[7]

Although the motivic design of this passage is not as strikingly original as the tonal organization, it too connects with the words in a most wonderful way. The piano's opening statement contains a four-note figure in an extremely high register: F³–E³–D³–C♯³. The four notes belong together, for they project into the melodic line the prevailing diminished seventh chord, of which the E³ and C♯³ are members. But the very slow pace and the strong subdivision into twos make it easier to hear two groups of two notes each than a coherent four-note figure. As example 10.4 shows, the vocal line uses the four-note figure as a motive, quoting it directly (bars 3–4) and elaborating on it (bars 5–8 and 9–12). When the tonally definitive cadence of bars 13–14 arrives, the character of the melodic line begins to change: the pace quickens; there are no chromatics and no dissonant leaps. Yet for all the contrast, there is a connecting thread: the melodic line over the

---

7. Both Capell (*Schubert's Songs*, 200) and Tovey have commented perceptively on the relation of the music's tonal structure to the syntax of the poem. See Donald Francis Tovey, *Essays and Lectures on Music* (London: Oxford University Press, 1949), 132.

Example 10.4. Dass sie hier gewesen, 1–16: F–E–D–C♯ motive

V^7 of bar 12 is our four-note figure—at a new pitch level, in a different harmonic context, in quicker time values, but nonetheless the same figure. Even the distribution of non-chord and chord tones remains the same. In its new form the motive no longer divides into two times two notes; the coherence of the four-note group has become manifest.

Let us now compare the central image of the poem and the motivic aspects of its setting. A perfume in the air signifies that the beloved has been here. The perfume—a melodic idea barely perceptible as such, floating in an improbably high register within a tonal context of the utmost ambiguity. The person—the same melodic idea but now with distinct outlines, a definite rhythmic shape, the greatest possible clarity of tonal direction. Certainly many compositional elements contribute to this astonishing example of text setting: rhythm, texture, register, and tonal organization, as well as motivic design. But only the motivic aspect conveys the *connection* between perfume and person, conveys the notion that, in a sense, the two—sign and signified—are one.

DER TOD UND DAS MÄDCHEN

The song was written in February 1817 and was published in 1821. The text, a poem by Matthias Claudius, is as follows:

Das Mädchen
Vorüber, ach vorüber
Geh, wilder Knochenmann!
Ich bin noch jung! Geh, Lieber,
Und rühre mich nicht an!

Der Tod
Gib deine Hand, du schön und zart Gebild!
Bin Freund und komme nicht zu strafen.
Sei gutes Muts! Ich bin nicht wild!
Sollst sanft in meinen Armen schlafen!

The Maiden
Go past, ah, go past
Wild skeleton!
I am still young! Go, dear,
And do not touch me!

Death
Give me your hand, you beautiful and tender creature!
I am a friend and do not come to punish.
Be of good courage! I am not wild!
You shall sleep softly in my arms!

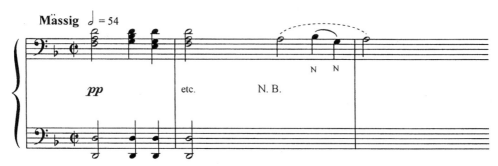

Example 10.5. Der Tod und das Mädchen, 1–2

The poem is a dialogue, and Schubert, altogether appropriately, composes the song as a dramatic scene.[8] The piano introduction clearly represents a vision of Death; the Maiden's outcry is an agitated recitative; Death's reply is set to a recomposition of the introductory material. In a piece as short as *Der Tod und das Mädchen* marked contrasts between sections can prove disruptive. That Schubert creates a continuous musical discourse despite the changes in tempo, rhythm, and texture is partly due to the presence throughout most of the song of a basic motive, which serves as a link between the contrasting sections. The first statement of the motive occurs at the very beginning of the introduction in the next-to-highest part. The motive is a double-neighbor figure decorating A: A–Bb–G–A (example 10.5). Note that this figure is the main melodic event at the beginning of the song, for the uppermost part, prefiguring the monotone character of Death's speech, simply repeats a single pitch.

The motive's first transformation occurs with the Maiden's first word, "Vorüber." The three syllables are set to three notes—A^1–Bb^1–A^1—a compression of the opening figure, with G omitted. In a sense this transformation is implicit in the first statement of the motive (bars 1–2), where the Bb is much more prominent than the G on account of its higher pitch and stronger metrical position. As example 10.6 shows, the first half of the Maiden's speech is permeated by the neighbor-note figure. After the first "Vorüber" an expansion of it stretches over four bars (9–12) of the middle voice. And with the despairing cry "Ich bin noch jung!" of bars 12–14 the figure breaks out into the open, transposed up a fourth.

In the second half of the Maiden's speech (bars 15–21) the motive does not appear. But it pervades the accompaniment to Death's reply, as can be seen in example 10.7. The figure resumes its original four-note form, but is altered by rhythmic enlargement (bars

Etwas geschwinder

Das Mädchen

Example 10.6. Der Tod und das Mädchen, mm. 9–12

8. Professor Christoph Wolff, in a highly interesting lecture at the International Schubert Congress (Detroit, November 1978), pointed out the operatic character of this song and suggested possible antecedents in the oracle scenes of Gluck's *Alceste* and Mozart's *Idomeneo* and in the two statue scenes of *Don Giovanni*.

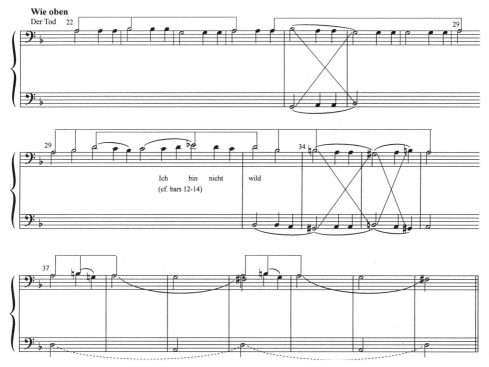

Example 10.7. Der Tod und das Mädchen, motive in the accompaniment

22–25, 25–29, etc.), voice exchange (bars 26–27 and 34–36), and the chromatic transformations B♭/B♮ and G♮/G♯ (bars 34–36, 37, and 40). In addition the phrase in B♭ (bars 30–33) most probably contains a statement of the motive, transposed up a fourth and with the two neighbors in reverse order. The similarity of the accompaniment at "Ich bin nicht wild" to the Maiden's "Ich bin noch jung" certainly seems to reflect the parallelism in the text.

The motivic design of *Der Tod und das Mädchen* parallels the emotional progress of the poem in a remarkable way. The basic motive itself—the double-neighbor figure—is a most appropriate one for a song about death. Its most prominent tones—A–B♭–A—form a musical idiom that has had an age-old association with ideas of death, grief, and lamentation. The musical basis of this association is surely the descending half-step (6–5 in minor) with its goal-directed and downward motion, its semitonal intensity, and the "sighing" quality it can so easily assume. Note that the three-note figure with its descending half-step occurs literally only when the Maiden speaks; Death's reply softens the B♭–A with the interpolated G and the very slow melodic pace. As Death continues to speak the motive undergoes subtle tonal changes. With his promise of sleep (bars 33–34), the B♭ changes to B♮; the despairing half-step descent is heard no more. At the same time the G changes to G♯. Owing to this upward inflection a half-step still remains in the double-neighbor figure, and with it melodic tension and goal-oriented progression. But now it is a rising half-step (G♯–A), signifying hope rather than despair.[9] With the D of bar 37, the Maiden surely dies. (This low tonic is far more expressive than the alternative higher one;

---

9. I would certainly not maintain that every rising half-step in music denotes hope and every falling one, despair. But in connection with a text that deals with death, upward and downward motion can easily take on extramusical significance, especially if the composer draws attention to it by varying previously heard material.

any singer who can reach it should certainly choose it.) At the Maiden's death, the double-neighbor figure appears in its original rhythmic shape for the first time since the introduction. It decorates a major tonic chord, and both neighboring notes lie a whole step from the main note. In this final statement there is no half-step, no strongly goal-oriented progression; the music, like the Maiden, is at peace.

NACHT UND TRÄUME

Universally regarded as one of Schubert's greatest songs, *Nacht und Träume* appeared in print in 1825, but was written much earlier, probably in 1822 or 1823.[10] The author of the poem was Matthäus von Collin, a friend of Schubert's, some of whose songs were first performed at Collin's home. According to the *Neue Schubert Ausgabe* Schubert possibly had the poem in manuscript, for the text of the song differs considerably from the published version of the poem.[11] The text, as Schubert set it, appears below.

Heil'ge Nacht, du sinkest nieder;
Nieder wallen auch die Träume,
Wie dein Mondlicht durch die Räume,
Durch der Menschen stille Brust.

Die belauschen sie mit Lust,
Rufen, wenn der Tag erwacht:
Kehre wieder, holde Nacht!
Holde Träume, kehret wieder!

Holy night, you descend
Dreams, too, float down,
Like your moonlight through space,
Through people's quiet breasts.

They listen in with pleasure,
And call out when day awakens:
Come back, lovely night!
Lovely dreams, come back!

Like *Der Tod und das Mädchen*, *Nacht und Träume* contains a tonal pattern that permeates the song and that helps to connect music and text. Here, however, the design is much less obvious than in the earlier song. The basic tonal pattern does not take on the form of a concrete melodic figure with a definite rhythmic shape, as does the double-neighbor figure at the beginning and end of *Der Tod und das Mädchen*. It is therefore not a pattern that would become evident through a conventional motivic analysis.[12] And it does not occur only at the **foreground,** but penetrates deep into the underlying tonal structure. Therefore the motivic design becomes accessible only if we take into account the song's large-scale linear and harmonic organization.

---

10. Revised Deutsch catalog, 522–23.

11. Franz Schubert, *Neue Ausgabe sämtlicher Werke*, Serie IV: Band 2, Teil b, ed. Walther Dürr (Kassel: Bärenreiter, 1975), 323.

12. A detailed analysis of *Nacht und Träume* appears in Diether de la Motte, *Musikalische Analyse (mit kritischen Anmerkungen von Carl Dahlhaus)*, 2 vols. (Kassel: Bärenreiter, 1968), 61–71. There is no mention of the basic motive.

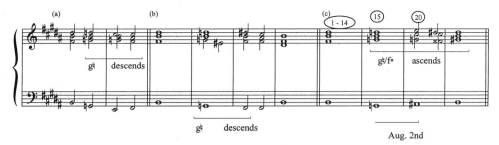

Example 10.8. Nacht und Träume, mm. 14–21

A good place to begin is with the G-major passage of bars 15–19. The passage is extraordinarily beautiful and is obviously of central significance to the song—"central" in an almost literal way, for the passage begins at the midpoint of the poem and, more or less, of the music. Its importance is underscored by the striking chromatic chord progression B major–G major of bars 14–15, by the long silence in the vocal part, and by the very slow pace of the chord progressions—six bars (14–19) of just one chord per bar.

What is the function of the prolonged G-major chord? At first one would probably think of it as ♭VI (♮VI)—the submediant triad borrowed from B minor. As a descriptive label, ♭VI would not be wrong, but it would not give us much insight into the behavior of this G major chord. That the behavior is most unusual can be seen from example 10.8. The progressions shown at (a) and (b) are typical for ♭VI. At (a) the bass moves down in thirds (bass arpeggio) to the II⁶₅ borrowed from the minor. At (b) the bass is sustained, and an augmented sixth is added above it. In both progressions, ♭$\hat6$ eventually *descends* to $\hat5$, either in the bass or in an upper part. This is what one would expect a chromatically *lowered* sound to do. How different is the progression shown at (c), a reduction of bars 14–21 of *Nacht und Träume*. "♭VI" does not occur within a connected bass line, either arpeggiated or scalar, for its lowest tone moves up an augmented second (bar 20). Nor does ♭$\hat6$ resolve to $\hat5$, either in the bass or in an upper part. In the bass, the augmented second leaves the G♮ hanging. In the "tenor" the G♮ is sustained into a diminished-seventh chord (bar 20), then transformed enharmonically to F^x, which *ascends* (bar 21) to G♯.

A glance at the score will show that a melodic progression F♯–F^x–G♯ occurs in bars 2–3 of the Introduction; the F^x functions as a chromatic passing tone. In bar 4 the reverse progression, G♯–G♮–F♯, answers the chromatic ascent; here the G♮ is a chromatic passing tone. In its rising form (F♯–F^x–G♯) the chromatic progression recurs twice before the G-major passage (in bars 7–8 and 9–10). It appears again immediately after the G-major passage as a consequence of the fact that bars 21–27 form an almost unaltered repetition of 8–14. And the postlude contains two G♮s, which obviously refer back to the F^{x}s and G♮s heard earlier on. F^x/G♮ appears far more often than any other chromatically altered sound—so often, in fact, and so characteristically that it must be regarded as a motivic element. In example 10.9, a voice-leading graph of the entire song, asterisks point out the various statements of F^x/G♮.

The interpretation of the piece shown in example 10.9 hinges on the idea that the section in G major derives from the earlier passages containing F^x or G♮. This idea is corroborated by the fact that the section is followed immediately by the restatement of one of these passages. And a careful study of the voice-leading context provides further substantiation. As example 10.9 shows, the prolonged G chord of bars 15–19 contains a middle-voice G♮ that comes from F♯ (bar 14) and that changes to F^x before moving up to G♯in bar 21. This melodic progression is the fantastic enlargement of the motivic F♯–F^x–G♯

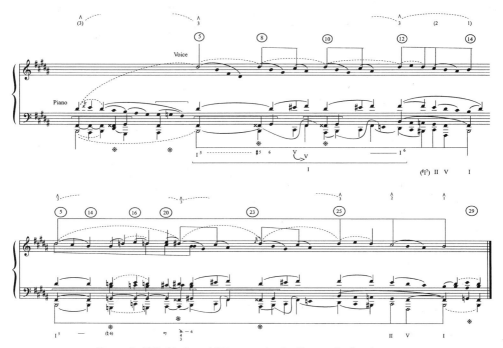

Example 10.9. Nacht und Träume, voice-leading graph of entire song

that occurs three times earlier in the song, as well as once in **inversion** (see the brackets on the lower stave of example 10.9). In this enlargement, the Fˣ, a chromatic passing tone, becomes transformed **enharmonically;** as part of a locally consonant triad it is stabilized and extended in time so that its passing function is disguised. Now we can begin to understand why ♭VI behaves so differently here from the typical usages shown at (a) and (b) in example 10.8: it is because the guiding idea of the passage is the rising middle-voice progression F♯–Fˣ–G♯. The G♮ of the middle voice represents the **foreground** transformation of an underlying Fˣ; that is why it moves up. And the G♮ of the bass does not function linearly—hence its lack of connection with the material that follows. Its purpose is to produce a root-position major triad—the most stable of all chords—and thus to provide support and emphasis for the G♮ (Fˣ) of the middle voice.

By combining in a single sonority two different and contrasting orders of musical reality, Schubert gives this song a great central image; the song embodies a musical symbol of dreams. The G-major section crystallizes around a most transitory musical event— a chromatic passing tone. Yet, while we are immersed in it, it assumes the guise of that most solid tonal structure, the major triad. Only at "wenn der Tag erwacht" does its insubstantiality become manifest; it vanishes, never to return except as an indistinct memory in the G♮'s of the coda. In *Nacht und Träume*, it seems to me, Schubert approaches the limits of what music composed to a text can achieve.

Quite apart from its fantastic relation to the text, the G-major passage is most remarkable, for the principles of tonal combination and succession that govern it are applied in a very special, perhaps unique, manner. Since its complex voice leading cannot be demonstrated adequately in a single graph of the whole piece, I should like to close this article by presenting a contrapuntal explanation of the passage (example 10.10). The graph proceeds from **background** to foreground and contains five levels:

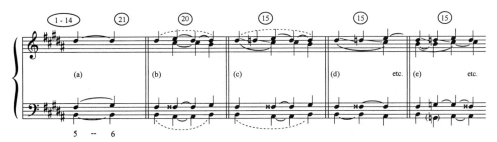

Example 10.10. Nacht und Träume, mm. 14–21, contrapuntal explanation

a. The basis of the passage is the connection of the prolonged B-major tonic of bars 1–14 to the G♯-minor $^6_3$ of bar 21. The inner-voice progression F♯–G♯ forms the intervals of a fifth and sixth (5–6) above the sustained tonic in the bass.

b. The motivic f♯–f^x–g♯ arises in the tenor, caused by the chromatic passing tone F^x. The F^x is incorporated into a diminished seventh chord that leads to the G♯-minor six-three. Note that the upper voice splits into two parts, one decorating D♯^{2} with its upper neighbor E^2, the other descending through C♯^{2} to an inner-voice B^1.

c. Another chromatic passing tone, D♮^{2}, appears in the uppermost voice.

d. The F^x of the tenor is anticipated so that it coincides with the soprano's D♮^{2}. Thus the two chromatic passing tones occur simultaneously, their coincidence producing a "chord" enharmonically equivalent to a G-major six-three (B–F^x–D♮^{2}).

e. The apparent G-major chord is stabilized. The F^x changes enharmonically to G♮ in order to produce a triadic structure. And G♮ is added in the bass, thus making a root-position sonority.

~11~

Isolde's Transfiguration in Words and Music

Patrick McCreless

Patrick McCreless (Yale University) is an organist and a conductor as well as an eclectic scholar. His research includes study of nineteenth-century music, especially the music of Wagner, as well as postmodern applications to music analysis.

    Tristan und Isolde, which Wagner composed from 1857 to 1859 and which was premiered in 1865, has long been recognized as marking a revolutionary step in the development of chromatic harmony in the nineteenth century. Music theorists, beginning in Wagner's time and continuing through the famous *Romantic Harmony and Its Crisis in Wagner's "Tristan"* (1920), by the Swiss theorist Ernst Kurth, and on to the present day, have been challenged by its original and powerful tonal language. The "Tristan chord," the first sonority in the opera, has inspired whole books. The essay below concerns not the beginning of the opera but the end, where Isolde, having just seen Tristan die, sings of love and death.

    McCreless's essay on Isolde's Transfiguration provides great insight into the workings of Wagner as poet and as composer. The essay also demonstrates the importance of understanding the dramatic context for operatic or other text-setting music.

The final stage direction in the score of Wagner's *Tristan und Isolde* appears precisely as Isolde's closing monologue—her *Verklärung,* or "Transfiguration"[1]—comes to its end: "Supported by Brangäne, Isolde, as though transfigured, gently sinks onto Tristan's body.

Another essay in this book that addresses the tragic finale of an opera is Schmalfeldt's, chapter 13.—Ed.

Some reminders: (1) all words in **bold** are defined in the glossary; (2) full citations for incomplete references are found in the selected bibliography; (3) the authors use their preferred notational system (e.g., Roman numeral, form label, and register notation). Most of the essays denote register by middle C as C^4.—Ed.

1. Robert Bailey has shown that Wagner himself used the title "Isolde's Transfiguration," not the familiar *"Liebestod,"* when referring to the final monologue as an orchestral piece coupled with the Prelude to act I. Bailey also makes it clear that, when Wagner used the term *"Liebestod"* to refer to an instrumental piece, he consistently used it in reference to the Prelude to Act I, *not* the conclusion of the opera. As he notes, *"Liebestod"* thus defines a musical representation of a 'state-of-mind' or psychological reference point, which exists *before* the action of the opera we witness." Accordingly, the century-old tradition of designating Isolde's final monologue as the *"Liebestod"* is not in keeping with Wagner's own usage. See Richard Wagner, *Prelude and Transfiguration from* Tristan und Isolde, ed. Robert Bailey (New York: W. W. Norton, 1985), 37, 41–43.

Great emotion among the bystanders." What is it that enables Isolde to be "transfigured" and that calls forth such a response among the bystanders? Surely it is in part the totality of her experience in the opera: her bitter resentment of Tristan when he first came to fetch her as the bride of King Mark, yet her falling in love with him after drinking the love potion that her maid Brangäne substituted for the death potion at the end of Act I; her tryst with him in the middle of Act II, the discovery of the lovers by Mark's associate, Melot, and the wounding of Tristan near the end of the same act; her returning to him again at the end of Act III, only to find him dying; and her then witnessing his death. Yet it is also some aspect of her character, some way in which she has found meaning in her experience and articulated that meaning, that has made possible her transformation and has empowered her to move those around her. How do words and music show Isolde's transfiguration and the effect of that upon those who see and hear her?

We can first understand her transfiguration through a brief reading of the text:

bar 1:	Gently, softly,		round me rings?
	how he smiles		Yet more clearly,
	how his eyes	35	wafting about me,
	he fondly opens!		are they waves
5	See ye, friends?		of gentle breezes?
	See ye not?		Are they clouds
	How he shines		of heavenly fragrance?
	even higher,	40	As they swell
	soaring on high,		and whisper
10	stars sparkling round him?		shall I breathe them,
bar 12:	See ye not?		shall I listen?
	How his heart		Shall I sip them,
	proudly swells	45	plunge beneath them,
	and, brave and full,		in sweet perfume
15	pulses in his breast?		breathe out my soul? [and]
	How softly and gently		in the surging swell,
	from his lips		in the soaring sound,
	sweet breath	50	in the vast wave of
	flutters—		the breath of the world,
20	Friends! See!		drown,
	Do ye not feel and see it?		sink down
bar 29:	Do I alone		unconscious—
	hear the melody		supreme bliss!
	which, so wondrous		
25	and tender		
	in its sad bliss,		
	all-revealing,		(Supported by Brangaene,
	reconciling,		Isolde, as though
	swelling from him,		transfigured, gently sinks
30	pierces me through,		onto Tristan's body. Great
	rises higher, [and]		emotion among the bystanders.
	gently sounding,		King Mark blesses the
			corpses.)[2]

_____

2. The translation of the text used here is the one that appears in Charles Burkhart, *Anthology for Musical Analysis,* 5th ed. (Fort Worth: Harcourt Brace, 1994), 356.

Wagner, of course, wrote his own libretto for *Tristan,* as he did for all his mature operas, and he probably had the music in mind, at least in a rudimentary way, when he wrote the poem. But it is instructive to discern the structure of the poem in and of itself and to interrogate its meaning, since it provides the foundation upon which the music is built.

A first look at the poem reveals that it is not divided into stanzas; it is an undivided poem of fifty-five lines (fifty-three in the original German). However, a closer look shows a clear sectionalization, even though division into stanzas or sections is not indicated by the orthography of the poem—that is, by spaces between units. Wagner clearly demarcates formal units early in the poem by means of a **refrain** ("See ye not?" or something similar) in lines 5–6, 11, and 20–21. These refrains set off units of six, five, and ten lines, respectively. The last refrain ("Friends! See! Do you not feel and see it?") is longer than the other two, and it serves to demarcate the first large division of the poem. The next two lines (lines 22–23) delineate the beginning of the next poetic section (lines 22–43), comprised of a series of questions, which in the original German are strictly in trochaic meter (long-short) with two stresses per line, and with strong rhymes (especially "-end" and "-en" rhymes) throughout. (The English translation does not maintain this important German meter and rhyme.) The final section (lines 44–55) is marked at first by a shift to a new poetic meter, anapestic (weak-weak-strong). Then, at the end of the poem, Isolde's language is transformed—transfigured, as it were—into lines of one or two words only. Looking back over the whole poem, we can see that it is thus divided into formal units of twenty-one (six + five + ten lines), twenty-two, and twelve lines.

How does Wagner the composer make musical use of the text of Wagner the poet? An initial impression that we might have of the music of the monologue is how extraordinarily seamless it is: it seems to flow in waves, moving smoothly from one moment to the next, without strong cadences and without obvious starting and stopping. This seamlessness is a well-known stylistic feature of *Tristan;* although the music does have cadences, they often resolve deceptively, and they often overlap with the beginning of the next phrase, creating **elisions.** Since phrases also tend not to fall into predictable groups of two or four measures, the overall effect is one of a constant flowing and surging of musical motion—a perfect analogue for the love of Tristan and Isolde. Wagner also uses two other well-known techniques for creating musical flow: leitmotives, which both provide symbols of what is going on in the drama and articulate musical form, and sequences, which provide a sense of progressive intensification.

Yet the music is like the poetry in that, despite its seeming lack of sectional divisions, close study reveals that it too is articulated into sections. The musical shape that Wagner derives from the text of the monologue takes its cue from the structural divisions of the poem to a degree, but it also works independently of those divisions in important respects. The fundamental musical partition of the scene in fact goes against the grain of the poetic sections noted above. Let us look at the music alone for a moment. The music of the monologue is divided into two large parts: mm. 1–43 and mm. 44–79. Two reasons can be adduced for positing such a division. First, a strong cadence occurs at mm. 43–44, where the music reaches a strong dominant seventh (m. 43) in the key of B major (the ultimate and principal key of the monologue), with a cadential trill on the leading tone; the dominant seventh then resolves, typically for the style, not to the tonic but deceptively—in this case, to the subdominant (m. 44). Second, motivic usage in the orchestra clearly differentiates the two parts. Part I uses primarily what I will call motive *a*—an ascending fourth followed by a repeated note and a descending second, all in quarter notes—although it also uses motives *b* and *c* (see example 11.1). Part II abandons these motives altogether and relies instead on two motives that often occur in conjunction with each other—motives *d* and *e* (see example 11.1). This part turns on the incessant use of motive *e,* a chromatic ascent, as a means of building to the climax

Example 11.1. Motives from Isolde's Transfiguration

at m. 61, after which the motivic pair *d* and *e* takes over as the music recedes from the climax.

But when we consider this bipartite musical structure in the light of our analysis of the text, we note that the primary division in the poem was *not* at m. 44 (line 34: "Yet more clearly" in the translation, "Heller schallend" in the German), the point of the primary musical division. Instead, as we have seen, the poetic structure suggests successive units of twenty-one (unit 1—six + five + ten lines), twenty-two (unit 2), and twelve (unit 3) lines. The crucial musical division of the monologue does not occur in conjunction with any of these textual divisions but rather in the middle of the twenty-two-line textual unit. Why did Wagner choose to put the musical division where he did? Before answering this central question, we must look first at the musical setting of the whole text and observe those ways in which Wagner does follow the natural divisions in the poem.

At a level of greater detail the textual divisions and the musical ones do coordinate closely, although not without certain complexities. The correspondence of the poetic and musical sections is shown in the diagram below:

Musical section	Poetic unit	Measure number
Part I		
Section 1	1 (lines 1–6, 7–11)	1–11 (orch.); 1–12 (voice)
Section 2	1 (lines 12–21)	12–28
Section 3	2, first question (lines 22–33)	29–43
Part II		
	2, remainder; 3 (lines 34–55)	44–79

Within Part I, the first musical section sets lines 1–11 of the poem, so that the two short verses with refrains (lines 1–6 and 7–11) are conflated into a single musical unit. However, the text and music overlap at the end of this first musical section: the orchestra begins in m. 12 with the same motive, motive *a,* now a minor third higher as that which began the Transfiguration, thereby articulating the beginning of a new section. Yet at this point the vocal part has yet to reach line 11 of the text, the second refrain, "Seht ihr's nicht?" In consequence, Isolde asks this concluding question of the second short poetic unit to the accompaniment of the new beginning in the orchestra, thus creating an elision between the first and second musical sections, so that the first musical section for the orchestra is eleven measures long, while the first unit for the voice is twelve measures long. Isolde then joins in with the orchestra, again with motive *a,* as in mm. 1 and 3, in m. 13. This second musical section (mm. 12–28) features an alternation, beginning in m. 18, of motive *a* with a new motive, motive *b* (see example 11.1). At the conclusion of the section, the end of the textual refrain ("Freunde! Seht! Fühlt und seht ihr's nicht?") coincides with the musical caesura of m. 28, so the textual and musical divisions are synchronized here in a way that they were not in mm. 11–12. A third musical section, setting lines 22–33 of the text, begins at m. 29 ("Höre ich nur diese Weise"), again with motive *a* as the initial motive, and it continues to the cadence at mm. 43–44. Now motive *a* is relegated only to the beginning of the section, as motive *b* becomes more prominent, occurring in successive measures beginning at m. 34 and feeding into four statements of motive *c* at mm. 38–42.

The beginning of Part II is, as we have seen, initiated by motives *d* and *e*—the first time a musical unit has not been initiated by motive *a.* Part II is not divided into musical sections, as was Part I, and so the last twelve-line unit of the poem is not given its own musical section. Rather, Part II builds in waves to the climax at m. 61 and then gradually falls back, the last lines "ertrinken-versinken-unbewusst-höchster Lust" each being articulated by the dying Isolde into separate musical gestures.

Musical section 1 (mm. 1–11) of Part I establishes a model harmonic sequence for the Transfiguration: it moves through four successive temporary keys, equally dividing the octave in minor thirds. Thus two measures of A♭ major (mm. 1–2) move to two of B major (mm. 3–4), followed by one-measure units of D major (m. 5) and F major (m. 6), before completing the cycle to A♭ major again in m. 7 (see the linear sketch—that is, a representation in musical notation of the essential linear, directional motion of a passage—of mm. 1–8 in example 11.2). This sequence in minor thirds represents a classic example of a nondiatonic sequence—a mechanical sequence that moves in exactly equal intervals, thus establishing a temporary, fleeting tonic in each leg of the sequence—rather than a *tonal* or *diatonic* sequence—one that adjusts intervals according to a single diatonic key.[3]

The sequence here is only the first of a number of such sequences to be encountered in the Transfiguration, and it perfectly exemplifies the chromatic style of *Tristan.* By transposing the motive consistently up exactly by minor third, with no diatonic adjustment, Wagner can have the music move through a dizzying succession of unrelated major keys that challenges our ability to retain a single tonal orientation. The instability of the harmonic sequence is also accentuated by the string tremolo, and especially by the fact that the individual triads are in inversions: the A♭, B, and D triads are in the particularly unstable second inversion, or ⁶₄ position, and the F and final A♭ triads are in first inversion,

---

3. Stefan Kostka calls sequences of this sort "real" sequences (*Materials and Structures of Twentieth-Century Music,* 7).

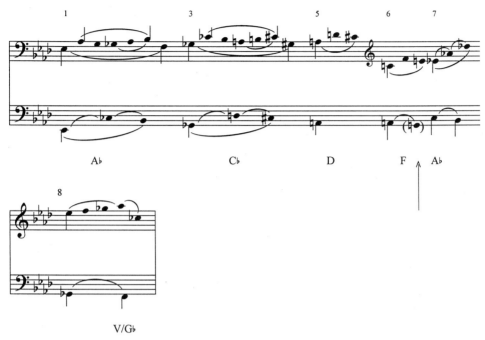

Example 11.2. Linear sketch of mm. 1–8

or ⁶₃ position.[4] Furthermore, each segment of the sequence arrives at what sounds like a dominant, but such dominants never resolve traditionally. Accordingly, at the end of m. 2 the B♭-major triad sounds like V/E♭ minor, or V/V in A♭ major, but it resolves in the next measure not to E♭ but to C♭, the equivalent of VI in E♭ minor. Once we reach m. 3 we have to realize that, although Wagner spells the progression in C♭ major, it is **enharmonically equivalent** to B major, from which the minor third progression up to D major can arise by m. 5. Again, the final chord of mm. 3–4 sounds like V in F♯ minor, or V/V in the home key of C♭/B major, but it resolves to VI of F♯: that is, to D rather than to F♯. Measures 5–7 move more quickly, with each measure temporarily establishing a key in the sequence D–F–A♭. If the orchestral accompaniment in mm. 5–7 were to continue the sequence exactly, the result would be the hypothetical music given in example 11.3. But Wagner **accelerates** the sequence here: the downbeats of mm. 6 and 7 provide the expected chords (F major and A♭ major, respectively), but, as is clearly seen by comparing example 11.3 to the actual music, he simply omits the second measure of what would have been two-measure units on D and F, and thus doubles the rate of the harmonic ascent from two measures per unit to one measure per unit.

When the tonic of A♭ is finally reached in m. 7, Wagner breaks the orchestral melodic pattern and writes successive ascending fourths (E♭^{1}–A♭^{1}, A♭^{1}–D♭^{2})—A change that makes possible the transfer of the E♭–A♭ motion an octave higher in m. 8, in both the orchestra and voice. Also, the change in the melodic line is accompanied by a new direction in the harmony: the sequence is finally broken, and for a moment, in m. 8, the music tonicizes

4. Leonard Meyer makes this point in his analysis of the Transfiguration in *Style and Music* (Philadelphia: University of Pennsylvania Press, 1989), 312. His perceptive stylistic analysis (311–25) offers many valuable insights into the monologue.

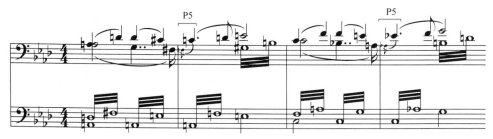

Example 11.3. Mm. 5–6, with hypothetical continuation

G♭ major. As is characteristic of the *Tristan* style, the key can be temporarily established simply by a short progression with a dominant chord—here IV$^6_4$–V$^6_5$ in G♭—without ever reaching a tonic. The final three measures of the first musical section also move freely in their harmony, quickly suggesting G minor (m. 9), C minor (m. 9, beats 1–2), and E♭ major (m. 9, beats 3–4), before m. 11 simply moves from an A♭-major triad to an E-major triad, without really suggesting a tonic orientation. Over the same measures, the primary melodic motion in the orchestra ascends slowly through a chromatic line that moves from the A♭^{2} of m. 8 to the B♮^{2} of m. 11 (see the linear sketch of mm. 8–12 in example 11.4). This is the first of a number of examples in Part I of the monologue in which, when a sequential pattern is broken, a linear pattern—that is, a slowly moving, stepwise voice in an upper voice or the bass—takes over the burden of continuity. (Of course, a sequence is also "linear motion," in the sense that it involves the repetition of a pattern at regular intervals in the same direction. But, although sequences most frequently move linearly by step, they—and especially nondiatonic sequences—can also move by thirds, as is the case with the sequence in mm. 1–7.)

The orchestral accompaniment to the second musical section of Part I begins with sequential motion based on motive *a,* as in the preceding section, though now it begins in B major (m. 12), the second key of the A♭–B–D–F motion of mm. 1–6. Now the individual segments of the sequence are only one measure long (as in mm. 5 and 6 before), and the sequence lasts for only two iterations of the motive. At m. 14, where a continuation of the sequence would bring an F-major triad, Wagner gives us instead a G-major $^6_4$ chord, thereby breaking the sequence. As was the case in the first section, when the sequential motion is broken off, linear motion takes over: we saw there how, once the sequence was concluded, the linear motion from A♭^{2} to B^2 tied the next few measures to-

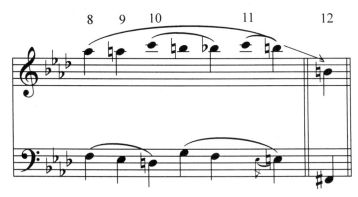

Example 11.4. Linear sketch of mm. 8–12

Example 11.5. Linear bass motion, mm. 14–18

gether. Here, however, the linear motion that follows the sequence is not in the upper register of the orchestra, as before, but in the bass. In this passage (mm. 14–17), the harmonic progression and the succession of temporarily tonicized keys do not form a comprehensible pattern, but the clear ascending linear motion (example 11.5) in the bass underlies the coherence of the passage and connects it to a goal—the new sequence that begins at m. 18. This sequence begins in E major, with motive *a,* as before, but makes a new two-measure unit by adding motive *b* (the turn figure and motion that follows it) in m. 19. Measure 20 then sequences the two-measure pattern a semitone higher, on F, and m. 22 brings us to F♯. In m. 23, however, the second measure of the sequence is displaced to a fourth higher (it brings an A-major, rather than the expected E-major, triad), and this, the final two-measure unit (mm. 24–25), occurs a fourth higher than it would have had the sequence continued exactly. As is now becoming predictable, once the sequence is broken off, linear motion—of a different sort here—takes over, this time with clear contrary motion in the leading upper and lower voices of the orchestra, so that a wedge leads to the octave F♯s at the beginning of Section 3 (m. 29; see example 11.6).

  The music thus far has set that part of the poetic text that is structured with refrains (in lines 5–6, 11, and 20–21 of the poem), although the poetic refrain is not matched with a musical one: here, as elsewhere, Wagner seems to seek continuity by avoiding simultaneous strong articulations of text and music. The words "Do I alone" (line 22, "Höre ich nur diese Weise") begin the poem's second large unit, which initiates the third musical section of Part I. The music here begins with motive *a,* as did Sections 1 and 2, yet for once the motive is not sequenced but rather flowers out into a full four-and-one-half-measure setting of the first line of the new section (m. 29–m. 33, beat 2)—again in B major, the goal key of the Transfiguration as a whole and the key that also began the second musical section. However, the setting of the lines that follow, beginning in the second half of m. 33, brings us back to a sequence, this one for the first time a descending rather than ascending sequence, and now in whole steps rather than semitones or minor thirds:

Example 11.6. Linear sketch of mm. 25–29

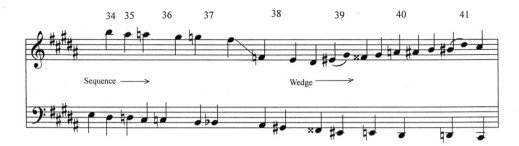

Example 11.7. Linear sketch of mm. 34–44

B major beginning in m. 34, beat 3; A major in m. 35, beat 3; G major in m. 36, beat 3 (note the rhythmic halving of note values here); and F major in m. 37, beat 3. Here the sequence accentuates the rhyming short lines of the text. When the rhyme changes, the melodic pattern changes: the shift from "-end" rhymes to "-get" rhymes (beginning in m. 39) brings a new, quasi-sequential vocal line (based on motive C) and, equally important, another linear wedge that prepares the beginning of Part II (example 11.7); in fact, the descending bass line of the wedge, beginning at m. 38, is traceable back to the beginning of the sequence at m. 34.[5]

With the arrival of Part II at m. 44, the task of the music becomes to build to and then recede from the climax at m. 61. To accomplish this task, Wagner first introduces motives *d* and *e*, leaving motives *a*, *b*, and *c* behind. He also shapes the music rather differently. In Part I, with the exception of the lyrical mm. 29–33, the music was either literally sequential or based on directed linear motion in melodic or bass voices, or both. Now, as the music begins to build to the climax of the whole monologue, the orchestra presents motives *d* and *e* as a pair in m. 44. But rather than sequencing this motivic pair at higher or lower pitches, he repeats it three times successively, in mm. 44–46, at the same pitch level. These repetitions, especially with the crescendos on motive *e* in the second half of mm. 44 and 45, initiate the buildup of tension in Part II. Then, in m. 47 the upper strings begin a long ascent, based on motive *e*. But this is a new kind of linear ascent in the monologue. Neither a sequence nor a straightforward linear pattern, the ascent behaves like the waves mentioned in the poem: beginning with the G#^{2} of motive *e* in m. 46, it drops back to F#^{2} and Fx^2 before reaching G#^{2} again on the last eighth note of the measure. The G#^{2} is then syncopated by being tied across the barline, and the pattern repeats twice in m. 47. Then in m. 48, an eighth-note triplet on the second beat pushes up

---

5. Meyer discusses this wedge in *Style and Music*, 319.

Example 11.8. Linear sketch of mm. 47–61

to a new high note, A^2, which is also **syncopated,** and which also falls back to the lower pitches in the motive before reaching the new high point again and repeating the whole pattern. This wavelike pattern of reaching a high point, syncopating it, then dropping back and repeating the whole pattern two or more times, then achieving a new high point becomes the basis for musical progression all the way from m. 46 to the climax at m. 61—from G#^{2} in m. 46–47 to B^3 at the climax in m. 61.[6] Isolde's vocal line also climbs by step, from B^1 in the second half of m. 46 to the G#^{2} of m. 61. These ascents in the orchestra and voice are accompanied by a corresponding descent in the bass, as shown in the wedge in example 11.8.[7] The insistence of the syncopated, wavelike ascending chromatic motive in the upper orchestral voices, constantly falling back only to rise incrementally higher and higher, makes possible, in conjunction with the descending bass line of the wedge and then a prolonged dominant pedal beginning at m. 54, beat 3, the most spectacular of all the climaxes in the monologue (though not too spectacular—Wagner's dynamic indication here is only forte, even though the Schirmer vocal score indicates fortissimo).

We can now see in more detail why Wagner chose to make the primary division in the music at line 34 of the poem, "Heller schallend." Since it is at this moment that Isolde begins to sing of giving herself up to the enveloping waves that surround her, it is only appropriate that the music at this point introduce motive *e,* which will be treated as a wavelike figure surging toward the climax. What is more, the essence of Isolde's transfiguration is embodied in lines 34–55 of the poem, and thus in Part II of the music. It is as if, at line 34, she suddenly realizes that the bystanders do not share her experience and that the answer to her question of the preceding lines is "yes": she *is* the only one to hear the glorious melody, and thus she can release herself to the waves that symbolize her joining Tristan in death—the act that "transfigures" her, that renders her "*verklärt,*" or "made clear." Tying this whole experience together musically are the two cadences at mm. 43–44 and 55–61. Both at the beginning of Part II, and at the climax, strong dominant seventh sonorities discharge into downbeat subdominant sonorities, each with motive *d* prominently in the orchestra. These two sonorities encompass the moments of Isolde's brightest radiance, before she sinks down into Brangäne's arms, and they musically embody her transfiguration. Just as Isolde's greatest heroic act is to give herself up to death, so is the harmony that is bound up with this act not the forward, directional dominant sonority, but the gentler, more placid subdominant.

---

6. Obviously, the climactic note here is C#^{4}. However, linearly speaking, the C#^{4} is a dramatically emphasized appoggiatura to the chord tone B^3, to which it resolves on the second half of the third beat.

7. Meyer also discusses this wedge in *Style and Music,* pp. 322–23. Note that in a sense this wedge continues the one of mm. 34–44. The earlier wedge ends on G#^{2} over EE in the bass. The wedge of mm. 47–61 begins on G#^{2} over E in the bass.

The subdominant remains in play as the accumulated tension from the climax of m. 61 is dissipated: first through the two successive IV–I motions in mm. 61–64, then through a more prolonged IV (iv)–I (mm. 65–74). The pairing of motives *d* and *e* returns in mm. 70–71, and an augmentation of this pair in mm. 72–74 effectively slows down the rhythmic momentum and prepares one of the most extraordinary moments in the entire score. At mm. 74–75, rather than reiterating yet again the melodic motion $C\sharp^3$–B^2–$A\sharp^2$–$G\sharp^2$–$G\sharp^2$–$F\sharp^2$–Fx^2–$G\sharp^2$–$A\sharp^2$–$C\sharp^3$, as one might expect after hearing mm. 70–72, the upper strings move $C\sharp^3$–B^2–$C\sharp^3$–$D\sharp^3$, such that accompanying the $D\sharp^3$ in the orchestra is none other than the Tristan chord, E♮–G♯–B–D♯, at m. 75.

This tonally ambiguous chord is emblematic of the entire harmonic language of *Tristan,* and it is worth taking a moment to discuss it. It is the first chord heard in the opera, in the famous Prelude to Act I, where it appears in the spelling F–G♯–B–D♯, in the context of A minor (example 11.9a). Later in the Prelude to Act I it appears in the context of E♭ minor (spelled F–A♭–C♭–E♭; see example 11.9b) and C minor (spelled F–A♭–B–E♭; see example 11.9c). In the Transfiguration it has appeared once before, at m. 8, beat 3, where it suggested G♭ major. Although in common harmonic parlance it is simply a half-diminished seventh chord, Wagner's usage of it to function in a wide variety of tonal contexts is what in particular characterizes it within *Tristan.* Its appearance here at the very end of the opera, now functioning in B major, makes us remember its other usages, and it specifically reminds us of its very first appearance in the Prelude to Act I. What connects the chord here to its appearance in the Prelude is that it brings in its wake, and on virtually the same instrument(s) (oboe and English horn here, oboe only there), the very melodic motive, often designated as the "Desire" motive, that was associated with the Tristan chord in the opening measures of the opera: the chromatic ascent G♯–A–A♯–B (refer again to example 11.9a). There the harmonic goal was an E-major dominant seventh chord, or V^7 of A minor, so the concluding b of the motive was a member of a nontonic triad. Here, however, the goal is the final B-major triad of the opera, and so the G♯–A–A♯–B pushes on up through C♯ to D♯, to resolve on a chord tone of the final triad, all over the harmonic progression moving from the Tristan chord to one last reiteration of the iv–I motion heard in mm. 68–70.[8]

The inclusion of the G♯–A–A♯–B motive has meaning even beyond its significance as recapitulating an idea from the very beginning of the opera. With respect just to the Transfiguration, the G♯ to B motive recalls (enharmonically) the A♭ to C♭ harmonic motion of mm. 1–3, as well as the large-scale A♭ to B motion of the beginning of Section 1 to the beginning of Section 2 (mm. 1 and 12). But the meaning of G♯–B goes even further. Bailey has shown that Act I of *Tristan* turns on what he calls a "double-tonic complex"—that is, an extensive musical unit that turns from one tonic at the beginning to another at the end—of A and C: Act I of the opera begins in A minor and ends in C major. Lawrence Kramer has shown that in the Prelude to Act I this A/C complex has a "shadow" complex of G♯/B—the opening oboe line, expressing the "Desire" motive, moves from $G\sharp^1$ to B^1, and then from B^1 to D^2, then D^2 to $F\sharp^2$. The oboe line thus outlines a Tristan-like half-diminished seventh chord G♯–B–D–F♯, which shadows the harmonic implications of the opening seventeen measures of the Prelude, which move A–C–E. (Because of space considerations I have not included the score of mm. 1–17 of the Prelude here;

---

8. Bailey has shown that Wagner thought of including the ascending chromatic motive (designated by Bailey as motive *y,* and by many earlier commentators as the "Desire" motive) *after* he had composed the first draft of the Transfiguration. The version including the motive appears by itself on the otherwise blank verso side of Wagner's preliminary draft manuscript. See Bailey, Analytical Study, 146.

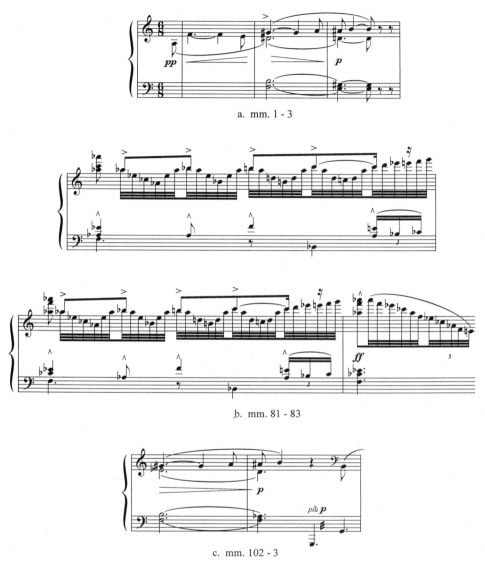

a. mm. 1 - 3

b. mm. 81 - 83

c. mm. 102 - 3

Example 11.9. Excerpts from *Tristan und Isolde,* Prelude to Act I

the score is readily available in numerous anthologies.) Kramer even claims that "the ruling musical process of *Tristan und Isolde* is the progressive reinterpretation of T [the Tristan chord], T' [the half-diminished seventh G♯–B–D–F♯], and the Desire motive—the outcome of which is nothing other than Isolde's Transfiguration."[9]

Although we cannot follow Kramer in detail here, the basic process is relatively straightforward. The first act of the opera moves from A minor to C major: at the end of the act, the ship pulls into port, with Tristan and Isolde now in love, even though he

---

9. Lawrence Kramer, *Music As Cultural Practice, 1800–1900* (Berkeley and Los Angeles: University of California Press, 1990), 154.

brought her to become the bride of King Mark, in C major—though with a shadow, as noted above, of G♯–B–D–F♯. When Tristan and Isolde meet again in Act II, their music initially tends toward the C major in which they were last together in Act I, but soon turns toward the two initial notes/keys of the shadow: the famous love duet "O sink' hernieder, Nacht der Liebe," which occurs precisely at the midpoint of the opera, begins in A♭ major (the enharmonic equivalent of G♯) but seeks a conclusion in B.[10] Act III begins in F minor, but it closes, with the Transfiguration, in a move from A♭ to B that recapitulates the A♭ to B motion of the love duet of Act II. As Kramer explains, "At its close, the Transfiguration circles back to mm. 2–3 of the Prelude [to Act I] and states the Desire motive, at pitch, on the oboes and English horn [at mm. 75–76 of the Transfiguration]. With this gesture, Wagner encourages us to hear the Transfiguration as a tonal projection of the Desire motive in the latter's primary structural form, the dyad G♯–B."[11] We can thus hear the motive G♯–B resonating through the entire opera, both as a melodic motive, as at the opening of the Prelude to Act I and at the conclusion of the opera, and as a tonal process, as in the Act II love duet and the Transfiguration.

In fact, if we were to study the entire score of *Tristan,* we would discover that the music of the Transfiguration, up to the climax at m. 61, is in large part a recapitulation of music from the love duet in Act II—that moment in the opera in which Tristan and Isolde come closest to consummating their love. Measures 1–11 recapitulate, now in 4/4 rather than 6/8, measures 178/1/1–178/3/4, and measures 12–60 recapitulate mm. 187/2/1–195/3/4, now in 4/4 rather than 2/2.[12] Wagner did make slight adjustments, which are beyond the scope of the present essay to describe, but which Bailey's study details carefully.[13] Suffice it to note here that, in the Act II version, the music that corresponds to mm. 1–11 of the Transfiguration is repeated, but this repeat is omitted in the Transfiguration; and that in both versions the prolonged dominant seventh at the end (see mm. 55–60 of the Transfiguration) leads not to a tonic resolution, but to a substitute for the tonic. In the Act II version it leads to the dissonant chord at m. 196/1/1, which articulates Kurvenal's sudden entrance to announce the arrival of Melot, Mark, and their retinue, and thus the shocking interruption of the lovers' tryst. In Act III, as we have seen, it leads to IV (m. 61), which, although it is a subdominant rather than a tonic, does constitute the climax of the monologue, and which, with its resolution in the next measure and beyond, solidly establishes B major as the ultimate tonic sonority of the Transfiguration.

What does this recapitulation mean? First, it suggests that Wagner must have already had the idea of recapitulating the Act II duet when he wrote the texts of the two passages; otherwise he could not have mapped the music of one onto the other. The extensive recapitulation also means that any analytical conclusions we drew for mm. 1–60 of the monologue are applicable to the corresponding measures of the Act II passage: thus the observation that each of the sections of the music combines literal, "real" sequences with directed linear motion, in either upper or lower voices, to a goal holds for both. But there must be a deeper meaning to a recall of music on this scale. What does it mean that the music that underlies the passage where Tristan and Isolde's love comes closest to being fulfilled in the real world, in Act II, is the same music that Isolde sings once Tristan is dead and the love can exist only in her imagination, in Act III? Kramer, commenting on the "recapitulatory character of the Transfiguration as a whole," suggests that "The mu-

---

10. Ibid., 156.

11. Ibid.

12. Measure numbers for the passage from Act II give page, system and measure of the Schirmer vocal score.

13. Bailey, *Analytical Study,* 140–46.

sic returns Isolde to the scene of her fullest earlier rapture and completes in fantasy the cadence/consummation that was shattered in reality."[14] So in the end there *is* an element of *Liebestod* here, even though that designation is an incorrect label for the monologue as a whole. For it is in death that Isolde experiences love on a higher spiritual plane and that she loses herself in the music, which, at the end of her monologue, unites her with Tristan in the shadow tonality of B, which emerges magnificently in the cadence of mm. 60–61 and undergirds the music as it dies away in the following measures. It is indeed her ability to give herself over to death—to allow her love of Tristan to envelop her wholly and to transcend the limitations of earthly love—that enables her to be transfigured, and at the end to move the bystanders by her experience.

14. Kramer, *Music As Cultural Practice,* 164.

~12~

MEANING IN A POPULAR SONG
The Representation of Masochistic Desire in
Sarah McLachlan's "Ice"

—————————————— *Lori Burns* ——————————————

For several years, Lori Burns (University of Ottawa) has pursued two relatively new analytical approaches in music theory: analysis of pop and rock music and analysis from a feminist perspective. Her work includes studies on music by k. d. lang, Tori Amos, P. J. Harvey, Courtney Love, and Meshell Ndgeocello, as well as other songs by McLachlan. Her most recent project is a study of blues and jazz song performances by early artists such as Billie Holiday, Bessie Smith, and Louis Armstrong, in comparison with contemporary performances of the same standard songs.

In the present essay, Burns demonstrates how rock music can be analyzed with concepts and methodologies formerly reserved for "classical" music; she also demonstrates how a feminist approach can uncover the gender issues in both the text and the musical setting. Readers are encouraged to read other essays in this volume that treat so-called popular genres: John Covach on rock music (chapter 6) and Ramon Satyendra on Chick Corea (chapter 5).

My motivation for writing this essay (beyond my fascination with the musical expression of McLachlan's beautiful song) stems from my pedagogical interest in demonstrating how to analyze a popular song in a manner sensitive to both its social message and its specific musical content. Students in popular music courses all over North America try their hands at content analysis of pop and rock songs (in a variety of genre contexts) and are motivated to make interpretive claims about lyrical expression and musical structure. However, within the existing literature on popular music and social meaning, scholars debate analytic methods and even the degree to which one should analyze structural musical elements such as voice leading and harmony.[1] With this essay, I set aside such theoretical

---

Some reminders: (1) all words in **bold** are defined in the glossary; (2) full citations for incomplete references are found in the selected bibliography; (3) the authors use their preferred notational system (e.g., Roman numeral, form label, and register notation). Most of the essays denote register by middle C as C^4.—Ed.

1. The various theoretical positions cannot be outlined in this paper, but the interested reader might wish to refer to the following publications: Richard Middleton, *Studying Popular Music* (Philadelphia: Open University Press, 1990), and "Popular Music Analysis and Musicology: Bridging the Gap," *Popular Music* 12, no. 2 (1993): 177–88; Allan Moore, *Rock: The Primary Text* (Buckingham: Open University Press, 1993); and Robert Walser, *Running with the Devil: Power, Gender and Madness in Heavy Metal Music* (Hanover: Wesleyan University Press, 1993). These are all references within the field of music; the reader should be aware that the debate over

debates and attempt to demonstrate the rewards of conducting a close reading of a popular song that engages structural analysis while remaining sensitive to the unique features of popular music and thus enabling analytic intersections between social message and musical content.[2]

SOCIAL MESSAGE OF "ICE"

In 1993 Sarah McLachlan traveled to Thailand and Cambodia to shoot a documentary for World Vision. She wrote the song "Ice" as a response to the blatant abuse of young women for prostitution that she witnessed in Thailand.[3] The song does not recount a particular scene or situation that she observed but rather translates her response to a general social problem into a story in which, as she herself says, "there isn't much hope for the characters." The song text can thus be considered on these two levels: (1) a general exploration of her disturbed response to the treatment of women for sexual hire; and (2) the specific story that the song relates about an unhealthy love relationship. The first level is more abstract, but its influence—as a global societal problem that bleeds into even a personal relationship—is heavily felt in the lyrical content of the song.

Feminist theorists give considerable attention to the ways in which social systems and institutions translate into personal values. Indeed, the historical treatment of female sexual power is of central import to the shaping of women's sociopolitical position in society, which in turn has a direct impact upon the shaping of women's private sexual identities.[4] Sandra Lee Bartky describes the feminist's discovery of the connections between larger social conditions and private sexual response:

> For the feminist, two things follow upon the discovery that sexuality too belongs to the sphere of the political. The first is that whatever pertains to sexuality—not only actual sexual behavior, but sexual desire and sexual fantasy as well—will have to be understood in relation to a larger system of subordination; the second, that the deformed sexuality of patriarchal culture must be moved from the hidden domain of "private life" into an arena for struggle, where a "politically correct" sexuality of mutual respect will contend with an "incorrect" sexuality of domination and submission.[5]

Bartky here raises the question of politically "correct" versus "incorrect" sexuality, suggesting that a feminist conscience would be adverse to the model of "feminine" sexual behavior that places women in a submissive role. It cannot be denied that a model of

---

the content of musical analysis in popular music studies is also explored in other disciplines, including cultural studies and communications, for example, Simon Frith, *Sound Effects: Youth, Leisure and the Politics of Rock'n'Roll* (New York: Pantheon Books, 1981), and Simon Frith and Andrew Goodwin, *On Record: Rock, Pop, and the Written Word* (New York: Pantheon Books, 1990).

2. By "structural analysis" I mean the detailed analysis of musical form, phrase, counterpoint, and harmony.

3. Sarah McLachlan, interview, "Egos and Icons," televised on Much Music, June 1998.

4. My discussion here cannot do justice to the subject of female sexual power and identity, but the interested reader could refer to the following selected publications: Sandra Lee Bartky, "Feminine Masochism and the Politics of Personal Transformation," in *Femininity and Domination: Studies in the Phenomenology of Oppression* Bartky, Sandra Lee. *Femininity and Domination: Studies in the Phenomenology of Oppression* (New York: Routledge, 1990), Ch. 1. (New York and London: Routledge Press, 1990); Paula Caplan, *The Myth of Women's Masochism* (1985; Toronto: University of Toronto Press, 1993); Lynn S. Chancer, *Sadomasochism in Everyday Life: The Dynamics of Power and Powerlessness* (New Brunswick, N.J.: Rutgers University Press, 1992); Lynda Hart, *Between the Body and the Flesh* (New York: Columbia University Press, 1998); and Carole S. Vance, ed., *Pleasure and Danger: Exploring Female Sexuality* (London: Pandora Press, 1992).

5. Bartky "Feminine Masochism," 323.

"feminine" submission is advanced and perpetuated in a variety of cultural forms.[6] Indeed, Jessica Benjamin makes the startling assertion that the "fantasy of erotic domination permeates *all* sexual imagery in our culture."[7]

Although I have barely introduced these feminist perspectives on women's sexual power, I would like these ideas to resonate as I present my analysis of McLachlan's song "Ice." Domination and subordination, sexual power, and masochism are essential themes at the heart of the song's message and meaning, with the context of prostitution as a larger social signifier.[8]

TEXT INTERPRETATION OF "ICE"

McLachlan claims to create song lyrics that can be interpreted in different ways by her diverse audience members. Although variant readings are certainly possible, I would argue that certain elements of a song text cannot be interpreted contrarily. The question I raise here of fixed meaning versus subjective interpretation is of tremendous import to the postmodern analyst. I am sensitive to the postmodern admission of various subjectivities, yet I believe that the solution is not to admit unlimited pluralism.[9] Popular music analyst Eric Clarke suggests that musical meaning can be likened to the meaning achieved through cinema, in which "a perceiver is encouraged, or *obliged*, by the film to adopt a particular attitude to what he or she is witnessing."[10] In that spirit, my reading is offered as my own particular response to this song text, yet I do not believe this reading to be a purely subjective response invented to suit my own ideological agenda. Rather, I believe that McLachlan has formulated a textual and musical expression that *obliges* the listener to share her deep concern for the social problem she engages.

"Ice" is based on the verse-chorus song form common to much rock music, in which a story is developed as each **verse** presents new lyrical material, while a more general message is repeated in the **chorus.** In this song, McLachlan only sings the chorus twice, placing it after verse 4 and then again after the final verse 6. The lyrics of the song with the formal sections marked are as follows:

Verse 1
The ice is thin come on dive in
underneath my lucid skin
the cold is lost, forgotten.

---

6. Bartky, for instance, refers to the popular "genre of historical romance known in the publishing trade as the 'bodice-ripper'" as an illustration of this cultural phenomenon (ibid, 324).

7. Jessica Benjamin, *The Bonds of Love: Psychoanalysis, Feminism, and the Problem of Domination* (New York: Pantheon Books, 1988), 281.

8. Masochism is simply defined as the inclination to find pleasure in pain; sadomasochism involves a partnership in which one takes pleasure from inflicting pain and the other finds pleasure in having that pain inflicted. I will not take the time here to develop the theme of masochism as it is addressed in sociocultural theory. I have written elsewhere on the subject of male dominance and female subordination as a theme in another song by Sarah McLachlan, the first track on the album on which "Ice" is produced. The interested reader may refer to "Sarah McLachlan's 'Possession': Representations of Dominance and Subordination in Lyrics, Music, and Images" in *Studies in Music at the University of Western Ontario* (forthcoming).

9. Walser makes a similar assertion when he says, "The range of possible interpretations may be theoretically infinite, but in fact certain preferred variant readings are commonly negotiated. . . . So while meanings are negotiated, discourse constructs the terms of the negotiation" (*Running with the Devil,* 33).

10. Eric Clarke, "Subject-Position and the Specification of Invariants in Music by Frank Zappa and P. J. Harvey," *Music Analysis* 18, no. 3 (1999): 347–74, p. 352.

Verse 2
Hours pass days pass time stands still
light gets dark and darkness fills
my secret heart forbidden . . .

Verse 3
I think you worried for me then
the subtle ways that I'd give in
but I know you liked the show.

Verse 4
Tied down to this bed of shame
you tried to move around the pain
but oh, your soul is anchored.

Chorus
The only comfort is the moving of the river.
You enter into me a lie upon your lips.
Offer what you can, I'll take all that I can get.
only a fool's here . . .

Verse 5
I don't like your tragic sighs
as if your god has passed you by
well hey fool that's your deception.

Verse 6
Your angels speak with jilted tongues
the serpent's tale has come undone
you have no strength to squander.

Chorus
The only comfort is the moving of the river.
You enter into me a lie upon your lips.
Offer what you can, I'll take all that I can get.
only a fool's here to stay.
only a fool's here . . . [11]

In verse 1, the poet establishes her vulnerable position in an unequal and possibly masochistic relationship.[12] With the metaphorical statement "the cold is lost, forgotten" she forgives some past cruelty; yet the opening of the song suggests her fragile state ("the ice is thin"); and her apparent willingness to risk injury again ("come on dive in"). Verse 2 invokes the value of time as a means of denoting again her subservience. The passing of hours and days and the loss of a sense of time defines her time as empty, valueless without the Other. Her fantasies are identified as clandestine, dark, and overcast with potentially negative consequences. Verse 3 attributes to the Other a concerned sympathy for the poet, but this sympathy is false, since the Other (according to the poet) enjoyed her

---

11. The text in figure 12.1 is based on the CD notes for *Fumbling towards Ecstasy* (Nettwerk, 1993). The sheet music is available at *Sarah McLachlan*, Hal Leonard, 1994.

12. In order to leave open the question of gender, I shall simply refer to the subject as the poet, and to the object as the Other. Because it is a woman singing the song, we would likely understand the poet to be female, but there is no explicit reference to the Other's gender.

efforts to please. In verse 4 the poet admits her shame that sexual desire is the reason that they are bound together. The second and third lines of verse 4 present a turning point in the text. They speak to the Other's feelings, although from her perspective ("*you* tried to move around the pain / but oh, *your* soul is anchored"). An accurate representation or not, the Other is now depicted as also being vulnerable. This complicates the relationship and offers a potential explanation for their ongoing involvement and sustained passion.

The chorus interrupts the verse narrative to express desire as the impetus for the relationship and to confirm the masochistic nature of that desire. The first line, "The only comfort is the moving of the river," connotes the satisfaction found in the fulfillment of her desire. Yet this satisfaction is expressed in such a way that it is tainted with the negative connotations of inequality and dishonesty: first, the "moving of the river" creates a textual link back to verse 1, in which "ice" was associated with past cruelties; second, the sexual embrace occurs simultaneously with the utterance of a lie; and third, she openly admits her masochism and declares her subservience ("I'll take all that I can get"). In the final line of the chorus, she pushes aside this passion and allows her conscience to speak the truth: she is a "fool" for putting herself in this position.

After the chorus we return to the verse narrative with verses 5 and 6. These verses offer a change in tone, a development of the poet's anger and resistance, inspired perhaps by the chorus's clear identification of the problem and its opportunity for self-criticism. In these final two verses, she criticizes the Other's power, which is rooted in religion, an institution from which she excludes herself—she refers to "*your* god" and "*your* angels." She identifies also a sense of entitlement (the Other's "tragic sighs" in the face of rejection), expresses her anger toward that sense of entitlement ("hey fool that's your deception"), and criticizes a fundamental story of Christianity (Adam, Eve, and the Serpent) that ascribes to all women the guilt of original sin. The last lines of verses 5 and 6 denounce these power sources as ultimately weak.[13]

Although these last two verses speak to her resistance, they are followed by a final statement of the chorus that reiterates her feelings of desire. We hear this statement differently than the first, not only because there are actual changes in the text, but also because of the preceding context. If she rejects so strongly what the Other stands for, as we have learned in verses 5 and 6, then why is she still affected by the desire that is expressed in the chorus? In addition, the line "only a fool's here" is expanded to conclude "to stay," suggesting that this situation is permanent. It expresses her resignation that despite her criticism, the relationship will continue. Just to confirm the problematic nature of her participation in the relationship, the very last utterance is a return to the unfinished and therefore more ambiguous earlier comment that "only a fool's here."

With this song text, McLachlan identifies a general societal problem as it is exemplified in a specific relationship. Her lyrics speak to the formation of "feminine" sexuality as subordinate in relation to a dominant male.[14] Given her broader goal of exploring the theme of prostitution and female sexual power, the story can be read not only as an account of this individual protagonist, but also of a greater problem in patriarchal culture at large. Although McLachlan does not attempt to resolve the problem, its mere identification is a form of resistance—with these lyrics, McLachlan illuminates the negative consequences when sexual power is not evenly distributed.

---

13. This reference to original sin is important given the context of McLachlan's other work. Her video for the song "Possession," which is the first track on the album *Fumbling Towards Ecstasy*, deals explicitly with images of women in the bible. I discuss her use of religious themes in "Captor or Captive." (forthcoming).

14. There exists a substantial literature in which feminist theorists discuss connections between power and desire in relation to the formation of female sexuality. I have already listed several references in n. 4.

MUSICAL INTERPRETATION OF "ICE"

The song begins with the sparse texture of a figurative pattern in the guitar. There is a brief entry of an electronic organ before the voice enters, which is accompanied by the continuing guitar part. The recording is "mixed" to place the voice very much in the foreground—high compression of the voice part, which results in a very "close" presentation of the vocal sounds, suggests she wants to communicate with us directly, personally.[15] The sparse guitar and voice texture continues through the first two verses. A strong downbeat in the electric bass initiates a short **bridge** passage that also introduces a saxophone melody. The bass deepens the guitar texture and focuses the ear on the functional bass movement. At the beginning of verse 3, the deep register is supported further by the addition of strong downbeat attacks in the kickdrum with an anticipatory rhythm in the bongo drum at the end of each bar. From that point on, the voice, guitar, bass, saxophone, percussion, and organ participate in a carefully constructed ensemble. The only addition to the texture after the beginning of verse 3 is in the introduction of backup vocals during the chorus (sparsely used in the first chorus but employed to create a rich harmonic texture in the final chorus).

The form of the song is articulated by the following distinctive textural changes: verses 1 and 2 form a structural unit with a fairly sparse texture, verses 3 and 4 add more instrumental layers, and the chorus adds the social element of backup voices. After the first chorus the sparse texture returns for verse 5, which features the voice and bass. Once again, more instrumental layers are added moving into verse 6 and the chorus, creating increased activity and ensemble involvement. The final chorus is a veritable web of sound with the dense backup vocal texture as well as the active ensemble, but the texture is reduced for the final lines "only a fool's here to stay."

The above comments on the musical texture of the song are intended to capture the somber quality that it achieves. The stylistic attention to instrumental detail plus the song's minor mode, slow tempo, and hushed dynamic signal a contemplative mood. In keeping with these features, the melodic and harmonic materials are simple and repetitive, allowing the listener to perceive subtle manipulations. I shall now illustrate how careful contemplation and subtle control are achieved by contrapuntal and harmonic means as well.

My analysis of "Ice" is based on an original transcription of the song as it was produced on the 1993 album *Fumbling Towards Ecstasy*.[16] Throughout my discussion, I shall refer to voice-leading graphs, which chart the melody (voice) and bass (guitar) relations as a contrapuntal framework.[17] In these graphs, *stemmed notes* indicate pitches that be-

---

15. "Compression" is a recording technique that brings all vocal dynamics within a restricted or compressed band of volume, with the result that even a whisper can sound as strong and direct as a full-voiced forte.

16. There is a score available for purchase (see n. 11), but as with all sheet music, the score does not reflect the details of the actual performance. When analyzing a popular song, it is important to acknowledge that different performances of the same work might have slight or even substantial variations. Given my interest in a close reading of the music, I have found it necessary to choose a performance and treat it as an authoritative version of the song.

17. The reader should be aware of the debate over the application of reductive analytic techniques to popular music. Applications of Schenkerian techniques to popular songs include the following: Walter Everett, "Voice-Leading and Harmony as Expressive Devices in the Early Music of the Beatles: 'She Loves You,'" *College Music Symposium* 32, no. 1 (1992): 19–35; and Burns, "Analytic Methodologies for Rock Music: Harmonic and Voice-Leading Strategies in Tori Amos's 'Crucify,'" in *Expression in Pop-Rock Music*, ed. Walter Everett (New York: Garland Press, 2000). Well-reasoned criticisms of Schenkerian applications to popular music can be found in Middleton, *Studying Popular Music*: 92–97; Allan Moore, "The So-Called 'Flattened Seventh' in Rock," *Popular Music* 14, no. 2 (1995): 195–201; John Covach, "We Won't Get Fooled Again: Rock Music and Musical Analysis," in *Keeping Score: Music, Disciplinarity, Culture*, ed. David Schwartz, Anahid Kassabian, and

Example 12.1. Basic harmonic progression (Verse)

long to the prevailing harmony for the measure or part of the measure. *Unstemmed note heads* are elaborative pitches—neighbor notes, passing tones, suspensions, triadic skips, and so forth. *Solid slurs* are analytic slurs; they connect elaborative pitches (such as neighbor notes) to structural pitches or group notes into a stepwise linear (passing) progression. *Dotted ties* connect notes that are anticipated to or suspended from the "structural attack" of the given note, that is, the moment when the note receives its harmonic support. The structural attack is a stemmed note; the anticipation or suspension is an unstemmed note head—this special notation indicates those moments when the structural counterpoint is offset by vocal anticipations or suspensions.

"Ice": Verses 1–4

The first verse establishes the key and the simple harmonic pattern that forms the basis of all six verses (example 12.1).[18] The basic pattern is i–VII–VI–V in F Aeolian in a parallel-fifth succession between bass (articulated by the guitar) and soprano (voice).[19] The overall movement is from tonic to dominant, creating an open-ended harmonic structure for the phrase, a half-cadence. The vocal line leads gradually down from scale degree $\hat{5}$ to $\hat{2}$, creating an expectation for melodic **closure** on scale degree $\hat{1}$. This coincides with the harmonic movement from i to V that creates an expectation for resolution to tonic. The basic progression of the phrase thus creates an unresolved dissonance or tension.

Lawrence Siegel (Charlottesville and London: University Press of Virginia, 1997). I am purposely avoiding Schenkerian notation in order to make this analysis more accessible to students who have not yet studied that analytic technique.

18. Although this paper is not intended as a theoretical guide to rock harmony, it will be useful to describe some general features of the language before I begin my analysis. First, rock music has a strong harmonic conception. That is, a harmonic progression forms the basis of each musical phrase; rock songs are usually organized such that the harmonic pattern is repeated, often with elaborations or variations. Second, the harmonic language borrows some common-practice tonal conventions, although the palette is expanded to include the use of modal scales and the harmonies that result from those modes. Third, the use of extended harmonies (beyond the simple triad) requires the analyst who is influenced by common-practice theory to adjust his or her definitions of dissonance. There are times when a seventh chord is used traditionally, as a dissonance that must resolve, but there are also nonfunctional dissonances, such as seventh chords, ninth chords, added sixth or fourth sonorities, which do not suggest a common-practice resolution or continuation. In my analysis, I argue for interpretation that is context-dependent, that is, in which dissonance is defined in relation to the surrounding treatment of harmony and voice leading.

19. For an explanation of the use of modes in rock, please see Moore, "The 'Flattened Seventh' in Rock," 49–50.

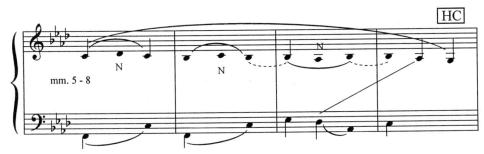

Example 12.2. Voice-leading graph, Verse 1, mm. 5–8

The voice-leading graph of verse 1, given in example 12.2, illustrates how McLachlan's performance develops further the inherent tension of this simple pattern. The contrapuntal "problem" explored in her musical phrase (example 12.2) is the offsetting of the parallel fifths (example 12.1) between melody and bass. The opening fifth, F to C, is clearly articulated between bass and soprano. As the bass holds onto its F in the next measure, the voice descends to B♭, but the consonant support for B♭ (E♭) does not arrive until the following bar. Once the VII chord is aligned in m. 7 (E♭ in the bass against B♭), the vocal B♭ is then sustained while the bass moves on to D♭ and then C. The voice does not move to its A♭ and G until after the bass has settled on the C. The A♭ in m. 8 "ought to" sound with the bass D♭ in m. 7, even though they are staggered. The remaining context of the song supports this interpretation: in verses 1 and 2, the A♭ does not arrive against the D♭, but in verses 3, 5, and 6, these pitches are vertically aligned.

Most of the harmonic movement and contrapuntal tension in verse 1 occurs in its two last measures (mm. 7 and 8). The rhythmic/metric distribution of the text also draws our attention to mm. 7 and 8, indicating that this is a purposeful musical strategy. It is worthwhile here to consider McLachlan's vocal line for the first verse, reproduced in example 12.3. Lines 1 and 2 of the lyrics each occupy one full measure of music. The rhythmic and metric structure is clear, with a downbeat emphasis that is logical for the text (for instance, "ice" in m. 5 and "underneath" in m. 6). The third and final line disrupts this regularity; it receives a more complex rhythmic/metric setting, as well as an emphasis of duration, as it occupies two full measures of music. The line features **syncopations, rests,** and varied note values. Indeed, line 3 follows closely on the heels of line 2 and enters at the very end of m. 6.

The harmony and voice leading, rhythmic and metric organization, and text distribution are calculated to underscore line 3 of the text. Line 3 of verse 1 suggests that there have been past cruelties ("the cold") but that they have been forgiven. This line constitutes an admission of her masochistic tendencies, and of pain, despite her claim that it "is lost, forgotten." In verse 2, line 3 also suggests that her desire has negative consequences; her desire is "forbidden." Her motivation for being submissive is identified in the third line of verse 3, "I know you liked the show." The third line of each of these verses explains the content of that verse and explores the poet's conflict between desire and power,

Example 12.3. Vocal line, Verse 1, mm. 20–23

Example 12.4. Voice-leading graph, Verse 4, mm. 20–23

relating the extent to which she is willing to yield power in order to satisfy a desire bound up in self-subordination and masochism.

In verse 4, the third line is pivotal in the presentation of the text, offering us, for the first time, a glimpse of the Other's vulnerability ("But oh, your soul is anchored") and a possible motivation for the protagonist's sustained passion. Verse 4 is also pivotal in articulating the musical structure, and once again, the latter part of the verse is underscored by the contrapuntal development. A voice-leading graph of verse 4 is given in example 12.4. The phrase begins with the same patter as verses 1 through 3, but in line 2 there is a melodic shift into the upper register. While the first three verses articulate a stepwise descent from C^4 down to G^3, now the C is abandoned and the upper register Ab^4 is established as the point of departure for a descending line to E. The linear progression from Ab down to E outlines a dissonant interval, a diminished fourth. The goal of the line, E♮, is the leading tone in the key of F, and this is its only vocal articulation in the entire song; indeed, the vocal E♮ is heard in contrast to the flattened seventh Eb that is heard frequently in the descending bass progression Eb–Db–C (VII–VI–V).[20] Not only does the leading tone inherently create a directional tension, in this case the effect is intensified because it is so seldom used in the song.

To sum up, by the end of the first four verse statements, the vocal line has presented two registral choices: the low C^4–G^3 descent, supported by the descending i–VII–VI–V movement (the parallel fifths), and then in verse 4, the higher register Ab^4–E♮ descent, supported by the same harmonic progression (but now in parallel thirds). These two melodic lines each suggest their own potential continuation. Both lines are initiated but are left unresolved, supported by dominant harmony. This poses an interpretive question for the listener: will the music ultimately resolve the lower line, to the tonic F^3, or will it resolve the upper line, to F^4? Given the context of the harmonic repetition, the musical tension that is being developed is heightened by the contrasting linear progressions in the lower and upper registers.

These two contrasting musical gestures are associated with a lyrical contrast: the poet's two modes of expression, rational criticism and passionate effusion. The opening verses offer a critical history of the painful relationship, expressed rationally and with self-reflection and control. In the fourth verse, however, a shift begins toward a more intense emotional expression upon which the chorus then builds. The poet's "rational" review of the relationship is placed in the lower registral descent from C^5 to G^3; the "passionate" shift at the end of verse 4 is accompanied by the upper registral span from Ab^4.

---

20. At the end of the third verse, the saxaphone anticipates this vocal E♮ with the gesture Ab–G–F–E–C over dominant harmony (immediately after the text "you liked the show").

The passionate thoughts are articulated in parallel thirds and indeed make the third of the dominant (the leading tone) the goal of the melodic descent; the rational thoughts, on the other hand, avoid the intensity of expression that comes with contrapuntal thirds, using instead the open sound of parallel fifths.

The contrast between rational criticism and passionate expression is next developed in the chorus. The textural contrast is signified musically by the contrast between low and high vocal registers as well as by the particular treatment (harmonic and contrapuntal) of the melodic progressions—the linear descents from A♭⁴ and from C⁴.

"Ice": Chorus

In contrast with the verse's narrative description of the relationship, the chorus is a more immediate and intense expression of her desire, its fulfillment, and the pain it brings. At the end of the chorus the poet attempts to return to the attitude of self-criticism or rational evaluation. In the last line, she comments on the situation with the thought "only a fool's here." The chorus thereby exposes the duality of her feelings—while invoking desire, she also criticizes the subservient role she plays in the relationship.

A voice-leading graph of the chorus is provided in example 12.5. The chorus comprises three statements of a pattern (the progression VI–V–i–[i6], or predominant–dominant–tonic), followed by a cadential gesture that is an incomplete statement of the pattern (VI–V). Similar to the bass, the voice repeats three times the pattern A♭⁴–G–A♭–C, but its incomplete fourth statement is transferred to the lower register A♭³–G (for the text "only a fool's here").

In this repeated melodic gesture A♭–G–A♭, harmonized by VI–V–i, the return to A♭ is noteworthy. The descent from A♭ to G suggests a continuation down to F, a resolution to scale degree 1̂. It is safe to assert that such a continuation is implied, not only by the conventionality of the progression 3̂–2̂–1̂ in association with the predominant–dominant–tonic resolution, but also by the context of the linear progression heard during verse 4, which established movement from A♭ down to the leading tone E♮, strongly suggesting the continuation to a tonic F. There, the cadence on dominant did not make such a continuation possible, but now in the chorus when a tonic resolution is offered, the voice avoids the descent to scale degree 1̂ and instead returns to the A♭. This return increases, rather than dissipates, tension: the A♭ holds the potential to initiate once again the melodic progression.

The intensification of the line through the movement back up to A♭ is important in the context of the song lyrics. The first statement of the repeated pattern sets the text "The only comfort is the moving of the river," a metaphorical admission of her motivation for remaining in the relationship. The notion of true comfort might have been represented by the resolving descent to F. Yet this "comfort" is not about security or resolution; rather, it is about her desire, which is intense despite the painful nature of the relationship. Instead of the resolving tonic, she thus returns to the pitch that initiated the linear progres-

Example 12.5. Voice-leading graph, Chorus, mm. 24–30

sion and that therefore has the potential for movement. We might anticipate that the renewed A♭ will now move to a resolution, but the line collapses into the low register, abandoning the tonal implications of the upper register.

The repeated pattern of the chorus manages to engage both of the registers that have been in play in this song. The stemmed pitches in example 12.5 show the dramatic shift from the upper A♭ to the lower C. These two pitches (and thus, the two registers) are—at the level of structural voice leading—unconnected. While the surface connection between the two is evident in the voice-leading graph, only the A♭ and C receive harmonic support. The voice-leading graph of m. 25 illustrates that over the prolonged tonic harmony (F), the voice descends by step from A♭ to F, and then moves through a modal gesture E♭–B♭–C (using the lowered seventh degree of F Aeolian).[21] The modal pattern has an interesting impact at this moment. A pattern that would have introduced E♮ (the leading tone) instead of E♭ might have been (potentially) the means by which a resolution to F could have occurred. Instead, however, we hear the E♭ leading down to C.

Although there is a great deal of emphasis on the upper register A♭^{4}, the chorus ultimately cadences in the lower octave, from A♭^{3} to G. The normative progression illustrates the chorus's emphasis on the upper register, dipping down to the low C but always returning to the high A♭^{4}. At the cadence, however, the voice remains in the lower register; indeed, it initiates a descending linear progression from the low A♭^{3}, although the progression ends, unresolved, on G^3. The text provides an explanation for this sudden shift in register at the end of the chorus. During the first three lines of the chorus, the protagonist is preoccupied with her desire, musically signified by the emphasis on the upper A♭. In the final line she shifts to a more critical perspective, with the thought "only a fool's here." This shift in perspective is represented by the musical shift to the low register. This gesture confirms what was already suggested by the music/text relations during the first four verses; the differentiation in the text between passion and reason is signified in the music by the opposition between the upper and lower registers, and by the specific treatment of the contrapuntal progressions that occur in these opposing registers.

"Ice": Verses 5 and 6

The chorus leads into a bridge, which in turn leads into the final pair of verses.[22] In these final verses, the poet explores her resistance to the Other's power. Verses 1 through 4 represent her as subservient within the masochistic relationship, and the chorus establishes desire as her motivation for sustaining the relationship. Even though she has the ability to criticize and evaluate the situation, the criticisms have served only to illuminate her own problematic role within the relationship. In verses 5 and 6 we now witness a strengthening of her anger, expressed in an outward criticism of the Other's power and sense of entitlement.

Verses 5 and 6 have the same basic voice-leading structure as verses 1 to 3. However, given the new direction of the text, we hear this music differently. As verses 5 and 6 reestablish the melodic descent from C^4 to G, it is heard in contrast to the higher register A♭^{4} established in verse 4 and the chorus. Her greater resistance and struggle for power occur within the lower register, thus confirming that musical space as the site for

---

21. The stepwise melodic gesture A♭–G–F in the repeated chorus pattern (mm. 25, 27, and 29) might be argued as a statement of the linear progression that I am listening for. However, the G and F in this case are not given individual harmonic support. The G is merely a passing note between A♭ and F.

22. I will not take the time here to discuss the bridge, despite the fact that it is a beautiful and fascinating moment in the song. Some interesting dissonances arise when a melodic saxophone line is offset against some sax chords, much as the vocal line is staggered against its harmonic backdrop elsewhere in the song.

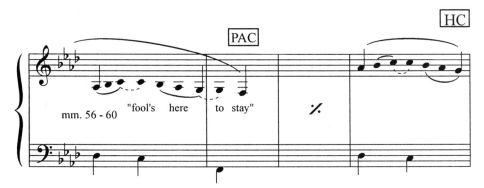

Example 12.6. Final chorus ending, mm. 56–60

her rational thoughts, now expressed as honesty and anger. To emphasize this shift in attitude, verse 5 is marked by a return to the sparse texture of voice and bass.

"Ice": Final Chorus

Following the expression of anger and resistance, the final chorus takes on new meaning. It reestablishes the registral conflict and the voice-leading tensions that result from the unresolved linear progression from A♭ to G (scale degrees $\hat{3}$ to $\hat{2}$). However, this chorus is altered to resolve that linear progression. A voice-leading graph of the final passage is given in example 12.6. The final line, "only a fool's here," is extended to conclude with the lyrical cadence "to stay." The low-register A♭^{3} and G now finally descend to F, with the dominant resolving to the tonic. Since we have been anticipating a structural melodic arrival on F throughout the song, the line is repeated to confirm the resolution. The poet thus concludes her thought in the lower register, the register associated with her rational/critical expression.

What does this textual and musical resolution mean for our interpretation of the poet's struggle? The admission that the "fool is here *to stay*" is a resignation that, despite her efforts to resist, she will continue to endure the situation. The musical choice to resolve the lower register F suggests that this admission is made with her full reasoning capacity. However, when this resolution occurs, despite its anticipated arrival, it is not particularly satisfying. The implications of her decision to persist in the relationship are ominous: the song's narrative has established the negative consequences of such a decision.

The musical continuation from this cadence confirms my interpretation that the cadential resolution is ultimately unsatisfying, that it is in fact marred by the threat of potential disruption. As her final musical gesture, the voice repeats—with one significant alteration—the unresolved version of the cadence, that is, the version that does *not* descend to tonic with the text ("to stay"). The alteration to which I refer is a registral shift from the low A♭^{3}–G^3 to the higher A♭^{4}–G^4, a change that I underscore as significant given the meaningful opposition of these contrasting registers throughout the song.

The final exposure of the very musical issue that was associated with the poet's struggle between desire and reason confirms that McLachlan means to interrogate the situation invoked in the song text, that is, the situation of a protagonist in a subordinate position to her desired Other. We have also to recall that McLachlan herself positions this song within the context of the serious social problem of young female prostitution. At the close of this carefully wrought musical narrative, at which point the unresolved version of the cadence is given the ultimate position and privilege of concluding the song, McLachlan represents her protagonist as continuing to struggle and therefore also continuing to resist. For feminist evaluation, the message of the song might be mixed. The exposed relationship is disturbing because of the unequal distribution of power, and in the end, there is no particular victory. Yet there is clearly self-reflection and resistance, and concomitantly the recognition that such a situation deserves critical attention.

The analysis presented here has illustrated that the musical structure of this song—specifically, its voice-leading structure—is an important vehicle for the communication of its textual meaning. Although my goal was to illustrate intersections between text and music, the reader should note that I began by considering each domain on its own, in order to gather analytic data thoroughly enough to do justice to each domain: the lyrical analysis went beyond literal poetic content to consider the specifics of the text within a broader social context, using McLachlan's own account of the song to determine that context; similarly, in the musical domain, specific harmonic and melodic events were not merely identified (labeled) but rather were considered for their connection to music-theoretical conventions and the expectations that derive from such conventions. Once familiar with the broader implications of the lyrical and musical content, it was then possible to make interpretive assertions about specific events in the song. The musical narrative as expressed in the harmony and voice leading was checked against the lyrical narrative. Again, the goal there was to go beyond claims to mere content associations between text and music and instead to integrate such claims with a more general understanding of the implied textual and musical conventions. Such an integration of song expression and conventional structure allows an interpreter to conduct a close reading of a chosen song and to unveil its social meaning, ultimately the aim of any analyst.

FURTHER READING

Burns, Lori, and Mélisse Lafrance. *Disruptive Divas: Feminism, Identity, and Popular Music.* New York: Routledge, 2002.

Covach, John, and Graeme Boone, eds. *Understanding Rock: Essays in Musical Analysis.* New York: Oxford University Press, 1997.

Everett, Walter, ed. *Expression in Pop-Rock Music.* New York: Garland Press, 2000.

Hisama, Ellie. "Voice, Race, and Sexuality in the Music of Joan Armatrading." In *Audible Traces: Gender, Identity, and Music*, edited by Elaine Barkin and Lydia Hamessley. Zürich and Los Angeles: Cariciofoli Verlagshaus, 1999, 115–130.

Moore, Allan. *Rock: The Primary Text.* Buckingham: Open University Press, 1993.

———, ed. *Analyzing Popular Music.* Cambridge and New York: Cambridge University Press, 2003.

~13~

In Search of Purcell's Dido

Janet Schmalfeldt

Since the publication of her book on Berg's *Wozzeck*, Janet Schmalfeldt (Tufts University) has especially focused her attention on issues of musical form. She is an active pianist and has also written about the relationship of analysis to performance.

As the present essay illustrates, Schmalfeldt advocates providing a historical context for music analysis. "Dido's Lament," from Henry Purcell's *Dido and Aeneas,* has long been a favored topic in academic courses on both the history and the analysis of Western tonal music. Schmalfeldt analyzes the Lament from both literary and recent historical perspectives.[1] Her essay considers how Purcell's seventeenth-century ground-bass techniques help to create the formal basis for one of the most eloquent moments in operatic literature. Like other essays in this unit, her study reveals the remarkable ability of composers to capture the nuances and complex meanings of poetic and dramatic texts.

"Remember me, but ah! forget my fate." With these famous last words, first sung in England in the late seventeenth century, Henry Purcell's Dido presents one of the most unforgettable farewells in the history of opera. As the ultimate irony within an acutely ironic tale, the heart-rending music of "Dido's Lament" makes it simply impossible not to remember this Dido or her fate. But who is it that we cannot forget? How did Purcell and his librettist Nahum Tate want us to remember Dido's character, and what might an analysis of her music tell us about this?

These questions are not meant to be **rhetorical,** nor can anything approaching definitive answers be reached. Certain ambiguities in Purcell's *Dido and Aeneas* as a whole would seem forever to confound attempts to know his Dido; and, for the many dedicated scholars of Purcell's work, a multitude of extramusical factors—literary, historical, sociological, even political—have continually required consideration. Here is a case, like so many, where an analysis of "the music itself," though rewarding in itself, can become immensely enriched when placed within the bigger contextual picture—in this case, the idea of Dido that evolved over many centuries on the way to becoming Purcell's Dido as por-

---

Some reminders: (1) all words in **bold** are defined in the glossary; (2) full citations for incomplete references are found in the selected bibliography; (3) the authors use their preferred notational system (e.g., Roman numeral, form label, and register notation). Most essays, but not this one, denote register by middle C as C[4].—Ed.

1. A more extended version of this essay may be found in "In Search of Dido," *Journal of Musicology* 18, no. 4 (2001): 584–613. Also note that the essay in this volume by McCreless (chapter 11) examines a heroine's tragic finale as well: Isolde's Transfiguration in *Tristan und Isolde.*—Ed.

trayed at the end of her life. My approach to an analysis of "Dido's Lament" begins, then, with a consideration of some historical and literary background. In this way I hope to suggest the considerable range of possibilities that Tate and Purcell faced when they chose to create Dido anew.

Let us briefly consider two of the earliest Didos—one probably a genuine historical figure, the other a fictional character. According to Greek and early Roman legend, the "real" Dido was a princess of Tyre, in Phoenicia, who became the founder and queen of ancient Carthage. This Dido was especially remembered for her chastity; devoted solely to her people and to the memory of her slain husband, she took her own life as a sacrifice to save her city from the unwanted consequences of a forced second marriage.[2] A second Dido, created by the Roman poet Virgil (70–19 BC), lives much further back in time, in about the twelfth century BC, when, in the aftermath of the Trojan War, the great Aeneas escapes from the victorious Greeks to fulfill his destiny in Italy as the founder of the Roman race. In the First and Fourth Books of Virgil's epic poem, the *Aeneid*, our second Dido emerges as again the widowed Carthaginian queen, though now the one upon whose shores Aeneas has been driven by the fates. His mother, the goddess Venus, is suspicious of Dido's hospitality, and so she determines to destroy her by enflaming her heart with a passion for Aeneas that is uncontrollable. Thus does the chaste "historical" Dido become the sexually overwrought queen of Virgil's *Aeneid*—an unknowing victim, to be sure, but also a temptress.

Ironically, the demise of Virgil's Dido begins when her own protector—Jupiter's wife and sister, Juno—devises a plan whereby Aeneas and Dido will go hunting together, be diverted into a cave for shelter from a thunderstorm, consummate their love, and then enter into a royal alliance. When word reaches the great Jupiter himself that Aeneas has thrown duty to the winds, has "reveled all the winter long" with Dido,[3] and is now even helping her people build their city walls, Jupiter sends Mercury posthaste to tell Aeneas that he *must* leave for Italy, right away. Shocked by Jupiter's admonishment, Aeneas instantly determines to set sail. "But what, oh what, was he to do? What words dare he use to approach the queen in all her passion?"[4]

Predictably, Aeneas does not find the right words, nor is he willing to try more than once. It appears that there has been a gross misunderstanding about what happened in the cave: Dido "called it marriage, using the word to cover her guilt"; Aeneas claims never to have "entered into that contract."[5] No words can console the outraged and heartbroken Dido, who realizes now that she has made a fool of herself for love, that she has neglected her responsibilities as queen, that she has been profoundly betrayed, and that there is nothing she can do to regain her honor or her integrity—nothing to do but die. When her pleas, threats, and, finally, vengeful curses fail to elicit even a single last word from Aeneas, Dido deceives her sister into building a pyre upon which to burn every last vestige of him; in fact, it is Dido herself who will climb to the top of the pyre and fall upon Aeneas's sword. For Virgil, Dido *must* die: she stands for a corruptive force—a wild, alien Other, whose suicide might even be interpreted as a sacrifice to the gods so that they will some-

---

2. What was once the Carthage of antiquity is now a residential suburb to the northeast of modern Tunis, on the north coast of Africa. For early accounts of the historical Dido, see James Davidson, "Domesticating Dido: History and Historicity," in *A Woman Scorn'd: Responses to the Dido Myth*, ed. Michael Burden (London: Faber and Faber, 1998), 65–88.

3. Virgil, *The Aeneid*, [poetic] trans. Robert Fitzgerald (New York: Random House, 1981), 102.

4. Virgil, *The Aeneid*, [prose] trans. David West (London: Penguin Books, 1990), 89.

5. Ibid., 86, 91.

day help Carthage take revenge upon Rome.[6] But Dido now also becomes an archetype of the abandoned woman.

Virgil's tale of Dido as reviewed here provides the basis for countless retellings of her story, including the one by Purcell and Tate. Tensions—ambiguities?—within Virgil's own narrative have continued, however, to invite multiple, and often sharply conflicting, views of her character. On the one hand, for all its verve and ravishing beauty, the *Aeneid* can easily be read as a flagrant case of moral and political propaganda.[7] Virgil's fiction of female instability and abandonment serves a didactic purpose while tapping into "the antifeminism . . . at the Augustan court" in Virgil's day.[8] On the other hand, when we first meet Virgil's Dido, she appears as Aeneas's *equal*, if not his superior, in a number of important respects. Both are widowed and in exile; both are obeying commands to found a new city, but Dido is way ahead of Aeneas in accomplishing that task. Virgil's Dido is a beautiful, beloved, and genuinely effective queen—just, industrious, knowledgeable, intelligent, and articulate; so gracious and generous is Dido that she invites Aeneas's men to settle in Carthage on an equal footing with her people—and this even before she has seen the princely Aeneas.

A dreadful irony emerges here. Like Aeneas, Dido has been destined to rule. But she *never learns that Venus has tricked her*—never discovers that she has been poisoned by love, only to serve as a detour in the march of history toward Rome. Virgil seems concerned to drive this point home: the very first thing he tells us about Dido is that she is "all unknowing / As to the fated future."[9] That Mercury twice comes to censure Aeneas, while *no god* ever warns Dido, is of course an essential element of Virgil's plot. But it also suggests considerable ambivalence on his part. He sanctions Dido's fate but then seems to lament it. He also portrays her frenzied love and her tragic death with language that captures an intimacy and anguish never before achieved in Western literature. By contrast, his Aeneas has struck more than one critic as "a cold fish, and finally a cad"; "he has no self, only his destiny."[10]

With the spread of Christianity in the West and the decline of the Roman Empire comes the need to reinterpret Virgil's pagan epic so that it would exemplify Christian virtues. An obvious strategy for Christianizing Virgil's queen begins with the simple reminder that "the true," historical Dido was chaste. Although a two-Dido thesis—chaste versus unchaste—remains dominant to this day, by the early sixteenth century the number and variety of different versions of Dido's tale reached an all-time high; and nearly every conceivable type of narrator—"commentators, allegorists, editors, homilists, storytellers, poets, painters, illustrators, and tapestry-makers"[11]—had by then gotten in on the act.

---

6. In other words, Dido's curses upon Aeneas were undoubtedly meant by Virgil to foreshadow the series of three brutal wars—the Punic Wars—waged between Carthage and Rome from the mid-third to the mid-second century BC. See Davidson, "Domesticating Dido," 77–78.

7. Whether pressured or not to do so, Virgil—the poet laureate of the Roman emperor Augustus Caesar—recasts the Homeric epic to accomplish for Rome what Homer's *Iliad* and *Odyssey* had done for the Greeks: Virgil creates "a legendary past for Rome, a great myth that would seem to predict, ordain, and bless the new imperial state"; "however you look at it, he performed an outrageous act of appropriation." David Denby, *Great Books: My Adventures with Homer, Rousseau, Woolf, and Other Indestructible Writers of the Western World* (New York: Simon and Schuster, 1996), 147.

8. John Watkins, *The Specter of Dido: Spenser and Virgilian Epic* (New Haven: Yale University Press, 1995), 6.

9. Virgil, *The Aeneid*, trans. Fitzgerald, 14.

10. Denby, *Great Books*, 149.

11. Watkins, *The Spector of Dido*, 30, 51.

As we move now into the late seventeenth century, where Purcell and Tate make their entrance, we must pause to acknowledge that we cannot be sure just *when* they composed their *Dido and Aeneas*, or *for whom*. The earliest known source—a single copy of Tate's libretto—gives no date; but scholars have held that the performance it confirms must have occurred early in 1689.[12] The problem of dating *Dido and Aeneas* has hampered speculation as to whether a political reason might account for why, after 1689, the work languished in near-complete obscurity until 1700. And no one has yet determined why the earliest surviving score of *Dido* dates from *after* 1777. In short, what has become Purcell's most beloved work—an ever-popular staple of the operatic repertoire—barely escaped obscurity in its own day; and the music that we are about to consider owes its survival to what may be a corrupt and incomplete source.

Just how well did Purcell and Tate know Virgil's Dido, or other Didos of the past? Here, at least, there is little mystery. Every seventeenth-century English schoolboy would have been expected to read the *Aeneid*—in Latin. In fact, Tate based his libretto upon an earlier play of his own (from 1678), in which his main characters were Virgil's Dido and Aeneas in all but name. Perhaps it was the opportunity, or necessity, to write a tremendously compressed version of Dido's tale—a performance of Purcell's complete opera lasts less than an hour—that helped Tate to return to a *Dido and Aeneas*. Virgil's story is the one that Tate and Purcell's opera assumed its audience would know; thus it is through Tate's *divergences* from Virgil, like those of so many earlier writers, that audiences then and now might especially be expected to discover what is unique about Purcell's Dido.

That this *Dido and Aeneas* will be fundamentally about Dido, rather than Aeneas, is clear from the outset. Act I finds Dido at center stage in her palace, accompanied by her train, as performed by Purcell's chorus, and by her sister qua confidante, Belinda.[13] We understand soon enough that Aeneas has arrived on Dido's shores; but we hear a full-scale Lully-like French overture, an air for Belinda with a choral conclusion, a profoundly melancholy air for Dido herself, and then four more discrete sections (rehearsal nos. 4–7 in the Norton Critical Score; see n. 13) before Aeneas finally makes his first, by now anticlimactic, appearance onstage. And it is Dido's present plight, rather than Aeneas's, that serves as the topic throughout this stretch—that is, until the last moments of Act I. But her plight is not completely clear. Since Tate's libretto never once suggests that Venus has impassioned Dido, we must at first guess why Dido "is pressed, / With torment not to be confess'd"—why she tells Belinda that she languishes till her "grief is known, / Yet would not have it guess'd."

Belinda and the chorus have no trouble guessing that Dido has fallen in love with "the Trojan guest," and so they urge her to marry him, thereby securing Carthage and achieving happiness (rehearsal no. 5). Dido fears that she pities Aeneas too much (no. 6);

---

12. Amazing as this may seem, it has long been assumed that the first person to perform the demanding role of Purcell's Dido must have been a schoolgirl; the title page of Tate's libretto announces a performance of this "Opera" by the "Young Gentlewomen" of a boarding school in Chelsea, a fashionable suburb of London. Over the last decade, newly discovered documents have convinced some Purcell scholars that the boarding-school production was probably a *revival* performance of a work whose premiere had already taken place earlier, in the more prestigious setting of the court. But the question of whose court, and in what political milieu—Charles II's (d. 1685), the Catholic James II's (ousted from the English throne in December 1688), or the Protestant William and Mary's—remains unanswered.

13. An authoritative critical edition of Tate's libretto and Purcell's music is provided in *Henry Purcell: Dido and Aeneas, an Opera*, ed. Curtis Price (New York: W. W. Norton, 1986); with permission of Novello and Co., this edition reproduces the Purcell Society Score, edited by Margaret Laurie and Thurston Dart. All subsequent citations from Tate's libretto and Purcell's music will be drawn from Price's Norton Critical Score.

taking this to mean that she fears she *loves* him too much, the chorus rushes to reassure her: "The hero loves as well as you" (no. 7). It is only when Aeneas enters to woo Dido that we find the clue, I think, as to why Dido's love for Aeneas has brought her to grief. Whether she senses that Aeneas does *not* "love as well" as she loves him, this Dido is historically well-informed(!)—or, rather, she has a strong intuition about her meager role in Aeneas's destiny: whereas Virgil's queen was "all unknowing / As to the fated future," the very first words of Tate and Purcell's Dido to Aeneas, and her *only* words to him in Act I, are: "Fate forbids what you pursue" (no. 8).

Only a cursory synopsis of the opera can be continued here; but it will take little time for readers of Tate's short libretto to note that, from this point forward, a new twist on Aeneas's fate unfolds. In Virgil's *Aeneid*, the gods themselves forbid Aeneas to remain with Dido. In Tate's tale, the gods play no such role; Aeneas falls instead for the deceit of an evil "Sorceress" and her "trusty elf" disguised as Mercury—Tate's most blatantly un-Virgilian inventions (no. 28, Act II). Thus when Aeneas tries to impart to Dido the "gods' decree" that they must part, we know (but Aeneas doesn't) that his words reek of the cruelest irony, and we cannot but take Dido's side in the hair-raising quarrel that ensues (no. 35, Act III). Damaging his image beyond repair, Aeneas suddenly promises— too late for Dido—to stay; she threatens to fly to her death if he doesn't leave immediately, and this seems to push him over the edge. His exit is stunningly abrupt; but her fury subsides the instant he leaves the stage. Left alone with her grief, and perhaps with a deep sense of shame, Dido knows that "Death must come when he is gone."

From the dark, low tessitura of Dido's perfect authentic cadence in D minor, at the end of no. 35, the chorus now lifts us gently into higher ranges in B♭ major and, like a Greek chorus, aspires to the wisdom of a proverb: "Great minds against themselves conspire, / And shun the cure they most desire" (no. 36). We might debate the applicability of this comment to Dido and Aeneas; but there could never be any question as to the exquisite effect of Purcell's choralelike sostenuto setting, a mere thirteen bars long: "It provides a release of tension . . . an outside point of balance from which to gauge Dido's grief . . . and a great passage of time, a lifetime of decision for Dido."[14] By its midpoint, the chorus completes a move from B♭ into its closing key of G minor—the key of "Dido's Lament" proper and her demise. But, as if to reflect upon that "lifetime" of experience she has suffered just since Aeneas's arrival in Carthage, Dido now returns to the tonal region in which Purcell's Act I began, the key in which she first told us of her grief—C minor (no. 3). Our search for Purcell's Dido brings us to the beginning of her end. Let us consider her final moments in detail.

Now that Aeneas has left, Dido finds herself almost alone onstage; only the faithful Belinda stands by Dido's side, and it is thus to her alone that Dido seems to speak. Here is the final seven-line stanza that Tate composes for Dido. Its fourth line emphasizes that only death can replace Aeneas, the now-absent "Trojan guest." Some have said that its fifth line doesn't properly scan, but Purcell clearly knew what to do (for one thing, he added the word "may"):

Thy hand, Belinda; darkness shades me,
On thy bosom let me rest.
More I would but death invades me,
Death is now a welcome guest.

---

14. Joseph Kerman, "[A Glimmer from the Dark Ages]," in *Henry Purcell: Dido and Aeneas, an Opera*, 225. (Extracted from Kerman's *Opera As Drama* [New York: Vintage Books, 1956].)

When I am laid in earth [may] my wrongs create
No trouble in thy breast,
Remember me, but ah! forget my fate.

Probably taking his cue from that longer fifth line, as well as from the clear *abab* rhyme scheme of the opening quatrain, Purcell divides Tate's stanza into two parts, using the quatrain to open with a recitative-like, yet measured, declamatory first section. As shown at example 13.1, only the harpsichord and the continuo bass accompany Dido within this introductory passage (no. 37); having provided only a bass line with its figures, Purcell entrusts his harpsichordist freely to improvise an accompaniment that accords with the figures and the somber mood.[15]

My harmonic analysis in the score at example 13.1 reads this passage as genuinely modulatory, thus tonally unstable. Phrygian half-cadences at mm. 5 and 9 mark the endings of Dido's second and fourth lines,[16] thus reinforcing the rhyme "rest-guest." But the first half-cadence (at m. 5) confirms the opening key, C minor, whereas the second—on V in G minor—achieves the key in which the rest of Purcell's opera will remain. The C-major chord at m. 7 might yet be heard as a Picardy transformation in C, but after this point we leave the key of C minor forever—there will be no turning back. What gives palpable coherence to this fluid but ultimately conclusive pull from one key into another is the skeletal structure of Dido's melody over the course of the complete passage—a slow, step-by-step descent from her initial C♮ (C²) to her arrival, at the word "guest," on the D♮ (D¹) a minor seventh below. The lengthened stems that I have superimposed upon the tones participating in Dido's descent propose that her line becomes chromatic at the point, within m. 7, where her tonal center begins to shift unequivocally toward G minor; my analysis of her submetric embellishing tones—neighbors (N), passing tones (+), and suspensions (figured)—substantiates that view, as do the two broad *voice exchanges* between her line and the bass, as shown at mm. 3–4 and 7–8.[17] I further propose that Dido's opening gesture here—the neighbor-motion C–B–C—urges us to remember that same gesture when it appeared both as the opening bass motion within the overture (example 13.2, m. 4) and as the **head bass motive** of Dido's air in Act I (no. 3), immediately imitated by Dido and later fully appropriated by her (example 13.3). Finally, there can be no question that her long, slow, fundamentally stepwise descent metaphorically summarizes her inevitable descent toward the grave over the span of Purcell's three acts.

Like Dido's first air and like two other numbers in the opera (nos. 13 and 25), "Dido's Lament" proper demonstrates a technique for which Purcell might best be known as a master, the type called "composition on a ground bass." Whether as an instrumental or an accompanied vocal work, the ground-bass composition is literally "based upon," or "grounded on," a single bass-line pattern, or melody, that will be continually repeated in the bass over the course of the complete movement. Also called a *basso ostinato*, a ground-

---

15. The figured-bass realization given in example 13.1 is the one provided in the Norton Critical Score. Purcell most probably served as his own harpsichordist when the work was first performed.

16. In tonal music the Phrygian half-cadence is the one in which the dominant as goal is approached in the bass by a semitone from above, generally via the progression iv⁶–V in minor, with the soprano voice moving in contrary motion from $\hat{4}$ to $\hat{5}$; the bass motion thus invokes the characteristic semitone relationship between the first and the second scale degree in the Phrygian mode.

17. A "voice exchange" expands a chord by means of an interchange of two of its tones within a pair of voices interacting in contrary motion. Thus at mm. 3–4 in example 13.1 the root-position iv chord in C minor expands to become a iv⁶ chord through the exchange of its tones A♭ and F♮ in the bass and Dido's voice. As a result, her A♭, now transferred to the bass, remains in effect until she descends to G♮ at m. 5

Example 13.1. Purcell, *Dido and Aeneas*, Act III (no. 37): "Dido's Lament"—declamatory introduction

bass line is often a regular four bars in length, as is the case with all three earlier grounds in *Dido*, and its ending tends to express an authentic cadence (endings on the dominant are also possible).

Unlike those earlier grounds, the bass line in "Dido's Lament," shown at example 13.4, directly invokes a well-established Italian "lament" tradition, initiated by Monteverdi and fully formalized in the operas of his successors by the 1640s: it had become com-

Example 13.2. *Dido and Aeneas*, Act I (No. 1): Overture, mm. 1–8

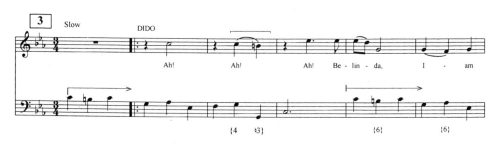

Example 13.3. *Dido and Aeneas*, Act I (No. 3): Dido's first air, mm. 1–8

monplace to set texts expressing lament to minor-mode arias with ground basses that feature a descent, often chromatic, through the *upper **tetrachord*** of the scale—that is, a descent through the four-note span from $\hat{1}$ to $\hat{5}$.[18]

Purcell's bass opens with precisely this descending-tetrachord pattern in G minor; it closes with a cadential progression that carries the descent all the way to the tonic in the lower octave. Together, the two segments of the ground—its opening and its closing—yield a notably irregular five-bar phrase; this length is not unusual for Purcell, but it is distinct from his earlier four-bar grounds and rich with compositional potential. With the change of meter and tempo, from 4/4 to 3/2, the initial, thrice-presented, short-long rhythm of the ground establishes new metric stability while at the same time creating a halting effect; conversely, the new rhythm within the cadential segment seems to impel the ground to its cadential goal. Two of the earlier grounds (nos. 3 and 13) demonstrate that ground-bass patterns can occasionally be **transposed** to effect modulations into the dominant; by contrast, the ground of "Dido's Lament" will remain immutable. Her air is about to assume a large-scale two-part form, followed by a coda; each of the two parts will be repeated—the first part taking an exact repetition, the second part ever so subtly varied, thus written out. What binds the two parts plus **coda** into one sustained and monumental whole are the inexorable repetitions of the five-bar ground-bass line, heard eleven times altogether, without a single alteration.

A cadential **elision** (indicated with ⟷) marks the end of the introductory statement of the ground and Dido's simultaneous beginning at m. 5 (example 13.4).[19] A string choir

Example 13.4. *Dido and Aeneas*, Act III (No. 38): "Dido's Lament" proper

(continued)

---

18. See Ellen Rosand, "The Descending Tetrachord: An Emblem of Lament," *The Musical Quarterly* 65 (1979): 346–59.

19. I use the term "cadential **elision**" to describe cases where the harmonic goal of a cadential progression simultaneously marks both the end of the phrase and the beginning of the next; in these cases, ending and beginning merge within a single moment in time, and what has thus been "elided" is actually the distinction between the two. For more on elision, see my "Cadential Processes: The Evaded Cadence and the 'One More Time' Technique."

Example 13.4. (*Continued*)

(presumed to have been composed and notated in full by Purcell) also enters here to support her; and now it will become clear that a ground-bass line not only serves as a repeated bass melody but also necessarily projects and controls a repeated harmonic progression. Indeed, a standard progression had by Purcell's time long become associated with the descending-tetrachord pattern (see example 13.4, mm. 5–10), and I shall describe it as a Descending-Step Sequence: with tonic harmony as the point of departure, each chromatic step in the bass supports a $\frac{6}{3}$-chord (V^6–v^6; IV^6–iv^6), the third of these embellished by a 7–6 suspension; taken together, the $\frac{6}{3}$-chords create a contrapuntal, sequential passing motion from the tonic to the dominant—in Purcell's case, the nonca-

Example 13.4. (*Continued*)

(*continued*)

dential dominant seventh chord on the bass note D♮. Purcell then draws upon a second convention—the traditional cadential progression i⁶–ii⁶–V–I—as his motion to an authentic cadence in the strings. Excepting just one awesome moment in the second part of the air, it can categorically be said that the harmonic progression just described fundamentally accompanies every repetition of the ground. In the face of such harmonic and bass-melodic constancy, it goes without saying that certain strongly opposing musical forces must be placed in the service of creating variation, providing contrast, and avoid-

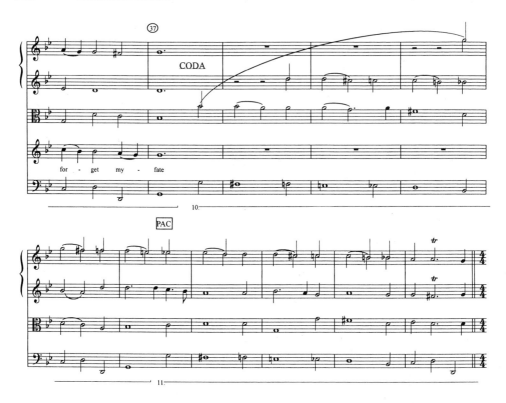

Example 13.4. (*Continued*)

ing monotony. In vocal ground-bass pieces, the vocal part itself creates the opposition. Put simply, in this case every aspect of contrast within the continuity will depend on Dido.

Since her opening phrase begins precisely at the point where the first statement of the ground ends, these two essential parts—bass and vocal soprano—fall out-of-phase with one another from the very outset: the second statement of the ground lags behind Dido's opening by one full bar. As the ground now begins its second chromatic descent, Dido's line has already started to do just the opposite: it is striving upward, in arduous stages, through the *lower pentachord* of the G-minor scale—that is, over the span from $\hat{1}$ to $\hat{5}$—but becoming delayed on $\hat{2}$ by a 4–3 suspension at m. 6, only to achieve $\hat{4}$ and then sink backward to the leading tone, F♯, at the conclusion of her words "When I am laid in earth" (in example 13.4 at mm. 5–8, see the lengthened stems and the unfolding of the tritone C–F♯ as superimposed on Dido's line). Her pause on the leading tone at m. 8 could well have accommodated a genuine half-cadence—indeed, it seems to be begging for this momentary cadential relief (Dido as singer *must* take a breath after the F♯). But the seventh (C♮ in Vln. II) within the ground's V^7 chord cancels the effect of a half-cadence because of its urge to resolve downward within the forthcoming i^6; and so the ground presses on toward its only genuine cadential goal—the tonic at m. 10. In fact, Dido's C♮, her $\hat{4}$ at m. 7, still in effect as the seventh in m. 8, should also want to pull downward to the B♭ in the i^6 chord; thus she achieves her apex—the D♮ as $\hat{5}$—only by dint of "reaching over" for it when the i^6 arrives at m. 8.[20]

Now, however, Dido determines to go higher—to the neighbor E♭ ($\hat{6}$) at m. 8, which she will strive to regain at mm. 10–11. But with the words "May my wrongs create no trouble," the tension between her line and the ground becomes extreme. Any self-respecting singer will affirm that Dido cannot rest on the crucial verb of her plea—"create"; nor would it be professionally acceptable for her to take an obvious breath before completing her thought—"create no trouble." And yet, at precisely the point where Dido reaches the word "create," the ground reaches its cadential goal. As Dido now rises to her E♭, it is as if she must *will herself* to overcome the inertia of the ground's cadence and, in doing so, to cancel its effect. Coinciding as it must with the F♯ in the ground's third chromatic descent, her E♭ on the word "trouble" at m. 11 gains indescribable poignancy. She fully relinquishes this dissonant diminished-seventh only after delaying and embellishing its resolution as a 7–6 suspension; but then, as if exhausted from her effort (and badly in need of a breath), she sequentially repeats the "no trouble" gesture as she now presses for her potential half-cadence at m. 13. Here again, the V^7 chord would seem to rule against a half-cadence, and so the ground moves onward to its authentic cadence; but the cadential elision at m. 15 (first ending) simply initiates a repetition of the entire process thus far. When that same cadential elision is achieved at the end of the repetition, the second part of the lament begins, and Dido enters her final stage.

However one chooses to interpret the spare final lines of "Dido's Lament," few would likely disagree that only the most sympathetic interpretation of Virgil's Dido could have produced the Dido of Tate and Purcell who will now say farewell. Gone is Virgil's blaz-

---

20. Technically speaking, "reaching over" (*Übergreifung*) involves the transfer of an inner voice to a position above a soprano tone that should (or will) descend by step. For an introduction to the concept, see Allen Cadwallader and David Gagné, *Analysis of Tonal Music: A Schenkerian Approach* (New York: Oxford University Press, 1998), 145–49. The "reaching-over" feature of Dido's ascent from $\hat{1}$ to $\hat{5}$ is not shown in Richard S. Parks's extensive series of voice-leading graphs for "Dido's Lament"; but these graphs provide an excellent overview of the lament's voice-leading structure; see Parks, *Eighteenth-Century Counterpoint and Tonal Structure* (Englewood Cliffs, N.J.: Prentice-Hall, 1984), 307–309, 186–88.

ing pyre; gone are the rage, the madness, and the vengefulness; even gone is the suicide: with no indication whatsoever in the libretto that Dido holds a sword or a knife, we are left to imagine that she is simply about to die of a broken heart. But she lingers to plead with us, even though the ongoing ground-bass repetitions would seem relentlessly to urge her toward her end. As she now twice declaims her plea—with each "Remember me!" insisting upon her hard-won $\hat{5}$ from m. 8—the string choir at last reacts as if in gentle response to her anguish; their "sighing" suspension gestures at mm. 18 and 20 each give her a full three half-rests for breathing and preparing to go on. But then the conflict between Dido's phrase structure and that of the ground reaches its climax: the ground's cadence at m. 22 ignores Dido's melisma on the word "Ah!"; and its initiating V^6 chord at m. 23 denies her a half-cadence on the word "fate." There is nothing left for Dido to do but repeat her entire plea, this time soaring to her highest tone—the majestic G♮ at m. 24—and then descending diatonically, step by step, through the full octave of the natural G-minor scale, finally to achieve (at m. 27) the first and only **closure** thus far that coincides with the ground's cadence.[21]

Performers of the role of Dido are invited by Purcell to search their own souls for how to portray her as she now repeats the second part of her Lament. Does Dido find new courage and greater vocal strength in these last moments, or has she nearly exhausted what remains of her will to live? Should her final high G♮, at m. 34, be the emotional climax of her Lament, or will her approach to it now be more subdued? The score is open-ended; but perhaps Purcell offers one wisp of a clue. Because Dido and the ground actually end together at m. 27, they must also begin together—for the first time—when the repetition begins at m. 28. But this means that the alignment of their parts has shifted (compare mm. 17–20 with mm. 28–30): Dido's "Remember me!" statements now lag behind the ground, relative to their alignment when we first heard them. Since the ground must remain immutable, Dido and the ground will end together again *only* if Dido's part "catches up" with the ground, thus regaining its original alignment. This is what happens at m. 30. Here, by eliminating the three half-rests in Dido's part from mm. 19–20—that is, by reducing these to a mere quarter-rest—Purcell regains the alignment of m. 21 at m. 31; from this point forward, his repetition becomes one measure shorter, but everything that follows will proceed as before to the cadence at m. 37. On the other hand, Dido now has less time for catching her breath at m. 30; and her necessarily quicker approach to "But ah!" at m. 31 might well be interpreted as conveying a greater urgency on her part. Dido's time is running out. Whether she makes one last heroic crescendo to her final high G, we sense, when she concludes, that Purcell's magnificent coda ushers in her death.

Here, one by one, the viola, the second violin, and then the first violin successively rise, each registrally "reaching over" one another until Dido's high G is regained in her honor. Her descent through the full octave is then recapitulated, but this time as slowly as possible over the span of the ground's final two statements: its fateful chromatically descending tetrachord now pervades the descent in the first violin, every step of which becomes chromatic. The coda's elided final cadence at m. 47 carries us without pause into what one writer has described as "an even greater achievement than Dido's aria"[22]; as if stunned by the tragedy it has just witnessed, Purcell's final chorus withdraws from

---

21. Dido's octave descent calls at m. 25 for the natural, rather than the raised, $\hat{7}$—F♮ as it leads to E♭; and this in turn produces the one moment in which the ground-bass progression must diverge from its basic scheme. Purcell's ingenious solution—the acutely intense double-suspension chord with which he harmonizes Dido's melismatic "Ah!" at m. 25—seems well beyond its time in affective power; perhaps this is because, for just one split second, the chord blesses Dido with the tenderness of a major triad (the mediant in first inversion).

22. Curtis Price, "Purcell: *Dido and Aeneas*," in *Henry Purcell: Dido and Aeneus, un Opera*, 17.

the chromaticism of her insistent ground, instead reiterating her own *diatonic* descent through the octave from high G and then paying hushed, solemn tribute to her "soft and gentle" heart. But there's a final irony here: the very Cupids who will now scatter roses on Dido's tomb, keep watch over it, and "never, never part" were last invoked at the end of Act I (no. 9) when, in a much different mood, the chorus joyously proclaimed, "Cupid only throws the dart, / That's dreadful to the warrior's heart."

Purcell and Tate may have had sensitive political reasons for eschewing Virgil's ultimately crazed, bitter, and obsessive Dido in favor of an utterly noble one.[23] That they go out of their way to do this seems particularly evident in their degrading of Aeneas as a foil: whereas every moment of this work would seem to lead inexorably toward the monumental achievement of "Dido's Lament," Aeneas is given not a single air. Instead, Dido's music urges us to forget him and identify entirely with her. As her vocal part gently struggles to overcome the ground, only in the end to be guided by it, so does Dido grip us with her courage: in her last moments, she struggles not for the sake of complaining or gaining sympathy, but only to reclaim herself while saying good-bye. We may never know just how or why Purcell's and Tate's Dido came into being; but no new discovery could ever discourage me from proposing that, of the several Didos this essay has explored, here is the one who comes closest to capturing the complexity of Virgil's Queen—ranging from her innate goodness and intelligence at the beginning of her tale to her tragic passion at the end. Where Virgil seemed sympathetic yet cautious, Purcell's music imbues Tate's modest text with exquisite passion while at the same time restoring Dido's dignity. We can appreciate this musical achievement all the more if we pause to remember the complex literary and historical tradition that Purcell and Tate faced when they undertook their Dido project. "Remember me," she says. And, thanks especially to Purcell, we shall always honor her request.

---

23. For example, Price argues that Tate was forced to adapt Virgil's tale in a manner that would "disengage Queen Mary from a symbolic link with [Virgil's] Queen Dido" (Price, "*Dido and Aeneas* in Context," 8). Price's argument of course hinges on the assumption that Queen Mary was the reigning monarch during the period when Tate wrote the libretto—an assumption no longer indisputable.

PART III

MODEL ESSAYS: INSTRUMENTAL

~ 14 ~

THE *PRESTO* FROM BACH'S G-MINOR SONATA FOR VIOLIN SOLO
Style, Rhythm, and Form in a Baroque *moto perpetuo*

Joel Lester

For many years an active violinist, Joel Lester has also been a teacher and scholar. Currently, he is dean of Mannes College of Music. His analysis of rhythm and meter in a Bach's G-Minor *Presto* offers insight into a performer's as well as a scholar's point of view. This essay derives from his recent book *Bach's Works for Solo Violin: Style, Structure, Performance*, winner of an ASCAP-Deems Taylor Award. The essay has two parts, an analysis of the rhythmic and metric complexities of the Presto followed by a formal analysis of the work's musical development.

In addition to his interest in performance and analysis, Lester also adds a historical perspective that is provided in his *Compositional Theory in the Eighteenth Century*. This adds another dimension to his analysis, namely, some eighteenth-century ways of thinking about musical structure.

The *Presto* from the Sonata no. 1 in G Minor for Violin Solo by Johann Sebastian Bach (1685–1750) with its constant sixteenth notes (broken only at the repeat sign that ends each large section) brings to mind nineteenth-century perpetual motions. But the quality of motion in Bach's *Presto*—indeed, in all such Baroque movements with continuous rhythms—differs from later perpetual motions at all levels of structure, from the note-to-note level to the form of the movement overall. This essay focuses on the characteristically Bachian qualities of motion in this *Presto* by examining the movement and by contrasting those traits with parallel ones in works from later eras.

A NINETEENTH-CENTURY PERPETUAL MOTION

The *Moto perpetuo* by Niccolò Paganini (1782–1840), excerpted in example 14.1a, is the nineteenth-century epitome of its genre. Its melodic fluidity encourages violinists (and even flutists, as in James Galway's famous recording!) to aim for a thrilling sense of speed. This fluidity arises not only from the actual speed, but even more from the rhythms inherent in the contours of the melodic line.

Some reminders: (1) all words in **bold** are defined in the glossary; (2) full citations for incomplete references are found in the selected bibliography; (3) the authors use their preferred notational system (e.g., Roman numeral, form label, and register notation). Most of the essays denote register by middle C as C^4.—Ed.

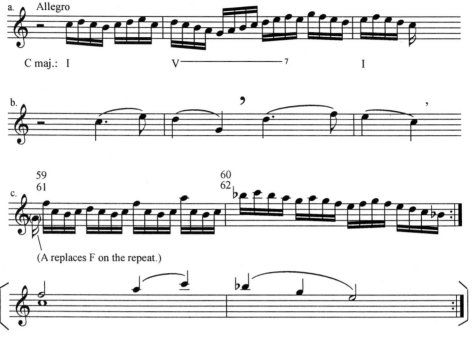

Example 14.1. Paganini, *Moto perpetuo* (New York: International, no date)

a. mm. 1–3
b. the underlying *bel canto* melody
c. mm. 59–62

In the first four beats of the melody, for instance, a chord tone appears on every strong, odd-numbered sixteenth (the first and third sixteenths of each beat) and a non-harmonic tone on almost every weak, even-numbered sixteenth. Each nonharmonic tone is a neighbor or passing tone that connects to the preceding and following notes by step, so that no nonharmonic tone jumps out of the texture because of a prominent skip. In addition, chord tones, not nonharmonic tones, form the tops and bottoms of most of the significant melodic spans: E atop the opening tonic chord, D and G during the following dominant, and so forth. As a result, every prominent note is a chord tone as well as a tone on a relatively strong metric point.

These melodic features contribute to the impression that the speedy sixteenths are merely filler in a leisurely *bel canto* melody with clearly marked phrase subdivisions, as example 14.1b illustrates. No significant level of rhythmic activity exists between this melody and the running sixteenths that fill in the melodic gaps; that is, one level of essential rhythmic activity (the actual notes of the piece) features fluid sixteenth notes, and another essential level of rhythmic activity delineates the underlying melody depicted in example 14.1b. No intermediate levels receive any strong articulation: nothing in the texture focuses regular attention on the eighth-note level, and quarter-note activity projects only when the underlying melody notes move at that pace. Figure 14.1 graphically depicts the levels of the metric hierarchy. With such a metric hierarchy, no matter how fast the sixteenths go (and the faster they go, the more thrilling the ride!), the *Moto perpetuo* unfolds with the Italianate grace and poise of a lyrical aria by one of Paganini's operatic contemporaries such as Gaetano Donizetti (1797 1848) or Vincenzo Bellini (1801–35).

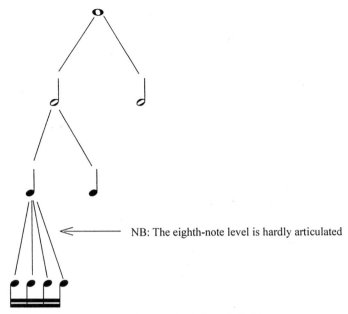

Figure 14.1. The metric hierarchy in Paganini's *Moto perpetuo*

To be sure, Paganini did not maintain exactly this state of affairs throughout the piece. Already in m. 2 there is a skip (not a smooth step motion) after the nonharmonic tone E at the end of the third beat, and the same nonharmonic E recurs as a passing tone on a relatively strong sixteenth (the third) of the next beat. Despite these minor disruptions to the alternation of chord tones and nonharmonic tones, the main melodic notes are all on the beats. Even when a more *agitato* effect emerges later in the *Moto perpetuo*, the same features predominate. The passage from the development section in example 14.1c has many more skips than the music at the opening of the piece, yet the main melodic notes are still entirely on the beat, and the figuration has the effect of reinforcing the disparity between the surface rhythm of rapid sixteenths and the essential melody activity in quarter and half notes. These metric and textural features of Paganini's *Moto perpetuo* characterize innumerable nineteenth-century rapid continuous-rhythm textures.

THE METRIC HIERARCHY OF BACH'S PRESTO

The nineteenth-century type of texture and the way different levels of rhythmic activity interact (which we call the metric hierarchy) in Paganini's *Moto perpetuo* are entirely foreign to Bach's style. Bach's continuous sixteenth-note textures almost always feature a metric hierarchy where all levels of motion are strongly active, with accentuations on metrically weak points enlivening the irregularities of the line. The metric accents of weak points often boldly conflict with one another and sometimes even create metric ambiguities. As Bach's continuous-rhythm movements proceed, increasing levels of significant rhythmic activity create a dynamism that continually heightens the intensity of the music even though the musical surface retains steady sixteenths.

Consider the opening of the G-Minor *Presto*. Excitement and ambiguity abound even in the first few measures: is the meter 3/8 or 6/16? Bach's pattern projects both of these duple and triple metric patternings. We call situations where the music projects more than

Example 14.2. Bach, Sonata in G Minor, *Presto*

a. mm. 1–4 interpreted in 6/16
b. mm. 1–5 interpreted in 3/8
c. the 3/8 vs. 6/16 metric conflict in mm. 9–11 and 25–29

one potential metric organization instances of "metric ambiguity." As shown in example 14.2a, each group of three notes replicates the opening three-note motive one stage lower in the downward arpeggiation of the tonic chord. At the same time, as example 14.2b shows, recurring pitches mark the eighth-note beats, outlining during the first five measures the voicing of the G-minor tonic chord that ends the *Presto*. (The same voicing of the G-minor tonic triad begins and ends the opening *Adagio* of this sonata and ends the *Fuga*. As a result, listeners hearing the beginning of the *Presto* will have that voicing of a G-minor triad in their ears.)

Passages with the 3/8 versus 6/16 metric ambiguity are not restricted to the opening measures of the *Presto*. Example 14.2c illustrates other figurations throughout the movement featuring the same metric ambiguity.

Both metric patternings are so strongly built into these passages that neither is strong enough to overwhelm the other. No matter which way violinists think they are playing the passage, the other interpretation remains quite audible in their performance. Even more strikingly, whichever metric interpretation a performer or listener desires for any of these passages, prominent notes conflict with it, beginning right in m. 1. The highest note in that measure, B♭, falls on a weak metric point in both the 3/8 and 6/16 interpretations. Yet that weak metric placement of the high B♭ is by no means a compositional miscalculation on Bach's part. The opening notes G–B♭ foreshadow the motion G–A–B♭ in the same register that underlies the opening G-minor music stretching from m. 1 to m. 9. (This suggests that violinists should clearly articulate that B♭ in m. 1 no matter which meter they hear.) The 1 + 5 slurring that begins in m. 5 initiates a different sort of metric conflict: a **syncopation** (accents on weak metric points) that the skips would have projected even if the measure were unslurred.

All this purposeful metric complexity stands in sharp contrast to Paganini's *bel canto*. Bach's figuration creates the metric hierarchy shown in figure 14.2. Instead of Paganini's fast surface flashily elaborating a much slower simple melody, Bach's metric hierarchy

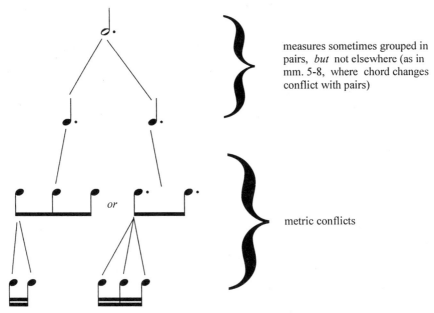

measures sometimes grouped in
pairs, *but* not elsewhere (as in
mm. 5-8, where chord changes
conflict with pairs)

or

metric conflicts

Figure 14.2. The metric hierarchy in Bach's *Presto*

offers musical interest at every level: in the prominent sixteenths contesting the meter, in
3/8 versus 6/16, and in the alternation of different patterns in mm. 5–8.

These ambiguities even affect interpretation of strong and weak measures. Consider
mm. 4–8. The return to the opening high G on the downbeat of m. 5 seems to begin a
new unit of phrasing: an alternation in two-measure units of two patterns, implying a
strong-weak alternation beginning in m. 5 that makes odd-numbered measures strong. But
the changes of harmony do not occur on the odd-numbered measures. Instead, the harmonies in these measures change on the even-numbered measures. Either the strong-weak
patterning changes to adjust to the harmonic rhythm (creating, at least in retrospect, a
three-measure unit in mm. 1–3), or a measure-level syncopation arises because of harmonic changes—the factor that is usually decisive in locating downbeats.

HEIGHTENING INTENSITY AND OVERALL STRUCTURE

The vibrant, continually changing interactions among the energized levels of the *Presto*'s
metric hierarchy intensify as the movement progresses. This intensification occurs on two
separate levels of structure. The more immediate level is the succession of music within
each half of the movement. Within these two large sections, each thematic element is
more intense than its predecessors in one or several ways. On a higher level of structure,
each musical element that appears in the first half of the movement recurs in the second
half, recomposed to heighten the level of activity. As a result, both on the local level (the
succession of ideas within each half) and on the larger level (the way the second half intensifies recurring elements from the first half), the levels of intensity are heightened.

Example 14.3 illustrates this process at work in six separate passages that appear in
both halves of the movement. The first passage so illustrated in example 14.3a features
the opening arpeggio at the beginning of the movement (mm. 1–5) and its recurrence

Example 14.3. Bach, Sonata in G Minor, *Presto*

a. mm. 1–5 and 55–59
b. mm. 5–9 vs. 59–67
c. mm. 9–17 vs. 67–74

opening the second half of the movement (mm. 55–59). At the beginning of the movement, the arpeggio proceeds downward, spelling out a single harmony—the tonic chord, the most stable of harmonies—with no nonharmonic tones. Nowhere else in the movement is there such a sustained harmony. But total stability is not the sole effect here. As discussed above (in connection with example 14.2), Bach uses the unchanging harmony as an opportunity to introduce metric ambiguity and rhythmic accentuations that conflict with either metric possibility (6/8 or 3/8). This opening arpeggio announces the registral limits of the entire first half of the *Presto*—the high B♭⁵ in m. 1 is the ceiling for high pitches until after the double bar.

Example 14.3. (*Continued*)

d. mm. 25–32 vs. 75–82
e. mm. 17–25 vs. 83–95

(*continued*)

The corresponding arpeggio that begins the movement's second half is a fairly literal inversion of the arpeggio in mm. 1–5. Because of that inversion, the arpeggio now ascends, gathering intensity as it quickly breaks through the first section's registral peak to attain the high D^5—the highest note of the entire *Presto*. The harmony is major, not minor—expressing the dominant of the key of G minor, a harmonic function that is not stable but pushes ahead.

The *Presto*'s next element, appearing in example 14.3b, introduces the movement's first harmonic motion. In mm. 5–9, the harmonic motion is the simplest possible: an alternation of tonic and dominant that defines the key. Above these harmonies, the melody once again ascends to the high $B\flat^5$ that was first stated in m. 1. In terms of contour (the shape of the melodic line as it rises or falls), there is a regular alternation of two-measure

Example 14.3. (*Continued*)

f. mm. 43–54 vs. 121–36

units: one measure descending, one measure ascending. The first measure of each pair features an irregular 1 + 5 contour—a pattern reinforced by the slurring. The second measure of each pair is an arpeggio that, like the pattern of mm. 1–4, can easily be heard in either 3/8 or 6/16, maintaining the metric ambiguity of mm. 1–4. As a result, these measures build on the elements of the opening arpeggio while at the same time intensifying the level of activity with new elements.

The recurrence of this passage in mm. 59–67 presents increased activity both in relation to mm. 5–9 and in relation to its immediately preceding music (mm. 55–59). Instead of the two-measure pacing of mm. 5–9, with its single ascent and descent within each pair of measures, mm. 59–67 feature a broader four-measure pacing with several registral undulations. Instead of the tonic-dominant-tonic progression of mm. 5–9 that reinforces the key, the recomposed passage in mm. 59–67 modulates to the subdominant by going around the circle of fifths (D to G to C, with each chord changing from a triad into a dominant ninth). The dissonance level heightens as the two dominant chords (the D chord in mm. 59–61 and the G chord in mm. 63–65) appear as full dominant ninths (D–F♯–A–C–E♭ and G–B–D–F–A♭).

In fact, the chord progression beginning in m. 59 is an intensification of the progression that appears in mm. 5–9—an intensification that builds on the norms of early-eighteenth-century harmony. Around 1720, while Bach was composing his Sonatas and Partitas for Solo Violin, the French composer and theorist Jean-Philippe Rameau (1683–

1764) was drawing together many different facets of knowledge about chords, voice lead-ing, and counterpoint into the first attempt at a comprehensive theory of harmony in his *Treatise on Harmony* in Paris in 1722.[1]

Rameau argued that dissonances, such as the seventh of a dominant chord, impelled an otherwise consonant chord toward a new harmonic goal. When that dominant resolved to its tonic, a key was defined (at least temporarily). We can apply this contemporary per-spective to the *Presto*. The opening G-minor harmony in mm. 1–5 announces a harmonic center that is confirmed by the dominant-to-tonic progression of the following measures. The intensified recurrence of this music beginning in m. 55 spells out the mechanics of the progression: the D-major triad in mm. 55–58 has no particular urge to move anywhere until a seventh and ninth are added in m. 59. Those added dissonances specify that the D chord is a dominant and impel it toward its goal of G in m. 60. But that G-minor triad is not the final chord of the piece. Instead, the G-minor chord itself (a temporary harmonic goal as a tonic preceded by its dominant) gains a major third and adds a seventh and ninth in the next measures, turning into a dominant of C, to which goal it then moves.

The next element, appearing in example 14.3c, quickens the pace of harmonic change and introduces new complexities in the unfolding rhythmic and metric patterning. The harmonic progression through all these measures is motion around the circle of fifths. But to hear the pattern that begins in m. 9 as a circle-of-fifths progression (G–C–F–B♭–E♭–A . . .) requires that one hear the meter as 3/8 (since the change of harmony within each measure occurs on the second eighth). But the contour of the progression, with its abrupt change in direction on the first and fourth sixteenths of each measure, strongly projects 6/16—maintaining the metric conflict begun in the very first measures. On both its first and second appearances (beginning in mm. 9 and 67), this progression expands on the preceding harmonic motions, which offer root motions by descending fifths but among a more constrained number of chordal roots.

When this element recurs in the second half of the *Presto*, it seems to be a simple **transposition** of its first appearance. But because that recurrence is a fifth lower, the notes bump into the lower registral limit of the violin (the open G string). This requires a less regular alternation of higher and lower notes: in particular, the F in m. 72 and E♭ in m. 74 are an octave higher than they would have been in a direct transposition. Such details may seem like an unfortunate result of the violin's registral limits; but it is striking that Bach, who was a fine violinist, invariably runs into such registral limits primarily on re-statements of such patterns, turning a registral disadvantage into a compositional advan-tage promoting heightened activity.[2]

The immediately following passage in the second half of the movement brings back a slightly later portion of the first half of the movement, as shown in example 14.3d. In the first half of the movement, the music in mm. 25–32 expresses a closed progression in B♭ major, beginning and ending on a tonic chord. The recurrence in mm. 75–82 also expresses a single key (C minor). But the music in C minor begins off the tonic chord, creating a more dynamic progression heading toward its conclusive goal. In both cases, the music is more varied and at a higher level of intensity than what precedes it. The har-monic progressions are no longer based solely on movement by fifths, and they express a wider range of chords from the key.

---

1. Rameau's *Trait de l'harmonie* (Paris, 1722) appears in English translation by Philip Gossett (New York: Dover, 1971). Comprehensive discussions of Rameau's theories appear in Joel Lester, *Compositional Theory in the Eighteenth Century*, chaps 4–5, and Thomas Christensen, *Rameau and Musical Thought in the Enlighten-ment* (Cambridge: Cambridge University Press, 1993).

2. Bach, most famous as a keyboard player, also held jobs as a violinist between 1703 and 1717.

The second half of the movement then doubles back to pick up the preparation for the music in B♭ from the first half. As shown in example 14.3e, mm. 83–95 greatly intensify the simpler figuration of mm. 17–25. Not only are the patterns expanded and interspersed with other figurations, but the direction of the pattern reverses between mm. 83–85 and 87–89. Furthermore, whereas there are only consonant triads from a single key in mm. 17–25, mm. 83–95 feature a change of key and many seventh chords.

The process of bringing back intensified parallel passages is itself greatly intensified approaching the cadence that ends each half of the movement. Example 14.3f shows the sequence in mm. 43–46 that prepares for the precadential dominant pedal during the first half of the movement and its dramatically intensified return in mm. 121–27. On its recurrence, the sequence is nearly twice the length, ascends rather than descends, is more irregular in figuration (as shown by the underlying counterpoint), and includes more chromaticism—even outlining an upper-voice diminished octave from E to E♭.

The final cadence itself is also intensified on its recurrence. The dominant pedal of mm. 47–49 recurs as an ascending bass scale in 129–31. Here again (as with mm. 9–17 versus 67–74 shown in example 14.4c), Bach has bumped into the lower registral limit of the violin—he could not place a low F in m. 47 parallel to the low B♭ in m. 129. Once again, he used the more dramatic version for the recurrence, with a more stable bass pedal during the first half of the movement but an ever-ascending bass driving toward the final cadence to end the second half. Even the seemingly slight alteration of the antepenultimate measure of the cadence (m. 134 versus 52) serves to heighten the drama: whereas the bass leading tone C♯ in m. 51 resolves to a bass D in m. 52, the bass F♯ in m. 133 moves, if at all, to a G in the higher octave in m. 134.

HEIGHTENING INTENSITY VERSUS MUSICAL FORM

These intensifications both within and between the two large sections of the movement are a powerful determinant of the overall shape of the movement. Form in the music of later periods (the classical period and the nineteenth century) results from the interaction of tonal structure with patterns of thematic contrast, variation, and return, all articulated by a variety of phrasing patterns. The last two of these classical period form-determining elements (thematic design and classical phrase patterns) are absent from much of Bach's music. Consistent rhythmic and thematic surfaces, not the alternation of different themes, are the norm. And continuous sections, not articulated phrase patterns, are the rule. For this reason, the formal types that theorists of the late eighteenth and early nineteenth centuries categorized to understand the music of their own time do not fit very well on Bach's compositions.

Instead, we can understand that the larger shapes of Bach's music can be understood from a perspective that viewed musical structures in terms of **rhetoric**. Bach's contemporary Johann Mattheson (1681–1764), a composer and writer on music, frequently stressed rhetoric in his 1739 composition treatise *Der vollkommene Capellmeister* (*The Complete Capellmeister*). Practical and witty, Mattheson urged composers to follow "the clever advice of the orators in offering the strongest points first; then the weaker ones in the middle, and, finally, convincing conclusions. That certainly seems to be the sort of trick which a musician can use."[3] Mattheson and other theorists of Bach's time extensively discuss

---

3. Mattheson's *Der vollkommene Capellmeister* (Hamburg, 1739) appears in an English translation by Ernest Harriss as *Johann Mattheson's Der vollkommene Capellmeister: A Translation and Commentary* (Ann Arbor: UMI Research Press, 1981).

Measures:	‖:	1 — 54	:‖:	55 — 136	:‖
Sections:	‖:	*A . . . . B* (=cadence in v):‖:		*A' . . . . B'* (=cadence in i)	:‖
Keys:	‖:	**i — III — v:**	:‖:	on **V — iv — i**	:‖

Notes:

- Both halves begin similarly, but with inverted motives.

- The cadence (approach and conclusion) that ends the second half is a modified transposition of the cadence that ends the first half.

Figure 14.3. Binary form in the *Presto*

issues such as permutations of figuration, which can lead to heightening activity, but hardly ever discuss the thematic and harmonic patterns of musical "forms."

The differences between conceptualizing the overall shape of the *Presto* in terms of an unfolding rhetoric and the binary form of later eras (with which this movement shares crucial traits) affect our interpretation of the dynamic of the movement as a whole. The *Presto* has two repeated sections—two "**reprises**," as eighteenth-century theorists would have called them. If considered as a binary form, the movement might be diagrammed as in figure 14.3.

The form, as taught by innumerable textbooks published during the past two centuries, is clearly binary because of the two sets of repeat signs. As in many such movements by Bach, each large section begins with the same thematic material, and each large section ends with similar cadential material. The middles of each half—the material between the opening and cadence—differ somewhat between the two large reprises. Also as is ubiquitous in Bach's two-reprise movements of any substantial size, the two reprises have opposite tonal orientations: the first reprise moves from tonic to nontonic keys (here, from G minor to B♭ Major and then D minor), while the second moves conversely from being away from the tonic to a cadence in the tonic (here, from beginning on the dominant to eventually returning to and remaining in the tonic).

Edward T. Cone has pointed out that in such Baroque binary forms, the combination of key scheme and tonal orientation creates a permutational relationship between the sections.[4] Every time the end of a reprise leads into the beginning of a reprise, the cadential material leads to some form of the opening thematic material but with a different tonal relationship. When the first repeat is taken, the cadence proceeds to the opening music in a nontonic to tonic relationship; the next time the first reprise ends, the same thematic events occur as nontonic to nontonic. When the second repeat is taken, the same thematic

---

4. Edward T. Cone, *Musical Form and Musical Performance*, 48. Nineteenth-century musicians viewed baroque forms in relation to the binary forms of their era (sonata forms and the like). A nineteenth-century interpretation of Bach's *Presto* appears in Robert Schumann's piano accompaniment to that movement. A discussion of that accompaniment that expands upon the present discussion appears in Joel Lester, *Bach's Works for Solo Violin*, 134–35.

events occur once again, but now as tonic to nontonic. As a result, three of the four possible tonal interactions occur (nontonic to tonic, nontonic to nontonic, and tonic to nontonic). The only possibility that does not occur is tonic to tonic, which would happen only if the entire movement were immediately repeated.

The two views of the movement's overall structure that are suggested here—Cone's suggestion that we hear the movement as the permutational interaction among the sections, and the view proposed in this essay that we hear the movement in terms of two large, parallel sections in which elements are continually heightening the levels of musical activity, both in relation to the immediately preceding music and in relation to previous appearances of the same music—are both consonant with Baroque-era perspectives on musical structure.

PERFORMANCE IMPLICATIONS

This essay compares the *Presto* of the G-Minor Sonata—and, by analogy, numerous continuous sixteenth-note movements by Bach—to nineteenth-century perpetual motions and nineteenth-century notions of musical form, both of which are fundamentally at odds with Bach's aesthetic. Considering these aspects of the *Presto*'s structure from Baroque perspectives rather than later perspectives inevitably affects performance of the movement. There is, of course, no single "correct" way to perform any piece of music. And any thoughts introduced in the present discussion are only intended as suggestions to stimulate a violinist's imagination.

Recordings of the movement vary fairly widely in tempo. Often, violinists known for extremely different styles of playing choose nearly identical tempos. For instance, two of the slowest recordings include one of the earliest recordings (by Yehudi Menuhin in 1935) and a performance by one of the violinists most concerned with replacing the legacy of nineteenth-century violin-playing by a return to greater historical authenticity (Jaap Schröder), both of whom recorded the *Presto* at just under 210 eighths per minute (just under 70 per measure). Likewise, among the fastest recordings are those by Gidon Kremer, who averages 263 eighths per minute (about 88 per measure), and Joseph Szigeti, who averages 247 eighths per minute (about 82.5 per measure).[5]

A striking feature common to almost all recordings is the uniformity of bow strokes used throughout the movement, despite all the changes in surface figuration. Exceptions are most obvious in Jascha Heifetz's 1935 recording, which includes a much wider palette of bow strokes in the second reprise, and Jaap Schröder's recording, which projects different affects or moods for the various sections of the movement.[6]

The uniformity of bow stroke and affect of most recordings approaches the implicit ideal behind the nineteenth-century *moto perpetuo* of the performer as a machine, producing an absolutely regular consistency of great speed and control despite the varying demands of different passages within a piece. To be sure, performances that attain that ideal are hair-raising—think, for instance, of Heifetz's unsurpassable tempo of sextuplets in his 1955 recording of the first movement of the *Suite*, op. 10, by Christian Sinding (1856–1941).[7] The speedy recordings of the *Presto* of the G-Minor Sonata by Kremer and

---

5. Menuhin's 1935 recording was reissued on CD by EMI in 1989 as CHS-763035 2. Schröder's recording is on CD by the Smithsonian Collection of Recordings Classics as 0777 7 64494 25. Gidon Kremer's 1980 recording was reissued on CD by Philips as 416 651-2. Originally recorded in 1946, Szigeti's recording was reissued in 1993 on CD under the Music and Arts label as CD-774.

6. Heifetz's recording was reissued on CD by EMI Classics in 1992 as 0777 7 64494 25.

7. RCA Victor LM 1832.

Szigeti—recordings that maintain their fast pace across all the changes in figuration—evoke the same ideal. The great nineteenth-century violin virtuoso Pablo de Sarasate (1844–1908) made a tradition of performing the E-Major *Preludio* in this manner, as witnessed by his turn-of-the-century recording.[8] Is that ideal appropriate, however, for this *Presto*, with its continual heightening of activity levels and its wide range of figurations?

Another quite different performance tradition of the nineteenth and early twentieth centuries embraces a great deal of tempo shift, both above and below the basis tempo of a movement. The bias against **rubatos** over the basic tempo is a fairly modern phenomenon, arising only in the twentieth century.[9] There is no reason to believe that in ages prior to the widespread use of the metronome there was any way that performers were even fully aware of their divergences over time from the basic tempo of a movement. (After all, anyone who has ever practiced with a metronome is aware of the wizardry of that marvelous invention, which seems always to speed up and slow down at exactly the same places!)

The predilection of performers for varying tempos surely extended to performances of Bach's unaccompanied violin works. Joseph Joachim's recording of the *Adagio* of the G-Minor Sonata includes noticeable tempo changes. And Adolf Busch (1891–1952), in a 1929 recording of the Chaconne (as part of a recording of the entire D-Minor Partita), takes different passages at a fairly wide range of tempos.[10]

In conclusion, Bach's *Presto* is not a nineteenth-century *moto perpetuo* in binary form, but a piece built according to different principles. An account of the *Presto* such as that given here opens performers and listeners to new perspectives on this timeless work.

FURTHER READING

Cone, Edward T. "The Picture Gallery: Form and Style." Chap. 3 in *Musical Form and Musical Performance*. (See the selected bibliography for full citation.)

Niedt, Friedrich Erhard. *The Musical Guide.* Translated by Pamela Poulin and Irmgard Taylor. New York: Oxford University Press, 1988. [Bach's favorite treatise on thoroughbass and composition (published in three parts between 1700 and 1721.)]

Tovey, Donald Francis. "Sonata Forms." In *The Forms of Music*. New York: Meridian Books, 1956, 208–232.

---

8. Sarasate's wax-cylinder recording was reissued on LP by the American Stereophonic Corporation around 1960. The scholar Andreas Moser (who co-edited the famous edition of the Bach solo-violin works with Joseph Joachim), probably recounting performances he had heard, reports that Sarasate "took pride in rushing [the *Preludio*] to death in the shortest possible time" ("Zu Joh. Seb. Bachs Sonaten und Partiten für Violine allein" ["On Bach's Sonatas and Partitas for Solo Violin"], *Bach-Jahrbuch* 17 [1920]: 62).

9. Robert Philip, *Early Recordings and Musical Style* (Cambridge: Cambridge University Press, 1993).

10. Joachim's recording was reissued on LP by the American Stereophonic Corporation around 1960. Busch's recording of the D-Minor Partita was reissued on CD by EMI in 1990 as CDH 7 63494 2.

~15~

DRAMATIC PROGRESSION IN HAYDN, SONATA NO. 46 IN A-FLAT, *ADAGIO*

Marion A. Guck

Marion A. Guck's work focuses on how one, usually as listener or performer, describes music so as to convey the qualities of his or her musical experiences. For years she has pursued an interest in how figurative language characterizes ephemeral and dynamic qualities of music, most recently turning to how amateurs and professional musicians alike think of music in terms of human abilities to move and feel.

Guck's analysis of Haydn's *Adagio* illustrates an eclectic approach, as she explores numerous aspects of the work. The essay is deceptively simple in its sparing use of technical language; however, analytical decisions and musical interpretations evolve from painstaking consideration of many facets of the piece. The essay is dramatically different from most of the others in the volume; it is written from the perspective of the work's performer and emphasizes how the interaction of musical events creates the temporal flow.

MOTIVATION AND METHODOLOGY[1]

The *Adagio* of Haydn's Piano Sonata no. 46 in A-flat Major has always evoked a particularly pronounced emotional response in me, a sympathetic attraction: it draws me out and toward it. This is true when I hear it; it's even more true when I play it, that is, when I'm calling it into being.[2]

The analysis of the *Adagio* below is therefore motivated and guided by my experience as its performer/enactor as well as its listener/appreciator.[3] That is, I understand the

---

Some reminders: (1) all words in **bold** are defined in the glossary; (2) full citations for incomplete references are found in the selected bibliography; (3) the authors use their preferred notational system (e.g., Roman numeral, form label, and register notation). Most of the essays denote register by middle C as C^4.—Ed.

1. The analytical approach taken in this essay grows out of my teaching practice, as does all my research. I am grateful to students who have studied with me for thinking these ideas through with me.

2. Anton Nel's performance of this movement (Musicmasters 7023-2-C) is concordant with my analytical perspective. By contrast, Paul Badura-Skoda's performance (Astrée E7711) would require a rather different analytical interpretation.

3. These perspectival distinctions will determine the orientation of the analysis, as any questions of analytical purpose do. Just how important the distinction can be was brought home to me in a graduate class meeting in 1998. The class was trying to pin down the effect of the opening of Beethoven's *Serioso* String Quartet, op. 95, and the discussion was circling around various images of surprise and lack of control, e.g., that hearing the opening had some of the effect of suddenly being dropped into a moving roller coaster car in mid-descent. These

piece both as it comes from me and as an entity separate from me. I don't, however, know it as a way to affect an audience since I typically play it for my own pleasure alone.[4]

I shall characterize the piece based on what I notice as a result of performing it as well as how I respond as listener/appreciator. Some of these observations are those I have needed in order to play the piece; others I've noticed in the wake of performance. Some of my description will be of what it feels like while playing a passage, because the feel of playing is part of the experience of the music for the performer, a part that may also have its effect on the sounds.[5]

My expressive decisions and my responses are no doubt to some degree personal, but they are also based on acculturation (including formal education in music); they can thus be expected to be intersubjective, that is, shared to a great degree by others suitably acculturated.[6]

I've taken this approach for three reasons: first, I'm curious about how the music elicits my response; second, I've found that exploring the relationship between response and musical source yields analyses that enrich my experience of the music; and, as a result, I have a more comprehensive web of connections to call on as I play.

The language in which this analysis is written will, as a result of examining experiences along with the musical reasons for the experiences, integrate characterizations that describe the piece as if it were human (e.g., in terms of emotions and behavior) with observations more typical of musical analysis.

Rhythm, broadly speaking, will be a constant preoccupation. Among the facets of rhythm that I'll consider is a contrast between harmonically framed passages and passages moving through **sequences**.[7] Harmonically framed passages tend to catch one's attention in the present moment, whereas sequential motion tends to direct one toward the future. The present–orientation of harmonic passages results from being enclosed within a harmonic progression and is often characterized by thematic statement.[8] The future-directedness of sequential passages is due to the regular repetition of voice leading (min-

---

were listeners' responses. The class included a cellist, and her response was quite different: the opening for her offered an opportunity to take control and to be powerful. Insofar as performer and listener have their attention drawn to the same events, what they would have to say about them can be rather different; and they may very well pay closest attention to different aspects of the music. Peter Westergaard has also pointed this out in *An Introduction to Tonal Theory* (New York: W. W. Norton, 1975), 3–4.

4. If it seems strange not to think of a larger audience, consider that pieces such as this sonata were written for the private pleasure of a performer (or a performer and her social circle) rather than for a wide public audience.

5. Alexandra Pierce has written insightfully on the role of the performer's acts as understanding; many of her articles are collected in *Spanning: Essays on Music Theory, Performance, and Movement* (Redlands, Calif.: published by the author). Suzanne G. Cusick made me think about how a piece might put a performer in particular physical situations in order to make a point about what the music portrays in "On a Lesbian Relationship with Music: A Serious Effort Not to Think Straight," in *Queering the Pitch: The New Lesbian and Gay Musicology*, ed. Philip Brett, Elizabeth Wood, and Gary C. Thomas (New York and London: Routledge, 1994), 77–78.

6. Acculturation: "**2** : the process beginning at infancy by which a human being acquires the culture of his [or her] society." Intersubjective: "**1** : involving or occurring between separate conscious minds . . . **2** : accessible to or capable of being established for two or more subjects." (*Webster's Ninth New Collegiate Dictionary*)

7. William Caplin addresses similar issues differently and more comprehensively in *Classical Form: A Theory of Formal Functions for the Instrumental Music of Haydn, Mozart, and Beethoven*. See especially chapters 1 and 2.

8. By "harmonic progression" I mean the conventional succession, at the very least, from an initial tonic to a cadence, whether half or authentic. The initial tonic and cadential chord(s) that frame the passage—a phrase—are usually in root position and therefore relatively stable and present-oriented.

imally a succession of parallel tenths or sixths), interval of repetition (e.g., repeated movement downward by diatonic seconds), and motive. A sequence, once it is established, implies its next move(s) and thereby encourages one to think of what is going to happen next, what will happen in the future.

Tracing the dramatic progress of the piece, as it has turned out, incorporates the *Adagio*'s **sonata form**. It also addresses such issues as phrase, motive, duration, texture, space, and harmony.

ANALYSIS

I can easily understand the **exposition** of the *Adagio* of Haydn's Sonata no. 46 as a kind of dramatic progression from very reserved, inward, and enclosed music blossoming to a moment of showy, extroverted, broad-gestured celebration.

(This dramatic progression, as I've said, also follows the lines of standard sonata form; successive moves from introvert to extrovert coincide with the successive stages of the sonata's exposition, which I'll outline briefly. The first two phrases [mm. 1–8] comprise the first theme; the **transition,** accomplished through a sequence leading to a half-cadence in A♭, begins at m. 9. The second theme begins with the arrival of A♭'s tonic at m. 13; it ends, unusually, with only a half-cadence [m. 20]. **Closure** continues to be deferred until the very end of the closing material, which begins at m. 21 and, like the first theme, includes two phrases. Delay of closure is even more extravagantly dramatized in the **coda** to the movement.)

The *Adagio* begins, as I said, in a reserved, understated way. In mm. 1–4 a phrase begins with a single D♭ in the middle of the piano and returns to the same single D♭ at the end of the phrase on the downbeat of m. 4. Between those points the topmost line rises directly and relatively quickly to one octave above and then descends quite slowly, with many turns aside, but fundamentally by step in a balanced, unbroken line. The bass line is also relatively simple: $\hat{1}$–$\hat{4}$–$\hat{5}$–$\hat{1}$ is just barely elaborated, by a neighbor figure that extends the opening tonic into the third measure. The associated harmonic progression is familiar, I–II^6–V–I; the initial I lasts until m. 3 thanks in part to the bass's neighbor figure. Bass and harmony **accelerate** in the third measure for the cadence. The phrase's perfect authentic cadence completely closes both harmony and voice leading. The phrase is quiet throughout. In outline it is entirely conventional and self-contained; it calls for nothing beyond itself. It is extremely simple, moderate, and subdued.

Perhaps I've made the phrase sound bland, and yet I find it extremely appealing. I hear a kind of grace in the languor of the way the quiet upper line falls back from the higher to the lower D♭. The music's intricacies make me attentive to each of its brief holds and dips and bends. As a performer, and even as a listener, it seems to ask for my care.[9]

It begins by quickly arpeggiating in eighth notes from D♭^{4} directly to D♭^{5}, and, turning around, it starts a descent, still in eighth notes but by step, which has the effect of slowing the line's downward progress. Then throughout the second and third measures, the line makes us follow carefully. There is a succession of delays—suspensions—but each is unlike any other, and as a result there is no pattern to fall into and ride forward.[10]

---

9. The quality of this opening reminds me of the *Adagio* of the *Mozart Piano Concerto in A Major* (K. 488), which my former colleague Roland Jordan has described as needing our care. Jordan is quoted in my paper "Music Loving, Or the Relationship with the Piece," in *Journal of Musicology* 15, no. 3 (1997): 350, first published in *Music Theory Online* 2, no. 2 (1996).

10. I'd like to remind readers, since we often seem to forget that a suspension is a holding of a pitch while others change. The term refers to the feel of the unchanging note in relation to its surroundings.

The beginning of the second measure delays arrival on A♭ by first holding B♭ and then dipping to G♮ to lead upward into A♭. The succeeding G♭ is reached only after a leap down a fourth to E♭ from which the line must rise through F to G♭. G♭ in its turn is held over the bar line, delaying F, which delays E♭. Having reached E♭, just a step away from the line's conclusion, the music moves regularly in eighths right through D♭ to its leading tone, from which it makes another small rise, on time, into the cadential D♭.

The usual expressiveness of the suspensions is enhanced by the individuality of each resolution. Each time we have to wait to hear how the line will make its next step. The music elicits attention that is acutely bound up in the present moment.

The sense of care that results from this close attention may be reinforced for the listener—and is certainly reinforced for the pianist—because the music of this phrase is intended to be performed by the left hand alone, and doing so is awkward. If the music asks for care—sympathetic attention—the pianist must exert literal physical care in order to shape the holds, dips, and bends expressively: connecting each note smoothly to the next, resolving each suspension while also holding the note of the lower voice. The physical care required to make the phrase graceful may very well have an effect on the sounds that also makes the phrase rather deliberate. Finally, when the music closes on the single D♭, it is reassuring both emotionally and physically.

Another effect of left-hand performance of both lines is the feeling that my hand is stretching about as far as it can in order to play both lines, and at the same time the two lines seem contained within the relatively small expanse that one hand can play. Still the music does not feel confined. Rather it feels like a single gesture, with the upper voice, especially, tracing a long, unhurried line. One must keep the thread spinning: if one were to sing the line, one would be sure to keep the energy of the voice alive to connect each note to the notes beyond.

This phrase having closed quite completely, I am somewhat surprised that the piece continues by beginning a literal repeat.[11] And then there's a second surprise when the beautiful tune falls into the shadow of a new, unexpectedly high melody that, beginning as it does with a passing tone, seems to enter out of nowhere. The higher melody is more complex than the lower, trilling A♭, splitting into two voice-leading lines at m. 6's leap from A♭ to E♭. After it splits in two, it twice regains its upper line only to descend by step to its lower. Unlike the original tune's continuous line, this one flakes apart at each leap upward; with each descent it introduces quicker figures and becomes more ornate. Its final, delayed rise to F makes the cadence and phrase less closed than the first.[12]

The two melodies are constantly responsive to each other, and at the same time the nature of their responsiveness changes frequently. The countermelody begins in parallel sixths with the original tune. In m. 6 the two voices exchange B♭ and G♮, both leading to A♭, and both going on to E♭, though the lower moves more quickly. The next measure be-

---

11. William Rothstein has discussed a resemblance between this movement and the music of C. P. E. Bach: "it is a deeply expressive *adagio*, basically in sonata form, but with a Baroque-like texture derived partly from the old ground bass forms (passacaglia or chaconne) and partly from the concerto grosso; the second group features two intertwining lines that are clearly meant to sound like two violins"; see *Phrase Rhythm in Tonal Music*, 135. Elaine Sisman also draws a parallel, proposing that two features of the movement, "the self-contained first period and archaic style," hint at the possibility of continuing "to become a passacaglia"; see *Haydn and the Classical Variation* (Cambridge: Harvard University Press, 1993), 99. With passacaglia or chaconne in mind, the repetition would not be surprising.

12. I prefer to think and speak of cadences in terms of relative degrees of openness or closedness. The most completely closed cadence is the perfect authentic cadence. Any other type is to a greater or lesser degree open. The cadence in m. 8 is authentic, and therefore quite—though not completely—closed, or, as I'll say below, "slightly open."

gins with simultaneous suspensions again in parallel sixths. The upper voice's leap brings the two lines into parallel tenths, the lower in even eighth notes while the upper embroiders a line around the tenths. In m. 8, the upper voice and its doubling third delay their cadential notes; both rise only on the measure's second beat.

At this point we have already heard a slight opening-out in the music. We have a new high voice moving in sympathy with the old melody. The new voice moves a bit more quickly and ornately. The upper voice and doubling make a slightly open cadence.

The phrase that follows (m. 9) again begins with middle D♭, and again a line rises to D♭ an octave above. But circumstances are beginning to change. The third voice enters even higher than before to drop and rise, drop and rise, in a pattern (vaguely familiar from the second measure) that outlines a new triad. The rising middle voice plays A♮ in place of A♭, transforming the D♭ harmony into a B♭ chord. The two upper voices are still responsive to each other, moving generally from a great distance toward each other, and at the same time nesting pairs of parallel tenths and sixths within the convergence.

The music has begun to change course: it is no longer formed within a slowly unfolding D♭ chord. When the next measure (m. 10) repeats what we've just heard, a step lower, the music begins to move measure by measure in a clearly future-directed way, leaving the phrase-long lines of the first theme behind. The feeling of moving onward that the sequence effects is enhanced by the leading tones within each occurrence of the sequence pattern. We hear the sequential music begin a third time (taking the lowest-voice C downward, not back up), but it is modified and it leads us away from D♭ into a half-cadence expectantly poised on the verge of A♭ major.

Thus in this phrase we have begun to move forward rather than being caught in the moment, and the step-by-step motion has taken us from one tonal region to another. The single chromatic note in m. 2, a secondary leading tone, has become the source of a succession of frequently chromatic leading tones (or lower neighbors). The music has spread from the middle register to very high; and the upper line has developed a pattern of momentary ear-catching flutters that highlight most of its unstable, forward-oriented notes.

The lowest voice begins to descend to lead into A♭'s tonic (m. 13), and by the end of the phrase's second measure (m. 14) a true bass is established continuously for the first time in the piece. We may have noticed the lack only subliminally, but we have not been grounded. The voice in the formerly lowest (the middle) register remains as a tenor, swelling the sound to four voices.

Our attention is elsewhere, however. The upper voice begins m. 13 with a figure that sits in place, pulsating lightly. When it shakes itself loose, it uncoils into a large leap upward, only to run back down into the note it had lingered on. That note holds on into the next measure (m. 14), now suspended, dissonant, until the line sinks another step. Below, the inner voice enters (m. 14) overlapping the upper, imitating it and rising above it momentarily with its leap, so that the two voices interlace. While the upper two voices are moving quickly and intricately, the lower voices are steady in quarters. The highest voice picks up again (m. 15) where it left off, repeats its sitting-leaping-running-down, and sinks another step. The inner voice follows again.

I've just described a sequence, and yet this passage is not particularly future–oriented. There are several reasons, I think. First, the upper voices' melodic pattern (example 15.1), lasting for two measures, is long by comparison with the melodic pattern of the sequence just ended. This melody is also rather intricate, especially in the embellishment of the opening stationary pitch and the floridness of the sixteenths, and the intricacy holds my attention.

Moreover, complexities between the lines are preoccupying. The duet between the upper two voices (example 15.1a and b) overlaps entries of the melody: at the same time

Example 15.1. Upper voices' duet with sequential bass, mm. 13–17

that I track the two-measure span that each entry lasts, I also track the measure-by-measure alternation of the two voices. In addition, as I've said, the two voices' registers overlap and intertwine.

Meanwhile, the bass is participating in the sequence in a strange way. It too has a two-measure pattern, but the pattern begins in m. 14 and repeats starting in m. 16, coinciding with the lower-voice entries of the right hand (example 15.1b and c). In fact the lower right-hand voice helps to bind these measure pairs (and not the uppermost voice's) by providing a seventh moving to its resolution in mm. 14–15 and mm. 16–17. Harmonically, the bass pattern begins a circle of fifths in m. 14 that continues until m. 17.

All of this means, among other things, that, though the music has cadenced on every fourth downbeat thus far, establishing a four-measure norm for phrase length, there is no cadence in m. 16. The music keeps moving into m. 17, where we hear the motivic surface again. But the right hand doesn't move down another step. It and most of the left hand of three measures earlier recur, though I'm not sure that I hear the repetition. Is the sequence breaking?

Indeed it is. In m. 18 only a bit of the sequential music is left: a voice sitting, trilling on Eb while a higher voice begins to ascend. As the rising voice continues to ascend, it begins to pull the inner voice, still sounding the little shake figure, with it. The ascent is drawn out for two measures, in striking contrast to the downward tendency of all that has gone before. As it continues, the upper voices pull away from the Eb chord, though the bass tenaciously holds Eb. It is a relief when the upper voices rejoin the Eb chord, though things still feel stretched upward.[13]

There are other reasons to feel stretched: this phrase has extended to eight measures, yet we've only reached a half-cadence, and the cadential dominant is held with a fermata . . .

So it's a relief—a release—for me, especially when I play this piece, to reach up to C and down to low Ab (m. 21) in order finally to play with confidence the so-much-desired Ab chord. The music has forgotten the inward-directedness of the first measures and become expansive, physically exuberant. The running triplet sixteenths feel like a pleasurable, celebratory flourish, even if they're descending. The right hand runs rather than stepping carefully, is lively rather than reflective.

The music slows and draws inward to a cadence (recalling m. 8's). Then it hurries right back up to repeat the confident Ab chord with its flourish. Again it draws inward to approach the cadence (closing completely this time). The moderation of the close is satisfying in the wake of the energetic Abs.

If the piece becomes more active as it goes along, becoming cheerful to a degree I would not have predicted from the opening, it is, or I am, always content with where

---

13. The stages in the story of this phrase track are in its harmonic movement: the four measures of right-hand sequence extend the tonic, the fifth measure nearly reiterates the second measure of the sequence but progresses harmonically to the predominant, and the measures that stretch out Eb stretch out the dominant into a half-cadence.

it is. And I'm happy to repeat the whole succession, from pensive opening to eventual ebullience.

Continuing in A♭ (m. 29), it is very gratifying to pace up through the triad again to meet the upper voice's sixths as both lines descend with the music of the second phrase. In the passage's third measure (m. 31), the music begins to change. The first two beats return to the first phrase's decorated suspension (m. 2, also recently heard as the middle voice of m. 30) but in parallel sixths, a pleasant sound and hand motion. The bass line, reintroducing G♭, suggests that the line might return us to D♭, but the middle voice abruptly replaces C♮ with C♭. This twists the tonality and conclusively forestalls the usual fourth-measure authentic cadence. The bass leads down to D♮, over which a B♭ dominant–seventh chord forms, and this dominant resolves to its tonic at the fifth downbeat of the phrase. Thus, the graceful, relatively closed second phrase of the piece turns in a new, more complicated direction, appropriate to the **development**.

While my right hand cadences (m. 33, downbeat), my left moves out of its E♭ into a rising arpeggio that is the beginning of the tune again. How pleasing that it's rising up in the bass (and without the left hand having to negotiate two lines). The countermelody joins it again, and all three voices move in parallel.

As my hands move here momentarily with particular ease, my attention is struck by the music's poignancy. The minor-mode color is evocative, especially since it has been heard very little, but I think there is something more specific about it than generalized modality.[14] The leap up to the modal C♭ enhances the minor effect. And the A♮ is evocative for several reasons: it is a nondiatonic leading tone; it explicitly denies A♭, which was so recently tonic; it participates in an augmented–sixth chord but leaps a tritone away, out of the register in which it would have resolved to B♭, and its leap is emphasized by the anticipating thirty-second note.

All three voices, including the bass, which is following the familiar melody, push through to the second beat of m. 34, a welcome moment of resolution. Immediately, while the bass smoothly continues the tune, the upper two voices break up into pairs of notes, tendency tone to resolution. The top voice seems especially discontinuous; it leaves D♮ to take up C♭ in order to provide the avoided B♭, and then it suddenly drops a sixth to D♮ rather than returning up to lead to E♭.

At the downbeat of m. 35, all the tendency tones of the dominant at the end of m. 34 move appropriately into the local tonic and immediately onward. The note pairs were an ephemeral idea of m. 34. A simple counterpoint outlining the E♭-minor triad continues through the measure, only to spring into the upward-leaping and chromatic lines of a new dominant (m. 36) that initiates another change of key reached on the fifth downbeat of a phrase. This, like the last phrase ending, simultaneously begins the next phrase with the well-recognized melody.

By now I am absorbed in keeping my hands in line. Though the first-theme melody begins each phrase, my reliance on it is misplaced. Its surroundings and its continuation change with each repetition. There are some patterns to rely on: the new five-measure phrase length, with its **elision** of cadence and beginning of new phrase, and the fact that the keys are moving backward around the circle of fifths. However, the backwardness of the harmonic movement contributes to the sense of being enmeshed.[15]

---

14. Here the word "mode" refers to use of minor versus major rather than use of church modes discussed elsewhere in this volume.—Ed.

15. Unlike a normal circle of fifths, which follows a familiar pattern of voice leading and harmonic order that easily creates the effect of forward impetus, this succession moves against the grain and some work is required to make a dominant (especially in this last case, where a diminished triad had to be made major).

If I thought I was caught up in the present moment in the opening phrase of the piece, I'm even more so here, though in a different way. The dips and rises of the second phrase of the piece no longer *attract* but rather *require* my constant attention as the familiar repeatedly turns into new paths, new tonalities. The frequent closeness of voices, particularly the upper pair, recalls the sense of inwardness of the opening but now seems like involution.[16]

I enjoy following and making the tonal moves, and my fingers still feel expressive as they play, yet I realize that I am more distant emotionally from this music than I was earlier. It feels much less intimate than in the exposition, more intellectual in its tonal and contrapuntal manipulations. As a musician I know the music has changed in a perfectly normal way—sonata developments do this. But its effect is to change the quality of the opening music so that it seems, as I've said, more exigent than inviting.

To return to the passage (m. 37), still in the minor mode, the melody is in the highest voice. With the shift upward of all three voices, this is the highest the melody has ever been; nevertheless a voice enters above. Both the bass, which is also very high, and the new countermelody are simpler than in the two previous phrases, letting the melody sound through. This third repetition, by contrast with the second, seems effortless. In effect, then, the melody has taken on three different characters in the development: first, beginning much as it was originally but becoming harder to predict near the end; second, more impassioned, perhaps falling apart a little; and, now, simple, even wistful.

The melody dissolves in the third measure as before—if "dissolves" is the right word, since the principal line immediately coalesces again in a tune that plays on the original top line (last half of m. 1 through the first half of m. 2), still with simple counterpoint. This measure-long pattern repeats down a step, and then down another step with an even livelier beginning. This sequence, with its unusually catchy opening rhythm, conveys a sense of lighthearted ease and pleasure while it also moves purposefully. The sense of purposeful motion continues beyond the sequence downward into a half-cadence (m. 44), whose left hand continues to descend (as in m. 12) to begin again.

As the **recapitulation** begins (m. 45) the music returns to the opening melody in a transformed texture. The melody sounds in its original register and for the first time since the beginning, without its countermelody, but it is accompanied by a proper low bass. This return seems, perhaps especially to the pianist, both a relaxed, expansive version of the opening—no longer contained and inward-directed—and a relief from the convoluted voice leading of so much of the development.

The repetition reaches only to the second measure's A♭, however, and is abruptly finished off with a flippant, high little figure leading into another A♭. This figure sounds familiar: most immediately, it summarizes the descent of the last few beats; more remotely it is a lighthearted reinterpretation of the high, descending triads of the **transition** (m. 9). As the passage continues, it becomes clearer that it is a fusion of the first theme's opening with the transitional sequence, represented not only within each measure by the descending triad figure but also across measures by the descending step motion, which is chromatically intensified. Each repetition contrasts the seriousness of the measured though now effortless opening figure with the flippancy of the high, quick figure. As a result, the music and we repeatedly "turn on a dime" emotionally, an unanticipated development given the slow emotional transformation of the exposition.

The sequential descent continues until it is cut off by the dominant, which extends, with elaborate ornamentation, through two measures (mm. 50–51), heightening expectation. The right hand slips smoothly into the second theme, which is recalled perfectly

---

16. By "involution" I mean inward-turning complexity.

from the exposition (albeit in D♭).[17] Of course it seems less intricate now, following the development.

In fact, thinking back from this point, the development seems the first theme enlarged and complicated by both its counterpoint and its chromaticism, and in these and other ways made weighty. The first theme of the recapitulation acts more like the transition. The second theme now seems to contrast with the development, and by comparison it is both less intricate (remember that in the exposition it seemed more intricate than what preceded) and completely familiar. If the exposition moved from seriousness to this livelier theme on its way to exuberance, the development-plus-recapitulation moves from a different kind of seriousness to this agile theme, on its way, perhaps, to some transformation of the **codetta's** affect.

After the second theme's half-cadence, I anticipate reaching out high and low to a broad tonic chord (m. 60, parallel to m. 21). Instead, from a low D♭ my hands roll up through a flourish that fuses the measured opening arpeggio with the celebratory feel of the A♭ chord in the exposition. I wonder if some of the pleasure felt in playing this figure derives from the fact that a flourish seems, now that the piece makes me think of it, like what was really called for at m. 21. There is no answering run falling toward the cadence, as in the exposition, however. Instead, the music moves directly into a moderate descent to the cadence, in the character of mm. 22–23.

Immediately the flourish sounds and sounds again, sweeping across almost the entire registral expanse of the piece in gestures as broad as the opening was contained. It is very satisfying to play so freely. Again the descent approaching the cadence recurs, but the expanded flourish has led the music so high that m. 65's bass is in the treble register.

Instead of a cadence, a sequence takes shape (m. 66). Afterbeat sixteenths reiterating a single octave through a whole measure ensure that time will be taken with each step of its leisurely descent. The figure seems entirely new, and the lower voices lead unobtrusively to an ephemeral E♭ minor.[18] The music seems to have drifted off someplace far from the piece and its imminent cadence, but it's an agreeable place—in addition to the octave alternation, I enjoy the simple, beautiful voice leading of the sonorities changing under them—and I don't mind. I'm in no hurry.

The slowly descending steps soon put D♭ major back together and reach its tonic in m. 70. There, the lowest voice leaps back into the bass register. At the same time, the music develops more impetus than the sequence has had, thanks both to the right-hand movement upward in sixteenths through the D♭ arpeggio and its first-inversion impulse toward IV, which follows, also with rising arpeggio. This arpeggio seems even more intensely forward-directed—toward V and a substantial cadence—until the last beat of the measure, when it stays with the predominant even though the rising arpeggio has ended.

Indeed, at the next downbeat the dominant is not reached, because the cadential $^6_4$ is unexpectedly minor. It thus diverts the music into near immobility, caught in repetitions of the sonority, with chromatic neighbors further extending the unwonted turn. The chromatic adjustments that return the music to D♭ major seem to force it awkwardly out of its tangent, into a major cadential $^6_4$ (m. 77), which is nevertheless especially appreciated and

---

17. One small change occurs in some editions: where m. 14 has D♮s on the second and third beats, the parallel point 8 at m. 53 have G♭.

18. The sixteenths may recall the second theme's repeated notes, particularly since both begin with E♭⁵ but, if the similarity is noticed, it emphasizes how far away this passage seems. E♭ minor makes the shift to the minor mode in the development, but again, if the relation is noticed, it is striking how much distance there is between the musical and emotional states of the two passages.

is celebrated by a cadenza. The piece ends without further fuss, except for the **syncopations**, heard also at earlier cadential approaches (mm. 22–23, 26–27 and mm. 61–62, 65), maintaining impetus to downbeats right up until the final one.

The coda (mm. 60–80) begins with greater exuberance than the closing material of the exposition. At the same time it counters the weightiness and involution of the development with its flight across the keyboard. And then it refuses to end: straying into an unhurried sequence, forestalling the cadential $^6_4$. It cadences, finally, but it barely stops. Given the opening phrase of the piece, with its closed cadence, who would have thought that, when the movement came to its end, it wouldn't want to stop?

This analysis has pointed out features of the music's passage in time that I hope will provide more to notice and appreciate about the Haydn *Adagio*. In conclusion, I have only three brief points to make.

First, I've come to understand the movement's sonata form in two closely parallel parts, though one is short (the exposition) and one long (the development, recapitulation, and coda).

Second, the distinction of temporal quality between harmonically framed passages (which are oriented in the present) and sequences (which are impelled into the future) is not always clear. It holds for the first theme and transition in the exposition. However, the first half of the second theme is sequential, and yet that sequence's forward impetus is very gentle (the displacement between upper- and lower-voice sequential patterns seems to moderate impetus). More strikingly, the diverging sequence in the coda (mm. 66–70) temporarily releases me from the progress of the piece and buoys me in a slow-moving present.

Finally, to return to the dramatic progression, if the opening of the piece makes me think of a reserved personality, the movement's course has repeatedly returned to the opening material, especially the rising arpeggio, to place it in different contexts and change its character or mood: pensive at the opening, involved in the development, flippant at the recapitulation, and animated at the beginning of the coda. The character of the opening is not immutable; we hear it in different frames of mind, or trying out different modes of behavior, or even different identities.

FURTHER READING

Cusick, Suzanne. "'There was not one lady who failed to shed a tear': Arianna's Lament and the Construction of Modern Womanhood." *Early Music* 22 (1994): 21–41.

———. "'Who is this woman? . . .': Self-Presentation, *Imitatio Virgine*, and Compositional Voice in Francesca Caccini's *Primo Libro delle Musiche* (1618)." *Il Saggiatore musicale* 5 (1998): 5–41.

Dubiel, Joseph. "Hearing, Remembering, Cold Storage, Purism, Evidence, and Attitude Adjustment." *Current Musicology* 60 and 61 (1996): 26–50.

Fisk, Charles. "Performance, Analysis and Musical Imagining, Part I: Schumann's *Arabesque*" *College Music Symposium* 36 (1996): 59–72.

———. "Performance, Analysis and Musical Imagining, Part II: Schumann's *Kreisleriana*, No. 2." *College Music Symposium* 37 (1997): 95–108.

———. *Returning Cycles: Contexts for the Interpretation of Schubert's Impromptus and Last Sonatas.* Berkeley, Los Angeles, and London: University of California Press, 2001.

Kielian-Gilbert, Marianne. "On Rebecca Clarke's Sonata for Viola and Piano: Feminine Spaces and Metaphors of Reading." In *Audible Traces: Gender, Identity, and Music*, 71–114. Edited by Elaine Barkin and Lydia Hammesley. Zurich and Los Angeles: Carciofoli Verlagshaus, 1999.

Lewin, David B. "*Auf dem Flusse:* Image and Background in a Schubert Song." In Schubert: *Critical and Analytical Studies*, edited by Walter Frisch, 126–52. Lincoln: University of Nebraska Press, 1986.

Maus, Fred Everett. "Music As Drama." *Music Theory Spectrum* 10 (1988): 56–73.

———. "Musical Performance as Analytical Communication." In *Performance and Authenticity in the Arts*, edited by Ivan Gaskell and Salim Kemal, 129–53. Cambridge: Cambridge University Press, 1999.

Treitler, Leo. "Mozart and the Idea of Absolute Music." In Leo Treitler, *Music and the Historical Imagination*, 176–214. Cambridge and London: Harvard University Press, 1989.

~16~

FORMAL AND EXPRESSIVE INTENSIFICATION IN SHOSTAKOVICH'S STRING QUARTET NO. 8, SECOND MOVEMENT

Roger Graybill

Roger Graybill (New England Conservatory) has published on the music of Brahms, pedagogy, and rhythmic theory. His approach to rhythm has largely been influenced by Dalcroze eurhythmics, which utilizes body movement as a pedagogical tool for teaching rhythm. He is especially interested in the ways that musical gesture interacts with tonality to create the impression of musical motion.

According to Graybill, the present essay "focuses on the kinetic quality of the second movement of Shostakovich's Eighth String Quartet. At its outset, this movement immediately strikes the listener with its intensity and forward-driving energy, which is generated through the interaction of dynamics, texture, tempo, and articulation. The thesis of this paper, however, is that the movement also exhibits such dynamism in a less immediately obvious way—that is, by its large-scale formal structure. Through a variety of means, Shostakovich creates a structure that accelerates and intensifies as it progresses toward its end. This intensification in turn contributes to the expressive impact that the movement makes on the listener."

While discussions of expressive character typically adopt the perspective of the listener, Graybill goes a step further, suggesting that the expressive content of this movement may provide a window into Shostakovich's psyche at the time he composed the Eighth Quartet.

INTRODUCTION AND OVERVIEW

Any attempt to analyze the second movement of Shostakovich's Eighth Quartet is complicated by a special structural feature of the quartet as a whole. Of its five movements, only the last attains **closure**; the preceding four are all open-ended, either leading without a break into the following movement (movements one, three, and four) or ending

---

Some reminders: (1) all words in **bold** are defined in the glossary; (2) full citations for incomplete references are found in the selected bibliography; (3) the authors use their preferred notational system (e.g., Roman numeral, form label, and register notation). Most of the essays denote register by middle C as C^4.—Ed.

	Part I					Part II		
Section	A1	A2	B	trans.	C	A	C	B
Tonal center	g♯	b	c	$--\rightarrow$ c		g♯/b	c	c
Rehearsal no.	11	18	21	22.	23+4	27	31+9	33

Figure 16.1. Formal/Tonal Plan of Movement II

abruptly in the middle of a phrase (second movement). Shostakovich also indicates "attacca" at the end of each of the first four movements, ensuring that the performers will connect the movements without any breaks in the musical flow. Moreover, the five movements are interconnected motivically through Shostakovich's use of his musical signature, DSCH, within each of the movements.[1] Thus the second movement is not a completely independent entity, and the analyst must keep an eye open to ways in which it is shaped by its larger context and how it contributes to that context. Yet this movement, like the others in this quartet, does project a coherent structure in its own right, thereby displaying a considerable degree of autonomy. This essay will focus primarily on those factors that lend the movement such coherence; at the end of the essay, however, I will consider the role played by this movement within the quartet as a whole. We shall see that the second movement poses and works through an interesting formal problem that indirectly bears on the extramusical significance of the entire quartet.

A structural overview of the second movement yields the formal plan shown in figure 16.1.[2]

Certain aspects of the formal/tonal scheme pose little difficulty for the analyst. Shostakovich articulates each of the sections with distinctive thematic material. Example 16.1 shows the opening measures of each theme. Theme A has a propulsive, motoric quality; it has no clear goal, tending either to circle back to its beginning (as seen in example 16.1) or to spin off toward a new section without reaching closure (R13 ff or R19+7 ff). Theme B, a quotation from Shostakovich's E Minor Piano Trio, is more self-contained, closing on a tonic C in R21+26 (not shown in example 16.1). Theme C, like theme A, lacks a definite cadential goal. It features two primary motivic ideas, C^x and C^y, the first of which is Shostakovich's "DSCH" **motto** (D–E♭–C–B), which permeates all five movements of this quartet. Since Shostakovich uses this motto throughout the quartet as a sort of personal signature, its incorporation within theme C automatically lends a special significance to that theme. The following analysis will in fact assign a central role to theme C by focusing on its relationship to the other thematic material in the movement; moreover, I will suggest that these thematic connections ultimately provide possible clues to Shostakovich's state of mind at the time he wrote the quartet.

Like the thematic material, the pitch centers shown in example 16.1 are relatively easy to identify by ear. These centers are projected by a variety of means. For instance, theme A asserts G♯ through melodic reiteration in the first violin, along with a supporting G♯–B harmonic **dyad** in the lower three strings. Theme B projects its pitch center by strongly outlining the C–G fifth; in addition, the pitch C receives emphasis as a pedal in

---

1. "DSCH" is a shorthand reference to Shostakovich's name, with "D" an abbreviation for "Dmitri" and "SCH" taken from the German spelling of his last name. These four letters correspond to the pitches D–E♭–C–B. ("S" is an abbreviated form of the German "Es," or E♭, while "H" is the German name for the pitch B.)

2. Rehearsal numbers refer to points in time—i.e., the bar lines over which they appear—not to the first measure following that bar line. Thus "R23+4" refers to the fourth measure following the bar line over which R23 appears. There will be one exception to this labeling system: references to measures that begin right at a rehearsal number will omit the "+1" suffix; thus, "R11" rather than "R11+1."

Example 16.1. Themes A, B, and C

the cello. Finally, theme C produces an impression of pitch centricity through a scale-degree succession that is characteristic of C harmonic minor (note in particular the diminished seventh between B♮ and A♭).

However, at no time does this movement establish a pitch center through a functional *harmonic* progression such as V–I. For this reason, it is best to regard the tonal areas in example 16.1 as pitch centers rather than true tonics. Moreover, not all of these pitch centers are equally strong. For instance, while Section A2 begins with an implied B pitch center due to the thematic material in the viola, the cello line at that point reiterates F♯–A (not B–D), which considerably weakens B as a pitch center.

As shown in figure 16.1, Shostakovich's distribution of theme areas helps to articulate the larger two-part form. The return of A at its original pitch level (R27) sounds like a "starting over," and the fact that all three themes heard prior to R27 reappear again after that point further delineates the bipartite structure of the movement. Furthermore, the return of all three themes in the second part suggests that this movement might be interpreted as **sonata form** without a **development**, with Parts I and II corresponding to **exposition** and **recapitulation**, respectively. The tonal design of Part I supports such an interpretation, since the G♯ pitch center at the opening is counterbalanced by an emphasis on C in the last two subsections. (The role of the B pitch center in Section A2 with respect to this larger tonal opposition will be discussed later.) However, Part II exhibits several features that resist any attempt to regard it as a recapitulation. First, and most notably, it fails to resolve the tonal conflict presented within the first part, simply restating all the thematic elements from the first part at their original tonal levels. (The resulting lack of large-scale tonal closure confirms that this movement is ultimately not a self-contained entity.) Second, the thematic plan of Part II is a bit irregular for a recapitulation: Sections A1 and A2 of Part I are collapsed into a single A section in Part II, and the order of themes B and C are reversed in Part II. Third, a closer look at the score reveals further thematic discrepancies between Parts I and II beyond those shown in figure 16.1. Most remarkably, Part II radically *compresses* the material of Part I from 232 measures down to 116—exactly by half.[3] Figure 16.1 of course hints at such compression with its reduction of two A sections to one section, but themes B and C are also abridged upon their return. Moreover, the thematic material from Part I undergoes considerable alteration in Part II. While the just-mentioned formal compression is partly responsible for this, the degree of thematic transformation far exceeds what we would normally expect to follow from such compression.

The preceding overview of the formal plan raises two large questions that will launch the forthcoming in-depth analysis. First, to what extent does the sonata-form model serve as a useful prism for viewing this movement? On the one hand, we have seen that Part I exhibits certain similarities with a sonata-form exposition; on the other hand, Part II does not lend itself well to a "recapitulation" label. The failure of Part II to exhibit a clear recapitulatory function may seem to indicate that we must simply abandon a sonata-form interpretation for this movement as a whole. But a closer analysis will lead us to an alternate possibility: instead of rejecting a sonata-form interpretation altogether, we might interpret Part I as the first stage of a *potential* sonata-form plan that is subsequently frustrated in Part II.

A second large question focuses more explicitly on the thematic plan shown in figure 16.1. We have seen that this plan exhibits a striking tension. One the one hand, it strongly projects a two-part formal division on the basis of a thematic parallelism (albeit not exact); in abstract formal terms, then, the two parts balance each other. Yet the two parts display an extreme *imbalance* in another sense, most notably with respect to their lengths; indeed, the extent to which Part II compresses (and alters) the earlier material challenges the very notion that Part II functions formally as a symmetrical response to Part I. This tension in our account in turn raises a question: assuming that we do understand Part II to be a varied repetition of Part I, how do we make sense of its radical reworking and compression of the earlier material? One reason is immediately palpable: Part II carries forward and intensifies the momentum generated by Part I; hurtling through time with increasing velocity, it seems by its end to be close to spinning out of control. But the forthcoming analysis will demonstrate that the transformation of material in Part II serves another purpose as well, one that is less immediately obvious: it draws our attention to thematic relationships that were presented within Part I in only an indirect or superficial way. Specifically, Part II brings to the fore connections between theme C—the "motto" theme—and the other two themes, thereby linking all the important thematic content of this movement with the quartet as a whole. The following discussion shines

---

3. In counting 116 measures for Part II, I do not include the "empty" measure with a fermata that ends the movement. While one could argue that this measure belongs within the second movement, I interpret it as a transitional moment of silence *between* movements.

light on this thematic interplay, first focusing on the embryonic thematic relationships that do emerge within Part I, then turning to Part II to consider its relationship to Part I in light of the thesis just put forth.

THEMATIC INTERPLAY WITHIN PART I

The beginning of theme A exhibits no clear relationship to either themes B or C (see example 16.1). However, the DSCH motto, which will eventually appear at the beginning of theme C, does appear later within the A1 section in rhythmic diminution, first as a single transposed statement just before R14, and then in multiple statements at its "proper" pitch level between R16 and R18. Indeed, this latter passage could easily act as a segue to theme C, but instead we hear a return of the opening A material at R18, **transposed** up a minor third (Section A2). In thus juxtaposing the motto with the transposed return of the opening material, Shostakovich draws a subtle connection between the two. This new transposition of theme A uses three of the four motto pitches, B, C, and D; Shostakovich further strengthens this connection in R18+5, where he restores the missing E♭ to yield the complete pitch content of the motto.

While the opening of the A2 Section thus foreshadows the motto opening of theme C with respect to pitch content, it obviously bears no more *thematic* resemblance to that motto than the very opening of the movement did. However, as Section A2 progresses, it does incorporate multiple statements of the motto at its literal "DSCH" pitch level, as did Section A1; see the first violin between R19 and R20, the cello after R20, and the two violins in the measures preceding R21. But again, these motivic references do not lead directly to the motto theme (C) but rather to theme B, which bears no apparent affinity to the motto. Thus, Sections A1 and A2 both foreshadow the arrival of theme C only from a distance, as it were.

As noted earlier, theme B is tonally self-contained, coming to a cadence just before R22. Immediately following this cadence is a **transition,** which reintroduces the motto in R22+17; this time the churning repetitions of the motto lead directly to theme C. It should be noted that while theme C emerges seamlessly from the preceding transitional measures, it bears little overt relationship to theme B itself. The only hint of a similarity is their common tonal center, C, and their emphasis on the pitch F♯ (which, however, is far more pronounced in theme B than C).

FORMAL SIGNIFICANCE OF THE THEMATIC INTERPLAY IN PART I

In sum, the thematic relationships within Part I may be understood in two different ways. First, we can hear its thematic succession as roughly analogous to that of a sonata-form exposition, as suggested at the outset of this paper. The shift of pitch center between Sections A2 and B supports such an interpretation, as does the striking thematic contrast between those sections. Furthermore, the passage immediately preceding section B has the character of a sonata-form transition, since it seems expressly designed to lead to the new theme: beginning in R19, the first violin projects a long-range melodic ascent from B^4 to $F\sharp^6$—the very pitch that initiates theme B. It should be noted that the C section plays a less pivotal role with respect to this sonata-form paradigm, since the A and B sections have already accomplished the requisite thematic/tonal opposition. Nevertheless, the fact that the C theme reinforces the tonal center that was established by theme B suggests a higher-level link between those two thematic areas.

A second possible interpretation of Part I focuses not on the thematic contrast between themes A and B, but rather on the motivic connections between the A and C sections. While the material that opens the two A sections lacks a surface relationship to either theme B or C, both those sections gradually incorporate the motto, thus anticipating from afar the beginning of the C theme. Moreover, we have seen that the new transpositional level of the A theme at R18 utilizes the exact **pitch-classes** associated with the motto that opens theme C (B–C–D, with E♭ added a few measures later). Turning to theme B, we have observed that the relationship between it and the other two themes is much weaker than that between A and C. Thus, to the extent that we interpret the thematic material of Part I in the second way, we will hear theme B as a disruptive agent within a linear process of thematic development that culminates with the arrival of theme C.

These two different interpretations for Part I suggest two different future paths that the movement might take after R27. If we hear theme B as the articulation of a second key area within a sonata-form exposition, we would probably expect a transposition of that material upon its return. But that is precisely what does *not* happen within Part II, as noted earlier. The second interpretation, in which theme B interrupts a motivic narrative involving the motto, suggests a very different course for the rest of the movement. It is difficult to foresee exactly what that course might be, though we would probably expect some kind of motivic reworking of the material in Part I, with the motto playing a central role. In the following discussion of Part II, it will be shown that Shostakovich in fact takes this path.

THEMATIC INTENSIFICATION IN PART II

As noted earlier, Part II alters the thematic design of Part I by switching the positions of themes B and C and by collapsing the two original A sections into one. Switching the order of B and C now produces a direct temporal link between the thematically related A and C sections, thus eliminating the disruption produced by section B in the first part. In a less obvious way, condensing the two A sections into one also strengthens the link between the A and C material. In Part I, the tonal shift from G♯ (Section A1) up a minor third to B (Section A2) required seventy-five measures; but in the recapitulation, the A theme pushes from G♯ to B after a mere thirteen bars (R28)—an immediate and dramatic **acceleration** that sets the new pace for the recapitulation. In thus skipping over most of the first A section and jumping ahead to the tonal center associated with the *second* A section, Shostakovich quickly brings the B–C–D **trichord** to the fore; this in turn sets the stage for the impending return of the forthcoming C theme with its opening DSCH motto.[4]

Since section A now leads immediately into theme C rather than B, one might now expect more emphasis on the motto to set up the opening of theme C. But remarkably, the very opposite occurs; the motto is completely absent from the A section and does not resurface until the actual arrival of theme C at R31+9. Shostakovich thus eliminates an important thread that had indirectly linked themes A and C in Part I, a strategy that at first seems puzzling.

Rather than emphasizing the motto in this recapitulatory A section, Shostakovich pursues a different route that ultimately sets up theme C far more effectively. Starting at R29, he introduces a melodic figure consisting of three pitches, E–G–A♭; these pitches form an **intervallic cell** containing a minor third on the bottom (E–G) and a minor second on top (G–A♭). This "m3/m2 cell" had already appeared earlier at a different transpositional level

---

4. Note that this pitch-specific link would have been impossible if Shostakovich had followed standard sonata-form procedure by transposing the C theme to the "tonic" G♯.

Example 16.2. Five different transpositions of the m2/m3 cell in Part II, Section A

(F♯–A–B♭) in the viola line within the A2 section of Part I (see R18+14 through R20).[5] But while that cell played only a subordinate role in the A2 section as a whole, it now dominates the melodic line up to the arrival of theme C, appearing at five different transpositional levels (example 16.2). (Note how the gradual ascent of this m3/m2 cell through pitch space recalls the gradual ascent leading from theme A2 to theme B in Part I.) The final statement of this cell at R31 repeatedly circles around the pitches B, D, and E♭, a literal subset of the forthcoming motto. The only pitch that is missing is C, which is finally brought in by the arrival of theme C at R31+9.

Retrospectively, then, the cell formed by B, D, and E♭ sounds like an incomplete version of the four-note collection formed by the DSCH motto that initiates theme C. Thus the arrival of theme C (or more specifically, its opening motto) appears to fulfill an incomplete aspect of the material that immediately precedes it. This represents a different kind of motivic link between sections A and C from that heard in Part I. In that initial presentation, Shostakovich foreshadowed theme C with complete statements of the motto within the A1 and A2 sections, producing a connection through *correlation*. In contrast, the arrival of theme C in Part II completes an entity that was incomplete within the A section (the "incomplete motto" as represented by the m3/m2 cell), effecting a connection by means of a *process* that only reaches completion at R31+12. By linking the sections in this way, Shostakovich creates an especially tight continuity between them.

We can also identify deeper-level connections between sections A and C. The return of the motto at R31+9 not only literally completes the B–D–E♭ cell of the preceding eight measures. On a more abstract level, that return also culminates a larger span of music beginning back at R29, since that entire passage is permeated with various transpositions of the m3/m2 cell, as explained earlier. But that is not the whole story: the material from the very beginning of section A—that is, theme A itself—is built on a *different* cell that may similarly be understood as an incomplete version of the motto. It will be recalled that in Part I, Shostakovich juxtaposed the motto with the return of theme A at R18 so as to reveal a connection between the theme's opening three pitches (B–C–D) and the pitch content of the motto. This B–C–D collection forms a m2/M2 intervallic cell, which will of course return at the beginning of section A in Part II, first at a G♯–A–B transpositional level (as at the very opening of the movement), and then again at its B–C–D level a mere fourteen measures later.[6]

Thus the A section of Part II is saturated with *two* different cells, m2/M2 and m3/m2, which combine to form the pitches of the four-note motto. See example 16.3; the transpositional levels of the cells are chosen to highlight the fact that they are literal subsets

---

5. This "m3/m2" cell is not equivalent to a melodic motive. Rather, it is to be understood more abstractly as the set of pitches providing the raw material for this particular passage—much as the major triad forms the raw material for the opening measures of Beethoven's *Eroica* Symphony or Mozart's *Eine Kleine Nachtmusik*. Thus an intervallic cell is essentially equivalent to a "pitch-class set"; see Joseph Straus's *Introduction to Post-tonal Theory*. The pitch-class set label for the m3/m2 cell would be [0,1,4]. The term "intervallic cell" is used by George Perle in *Serial Composition and Atonality*, 6th ed., 9–10.

6. The m2/M2 cell is equivalent to (0,1,3) in pitch-class set theory.

Example 16.3. The motto pitches (B, C, D, E♭) resulting from a union of the m2/M2 and m3/m2 cells.

of the motto. These cells both contain a semitone and a minor third, a relationship that is aurally perceivable even at the beginning of the piece (compare the m2/M2 cell of the first two measures with the m3/m2 cell between R12 and R13). But only in Part II is the m3/m2 cell elevated to a level of importance equal to that of the other cell. And unlike Part I, Part II presents this m3/m2 cell as a literal subset of the motto (R31); in Part I, none of the statements of that cell appeared at the B–D–E♭ pitch level.

In short, the arrival of theme C in Part II effects a union of the two intervallic cells that generated most of the motivic content in the preceding A section. Moreover, the union also occurs in a literal sense, through a joining of the highly salient B–C–D and B–D–E♭ subsets from section A. Looking back on Part I, we now see that the multiple appearances of the motto within A1 and A2 provided a relatively superficial link with theme C. In lieu of such literal motivic foreshadowing, Part II substitutes a deep-level processive connection in which theme C *fulfills* the motivic content of A.

Theme C itself makes a much briefer appearance in Part II than it did in Part I, compressing the original fifty-five measures down to twenty-seven; moreover, the recapitulated theme C is greatly simplified. Utilizing the motivic labels shown in example 16.1c, we may describe it as two statements of motives x and y in alternation, with the second y extended by three more repetitions (xy xy yyy). The repetitions of motive y lend extraordinary weight to the pitch F♯, which in the original theme C made only a fleeting appearance. This striking alteration to theme C beautifully sets up the arrival of theme B, which takes up the F♯ and resolves it to G. By linking theme C with B in this way, Shostakovich is able to dispense with a transition, which had occurred within Part I between themes B and C. More important, by leaving F♯ unresolved at the end of theme C and subsequently resolving it at the beginning of theme B, he provides a processive link between these sections, just as he did between sections A and C. (Note that this voice-leading connection would have been less noticeable if the common tone between themes had been a stable pitch; it is the very instability of the F♯ that forces us to hear a powerful tonal push *through* the formal division between sections C and B.) Theme C, the common element in these two processes, both emerges from theme A *and* sets up the arrival of theme B, thereby assuming a central role that it was lacking in Part I.

Theme B (R33 ff.) is stated in the viola and cello while the two violins arpeggiate an accompanimental figure, reversing the instrumentation heard in Part I. The theme essentially matches its earlier appearance for twenty-four bars (except for a change of harmony to a fully diminished chord on C♯ at R34) and then extends it one more measure before suddenly breaking off into complete silence just prior to its expected closure on C. A full measure in duration, this rest brings the second movement to an abrupt stop; there is no sense of closure, since the movement simply ends without warning. By cutting short theme B at this point, Shostakovich also intensifies one of its structural features that was already apparent in Part I—that is, its increasing motivic **fragmentation**, with **groupings** of four measures yielding to groupings of two (R34+3), and finally to groupings of one (R34+11). Thus the process of formal compression that has predominated throughout Part II accelerates and comes to a head at the very end of the movement.

Extramusical Implications of the Analysis

While most of the foregoing analysis has largely treated the second movement as if it is a self-contained structure, the failure of this movement to reach closure brings us back to the point raised at the outset of the essay. That is, this movement is only partially autonomous; it also functions within a larger entity, the quartet itself. Our analysis sheds light on the role played by the second movement within that larger context. Such a role can be described in purely musical terms, but it also bears on a possible extramusical interpretation for the quartet as a whole.

We have seen that Part II of the second movement strengthens the links between the "motto" theme (theme C) and the other two themes. Since the motto that initiates theme C appears in all five movements, this process of thematic integration brings the entire second movement into a closer relationship with the other movements. Our awareness of this connection emerges only within Part II; within Part I, the A and B themes bear only a superficial or indirect relationship to the C theme, and to that extent they seem to stand apart from the other thematic material in the quartet. This is most obviously true of theme B, since it is a quotation from a different work, but it is equally true of theme A. The beginning of that theme explodes with a sudden burst of energy and bears no apparent relation to the subdued and somber first movement, either expressively or motivically. In addition, the sudden kinetic jolt at R11 is reinforced by a harmonic surprise; the G♯ at the end of the first movement sounds like an A♭ that wants to resolve down to G (as actually occurred two measures prior to the arrival of G♯), but instead of moving down, that pitch crescendos into R11, where it is instantly transformed into a stable tonic pitch. Indeed, this transformation enhances the terrifying character of the A theme; one feels as if we have suddenly entered a nightmare, far removed from the quietly somber world of the first movement.

But if themes A and B at first sound remotely related to the rest of the quartet, their emerging association with the motto theme (C) within Part II eventually brings them into the fold. In purely musical terms, the result is a more tightly integrated quartet. But the thematic processes outlined in this essay also may shed light on an issue that has been of great interest to Shostakovich scholars—specifically, the extramusical meaning of this quartet. Shostakovich composed this work shortly after visiting Dresden in July 1960; there he observed firsthand the devastation that had been brought on the city by bombing raids during World War II. The Eighth Quartet is an apparent response to this visit, as seen in Shostakovich's inscription at the head of the first movement, "To the memory of the victims of fascism and war" ("Dem Gedächtnis der Opfer des Faschismus und Krieges"). But there is evidence to suggest that this inscription was intended to conceal a deeper meaning. In 1960 Shostakovich came under especially intense pressure to join the Communist Party, which he did just prior to his visit to Germany. According to his friend Lev Lebedinksy, Shostakovich "dedicated the Quartet to the victims of fascism to disguise his intentions, although, as he considered himself a victim of a fascist regime, the dedication was apt. . . . He associated joining the Party with a moral, as well as physical death."[7] The last phrase alludes to Lebedinsky's belief that Shostakovich was actually contemplating suicide at this time.

---

7. As quoted in Elizabeth Wilson, *Shostakovich: A Life Remembered* (London: Faber and Faber, 1994), 340.

In a letter to his friend Isaak Glikman, Shostakovich himself suggests that Lebedinsky's interpretation of the inscription is correct:

> When I die, it's hardly likely that someone will write a quartet dedicated to my memory. So I decided to write it myself. One could write on the frontispiece, "Dedicated to the author of this quartet." The main theme is the monogram D, Es, C, H, that is—my initials.[8]

The second movement therefore can be heard in two ways, reflecting the double meaning that has been attributed to the quartet as a whole. First, we can take Shostakovich's inscription at face value and hear the almost demonic energy of this movement as a depiction of a bombing raid in progress. This reading is supported by the overt ferocity of the music—in particular, the explosive accompanying chords within the A section.[9] Or we could hear the movement as a personal expression of Shostakovich's intense suffering at the hands of the Soviet authorities. Considered by itself, of course, theme C is automatically linked to Shostakovich because of its motto opening, and its agitated quality could be taken as a depiction of Shostakovich's emotional state. But the foregoing analysis suggests that themes A and B also take on an autobiographical meaning as Part II progresses. Tightly bound to theme C through the processes described earlier, both seem to be inexorably pulled into the vortex of Shostakovich's tortured psyche; like theme C, they become expressions of his inner world. The movement therefore progressively shifts its emphasis from outer objective reality at the beginning of Part I to a private realm during the course of Part II. The beginning convincingly depicts a war scene, but as the motto begins to appear within Sections A1 and A2, we sense a slight blurring between that reality and Shostakovich's psychological state. The arrival of the "Jewish" B theme clearly reestablishes the world of outer reality, as we are reminded of the "victims of fascism" referred to in the dedication. But the bold reemergence of the motto in theme C marks a decisive turn toward the personal, setting the stage for Part II, where the earlier depictions of the outer world in Part I are transmuted into expressions of an internal psychic state. Insofar as it asserts such a transformation, this interpretation lends strong support to the idea that the quartet as a whole is an autobiographical work. Of course, the ubiquitous use of the motto throughout the quartet supports that reading anyway; but within the second movement Shostakovich seems to *lead* the listener away from the officially sanctioned interpretation indicated in the dedication toward the subversive private reading. Thus one might hear this movement as a coded message warning the listener not to take the dedication at face value.

Finally, the structural open-endedness of the second movement also bears on an autobiographical interpretation for the entire quartet. Throughout the entire second part we are witness to Shostakovich's anxiety and terror, which intensify until it reaches fever pitch. The trajectory of the music points toward a terrible cataclysm of some kind—perhaps even a descent into madness—but just before reaching that point, Shostakovich simply stops the music, as if flipping off a psychic switch. The sardonic parody of a waltz that follows (movement three) seems a perfectly appropriate response, conveying a chilling sense of detachment. Fortunately, the remaining portion of the quartet works past that response, leading through a wide range of emotional states in the last three movements. While the final movement ends in a state of desolation, it at least conveys the deeply felt emotions of a persona who has experienced grief and yet has learned to live with it.

---

8. Ibid.

9. The inclusion of the "Jewish" theme from the E Minor Piano Trio suggests a variant of this interpretation: perhaps the movement is not merely a musical representation of a literal war scene but also a depiction of the spiritual and physical terrors that German fascism held for its victims.

FURTHER READING[10]

Fanning, David. *Shostakovich: String Quartet No. 8 (Landmarks in Music Since 1950)*. Aldershot, Eng.: Ashgate Publishing Company, 2004.

Karl, Gregory, and Jenefer Robinson. "Shostakovich's Tenth Symphony and the Musical Expression of Cognitively Complex Emotions." In *Music and Meaning*, edited by Jenefer Robinson, 154–78. Ithaca, N.Y.: Cornell University Press, 1997.

McCreless, Patrick. "The Cycle of Structure and the Cycle of Meaning: the Piano Trio in E Minor, Op. 67." In *Shostakovich Studies*, edited by David Fanning, 113–36. Cambridge: Cambridge University Press, 1995.

---

10. Of the three citations provided here, David Fanning's monograph should be of special interest because of its specific focus on the Eighth Quartet. Unfortunately, it was published too late for its findings to be incorporated into the present essay.

~17~

PLAYING WITH FORMS
Mozart's Rondo in D Major, K. 485

William Rothstein

William Rothstein (CUNY/Graduate Center and Queens College) has focused his scholarly energies on exploring Schenker's theory and analytical
system, particularly the implications for rhythm, meter, and phrase. Along
with Carl Schachter (see Schachter's essay in chapter 10), Rothstein has created a remarkable theory of phrase rhythm that extends Schenker's own rather
sketchy treatment of rhythm and meter while incorporating insights of both
earlier and later theorists. Two essays in this book concern themselves with
Schachter's and Rothstein's theories: Harald Krebs offers an introduction to
hypermeter in chapter 2, and Charles Burkhart demonstrates issues of "phrase
rhythm" in chapter 1. Rothstein's *Phrase Rhythm in Tonal Music* won the Society for Music Theory's Young Scholar Award.

One of Rothstein's current interests is musical form, and the present essay addresses formal concerns in a systematic and provocative way. He chose
Mozart's Rondo in D, K. 485, because it uses the same theme for every segment of the form. Because of the monothematic nature of the work, attention must be paid to musical elements other than thematic identity. In addition, the lack of apparent contrast in the piece suggests the composer
replaced thematic contrast with other formal processes.

Rothstein is a superb pianist and has studied the nuances of the piece—
for example, how the work's seemingly smallest details (such as the appoggiaturas) incorporate important motivic repetitions.[1]

Composers of the eighteenth century were neither expected nor particularly encouraged
to be "original" in the music they wrote. To appreciate the degree to which eighteenth-
century music was governed by convention—that is, by what audiences expected to hear—
one must compare it to popular rather than to art music of later centuries. A symphony,

---

Some reminders: (1) all words in **bold** are defined in the glossary; (2) full citations for incomplete references
are found in the selected bibliography; (3) the authors use their preferred notational system (e.g., Roman numeral, form label, and register notation). Most of the essays denote register by middle C as C^4.—Ed.

1. The Rondo, K. 485, has been extensively treated by scholars. More advanced students may wish to consult
Joel Galand's excellent article "Form, Genre, and Style in the Eighteenth-Century Rondo," *Music Theory Spectrum*. (See further reading for full citation.) Galand's analysis of K. 485 is similar to that presented here; he also
discusses several other analyses of the piece. Most helpful, perhaps, are his reflections on the rondo as a genre
and his listing of other pieces that share some of the peculiarities of K. 485.

a sonata, or an opera was expected to follow certain patterns that would make it sound reassuringly familiar even on first hearing, much like a popular song today. The idea of challenging the audience with radically new sounds belongs to a later period in musical history.

If Mozart's D-Major Rondo, K. 485, is "about" anything, it is about the uses of convention.[2] It could be termed a "crossover" piece because it mixes conventions stemming from at least three eighteenth-century genres: sonata, rondo, and (to a lesser extent) concerto. It contains just one main theme, and even that theme was not original, either to this piece or to this composer. Mozart had used the same theme in another piece just a few months earlier, and he was to use it again.[3] The theme seems to have originated with Mozart's friend and teacher Johann Christian Bach, the youngest son of J. S. Bach. By using a borrowed theme, repeating it frequently, and demonstrating how many different roles it could play in one piece, Mozart created not only a delightful piece of music but also a valuable lesson in composition.

We do not know precisely why Mozart composed K. 485 (it may have been intended for one of his piano students), but we do know *when* he composed it: the score, in his own hand, is dated January 10, 1786.[4] Presumably, then, the piece was written in just one day. The manuscript bears no title, only a tempo marking: Allegro. When the piece was published, however, it was called *Rondo très facile*, meaning "a very easy rondo." The title was probably not Mozart's but his publisher's; calling a piece "very easy" was a good way to increase sales of sheet music. It's a curious title, though, because this "rondo" does not follow the pattern of most pieces bearing the same name. All of which raises an obvious question: What is a rondo?

The answer depends very much on whom you ask—especially if you include in your question not only the Italian-derived *rondo* but also the French *rondeau* and the Italian variant *rondò*. The French term, at least, has been used since the late Middle Ages, when it denoted a poetic form and only secondarily the musical setting of such a poem. Characteristic of both poem and music were frequent repetitions of the opening lines. In French baroque music (seventeenth and early eighteenth centuries), a *rondeau* was generally an instrumental piece, often a dance, in which a recurring section of music alternated with a series of contrasting sections called *couplets*. The recurring section was also, somewhat confusingly, called *rondeau*, so the pattern of the piece was as follows: *rondeau-couplet-rondeau-couplet-rondeau*, etc. The *couplets* were all different, but the *rondeau* sections were always the same. The *rondeau* enjoyed a great vogue in the early eighteenth century, when it spread far beyond France. *Rondeaux* (the plural of *rondeau*) were most often composed for harpsichord; those by François Couperin became especially famous. Later composers of *rondeaux* included Jean-Philippe Rameau and J. S. Bach.

To Italians of the late eighteenth and early nineteenth centuries, a *rondò* was a type of aria—an aria being an operatic song for a single character, sometimes accompanied by secondary characters, chorus, or both. A *rondò* fell into two sections, first slow then fast. Many operas in the early nineteenth century ended with a *rondò*, which in that case was

---

2. The K. number refers to a list of Mozart's compositions first compiled by the musicologist Ludwig Köchel in 1862 and revised several times thereafter. The numbers run from K. 1 to K. 626.

3. The other pieces in which Mozart uses the theme of K. 485 are: the last movement (Rondo) of the G-Minor Piano Quartet, K. 478, and the aria "Tardi s'avvede" from the opera *La clemenza di Tito*, K. 621. A valuable list of Mozart's borrowings from J. C. Bach appears in Ellwood Derr, "Composition with Modules: Intersections of Musical Parlance in Works of Mozart and J. C. Bach," *Mozart-Jahrbuch* (1996): 249–91.

4. A facsimile of Mozart's autograph manuscript is included in the Urtext edition by Schott/Universal Edition (UT 51018).

known as a *rondò-finale*. Although Mozart included *rondò* arias in several of his Italian operas, this meaning of our term has no bearing on K. 485.

Now let us ask for a definition from a German musician of Mozart's generation. Heinrich Christoph Koch was a minor composer but an important theorist; seven years older than Mozart, he outlived his more famous contemporary by twenty-five years. In his *Musikalisches Lexikon* (*Musical Dictionary*) of 1802, Koch defined the *Rondo* or *Rondeau* (he offered both spellings) as, first of all, a type of poem. Such a poem, according to Koch, had exactly thirteen lines, but the first line—sometimes just half a line—was to be repeated after lines 5, 8, and 13. The meaning of the repeated line, however, was to be slightly different each time, depending on how it fit into each new verbal context. Although Koch did not use the term "**refrain**", that is what such repeated lines in poetry are generally called. When a poem containing a refrain is set to music, the same music is typically used for each statement of the refrain; thus the term "refrain" came to refer to the repeated music as well as the words. Koch asserts that the sung rondo inspired the instrumental rondo, which similarly repeats a refrain several times (without words, obviously).

Koch has some interesting things to say about the character of rondos. Because of the frequent repetitions, he states, rondos are not well suited to the expression of lofty sentiments. Frequent repetition suggests naïveté, so rondos tend to be simple and naïve in style. Most eighteenth-century rondos fit this description, and Mozart's K. 485 is no exception.

Mozart's rondo fits Koch's description in two other ways. First, it contains a refrain: the music of the first sixteen measures is heard several times throughout the piece. Second, Mozart's refrain follows Koch's plan exactly. Koch says that a refrain should contain two melodic phrases of equal length—in this case, eight measures each. The melody of the first phrase should end on a note of the dominant triad, supported by a simple V chord; Koch calls this a *half cadence*. The second phrase should be much the same, except that it should end with what Koch calls a *cadence*. By *cadence* Koch means what North Americans call a *perfect authentic cadence*, where the harmonic ending is V–I or V⁷–I (both chords being in root position) and the melody ends on the tonic note. To qualify as a perfect authentic cadence (henceforth PAC), the tonic note must arrive together *with* the concluding tonic harmony; at most, the tonic note may be delayed by a suspension or **appoggiatura**.

Koch goes on to suggest what the later sections of a rondo should sound like, assigning a key to each. He offers three slightly different plans for the piece as a whole: these may be symbolized as ABACA, ABACADA, and ABACABA, where A represents the refrain. The first two plans differ not at all from the Baroque *rondeau*; they differ from each other only in that the second plan includes one *couplet* more than the first. (The refrain is repeated after each *couplet*.) The third plan differs from its baroque predecessors in that one *couplet*, B, appears twice.

When he composed K. 485, Mozart did not follow any of these plans. He was no musical rebel; indeed, most of his rondos fall into patterns similar to those described by Koch. (Remember, too, that calling the piece "Rondo" may not have been his idea.) Instead, Mozart followed a different plan. K. 485 is not composed in what later theorists would call *rondo form*—meaning a form conforming to one of Koch's plans—but in what those same theorists would call "**sonata form**." It is a sonata form, however, in which there is only one main theme. Since sonata form is often thought, erroneously, to depend on thematic contrast, the existence of an essentially *monothematic* sonata form is of special interest. Mozart must have known that he was writing a sonata form, even though he wouldn't have called it that (the term didn't exist yet). He wrote *a sonata form in the style of a*

(A truthful heart, full of honor...)

Example 17.1. Mozart, *La clemenza di Tito*, K. 621: Aria, "Tardi s'avvede," mm. 11–14

rondo, in that the main theme sounds like a refrain and is treated like a refrain. Since, however, *every* section of the piece is based on the refrain, the piece is quite unlike a conventional rondo. The piece is not without contrasts, but those contrasts are created by differing treatments of the theme and by different ways of continuing it. How Mozart formed a moderately substantial piece out of a minimum of melodic material will be the focus of our analysis.

Nothing could be simpler than the raw material of Mozart's (or Bach's) theme. The melody is based on a descending arpeggiation of the tonic triad: $\hat5$–$\hat3$–$\hat1$. That arpeggio is followed by an arpeggiated leading-tone triad, also descending: $\hat4$–$\hat2$–$\hat7$. This latter triad is, of course, diminished. Example 17.1 shows how Mozart used the same idea in his opera *La clemenza di Tito* (see note 3). The theme appears here in the key of G major; only the melody and the bass are shown.

The leading-tone triad in the second measure of example 17.1 is harmonized by the dominant note in the bass, resulting in a complete V^7 chord. Then the two arpeggios are repeated in reverse order. This means that the diminished triad in m. 3 resolves irregularly, since its top note, C, is heard to go up to D (m. 4) instead of down to B. (The diminished fifth F♯–C would normally resolve to a third, G–B.) C is the seventh of the V^7 chord, so its ascent is all the more striking. Notice, though, that the expected note of resolution appears in the bass, resulting in a first-inversion tonic triad, I^6, in m. 4. The seventh of V^7 thus receives a transferred resolution.

Example 17.2 shows the first nine measures of K. 485. The arpeggios in mm. 1 and 3 are filled in with appoggiaturas, each roughly a sixteenth note in length.[5] (The appoggiaturas are played *on* the beat; their length is subtracted from the following note.) The bass line contains very little motion, only a step from D to E and back again. The interval to which the diminished triad in m. 3 "should" have resolved, D–F♯, is sounded in the left hand on the downbeat of m. 4; in fact, it is the left hand that resolves the seventh of the inverted V^7 chord that fills mm. 2–3. As in the aria (example 17.1), the irregular upward motion from the seventh in the melody creates a marvelous feeling of "lift" at the beginning of m. 4. Also contributing to this feeling is the delayed resolution of the leading tone, C♯, which reaches D only at the third beat of m. 4. Notice the pattern formed by the top notes of the four arpeggios, A–G–G–A, and how this pattern mirrors the bass line in mm. 1–4.

---

5. In this essay, the term "appoggiatura" is used to indicate any embellishing note that precedes the main note, is not tied, and is played "on the beat," regardless of how the embellishing note is approached and regardless of whether it is consonant or dissonant. The term thus includes notes that might also be called rearticulated suspensions or accented passing tones. It even includes some chord tones. Example 17.3, for instance, shows that the high A in m. 7 (first beat) acts as an appoggiatura to G♮ (second beat), even though A is the root of the chord (an inverted V^7).

Example 17.2. Rondo, K. 485, mm. 1–9

The series of descending arpeggios is followed by a repeated *ascent* from A to D. (See the beams above the treble staff in example 17.2; the ascending fourth is clearer the second time than the first.) The motion then reverses itself, descending a fourth from A to E. Each note of this descent, except the first, is delayed by a written-out and embellished appoggiatura: first A–G, then G–F♯ and F♯–E. (The appoggiaturas function as suspensions here.) Finally the melody rushes past the E of m. 8 to the low A—itself decorated with a lower neighbor—and back up again to connect to the beginning of the second phrase (m. 9).

In example 17.3, the melody of mm. 5–9 is rewritten to highlight the appoggiaturas, the descending fourth, and—perhaps most interesting—the concealed arpeggio in m. 8. This arpeggio helps to prepare the return of the theme in m. 9. (Please note: From here on I will refer to mm. 1–4 as "the theme," mm. 1–16 as "the refrain.")

The entire first phrase, mm. 1–8, illustrates a common melodic pattern that theorists call a sentence. A sentence involves two statements of a basic idea—usually slightly different from each other—followed by a continuation that leads to some kind of *cadence*.[6] Here the basic idea is two measures long (mm. 1–2), and its restatement is varied by the reversal of the two arpeggios, something we noted earlier. The part of a sentence known as the continuation is generally characterized by **acceleration**, a quickening of musical activity. Here acceleration is created in two ways: by reducing the size of melodic statements from two measures to one measure; and by increasing the rate of chord change, also known as **harmonic rhythm**. Finally the melody moves to a half-cadence (mm. 7–8). These last two measures contain further acceleration: the melodic pattern repeats after only half a measure (m. 7), and the melodic rhythm accelerates through the disappearance of quarter notes, the absence of rests, and a change from eighth notes to sixteenths (m. 8). This is a typical sentence in that its lengths are—in measures—2 + 2 + 4, with

Example 17.3. Measures 5–8, renotated (melody only)

the second half subdividing along similar lines, 1 + 1 + 2. Even the last two measures subdivide as 1/2 + 1/2 + 1, maintaining the same proportions.

The refrain ends at m. 16 with a PAC. Its two phrases, mm. 1–8 and 9–16, will be called respectively the **antecedent** phrase and the **consequent** phrase. The next four measures, 17–20, stand curiously apart from their surroundings. The right hand is based on the earlier left-hand accompaniment—specifically, on the eighth-note layer in that accompaniment, which uses the same pitches. The left hand moves no farther than a step above and a step below the tonic, much like the bass line in mm. 1–7. There is little here that can be called melody. There is, however, a distinctive rhythm, which will make this musical idea instantly recognizable each time it returns. For now, though, the purpose of this little idea seems to be to separate the end of the refrain from the theme's varied repetition, which begins at m. 21.

With m. 21 we enter a new part of the form; we also begin to leave the key of D major. Koch states that, at this point in a rondo, there is a modulation to the key of the dominant (or, in a minor key, to the relative major), followed by a relatively stable section of music in the new key; this section will end with a PAC.[7] Since the main key of this piece is D major, Koch's plan calls for a modulation to A major. A more or less extended section in A major should follow, ending with a PAC in that key.

The modulating section in K. 485 extends from m. 21 to m. 34. Keys touched upon include B minor (mm. 21–22), A major and minor (mm. 23–24), and A minor (mm. 27–33). The music comes to rest on V of A minor (mm. 32–34). The progression in mm. 25–26—V^7 of E resolving to V^7 of A—makes it very difficult for a listener to hold onto the feeling that D is the tonic; even after m. 24, an immediate return to D major remained possible. To use a favorite expression of the British critic Donald F. Tovey, mm. 25–26 represent the moment at which the key of D major sinks below the horizon.[8] After m. 34, therefore, the listener awaits a new section in which A will be the tonic. An ascending chromatic scale fails to give away the mode, but A *major* is firmly established at m. 36. Here begins the relatively stable section in A major called for by Koch's plan.

The modulating section, or **bridge**, is based on the refrain. The rhythm of m. 2 is heard several times. The sentential arrangement of mm. 1–8 is also preserved: the basic idea, mm. 21–22, is repeated a step lower; the continuation, mm. 25–26, features one-measure instead of two-measure units; mm. 27–28 bring the melodic descent to a provisional close on the leading tone, G♯, accompanied by a root-position dominant. (The presence of the seventh in the V chord prevents m. 28 from sounding like a fully achieved half-cadence.) The motion leading to G♯ is repeated twice more, but the last time the melody leaps upward to a quarter-note E, accompanied for the first time by a pure V triad (m. 32, half-cadence). Now comes a new acceleration, as the alternation of E major and A minor chords speeds up to two chords per measure.

---

7. Koch implies the PAC by calling the section in question a "main period." A "main period," for Koch, always ends with a PAC.

8. See Donald Tovey, *Essays in Musical Analysis: Symphonies and Other Orchestral Works* (Oxford and New York: Oxford University Press, 1981), 12: "By firmly establishing another key, we understand some process which causes the original tonic as it were to sink below the horizon."

The section in A major is lengthy, extending from m. 36 to the repeat sign (m. 59). The PAC called for by Koch is heard in mm. 52–53, where it is emphasized by a long trill on $\hat{2}$. Such a trill is a conventional signal, in music of the classic period, for the PAC that concludes a lengthy section; it occurs especially often in concertos. Often, as here, the trill forms the climax of a general rhythmic acceleration; notice the prevalence of sixteenth notes from m. 43 on.[9] The passage from m. 53 to the repeat sign forms a **coda**—literally, "tail"—to the A-major section.[10] Mozart uses two conventional signals to indicate that this is a coda. Bass motion disappears; there is only a tonic pedal. Also, repeated use is made of the chord V^7 of IV, resolving to IV over the tonic pedal (notice the G♯'s in mm. 53, 55, and 57). A tonicization of IV is typically felt as a relaxation, so it is especially appropriate in codas.[11]

The A-major section is clearly subdivided into two parts (not including the coda) at m. 43; the division is defined by a change of texture, including a new statement of the theme in the left hand. Both subdivisions are based on the theme, as is the coda. Example 17.4 compares several occurrences of the theme throughout the first two-thirds of the piece; mm. 36–43 appear on the fourth line (d). The example makes it easier to recognize both similarities and differences between any two of the theme's many appearances.

In m. 39, Mozart arpeggiates a diminished triad (part of a diminished seventh chord) instead of the A-major triad that was expected; mm. 38–39 are also placed in a higher octave. Thus the fourth measure of the refrain is no longer a resolution of the third measure; instead it represents a heightening of harmonic and melodic tension. Measure 40 is surprisingly similar to m. 5 despite the difference of key (A major versus D major); the relation of m. 40 to m. 41 is sequential (compare mm. 21–24). Mozart models m. 42 after m. 27 (example 17.4c) instead of m. 7 (example 17.4a), but he reverses the melodic motion across the bar line: it is now G♯–A instead of A–G♯. Concluding the phrase in this way strongly suggests a cadence, and Mozart could easily have written a PAC here, effectively ending the section (example 17.5). Instead he begins the theme in the left hand, still in A major. Since m. 43 is the eighth measure of a phrase, a new beginning was not expected here (compare mm. 8 and 16). Since a cadence *was* expected, the new beginning sounds especially abrupt, especially since the tonic chord is heard in its least stable inversion, $^6_4$. The texture in mm. 43–46 strongly suggests the string section of an orchestra, with the theme in the cellos (perhaps with double basses an octave lower) beneath a measured tremolo in the upper strings (example 17.6). This time the theme's first two measures are repeated *without* reversing the order of arpeggios. The fourth measure of the theme is thus again unstable, ending on V^6_5.

Except for the use of one-measure units in mm. 47–48, it is difficult to recognize the continuation of the theme as having much to do with the refrain. Mozart's main purpose here is to lead in an exciting way to the conclusive PAC in mm. 52–53. The right-hand

---

9. See Edward Lowinsky, "On Mozart's Rhythm," in *The Creative World of Mozart*. This essay first appeared in 1956 in *The Musical Quarterly*. Passages resembling mm. 47–53 may be found in the first movement of virtually any Mozart piano concerto at the close of the solo exposition; a similar passage ends the recapitulation. For an example, see the Concerto in C Major, K. 467, mm. 184–94.

10. A **coda** in the middle of a piece is usually called a **codetta**.

11. In eighteenth-century music, pieces in major keys usually modulate to the key of the dominant (V). Once the tonic key returns, a brief tonicization of the subdominant (IV) is often used to counterbalance the dominant. The move from tonic to dominant, an ascent of one step on the circle of fifths, is experienced by listeners as an intensification. A later move from tonic to subdominant—a step downward from the same starting point—is felt as a corresponding relaxation.

Example 17.4. Eight appearances of the theme

a. mm. 1–8
b. mm. 9–16
c. mm. 21–28
d. mm. 36–43
e. mm. 43–53
f. mm. 54–59
g. mm. 71–78
h. mm. 95–102

flourishes in mm. 47–51 strongly resemble the solo part of a concerto, while the left-hand octaves maintain the illusion that we are hearing the cellos and double basses of an orchestra.

The coda (or codetta) acts in part as a response to mm. 43–46. Instead of arpeggiating the progression from I to viiº, the melody twice arpeggiates the reverse progression,

Example 17.5. Mm. 42–43, recomposed

Example 17.6. Mm. 43–46, orchestrated

from vii° to I.[12] Thus the theme is resolved firmly to the tonic of A major. The "lift" from m. 3 to m. 4 is also reproduced, including the delayed resolution of the leading tone (now G♯ to A). The arpeggios in mm. 56–58 are embellished, recalling m. 1. Finally, m. 59 resolves G♯ *directly* to A as part of a root-position A-major chord. A major is now as firmly established as it can possibly be, considering that this is not the main key of the piece.

If this were a piece in rondo form, there would be no repeat sign following m. 59. Instead there would be a short passage emphasizing V⁷ of D major, followed by a re-statement of the refrain in that key. The presence of the repeat sign (assuming the per-former observes it) means that the next thing we hear *is* the refrain, but there is no link-ing passage—the technical term is **retransition**—and no V⁷.[13] The very lack of these things is an important clue to the listener, like the dog that didn't bark in a famous Sher-lock Holmes story. This is, in fact, the *first* unambiguous sign that the piece will not fol-low the usual pattern of a rondo. Once the listener realizes that mm. 1–59 are being re-peated in their entirety, it is clear that the piece is following the pattern of a sonata form. Measures 1–59 constitute the **exposition**, which is that part of the form in which the main themes are first exposed, and in which there is a both *a modulation to* and *a PAC in* a key other than the tonic. Almost always, the exposition of a classical sonata form is repeated.[14]

Measures 60–94 form the **development** section, and mm. 95–156 the **recapitulation**. Together with the exposition, these form the three main parts of a sonata form. Example

---

12. As has been true in several earlier passages, including mm. 2–3 and m. 39 (also example 17.1, mm. 2–3), the arpeggiated vii° triad constitutes only part of the harmony. In this case (m. 54), the harmony moves from IV to vii° over the tonic pedal.

13. A **retransition** is a linking passage that leads to a restatement of a piece's opening theme. Other linking passages are called, simply, transitions.

14. Students who are familiar with binary form will recognize that the exposition of a sonata form is, in effect, an enlarged version of a binary form's first section.

EXPOSITION

Section:	Principal (tonic) group	New motive	Bridge	Subordinate (dominant) group	Codetta
Measures:	1-16	17-20	21-35	36-53	53-59
Main key(s):	D	D	D→A	A	A
Final cadence:	PAC in D (16)	(on I of D)	HC in A (32-35)	PAC in A (53)	(tonic pedal in A)

DEVELOPMENT

Section:	Modulating passage	Theme	Sequences (ascending and descending)	Retransition
Measures:	60-70	71-78	79-90	91-94
Main key(s):	A→G	G	G→D	D
Final cadence:		PAC in G (78)	HC in D (90-94)	(on V^7 of D)

RECAPITULATION AND CODA

Section:	Principal group plus Bridge	Subordinate group	Codetta	Coda
Measures:	95-124	125-48	148-56	156-67
Main key(s):	D→d→F→d	D→Bb→D	D	D
Final cadence:	HC in d (120-24)	PAC in D (148)	PAC in D (156)	PAC in D (166-67)

Example 17.7. An overview of the form

17.7 provides an overview. Measures 148–56 correspond to mm. 53–59, the little coda (or codetta) that ended the exposition. Measures 156–67 form a coda to the entire piece. Now we will examine the development section, followed by the recapitulation and coda.

As a general rule, the development section in a classical sonata form leads from the dominant *key* at the end of the exposition to a dominant *chord* (generally V^7) just before the recapitulation. The dominant chord leads back to the music that began the movement, marking the beginning of the recapitulation.[15] The dominant's change of meaning—from tonic of its own key to V^7 of the original key—represents the main *harmonic* task of the development section. This task may be accomplished in a few measures, or it may be spread out over a hundred measures or more. K. 485 has a relatively short development section. Turning A major from a tonic into a dominant requires removing G♯ from the scale and replacing it with G♮. Mozart introduces G♮ as early as m. 62, but he emphasizes this note most strongly by writing an eight-measure statement of the refrain in the key of G major (see example 17.4). G♮ is also stressed as part of the V^7 chord in the retransition (mm. 91–94).

The development section opens with an ingenious reshaping of the theme. After the first two measures have been stated, *forte*, in A major, the diminished arpeggio of the second measure is imitated twice in succession, *piano*, on dominant seventh chords of IV (D major) and ii (B minor), respectively. Thus there are three dissonant harmonies in a row, and none of them resolves exactly as expected. (The bass line in mm. 61–63 is chromatic, G♯–A–A♯; A♯ resolves by implication to B in m. 64.) As a result, the music of these measures has a "searching" quality that is highly effective as a contrast to the repeated affirmations of A major we have just heard. The rhythm, with its starts and stops, also contributes to this "searching" quality. Measures 60–61 are then transposed to B minor, reversing the pattern of mm. 21–24: then we were moving toward A major, now we are

---

15. There are recapitulations that begin in other ways, but they are relatively uncommon. Sonata forms in minor keys usually end the exposition in the relative major.

moving away from it. The turn toward G major in m. 67 comes as a slight surprise, since the bass descends instead of ascending further.[16]

The G-major statement of the refrain includes only the consequent phrase; thus a PAC is heard in m. 78. Next comes the little idea from mm. 17–20, used now in an ascending sequence over a chromatic bass line: F#–G–G#–A–A#–B. Again B minor acts as a temporary goal. A quick series of descending $^6_3$ chords, which is repeated with sixteenth-note figuration, leads to I^6 of D major (mm. 86 and 88) in preparation for the important half-cadence on the downbeat of m. 90. This half-cadence is followed by the retransition and its crucial V^7.

It is in the recapitulation that Mozart strays furthest from any conventional pattern, whether of sonata form or rondo. The music launches one surprise after another. Typically, the recapitulation of a sonata form repeats all sections of the exposition in their original order; any sections that were first heard in the dominant key, however, are transposed to the main (tonic) key, so that the movement ends in the key in which it began. If Mozart had followed this plan the results would have been stupefyingly dull, and the piece would have died a well-deserved death. Since, in the exposition, the theme was heard no fewer than six times—see example 17.4, a through f—the conventional plan would call for repeating all six statements in the same key, D major. This is, clearly, a recipe for monotony. It is also a dilemma that Mozart surely anticipated. He probably expected his audience, attuned as they were to eighteenth-century genres and forms, to foresee it as well, once the music reached the recapitulation. Escaping the threat of monotony, and being *heard* to escape it, is how Mozart demonstrates his compositional virtuosity in this piece.

Example 17.8 completes the table of thematic statements begun in example 17.4; it shows all statements in the recapitulation and coda. The first statement, mm. 95–102, also appeared in the earlier example; it is, of course, identical to mm. 1–8. Subsequent statements are heard in the following keys: D minor moving to F major; F major moving back to D minor; D major; Bb major moving to D major; D major; and D major again. Thus, beginning at m. 95, there are seven statements of the theme, six in the recapitulation and one in the coda. Four statements are in D major throughout, including three—exactly half—of those in the recapitulation itself. It is probably no accident that Mozart included the same number of thematic statements in the recapitulation as in the exposition, even though statements corresponding to examples 17.4c (the bridge) and 17.4d (the beginning of the subordinate theme group) are missing. Two statements we had reason to expect are absent; instead, Mozart gives us statements where we don't expect them. The appearance of the theme in Bb major (m. 138) is, perhaps, the most surprising of all, and its effect is consequently comical.

Before we explain Mozart's joke—something that is, after all, much less fun than hearing the joke itself—we should note that three of the keys Mozart uses in the recapitulation belong to the harmonic realm of D *minor* rather than D major. There is, of course, D minor itself, entering unexpectedly at m. 103. In addition, F major is III of D minor, and Bb major is VI. Much of the recapitulation thus falls in the shadow of the minor mode, constituting a little tour of D minor and two of its closely related keys. As in the exposition, an ascending chromatic scale is used (mm. 123–24) to keep the listener in suspense: Will the next section continue the minor mode, or will it revert to the major? It is remarkable how, even the second time around, Mozart succeeds in making the suspense real.

---

16. If Mozart had adhered strictly to the ascending sequence, the next key after B minor would have been C# minor (iii). Alternatively, he could have modulated from B minor to C major without fundamentally breaking the sequence.

Example 17.8. Seven appearances of the theme

a. mm. 95–102
b. mm. 103–10
c. mm. 112–20
d. mm. 125–36 (not all measures are shown)
e. mm. 138–48 (not all measures are shown)
f. mm. 149–156
g. mm. 158–66

To appreciate the comic effect of m. 138, it will help to trace the course of the music from m. 125; the latter measure corresponds to m. 43 in the exposition. Measure 43 began the *second* thematic statement within the subordinate theme group; here, following an emphatic dominant, m. 125 *begins* the group. If we compare the fourth measures of corresponding statements—mm. 46 and 128—we see that Mozart has now incorporated the same diminished seventh chord (vii°$^6_5$ of B minor) that he used in m. 39, the fourth measure of example 17.4d. This leads to a harmonic digression emphasizing first B minor (vi), then E minor (ii). At m. 134, Mozart returns to the cadential formula he had used at the end of the subordinate theme group in the exposition (mm. 51–53).[17] The surprise comes when the cadence at m. 136 is not a PAC, as the trill seemed to promise, but a deceptive cadence to B♭ major (♭VI). The thematic statement at m. 138 is part of Mozart's way of returning to the cadential $^6_4$ in order to complete the PAC (m. 148). This time the $^6_4$ chord lasts much longer than before—three measures—and its bass is doubled in a low register: Mozart is saying he really means it this time!

Although by this point the recapitulation is almost over, m. 148 is the *first* PAC in D major we have heard since m. 16, the end of the first refrain. Mozart has intentionally omitted the refrain's consequent phrase from the recapitulation (we heard it in the development section) so that a PAC in D major, with its implication of full **closure,** could be avoided until just this point. Even here, the lack of a bass note on the downbeat of m. 148 impels the music forward, into the codetta.

---

17. The right-hand flourish in m. 134 is adjusted to avoid exceeding the upper limit of Mozart's piano.

Example 17.9. The coda (mm. 158 ff.) compared to mm. 1–4

The codetta is expanded from its original six measures to full eight-measure length. The extra length includes another PAC, and this one finally places D on the downbeat in both melody and bass (m. 156). The following coda dissolves the theme quite wonderfully—separating the two initial arpeggios, using three-measure units (mm. 158–60 and 162–64), and emphasizing the new cadential figure heard at the end of the codetta.[18]

Most ingenious is the way that m. 161 stands simultaneously for m. 2 (which went unstated after m. 158) and for m. 3, while m. 162 stands for m. 4 and m. 1. Example 17.9 illustrates. The grace note in m. 162 is perhaps the single most delightful note in the piece: no mere embellishment, it stands for the first note of m. 4. For this reason, it is especially important to play this A *with* the bass note, *on* the beat, thus delaying the higher A by a fraction of a beat. Endings and beginnings have become confused; the piece has returned to its starting point. What could be more appropriate? The word *rondo*, after all, refers to something *round*.

FURTHER READING

Cadwallader, Allen, and David Gagné. *Analysis of Tonal Music: A Schenkerian Approach.*

Caplin, William. *Classical Form.*

Galand, Joel. "Form, Genre, and Style in the Eighteenth-Century Rondo." *Music Theory Spectrum* 17 (1995): 27–52.

Lowinsky, Edward. "On Mozart's Rhythm." In *The Creative World of Mozart*, edited by Paul Henry Lang, 31–55. New York: W. W. Norton, 1963.

---

18. Resolution of the leading tone, and of the tritone G–C♯, is a preoccupation of the coda. The theme was conspicuously nonchalant about both of these resolutions.

~18~

TWO POST-TONAL ANALYSES
Webern, "Wie bin ich froh!" from *Three Songs*, Op. 25
Schoenberg, "Nacht," from *Pierrot Lunaire*, Op. 21

Joseph N. Straus

Joseph Straus (CUNY) has written primarily on twentieth-century topics, including Ruth Crawford Seeger and Milton Babbitt, and especially the music of Stravinsky. In addition, his collection of writings by Carl Schachter, *Unfoldings: Essays in Schenkerian Theory and Analysis*, begins with a fascinating discussion between Straus and Schachter that illuminates some of the most interesting aspects of Schenkerian analysis.[1] Straus's book *Remaking the Past: Musical Modernism and the Influence of the Tonal Tradition* won the Society for Music Theory's Outstanding Publication Award.

The present essay was derived from his popular text *Introduction to Post-tonal Theory*, written in 1990 and now in its 3d edition (2005). Like the text, the essay is clear and easy to read. The essay also demonstrates how musical examples can be used to demonstrate a variety of points.

The analytical method we call "set theory," with the use of so many numbers and letters, can seem intimidating. However, as this essay will show, the system is essentially simple, a numerical short-hand for uncovering pitch relations in nontonal music.

AUTHOR'S NOTE Here are brief definitions of some of the technical terms used in the essay that follows.

*A pitch is a tone with a certain frequency. A **pitch-class** is a group of pitches related by one or more octaves. For example, all of the E♭s (and D♯s) in any register are members of the same pitch-class. The resulting twelve pitch-classes are frequently identified with integers from 0 through 11: 0 stands for C (and B♯ and D♭♭); 1 stands for C♯ (and D♭); 2 stands for D (and C♯♯ and E♭♭); and so on.*

A pitch interval is the distance between two pitches, measured by the number of semitones between them. Sometimes we will be concerned about the order of

---

Some reminders: (1) all words in **bold** are defined in the glossary; (2) full citations for incomplete references are found in the selected bibliography; (3) the authors use their preferred notational system (e.g., Roman numeral, form label, and register notation). Most of the essays denote register by middle C as C[4].—Ed.

1. For more on Schenkerian analysis, see the essays by Burkhart (chapter 1), Forte (chapter 3), and Schachter (chapter 10); also note the Schenkerian texts in the selected bibliography.—Ed.

*the two pitches and thus with the direction of the interval, whether ascending or de-
scending. In identifying such ordered pitch intervals, the number of semitones will
be preceded by a plus sign (ascending) or a minus sign (descending). (Example: the
ordered pitch interval from the lowest string on the violin [G3] to the highest [E5]
is +21; from the highest string to the lowest is −21.) At other times, we will be
concerned only with the absolute space between two pitches.* For such unordered
pitch intervals, *only the number will be provided. (Example: the space between
the lowest and highest strings of the violin, the unordered pitch interval, is 21.)*

A pitch-class interval *is the distance between two pitch-classes, again measured in semitones. As with pitch intervals, we will sometimes be concerned about
the order of the two pitch-classes (resulting in an* ordered pitch-class interval) *and
other times only with the absolute space between two pitch-classes (resulting in an*
unordered pitch-class interval). *To determine an ordered pitch-class interval,
imagine a circular clock face and count the number of semitones upward (clock-
wise) from the first pitch-class to the second. That number will never be higher than
11. (Example: the ordered pitch-class interval from the lowest string of the violin
[G] to the highest [E] is 9; from the highest string to the lowest is 3.) To determine
an unordered pitch-class interval, count upward from the first pitch-class to the second and upward from the second to the first, then choose whichever of these numbers is smaller. (Example: the space between the lowest and highest strings of the
violin, G and E, measured as an unordered pitch-class interval, is 3.)*

An unordered pitch-class interval *is also called an* interval class: *just as a
pitch-class contains many equivalent pitches, an interval class contains many equivalent intervals. The interval-class content of a motive or a harmony—that is, the
interval classes it contains—determines its basic sound.*

Listen several times to a recording of "Wie bin ich froh!"—a song written by Anton Webern in 1935. We will concentrate on the first five measures, shown in example 18.1.
Here is a translation of the first part of the text, a poem by Hildegarde Jone.

Wie bin ich froh!	How happy I am!
noch einmal wird mir alles grün	Once more all grows green around me
und leuchtet so!	And shines so!

The music may sound at first like disconnected blips of pitch and timbre. A texture that
sounds fragmented, that shimmers with hard, bright colors, is typical of Webern. Such a
texture is sometimes called "pointillistic," after the technique of painting with sharply defined dots or points of paint. Gradually, with familiarity and with some knowledge of
pitch and pitch-class intervals, the sense of each musical fragment and the interrelations
among the fragments will come into focus.

The lack of a steady meter may initially contribute to the listener's disorientation.
The notated meters, 3/4 and 4/4, are hard to discern by ear, since there is no regular pattern of strong and weak beats. The shifting tempo—there are three ritards in this short
passage—confuses matters further. The music ebbs and flows rhythmically rather than
following some strict pattern. Instead of searching for a regular meter, which certainly

Example 18.1. Webern, "Wie bin ich froh!" from *Three Songs*, op. 25 (mm. 1–5)

does not exist here, let's focus instead on the smaller rhythmic figures in the piano part, and the ways they group to form larger rhythmic shapes.

The piano part begins with a rhythmic gesture consisting of three brief figures: a sixteenth-note triplet, a pair of eighth notes, and a four-note chord. Except for two isolated single tones, the entire piano part uses only these three rhythmic figures. But, except for m. 2, the three figures never again occur in the same order or with the same amount of space between them. The subsequent music pulls apart, plays with, and reassembles the opening figures. Consider the placement of the sixteenth-note triplet, which becomes progressively more isolated as the passage progresses. In the pickup to m. 1 and in m. 2, it is followed immediately by the pair of eighth notes. In m. 3, it is followed immediately, not by a pair of eighth notes, but by a single note. At the beginning of m. 4, it is again followed by a single note, but only after an eighth-note rest. At the end of m. 4, it is even more isolated—it is followed by a long silence. The shifting placement of the rhythmic figures gives a gently **syncopated** feeling to the piano part. You can sense this best if you play the piano part or tap out its rhythms.

Now let's turn to the melodic line. Begin by learning to sing it smoothly and accurately. This is made more difficult by the wide skips so typical of Webern's melodic lines. Singing the line will become easier once its organization is better understood. Using the concepts of pitch and pitch-class, and of pitch and pitch-class intervals, we can begin to understand how the melody is put together.

There is no way of knowing, in advance, which intervals or groups of intervals will turn out to be important in organizing this, or any, post-tonal work. Post-tonal pieces tend to create and inhabit their own musical world, with musical content and modes of progression that may be, to a significant extent, independent of other pieces. As a result, each time we approach a new piece, we will have to pull ourselves up by our analytical bootstraps. The process is going to be one of trial and error. We will look, initially, for recurrences (of notes and intervals) and patterns of recurrence. It often works well to start right at the beginning, to see the ways in which the initial musical ideas echo throughout the line.

In "Wie bin ich froh," it turns out that the first three notes, G–E–D♯, and the intervals they describe play a particularly central role in shaping the melody. Let's begin by considering their ordered pitch intervals (see figure 18.1).

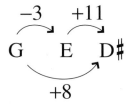

Figure 18.1. Ordered pitch intervals

The same ordered pitch intervals occur in the voice in two other places, in m. 3 (D–B–B♭) and again in m. 4 (C–A–G♯). (See example 18.2.)

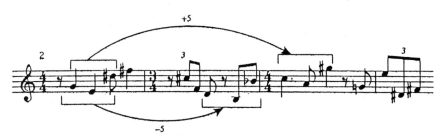

Example 18.2. Three fragments with the same ordered pitch intervals

Sing these three fragments, then sing the whole melody and listen to how these fragments help give it shape. The second fragment starts five semitones lower than first, while the third fragment starts five semitones higher. That gives a sense of symmetry and balance to the melody, with the initial fragment lying halfway between its two direct repetitions. Furthermore, the second fragment brings in the lowest note of the melody, B, while the third fragment brings in the highest note, G♯. These notes, together with the initial G, create a distinctive frame for the melody as a whole, one which replicates the ordered pitch-class intervals of the initial fragment (see example 18.3). Composers of post-tonal music often find ways of projecting a musical idea simultaneously on the musical surface and over larger musical spans.

The three melody notes at the beginning of measure 3, C♯–F–D, also relate to the opening three-note figure, but in a more subtle way. They use the same pitch intervals as

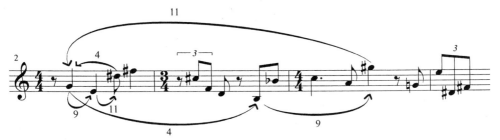

Example 18.3. Melodic frame (first note, lowest note, highest note) that replicates the ordered pitch-class intervals of the initial fragment

the first three notes of the melody (3, 8, and 11), but the intervals occur in a different order. In addition, two of the three intervals have changed direction (see figure 18.2).

Figure 18.2. Reordered intervals with changed directions

In other words, the fragment C♯–F–D has the same unordered pitch intervals as the opening figure, G–E–D♯. The relationship is not as obvious as the one shown in example 18.2, but it is still not hard to hear. Sing the two fragments, then sing the entire melody and listen for the resemblance (see example 18.4).

Example 18.4. Two fragments with the same unordered pitch intervals

The first four pitch-classes of the melody are the same, and in the same order, as the last four: G–E–D♯–F♯ (see example 18.5).

Example 18.5. The first four notes and the last four have the same ordered pitch-class intervals

The contours of the two phrases (their successive ordered pitch intervals) are different, but the ordered pitch-class intervals are the same: 9–11–3. This similarity between the beginning and end of the melody is a nice way of rounding off the melodic phrase and of reinforcing the rhyme in the text: "Wie bin ich froh! . . . und leuchtet so!" Sing these two fragments and listen for the intervallic equivalence that lies beneath the change in contour.

By changing the **contour** the second time around, Webern makes something interesting happen. He puts the E up in a high register, while keeping the G, D♯, and F♯ together in a low register. Consider the unordered pitch-class intervals in that registrally defined three-note collection (G–D♯–F♯). It contains interval classes 1 (G–F♯), 3 (D♯–F♯), and 4 (G–D♯). These are exactly the same as those formed by the first three notes (G–E–D♯) of the figure: E–D♯ is 1, G–E is 3, and G–D♯ is 4 (see example 18.6).

Example 18.6. A registral grouping and a melodic figure contain the same unordered pitch-class intervals

The melodic line is thus supercharged with a single basic motive. The entire melody develops musical ideas presented in the opening figure, sometimes by imitating its ordered pitch intervals, sometimes by imitating only its unordered pitch intervals, and sometimes, still more subtly, by imitating its ordered or unordered pitch-class intervals (see example 18.7).

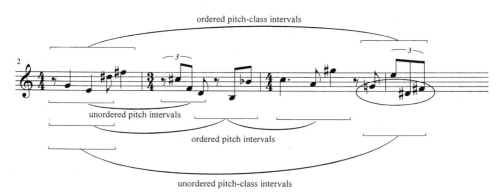

Example 18.7. Development of the initial melodic figure

Knowledge of the intervallic structure of the melody should make it easier to hear it clearly and to sing it accurately. Sing the melody again, concentrating on the motivic and intervallic interplay shown in example 18.7.

The piano accompaniment develops and reinforces the same musical ideas. Rather than trying to deal with every note, let's just concentrate on the sixteenth-note triplet figure that comes five times in the passage. When it occurs in m. 2 (G–E–D♯), it contains the same pitches and thus the same ordered pitch intervals as the beginning of the melody: −3, +11. In m. 3, different pitches are used (C–A–G♯), but the ordered pitch intervals are the same: −3, +11. When it occurs in the pickup to m. 1 (F♯–F–D) and at the end of m. 4 (B–B♭–G), it has the same ordered pitch intervals, but reversed: +11, −3.

The remaining occurrence of the figure, at the beginning of m. 4 (C–A–C♯), is somewhat different from these. Its ordered pitch intervals are −3, +16. It is not comparable to the others in terms of its pitch intervals or even its ordered pitch-class intervals. To understand its relationship to the other figures we will have to consider its interval classes. It contains a 3 (C–A), a 1 (C–C♯), and a 4 (A–C♯). Its interval-class content is thus the same as the first three notes of the voice melody (see example 18.8).

Wie bin ich

Example 18.8. Accompanimental figures derived from the initial melodic idea

In fact, all of the three-note figures we have discussed in both the vocal and piano parts have this same interval-class content. That is one reason the piece sounds so unified. Play each of the three-note figures in the piano part and listen for the ways they echo the beginning of the voice part—sometimes overtly, sometimes more subtly.

So far, we have talked about the voice part and the piano part separately. But, as in more traditional songs, the piano part both makes sense on its own and accompanies and supports the voice. For a brief example, consider the two single notes in the piano part, the F♯ in m. 3 and the G♯ in m. 4. In both cases, the piano note, together with nearby notes in the voice, creates a three-note collection with that familiar interval-class content: a 1, a 3, a 4, and no others (see example 18.9).

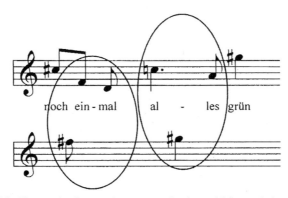

noch ein - mal   al   -   les grün

Example 18.9. Piano and voice together create collections with interval classes 1, 3, and 4

Example 18.10. Schoenberg, "Nacht," from *Pierrot Lunaire* (mm. 1–10)

The passage, at least as far as we have discussed it, is remarkably unified intervalli-
cally. It focuses intensively on the pitch intervals 3, 8, and 11 and, more abstractly, on
interval classes 1, 3, and 4. The passage is saturated with these intervals and with motivic
shapes created from them. Some of the relationships are simple and direct—we can discuss them in terms of shared pitch intervals. Others are subtly concealed and depend on
the more abstract concepts of pitch-class interval and interval-class content. With our
knowledge of pitch and pitch-class intervals, we can accurately describe a whole range
of motivic and intervallic relationships.

The same sort of intensive intervallic concentration is at work in "Nacht," one of the twenty-one short movements that make up Arnold Schoenberg's *Pierrot Lunaire*. *Pierrot* is probably Schoenberg's best-known work, and many factors contribute to its stunning effect. The instrumentation is wonderfully varied. The work is scored for a singer and a small instrumental ensemble (piano, flute/piccolo, clarinet/bass clarinet, violin/viola, and cello) in such a way that no two of the twenty-one movements have the same instrumentation.

The singer uses a vocal technique known as *Sprechstimme* (speech-song), a kind of declamation that is halfway between speech and song. The notated pitch should not be sustained but should be slid away from, in the manner of speech. As to whether the no-tated pitch need be sung accurately in the first place, there is considerable controversy. Some singers lean toward the speech part of speech-song, following only the approximate contours of the notated line; others try to give a clear indication of the actual pitches spec-ified. As we will see, the pitches in the vocal part so consistently reproduce intervals and motives from the instrumental parts that singers should probably touch the notated pitches accurately before sliding away. Listen to a recording of *Pierrot Lunaire,* concentrating on "Nacht," the eighth movement. The score for mm. 1–10 is given in example 18.10, with a translation of the first stanza of the text, itself a German translation of a poem by Al-bert Giraud.

Finstre, schwarze Riesenfalter	Dark, black giant butterflies
Töteten der Sonne Glanz.	Have obliterated the rays of the sun.
Ein geschlossnes Zauberbuch,	Like an unopened magic-book,
Ruht der Horizont—verschwiegen.	The horizon rests—concealed.

Schoenberg calls this piece a passacaglia. A passacaglia is a continuous variation form that uses a bass ostinato. In this piece, the ostinato consists of the three-note figure E–G–E♭. After the Introduction (mm. 1–3), this figure occurs once in each measure of this passage. Play this figure as it occurs in each measure, noticing how it moves from voice to voice and register to register. In mm. 8 and 9, each tone of the figure is elabo-rated, in diminution, by a rapid statement of the same figure transposed (see example 18.11).

Example 18.11. E–G–E♭ elaborated, in diminution, by transposed versions of itself

In m. 10, the passage comes to a striking conclusion when the same figure appears in the voice part. This is the only time in the piece that the singer actually *sings*. Her do-ing so in such a low, dark register and on such musically significant notes adds to the emotional impact of the word *verschwiegen* (concealed), a word that seems to crystallize the ominous, foreboding nature of the entire text.

Let's examine the intervallic makeup of that repeated figure: E–G–E♭. Its ordered pitch intervals are +3, −4, and (from the first note to the last) −1. These intervals per-meate the entire musical fabric. Consider, for example, the tune stated first in the bass clarinet beginning in m. 4, and then imitated in the cello (m. 5), the left hand of the pi-ano (m. 6), and, in part, the right hand of the piano (m. 7) (see example 18.12).

Example 18.12. The initial motive expanded and developed into a recurring melody

The tune begins, of course, with E–G–E♭. It then takes the interval −1, spanned by E–E♭, and extends it into a lengthy chromatic descent. The tune ends with a three-note figure that introduces two new pitch intervals, +9 and +8.

This new figure, B♭–A–G♭, does not have any obvious relationship to the initial motive, E–G–E♭. It has a different contour and different pitch intervals. To understand the relationship, we will have to consider the unordered pitch-class intervals of the two figures. Both have a 1, a 3, and a 4. (Their shared interval content is thus coincidentally the same as that of the main motive in Webern's song, discussed earlier.) Find those three intervals in each of the figures. From the perspective of interval class, we can hear the second figure as a development of the first. Sing the tune shown in example 18.12 and listen for the familiar initial motive, its continuation into a chromatic descent, and its development in the concluding figure.

In light of these observations, it becomes clear how carefully Schoenberg has notated the pitches of the voice part. Consider its first melodic gesture, shown in example 18.13.

Example 18.13. Motivic penetration of the *Sprechstimme* part

In its initial chromatic descent from D♭ to A and the leap upward from A to G♭, it exactly traces the last part of the melody shown in example 18.12. Then, by moving down to F, it tacks on an additional, overlapping version of the three-note figure involving pitch intervals 8 and 9. Surely these pitches should be clearly indicated by the performer! Try it yourself, first trying to indicate the notated pitches and then mainly chanting. Which do you prefer?

The Introduction (mm. 1–3) not only sets an appropriately gloomy mood with its use of the lowest, darkest possible register, but also introduces the main intervallic material in a subtle way. To make it easier to see and hear what is going on, the music is written an octave higher in example 18.14.

Of the six distinct musical lines here, all but one descend by semitone from the initial pitch. The melodic interval of −1, of course, anticipates the many chromatic descents that are coming up later in the music. Even more striking, however, are the relationships between the lines. In the lowest register, the first three notes are E–G–E♭, our familiar

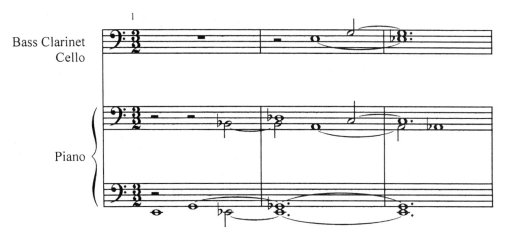

Example 18.14. Motivic saturation of the introduction

motive. The second note of the motive, the G, is also the first note of a **transposed** statement of the motive: G–B♭–G♭. The second note of that statement, the B♭, becomes the first
note of a new statement: B♭–D♭–A. This process continues upward until the cello and bass
clarinet come in with a restatement, an octave higher, of the original E–G–E♭. One additional statement of the motive, A–C–A♭, begins in the middle of the texture on the second beat of m. 2. In all there are six statements of the motive packed into these three measures. The density is extraordinary; the music of the Introduction is motivically saturated.
Play these measures and listen for each statement of the motive. The music that follows
can be heard as an unpacking of material so intensely presented in the introduction.

~19~

"THIS MUSIC CREPT BY ME UPON THE WATERS"
Introverted Motives in Beethoven's "Tempest" Sonata

Richard Cohn

Richard Cohn (University of Chicago) is a prolific scholar who has written on a wide range of topics, including atonal pitch-class theory, nineteenth-century chromatic harmony, meter and metric dissonance, Schenkerian theory, and transformational theory. He is a two-time winner of the Society for Music Theory Outstanding Publication Award.

This essay models one kind of motivic analysis in tonal music. Cohn traces certain important motives—both overt and subtle—in the first movement of Beethoven's "Tempest" Sonata, op. 31, no. 2. The author also addresses the allusion to Shakespeare's play, offering speculation about where the performer or listener might find a musical reference to the drama. Shakespeare's drama was written in 1611 and was based in part on actual written reports of daily events. It is the playwright's last comedy and contains many scenes with music, where the music accompanies acts of magic.

In music, a motive is a recurring element that both unifies a composition and marks its individuality. Like traits of human personality, some motives are extroverted, seizing a listener's attention immediately, while others are introverted, revealing themselves over longer acquaintance. The first movement of Beethoven's seventeenth Piano Sonata in D Minor (op. 31, no. 2), written in 1802 and nicknamed "The Tempest" after Shakespeare's play, contains motives of both types.[1] The upward octave arpeggio of the opening measure, which recurs in the bass at the phrase beginning in m. 21 (and elsewhere), is an example of an extroverted motive. These arpeggios quickly come to the attention of the listener, and, despite distinctions in tempo, loudness, and register, a listener quickly recognizes their similarity, in part because they are outfitted with identical ♩♩♩♩. rhythms.

But the "Tempest" is also unified and individuated by motivic connections that are less evident on first encounter. The motivic fragments that participate in such connections may occur during less-prominent moments, may be buried in an inner voice, or may lack

---

Some reminders: (1) all words in **bold** are defined in the glossary; (2) full citations for incomplete references are found in the selected bibliography; (3) the authors use their preferred notational system (e.g., Roman numeral, form label, and register notation). Most of the essays denote register by middle C as C^4.—Ed.

1. The origin of the nickname is shrouded in obscurity. The speculations on this question are reviewed in Theodore Albrecht, "Beethoven and Shakespeare's *Tempest*: New Light on an Old Allusion," in *Beethoven Forum* 1 (Lincoln: University of Nebraska Press, 1992), 81–92.

a characteristic rhythm. They may be compressed into flitting wisps of musical time that, like pesky flies, leave the grasping listener in the dust. Conversely, they may be stretched across such large temporal canvases that they only come to the attention of a performer or listener who adopts a bird's-eye perspective.

To bring such introverted connections to conscious awareness requires a special sensitivity. Like most mental activities that involve pattern matching, attunement to motivic connections results from a combination of intuition and technique. As a performing musician, one can—indeed must—train oneself to peer into the dark corners of a piece, to expand and contract one's temporal horizons, and to explore those moments in a piece that seem least charismatic. As with human interactions, individualizing traits that elude a first encounter are frequently the ones that are the more rewarding, those more cherished across a lifetime of exposure.

Where does one begin a motivic analysis? One way is to start labeling from the outset, noting for example that the piece begins with an upward arpeggio, followed by the stepwise filling of a descending perfect fifth, and so forth. Another way is to focus on a moment that draws one's attention and to explore its relationships to other moments in the piece. Early in my own encounter with this movement, my attention was drawn to the music presented in example 19.1, a five-measure segment of progressively quieter, slowly changing chords over a dominant pedal point.

These measures are not particularly remarkable in and of themselves. What drew my attention to them was the context in which they were presented: they occurred at the end of the **development** section. A decrease in intensity is what we least expect to hear at the approach to a **recapitulation**, especially after a development section as compact and intense as this one. The development, which begins at m. 99, is continuous, rhythmically propulsive, and tonally unstable until m. 121, where the harmony stabilizes on a dominant chord. The active surface rhythm continues while the dominant is extended through the next twelve measures by melodic double-neighbor motion. This dominant **extension** resembles an earlier moment in the movement, from mm. 13–21, where the harmonic motion also stood still over a rhythmically charged dominant pedal. That earlier dominant boiled over into a dramatically articulated tonic at m. 21. We are thus doubly conditioned, by prior events in the movement and by the conventions of classical first-movement form, to expect at m. 133 either a continued intensification or a resolution of the dominant.

Why does Beethoven turn down the flame at the very moment that the pot is about to brim over? A close look at these five measures will take us into the heart of the rich motivic world of this movement. The upper voice descends stepwise in whole notes from E^4 to A^3, covering the interval of a perfect fifth. We've heard similar stepwise fillings of a perfect fifth earlier in the movement. In mm. 75–76, the highest pitches of the left hand descend stepwise from E^4 to A^3 in half notes, while the highest pitches of the right hand

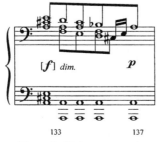

Example 19.1. Mm. 133–37

Example 19.2. Ascending and descending fifths, mm. 75–77

ascend from A^5 to E^6 at the same pace (see example 19.2). These measures are immediately repeated, with registers exchanged, in mm. 77–78. The entire four-measure unit is then repeated at mm. 79–82 and partially repeated again at mm. 83–84, leading to the cadence at m. 87 that signals the close of the **exposition**. Throughout these precadential measures, the voices resemble a pair of inverse sine waves, moving in contrary motion up and down through the perfect fifth between A and E in their respective registers (example 19.3).

The two stepwise motions, however, fill their perfect fifths in different ways. The *descending* motion from E to A is always a fragment of the natural minor scale, consisting exclusively of diatonic steps. The *ascending* motion from A to E contains an augmented second between its third and fourth notes, C and D♯, and thus is a component of the harmonic minor scale. It will be useful to honor this distinction with separate labels: "5N" when a fifth-fill melody consists exclusively of diatonic steps, as in the *natural* minor scale; "5H" when the fifth-fill melody contains the augmented second that is characteristic of the *harmonic* minor scale.

These observations begin to create a context in which to interpret the details of mm. 133–37, which we now recognize as an instance of 5H. Here, the augmented second is present between the third and fourth notes of mm. 133–37, but this time in descent. Indeed these measures are an exact **inversion** and augmentation of the ascent from A up to E that occurs multiple times at the end of the exposition (mm. 75–86).

Examples 19.4 and 19.5 broaden the context further by indicating some fifth-fills in the first part of the exposition. Descending fifths are prominent in the opening phrase of the Allegro. After the initial arpeggio, the right hand presents and then repeats a stepwise descent of a perfect fifth, from A^4 down to D^4. This melodic gesture is then **transposed**

Example 19.3. Ascending and descending fifths, mm. 75–87

Example 19.4. Mm. 3–6

upward by perfect fourth, moving from D^5 down to G^4 before cadencing on A^4 at m. 6 (see example 19.4).

Example 19.5 models the first occurrence of the ascending fifth-fill in the passage beginning at m. 21. The bass sweeps in a single gesture from the D-minor tonic articulation of m. 21 to the arrival of E major, the dominant of A minor, at the downbeat of m. 41.

Among the factors contributing to the explosive intensity of this twenty-measure phrase are its propulsive surface rhythm in the right hand and its upward thrusting arpeggios in the left hand. More subtle is the phrase's **accelerating** harmonic rhythm: the first two chords have a duration of four measures each, but a shortening to two-measure harmonic segments begins at m. 29. At m. 37, the A minor $^6_3$ harmony has a duration of a single measure, where it is prematurely displaced by a diminished seventh chord that prolongs the tension, at a maximum volume and maximum degree of dissonance, for three full measures. The diminished seventh chord, which functions as viiº^7/V in A minor, discharges onto an E dominant seventh at the downbeat of m. 41, at which point the bass becomes stabilized for the next thirteen measures.

The centrifugal energy of the passage is reined in by the orderly progression of the bass, which moves from D^2 (m. 21) to E^3 (m. 41), providing a "through-line" that directs the listening ear.[2] The motion is directly stepwise, with the exception of the temporary octave adjustment upward of the D♯ at m. 38. The bass of mm. 21–41 fills out the space of a major ninth and partitions that space into two perfect fifths, whose point of conjunction is the A^2 of m. 33. Both fifths contain an augmented second, marking each as an instance of the 5H motive.

The prevalence of the 5H motive in mm. 21–41 is crowned by events in the treble register. Throughout the first eight measures of the passage, the highest register, sounded by the crossing left hand, plays a legato double-neighbor figure about A^4. At m. 30, the

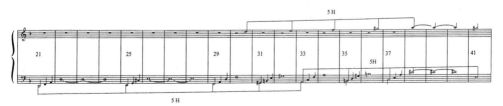

Example 19.5. Three slowly unfolding instances of the 5H motive in mm. 21–41

2. Not every note sounded by the left hand in the lowest register participates in the "bass line." That privilege is accorded only to the pitches that sound at the arrival of a new harmony. Without exception, those notes are metrically accented and are lower than any of the other pitches that accompany the same harmony.

crossing left hand opens up to a higher register and begins to articulate the 5H motive, *sforzando marcato*, from D^5 up to A^5. This treble line both responds imitatively at the (triple) octave to the bass (mm. 21–33), and in turn gives the bass (m. 33–41) something to imitate at the compound fourth.[3]

In exploring the motivic implications of the upper voice of mm. 133–37, we have not exhausted the potential of these measures to serve as a motivic source for the movement. Consider now the tenor line in the last four of these measures, consisting of the notes articulated by the right thumb of the pianist, $\langle$F, E, D, C#$\rangle$,[4] which we will call the "4D" motive in recognition of the diminished fourth between its first and last notes. Although the line is mostly concealed by the upper two voices, the arpeggiation of the chord at m. 137 causes its final C# to emerge more prominently.

The 4D motive has its source in the left hand of m. 3, which presents its pitches in reverse order, $\langle$C#, D, E, F$\rangle$, in the same register (see example 19.4). Like the 5N motive with which it is counterpointed, the 4D motive is repeated at m. 4 and then transposed upward by perfect fourth at mm. 5–6. As in its presentation in the tenor voice of mm. 134–37, the 4D motive is concealed at mm. 3–6 by a higher line.

With a single exception, the characteristic of concealment is a feature of the 4D motive in all of its presentations throughout the movement. The exception comes at mm. 61–62, where the motive is prominently articulated in the upper register, culminating at F^6, the highest note available on a standard 1802 fortepiano.[5] This overt quotation of the 4D motive, the first since the opening measures, triggers a clandestine obsession that endures for the remainder of the exposition and for the entire development, eventually linking back to the **reprise** of the opening bass line beginning at m. 148.

Example 19.6 indicates each appearance of the 4D motive between m. 61 and the closing theme at m. 74. The initial appearance of the motive at mm. 61–62 is multifaceted. The upper melodic line is accompanied by a lower line that presents the same notes in a different order, beginning with the last two notes, $\langle$E, F$\rangle$, and then presenting the first two, $\langle$C#, D$\rangle$. The four notes of the motive are present not only in each melodic line, but also within each two-beat segment, where they are distributed between the two voices. The first two-beat segment features parallel major sixths, ($\langle$C#, D$\rangle$ over $\langle$E, F$\rangle$), while the second two-beat segment features parallel minor tenths, $\begin{smallmatrix}E & F\\C\# & D\end{smallmatrix}$.

The presentation of the notes of the 4D motives in parallel sixths and tenths is continued in the following measures. At m. 62, immediately following the parallel tenths, the same configuration appears transposed and retrograded as parallel thirds in the tenor, $\begin{smallmatrix}C & B\\A & G\#\end{smallmatrix}$. In the following six measures (63–68), the $\begin{smallmatrix}E & F\\C\# & D\end{smallmatrix}$ configuration is presented three times in the middle register, at an interval of two measures. Each presentation is answered by a progressively higher version in thirds or sixths in reverse order, until the zenith F^6 is regained at m. 68. This latter event triggers a stepwise descent in diatonic parallel thirds in the right hand, distributed between two different registers. The last set of such thirds,

---

3. The imitative features of this music are noted in Rudolph Réti, *Thematic Patterns in Sonatas of Beethoven* (New York: MacMillan, 1967), 181.

4. A standard convention of music analysis is to enclose a list of pitches in angled brackets if one is referring to their presentation in a particular melodic order. If the order does not matter (as when one lists the tones of a chord), the pitches are enclosed in curly brackets.

5. See Sandra P. Rosenblum, *Performance Practices in Classic Piano Music* (Bloomington: Indiana University Press, 1988), 32. All three of the op. 31 Sonatas extend up to F^6 and no further, suggesting either that Beethoven lacked higher pitches on his fortepiano at that time or that he assumed the same of his "software clients."

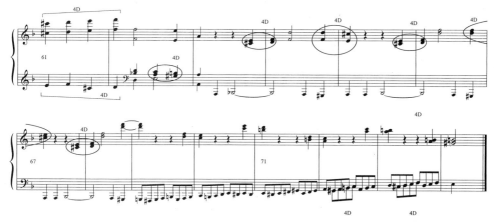

Example 19.6. Eleven instances of the 4D motive, mm. 61–74

at mm. 72–74, again reproduces the 4D motive as a two-voice counterpoint, $^{C\ B}_{A\ G\sharp}$, but with the A suspended, $^{C-\ B\ -(B)}_{A-(A)-\ G\sharp}$.

Counterpointed against the right-hand descent in mm. 68–74 is a more rapid rumble that ascends from the lowest register of the keyboard. The 4D figure is worked in here as well: ⟨G♯, A, B, C⟩ is presented at m. 72 and immediately transposed upward by perfect fourth as ⟨C♯, D, E, F⟩ at m. 73. The concatenation of these two transpositions in the bass echoes the opening five measures of the movement. Indeed, when this passage is transposed in the recapitulation at mm. 202–203, it will cause the exact pitches of the opening bass line to recur (see example 19.7).

The music modeled at example 19.6 is immediately followed by the music that closes the exposition, which we already discussed with reference to example 19.2. Our earlier model focused on the appearance of the fifth-fill motives, but we are now in a position to observe that the 4D motive continues to be present in these measures as well. Each time that the descending 5N motive ⟨E, D, C, B, A⟩ occurs, in either register, it is accompanied in parallel thirds by a lower voice that sounds ⟨C, B, A, G♯⟩. We can thus see that the closing of the exposition draws together all three motives that we have been documenting, sounding them in a three-voice counterpoint. This same combination is repeated, in transposed form, at the close of the movement.[6]

The 4D motive, then, is present in virtually all of the last twenty-six measures of the exposition, yet only at its initial appearance (61–62) is it brought to the forefront of consciousness. I like to think of the motive as popping its head out of a manhole cover at this moment. To the casual listener, it presents the sole indicator of an underground system of pipes and tunnels that is laid through the heart of the movement. Beethoven's strategies for "working out" the 4D motive at the end of the exposition allow us to compile a handbook of smuggler's techniques: the motive is disguised through reordering; it is tucked into an "inside pocket"; it is bootlegged inside a stampede of bass notes. As we turn the corner into the development section, our smuggler's inventory will expand even further.

---

6. The technique of combining distinct melodies into a multivoiced counterpoint and assigning such a combination a closing function has affinities with the perorational combination of distinct subjects at the close of a baroque fugue, and it anticipates the virtuosic writing at the end of Wagner's Overture to *Der Meistersinger*.

Mm. 3 - 6

Mm. 72 - 74

Mm. 202 - 204

Example 19.7. The recapitulation (mm. 202–203) restores the 4D motive to its original pitch level (mm. 3–6)

After a six-measure introductory *Largo*, the development proper consists of a single twenty-two measure phrase whose upward arpeggiating bass, propulsive right-hand tremolo, and overcrossing left hand are modeled on the modulatory transition that extends from mm. 21–40. We studied some features of that earlier passage in connection with example 19.5, where our focus was on the 5H motive as it was articulated in imitative counterpoint in the two outer registers. In the corresponding section of the development section that concerns us here, the primary motivic significance is instead carried by the tremolo interior, whose highest voice stretches the 4D motive, at its original transposition, across the entire extended phrase (see example 19.8). The C♯ is present from m. 99 up to the downbeat of m. 109, where it is displaced by the D. The E arrives at m. 113, and the culminating F appears at the downbeat of m. 117, at exactly the moment that the tonic harmony first reappears. This moment is articulated by a reversal of direction in the bass line and the cessation of the left-hand arpeggios for the first time since the opening of the development.

The phrase that extends from mm. 99 through 117 thus displays a procedure that is opposite to the one we observed in the bass at mm. 72 and 73, which concealed the 4D

Example 19.8. The tenor slowly unfolds the 4D motive, mm. 99–117

motive like a needle in a haystack of notes. Here the motive is easy to overlook (or "overlisten") because its girth overflows the boundaries of the temporal frames in which melodic continuities are customarily sought.[7]

Four measures after the culmination of the expanded 4D motive, the **retransitional** dominant is reached. The twelve measures beginning at m. 121 are characterized by a double-neighbor figure in parallel thirds, $\begin{smallmatrix} E & F & D & E \\ C\sharp & D & B & C\sharp \end{smallmatrix}$, whose first two events present the notes of the 4D motive in parallel tenths, exactly as at mm. 63–68. At the end of these twelve measures we have reached the event that prompted our inquiry: the tenor 4D descent of mm. 134–37, whose final pitch (which, by virtue of the notated arpeggiation, is the first to be struck) marks the arrival of the opening chord that ushers in the recapitulation.

Many of our observations so far have taken the form of sightings, somewhat resembling a bird-watch: "there's that motive . . . right there through those trees . . . I see it again over there." Such a roster of motivic appearances is useful to the extent that it shows how a composition was conceived and may be heard as unified, how its particulars are stitched together with the design of the larger fabric in mind. Yet it is perhaps not entirely satisfactory, as it seems to ignore what we might call "behavioral" questions: why this transposition of the motive? Why in this register? Why does this version of the motive precede that one rather than follow it? Why is the motive iterated just here and not six measures later? We are not likely to find answers to all such questions, as each answer typically prompts new questions. But in addressing such questions of detail, order, and pacing, we can begin to approach topics of great concern to performers: How do I shape the piece? How can I make it "tell a story" or "enact a drama"? How can I conceive the piece as a whole yet keep a sense of moving forward, so that listeners will be persuaded to invest their keenest attention in my performance, to hang with me on every phrase?

I will keep my remarks on these topics brief and suggestive rather than fully explicit. The reader will benefit more from a self-guided exploration of their implications than from an authorial taking-by-the-hand.

We can begin by observing that each of the three motives whose appearances we have documented occur in three distinct transpositions, each corresponding to familiar tonal functions. The original, or "tonic" ("T"), version is followed by transpositions both up and down a perfect fifth, creating dominant ("D") and subdominant ("S") versions. Example 19.9 inventories the three motives in their three versions. We are accustomed to tracking musical form as a journey through harmonic regions affiliated with these three functions. Tracking our three motives through their three analogous "functional regions" can reveal syntactic principles that sometimes reinforce the harmonic journeys and sometimes conflict with them.

Consider, for example, the surfacing of the 4D motive in the treble at m. 61 in its tonic form, ⟨C♯, D, E, F⟩. The music has not been in the tonic D minor for many measures. Indeed, just before this sounding of the 4D motive, we have experienced a long-awaited (albeit weak) A-minor cadence (m. 55), and just after, we will soon be treated to

---

7. Such very slow motivic unfoldings are associated with the phenomenon of "distance hearing" or "structural hearing" and are characteristically exposed by techniques of linear analysis associated with the theories of Heinrich Schenker. In most cases, the motivic "scaffold" pitches that constitute such an unfolding are intermixed with additional pitches that are "reduced out" by Schenkerian analytic techniques. [See the glossary and the Forte essay in chapter 3 for more on Schenkerian analysis.—Ed.] What is remarkable about the development section of op. 31, no. 2, is that distance hearing does not require the listener to eliminate any such "ornamental" events. Beethoven's motivic technique here is reminiscent of the very long, slow unfoldings of fragments of Gregorian chant (*cantus firmus*) used by composers between the twelfth and fifteenth centuries.

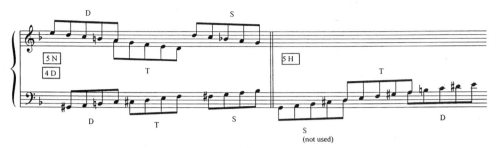

Example 19.9. The three motives in their tonic (T), subdominant (S), and dominant (D) transpositions

a stronger such cadence (m. 63). Are we then in D minor at m. 61? No. But the motive is still clinging to its tonic form in spite of the dominant tonal environment and will continue to do so until m. 70, at which point it will be replaced by its dominant form, ⟨C, B, A, G♯⟩, in an inner voice. The persistence of the tonic form of the motive, long after the key of A minor has been reached, accounts in part for the continuing sense of tension that energizes the second half of the exposition. The reader will find it instructive to label all three motives throughout the movement by transposition level and to consider how this perspective contributes to the shape of the piece, to its curve of departure and return.

A second observation is that motives appear in both ascending and descending forms, and that the two can have complementary or offsetting effects. We have already observed the inverse "sine waves" whose simultaneous unfolding was documented at example 19.3. A similar effect may be observed with respect to the 4D motive, which, as we have seen, ascends slowly in the middle register throughout the development section. Beginning at m. 121, the motive fragments into two-note pairs, which are quoted three times in the upper register (m. 122–24) and then six times in the middle register (126 through 132). At m. 133, as we have seen, the 4D motive is returned to its original lower register, where it is presented in descending order. The final pitch of this descent is the C♯^{3}, the same pitch that initiates the bass line of the recapitulatory Allegro, where the motive is again restored to its initial ascending form.

The progress of the 4D motive across the development section is summarized at example 19.10, which brings out the offsetting character of the ascending and descending versions across a long span of musical time. This model enriches yet further the story that we can tell about mm. 133–37. It suggests that the appearance of the 4D motive in the tenor voice plays two specific roles: it both reverses the ascent of the ⟨C♯, D, E, F⟩ motive that was so carefully cultivated across the development proper and it restores that motive to its native bass register for the return of the Allegro at the beginning of the recapitulation.

The analyst/listener who is able to identify the types of motivic resonances that we have been exploring will be in a position to internalize them, to sing them inwardly. Such an inward listener who also possesses the appropriate technical capacities will be in a position to become a performer who projects these resonances to a listener, to animate a narrative such as that suggested by example 19.10. Such a performer knows who the characters are in the "drama" of the piece, how they unfold, develop, interact, and reach their fate.

The reference to "drama" leads us to recall that the subtitle of the Beethoven sonata refers obscurely to a drama of William Shakespeare. I will conclude by showing how the motivic story that we have been telling suggests how we might beat a path, however tentatively and speculatively, through Beethoven back to Shakespeare. The reader should

Example 19.10. The tenor line at mm. 134–37 reverses the 4D motive and restores it to its original register in preparation for the recapitulation

consider the story of the 4D motive—its concealed introversion and its registral migrations—in light of the bewitching music perceived by the ship-wrecked Ferdinand in Act I Scene 2 of "The Tempest," and consider how such a story might be animated by a performance of the first movement of Beethoven's op. 31, no. 2:

> Where should this music be? i' th' air or th' earth?
> It sounds no more; and, sure, it waits upon
> Some god o' the island. Sitting on a bank,
> Weeping again the king my father's wreck,
> This music crept by me upon the waters,
> Allaying both their fury and my passion
> With its sweet air; thence I have followed it,
> Or it hath drawn me rather. But 'tis gone.
> No, it begins again.

The passage suggests a response to the question with which we began. Why does Beethoven turn down the flame at mm. 133–37, the very moment that the pot is about to brim over? Perhaps because he wishes to depict the allaying of the fury and passion of the development section, where the music ($\langle$C♯, D, E, F$\rangle$) crept by upon the waters of the middle register after inhabiting the air (mm. 61–62) and the earth (mm. 3–5).

Is this explanation "true"? We will never know. Does it provide an interesting story that provokes a riveting performance? Try it and hear.

FURTHER READING

Burkhart, Charles. "Schenker's Motivic Parallelisms." *Journal of Music Theory* 22, no. 2 (1978): 145–75.

Jonas, Oswald. *Introduction to the Theories of Heinrich Schenker*, New York and London: Longman Inc., 1982. Chap. 1.

Reti, Rudolph. *Thematic Patterns in Sonatas of Beethoven*. New York: MacMillan, 1967.

Stein, Deborah. "Schubert's 'Erlkönig': Motivic Parallelism and Motivic Transformation," *Nineteenth Century Music* XIII/2 (Fall 1989): 145–58.

~20~

"ROUNDING UP THE USUAL SUSPECTS?"

The Enigmatic Narrative of Chopin's C-sharp Minor Prelude

Charles J. Smith

Charles J. Smith (The University at Buffalo) has long been interested in the chromatic harmony of the nineteenth century and in the theories of Heinrich Schenker.[1] His article "Musical Form and Fundamental Structure: An Investigation of Schenker's *Formenlehre*" won the Society for Music Theory's Outstanding Publication Award.

Smith's essay on Chopin's C-sharp Minor Prelude analyzes the work as a narrative by explicitly relating it to a well-known recent suspense film, *The Usual Suspects*. In this unusual approach, Smith finds musical cognates for narrative devices that are familiar from the suspense genre. In particular, his discussion of musical form is based primarily on harmonic criteria rather than on thematic characteristics; this emphasis reflects his conviction that form is best approached as a musical phenomenon projecting harmonic relationships first and foremost.[2]

Chopin's Prelude in C-sharp Minor (op. 45, written in 1841) has been dismissed by many critics as strange, obscure, and insignificant.[3] The Prelude has seldom been rigorously analyzed—perhaps because it proves surprisingly resistant to traditional analytical strategies. This failure is not a misfortune, however, since, despite their usefulness for producing lots of significant data without overmuch effort, these strategies can conceal just how mysterious all music is—how hard it is to say anything coherent and persuasive about the fundamental issues of shape and narrative, in any piece of music whatsoever. "Diffi-

---

Some reminders: (1) all words in **bold** are defined in the glossary; (2) full citations for incomplete references are found in the selected bibliography; (3) the authors use their preferred notational system (e.g., Roman numeral, form label, and register notation). Most of the essays denote register by middle C as C^4.—Ed.

1. See "The Functional Extravagance of Chromatic Chords," *Music Theory Spectrum* 8 (spring 1986): 94–139.

2. Music scholars have debated for years about what aspect of musical form is more important: thematic structure or tonal design. Even though most analyses focus on one or the other, both are significant. For an explanation of tonal issues in classical music, see Charles Rosen, *The Classical Style: Haydn, Mozart, Beethoven*, chap. 1, "The Musical Language of the Late 18th Century."—Ed.

3. Jean-Jacques Eigeldinger, in "Chopin and 'La note bleue': An Interpretation of the Prelude, op. 45," *Music and Letters* 78, no. 2 (May 1997): 233–53, describes the circumstances of the Prelude's publication and provides an overview of its reception. Eigeldinger describes it as an "enigma waiting to be, if not decoded, at least examined" (234).

cult" pieces such as the C-sharp Minor Prelude force us to confront these issues, because there is so little else that can easily be said about them.

The approach proposed here is to interpret the piece as having the narrative trajectory of a thriller—that is, presenting puzzles to be solved, raising our expectations only to thwart them, and then at the end unmasking a hidden central character who has secretly controlled the whole story. This narrative is similar in many remarkable ways to that of Bryan Singer's well-known film *The Usual Suspects,* with its convoluted plot and series of escalating revelations.[4] In the absence of a simple picture of the Prelude, a comparison between the film and the piece can be eye-opening . . . and can help us grasp the overall shape of the narrative.[5]

THE LINE-UP: PUZZLES TO PONDER

The C-sharp Minor Prelude presents us with a unique set of puzzles, just as *The Usual Suspects* presents puzzles to the viewer. The first appears before the music starts—the title. In what sense is this piece a prelude? That name normally suggests prefatory music, designed to precede a longer or weightier piece in the same key. Chopin's understanding of the term was always somewhat unconventional,[6] but the 1841 Prelude is even more un-prelude-like than any of his other preludes, with an uncanny sense of spaciousness that makes it seem longer than its ninety-two measures. A hint to its character might be provided by the tendency of earlier composers to use the title "Prelude" for improvised pieces, or at least for pieces that sound like written-out improvisations. All of Chopin's music has a spur-of-the-moment flavor, but the C-sharp Minor Prelude suggests an ongoing improvisation even more strongly than most.[7] Likewise, first-time viewers of the film usually find it disjointed and difficult to follow—as if the director were improvising rather than working from a carefully thought-out script.

Another puzzle about the Prelude is its failure to present any distinctive melodies; the only memorable tune arrives in mm. 27–28 and reappears just three more times, in mm. 31, 51, and 55 (see scores 20.3 and 20.5).[8] A nineteenth-century piano piece without a singable melody is as anomalous as a thriller without a hero. And, indeed, the film includes almost no normally sympathetic characters; all of the investigators and other conventional hero types are flat and uninteresting. Without likeable heroes, viewers must identify with unrepentant criminals and a pathetic loser. Without distinctive melodies, listeners have to attend to less obvious musical gestures.

---

4. This 1995 film was written by Christopher McQuarrie (who received an Academy Award for best original screenplay). Readers of this essay are encouraged to watch the film several times before continuing; the DVD version with audio commentary by the director and writer is particularly helpful.

5. Reading a piece of music as analogous to a mystery story is a strategy with a distinguished precedent: Edward T. Cone's brilliant article, "Three Ways of Reading a Detective Story—Or a Brahms Intermezzo," *The Georgia Review* 31, no. 3 (fall 1977): 554–74.

6. Though most of the individual pieces in his set of Twenty-four Preludes (published as op. 28) are too short to stand convincingly on their own, none of them work all that well as introductions to other pieces. The op. 45 Prelude has no connection whatsoever with this earlier set, though publishers have typically included it as an unconvincing epilogue to scores of op. 28.

7. The similarity between parts of the Prelude and some introductory sections in Chopin's F Minor Fantasie (op. 49) and A-flat Polonaise-Fantasie (op. 61) is pointed out by Eigeldinger, "Chopin and 'La note bleue,'" 245.

8. An annotated score of the entire Prelude is distributed through scores 20.1 to 20.9. The boxes below the score enclose the names of keys that are clearly articulated by strong cadences; circles mark points of abrupt harmonic deflection. The significance of these moments will be explained shortly.

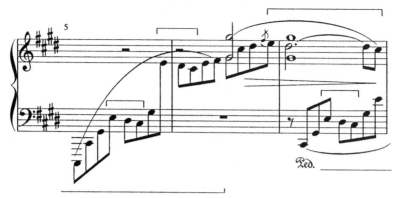

Figure 20.1. Appoggiatura motive in mm. 5 ff.

The surface of the Prelude is an amorphous texture of almost-imitative counterpoint, weaving long lines into an illusion of canonic pursuit. For example, in mm. 5 ff. (see the brackets in figure 20.1), an E–D♯–C♯ descending-third motive appears first in a bass register, then in the middle of the keyboard, and finally in the treble—as the whole process begins again in the left hand. Many of these overlapping lines span more than three octaves; most come to no definite end but seem instead to vanish into thin air, or rather into the middle of the ensuing texture. In such an environment, it is almost impossible to distinguish between theme and accompaniment. Lines that begin as accompaniments, usually chordal arpeggiations, gradually become more like melodies as they move into higher registers; likewise, lines that begin tunefully (e.g., the right-hand octave G♯s in mm. 6–7) tend to drift away into nothingness. If we try to follow the usual strategy of attending more to what's accompanied than to the accompaniment itself, we get into trouble at every turn. Similarly, the film is about an ensemble of characters rather than any one person as the clear center of the story. The narrative spotlight moves disconcertingly back and forth, from one crook to another; no one gets picked from the lineup as the fellow to watch.[9]

The Prelude's lines interact with their supporting harmonies in a way that is typified by the initial E–D♯–C♯ motive (scale-steps ♭$\hat{3}$–$\hat{2}$–$\hat{1}$ in C♯).[10] This line appears within a C♯-minor chord—a tonic harmony that coincides with the E and C♯ chord tones. It is, however, the second pitch, the D♯ passing tone, that is consistently accented (see figure 20.1) in the motive's initial appearances and in all of its many later re-appearances—whether supported by C♯-minor or any other triad. As a result, most of the recognizable chords in the Prelude begin with some kind of accented nonchord tone; the few that arrive without an initial decoration (e.g., the downbeat of m. 15 over a D-major chord) stand out as special. Likewise, few narrative episodes in the film begin cleanly; instead, most are set in

---

9. Our natural inclination to treat the narrator as the focus of the story is thwarted by the fact that Verbal Kint seems to be a dull-witted hanger-on, a physical cripple who will never amount to anything. The central figure of the story, the indomitable criminal genius Keyser Soze, hardly appears at all, and is not even mentioned until the film is well underway.

10. In this essay, flat signs in front of scale-step numbers and chord symbols indicate minor mode, as opposed to major mode, versions; thus scale-step ♭$\hat{6}$ of C♯ minor is A (as opposed to A♯, which is $\hat{6}$ of C♯ major). Upper- and lowercase symbols designate major- and minor-quality chords; therefore ♭VI in C♯ minor is an A-major triad (as opposed to A♯-minor, which is vi of C♯ major). This notational differentiation is necessary because Chopin's music seldom presents parallel major and minor modes as segregated; chord symbols need to be able to indicate whether a particular harmony is shaded with a major mode or a minor mode color.

mm.	Harmonic Motion between Cadences	Harmonically Defined Sections
1–5	[c♯]	Introduction
5–18 19–26 27–35	c♯ ↘ A … D? **f♯** ↘ (V⁷/D) – **B♭** (V⁷/B♭) – **G♭** … [G♭]	Section 1 (harmonically open—modulating away from the home key)
35–50 51–59	**G♭** ↗ (V/B♭) (V/A) — **F** … [F]	Section 2 (modulating to a second harmonic goal)
59–67	**F** … [c♯]	Retransition (return from this second goal to the original key)
67–85	c♯ ↘ A ↘ ↗ [c♯]	Reprise (w/cadenza) (rewrites material of section 1, so that it doesn't modulate)
85–92	c♯ ↗ D ↘ [c♯]	Codetta

LEGEND

Uppercase = Major mode key

Lowercase = Minor mode key

Boldface = Tonicized key (both its tonic and dominant appear, in close proximity)

Boxed = Key articulated by a strong dominant-to-tonic cadence

↘ = Harmonic sequence descending by 2ds

↗ = Harmonic sequence ascending by 2ds

… = Nonsequential progression of chords

— = Immediate succession of chords

Figure 20.2. Formal-harmonic shape

motion by bickering between at least two of the five protagonists. The few times when the five present a unified front invariably turn out to be pivotal moments in the narrative.[11]

---

11. Perhaps the most powerful of these unqualified episodes is the scene where they try to kill the lawyer—an attempt that backfires and demonstrates the futility of trying to outmaneuver Keyser Soze.

By definition of the genre, a mystery plants salient clues, concealing them within the stream of narrative details, for the alert viewer to use in figuring out what's actually going on.[12] Solving the mystery depends on recognizing which details are the clues, without getting distracted by what surrounds them. Chopin's Prelude also presents clues essential for unraveling its narrative. One important set of clues derives from the consistently linear organization of the harmonic language: the usual pattern is for a short progression to be repeated one or more times, transposed successively either up or down. The result (referred to as a harmonic sequence) organizes complex harmony as a linear phenomenon, typically as passing chords subordinate to the framing moments of the sequence.[13] Figure 20.2 summarizes the Prelude's most important sequences, labeled with descending and ascending arrows. Sequential patterning invites us to focus our attention on the beginning and end of each sequence—which is why figure 20.2 identifies just their framing points. Sequences help us to organize and make large-scale sense of what we're hearing, without getting distracted by intervening harmonic details. If we ignore this aspect of harmonic organization, we have little chance of finding our way through the form of the Prelude.

THE SET-UP: PLOTTING THE FORM

Musical form is something like the plot of a film. In both cases, it usually provides the central narrative—the story of how time unfolds as we attend to what's going on, and an essential starting point if we want to make sense of things.[14] The plot of *The Usual Suspects* is notoriously convoluted and difficult. The story begins with a climactic shooting and its investigation, which uncovers what seems to have happened, told mostly in flashbacks; this same climax eventually reappears even more enigmatically. A final revelation solves the principal mystery by unveiling the central figure but also entails a wholesale reevaluation of almost everything seen up to that point, with unsettling implications. This intricate confusion of truth and deception turns out to be essentially a variation on a familiar type of mystery story, which might be described as the "hidden in plain sight" maneuver. After repeated viewings, what seemed to be an erratic and unpredictable narrative turns out to be a brilliant embellishment of this standard plot paradigm.

On first listenings, the C-sharp Minor Prelude seems just as convoluted—certainly a difficult piece to fit into any of the familiar musical forms.[15] Indeed, the erratic and meandering phrases of the Prelude might suggest that, instead of proceeding as other pieces do, it develops, right before our ears, into a shape for which there are no precedents. Just

---

12. An example of this kind of clue in *The Usual Suspects* is the gold cigarette lighter used by Keyser Soze in the very first scene; near the end of the film, it reappears in the possession of another character.

13. Many of the Prelude's sequences are highlighted in the scores by visual alignment. Thus in score 20.2, the aligned beginnings of the four systems all contain essentially the same pattern, in sequential repetition; scores 20.3 and 20.5 each contain two systems whose patterns are sequentially related (as aligned) despite slightly different beginnings and endings; scores 20.1, 20.6, 20.8, and 20.9 also contain sequential patterns but of a sort that cannot be shown easily by stacking—and also of less significance to the large-scale shape of this piece.

14. In Donald Francis Tovey's words, "How many plays or stories could you describe clearly if you conscientiously omitted the plot?" See *The Main Stream of Music and Other Essays*, 181.

15. An excellent strategy for analyzing most tonal pieces is to start by classifying them in terms of familiar stereotypical forms (e.g., binary or ternary, sonata or rondo). Of course, this strategy does not work well for pieces with unique or unprecedented forms, so it should be jettisoned if the familiar forms turn out to distort more than they clarify. In any case, applying a formal label and considering the implications of that label upon a piece's details must be one of the first things we do in analyzing, not one of the last.

as *The Usual Suspects* builds deceptively upon a familiar mystery plot, however, the Prelude also conceals a familiar large-scale formal organization underneath its improvisatory surface and harmonic idiosyncrasies. The analyst's problem is how to unravel this form; the solution depends on following the clues, which depend only on some basic principles of harmony.

Functional harmony is based on dominant-to-tonic cadences, normally over $\hat{5}$-to-$\hat{1}$ bass lines. These are the fundamental cadential progressions; the phrases and (especially) the sections of tonal pieces are typically closed off by them. The following analysis of the formal shape of this Prelude begins by locating all of its strong cadences. Figure 20.2 lists these cadences; each is identified by the name of its tonicized key inside of a box.

- M. 5, in C♯ minor, closing a four-measure introduction (see score 20.2) and announcing the beginning of the main body of the Prelude.

- M. 35, in G♭ major (score 20.3)—the first strong nontonic cadence of the piece.

- M. 59, in F major (score 20.5)—a cadence much like the previous, transposed down a half-step.

- M. 67, back in C♯ minor (score 20.6).[16]

- M. 85, again in C♯ minor (score 20.8). This is the only cadence that moves to a tonic chord without any embellishing nonchord tones[17]—as a wrap-up to an impassioned, almost nonfunctional cadenza.

- The final C♯ minor cadence in mm. 88–89 (score 20.9), which ends the Prelude.

In addition to listing these cadences, figure 20.2 develops a large-scale shape for the Prelude, with each formal division closed off by one of these cadences. This harmonic shape (shown in the far right column) consists of three large sections with three connecting episodes before, between, and after them.

- A brief introduction, mm. 1–5, establishing C♯ minor, with almost all first-inversion triads in a pattern that is almost but not quite sequential (score 20.1).

- A first section, mm. 5–35, modulating from C♯ minor to G♭ major, by means of a complicated series of several different sequences (scores 20.2 and 20.3).

- A middle section, mm. 35–59, whose harmonic goal is unclear until it finally comes to rest in F major (scores 20.4 and 20.5).

- A quick **retransition** from F major to C♯ minor, mm. 59–67—a breathtakingly expeditious return from such a distant key (score 20.6).

- A third section, consisting of a **reprise** of the opening material in C♯ minor, moving through a cadenza and a definitive close in the home key, mm. 67–85 (scores 20.7 and 20.8).

---

16. The keys of G♭ major and F major appear to be very distant from the overall key of C♯ minor, and indeed one of the most puzzling aspects of the Prelude is the way it wanders so far from its tonal home. Even if these keys are understood as enharmonic respellings, of F♯ major and E♯ major respectively, the relationships are not close. Both are modal variants: the former of the normal subdominant of C♯ minor (i.e., of F♯ minor), and the latter of E♯ minor (the normal mediant of C♯ major, which is the parallel major of C♯ minor).

17. The cadences in G♭ and F major conclude with tonic chords decorated with ascending embellishments ($\hat{7}$–$\hat{1}$ in their respective keys), in contrast with the C♯-minor tonics in m. 5 and m. 67, whose embellishing nonchord tones descend ($\hat{2}$–$\hat{1}$). The final C♯-minor cadence (m. 89, score 20.9) is different from all three previous C♯-minor cadences, in that the final tonic chord of the piece appears (as did the middle section tonics) beneath $\hat{7}$–$\hat{1}$ nonchord tones.

- A brief concluding passage (which might be described as a **codetta**), mm. 85–92, which at first hearing seems to do little of significance, beyond balancing the equally brief introduction (score 20.9).

The underlying formal picture (often referred to as a **rounded binary form**) is strikingly similar to that presented by many other tonal pieces.[18] What disguises it here is the strangeness of the harmonic relationships; this kind of form is easier to recognize when the first section modulates to the dominant or another close-related key. The underlying formal narrative is no less powerful for being disguised, however.

It is important to realize that this formal picture of the Prelude is derived from harmonic rather than thematic criteria. The beginning analyst often considers it more natural to track musical form by following themes, but such a strategy is misleading here. Since the only even moderately distinctive melody occurs just four times, in four different keys,[19] a thematic analysis would probably assemble these four statements as the middle section of the Prelude, beginning in m. 27.[20] This thematically derived picture is problematic but revealing: problematic because it leaves the first section without a convincing ending, revealing because it focuses our attention on m. 27. It is there that this tune first appears, before the end of the first harmonically defined section; for most listeners this is a telling moment—as unsettling as when the crooks are handed the dossiers and shown that Keyser Soze controls their destinies.

CYCLES OF DECEPTION

That m. 27 turns out to be a pivotal moment within the Prelude's narrative is a direct consequence of its shockingly abrupt deceptive cadence. This lunge from V^7 of D to the ♭VI chord of D turns out to be the first of four abrupt moments of harmonic redirection (in mm. 27, 31, 49, and 51).[21] The narrative of the Prelude is built around these harmonic shocks; all of its secondary harmonic goals are approached and enhanced by some kind of deceptive progression. Figure 20.3 is a schematic diagram of the Prelude's overall harmonic shape, in which these four pivotal moments are marked with asterisks.

The first two deceptions work in much the same way: in m. 27 (score 20.2), a sequentially approached V^7 of D moves to B♭, ♭VI of D minor, setting up the first appearance of the middle-section melody; shortly thereafter in m. 31 (score 20.3), a V^7 of B♭ moves to G♭, ♭VI of B♭ minor. In both cases, the actual chord is a major triad a major third lower than the tonic that is expected; instead of a D tonic, B♭ appears, and, instead of a B♭ tonic, G♭. If a comparable deceptive progression had followed in G♭, the result would have been ♭VI of that key, namely E♭♭, which is enharmonically equivalent to D—that is, back where the first deceptive progression began. These three keys, D, B♭, and G♭, form

---

18. Rounded binary is the most common short form in Classical music, found in vast numbers of minuets, trios, variation themes, and the like; an often-analyzed example is the theme to the variation movement of Mozart's D Major Sonata (K. 284). Nineteenth-century versions can be found in several of Mendelssohn's Songs without Words (e.g., op. 62, no. 1, in G) and Brahms's shorter piano pieces (e.g., the Intermezzo in C, op. 119, no. 3)—though here the form is harder to recognize, in the absence of the signaling double bars.

19. These four tunes begin in m. 27 (B♭ major) and in m. 31 (G♭ major), both in score 20.3, and then in m. 51 (A major) and in m. 55 (F major), both in Score 20.5.

20. That these four statements are separated by an ascending sequence of material reminiscent of mm. 5 ff. has a flashback effect. Narrative flashbacks are common in mysteries and pivotal to *The Usual Suspects*.

21. As explained in n. 10, this ♭VI chord symbol represents a major triad with a root of the flat submediant. The uppercase symbol indicates that the quality of the chord is major. The incorporation of the flat sign is a reminder that the root of the chord is the sixth scale-step of the minor mode, that is, ♭6̂, which in D minor is B♭.

Score 20.1. Introduction (mm. 1–5)

Score 20.2. Section 1, first two parts (mm. 6–27)

Score 20.3. Section 1, third part (mm. 27–35)

243

Score 20.4. Section 2, first part (mm. 36–51)

Score 20.5. Section 2, second part (mm. 51–59)

Score 20.6. Retransition (mm. 60–67)

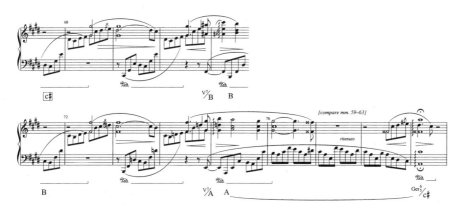

Score 20.7. Reprise, part 1 (mm. 68–79)

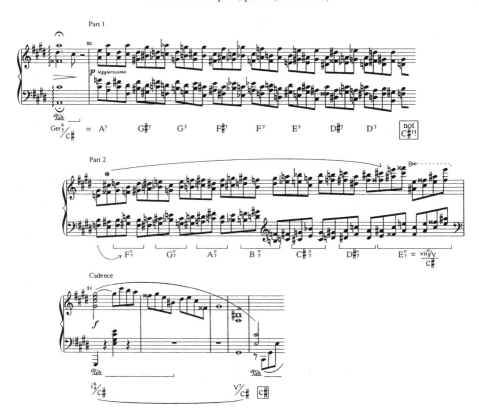

Score 20.8. Reprise, part 2 (mm. 79–85, including cadenza)

Score 20.9. Codetta (mm. 86–92)

245

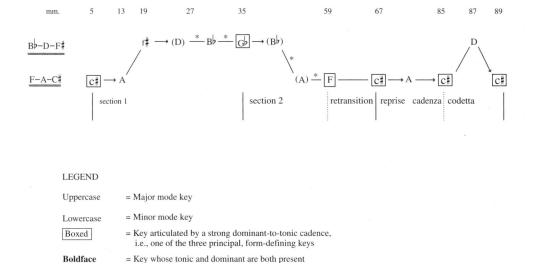

Figure 20.3. Schematic form

a **cycle of major-third–related keys**, a configuration that is laid out horizontally across the top of figure 20.3.[22]

Instead of a third deceptive progression, a strong cadence, with an elaborated cadential $^6_4$ resolution over a two-measure D♭ pedal, establishes G♭ as the first substantial harmonic goal of the Prelude. From G♭, the cyclic direction is reversed by means of an ascending sequential pattern that appears to be heading back to B♭.

From here, a second pair of deceptive progressions reorients the Prelude's harmonic direction. Instead of a sequentially prepared cadence in B♭, the third deception, in m. 51 (score 20.4), reinterprets a V of B♭ (F) as a ♭VI of A, which moves to a dominant of that key.[23] This dominant never resolves to its tonic but instead, in m. 55 (score 20.5), moves deceptively back to F, ♭VI of A minor.[24] Finally, a strong cadence (comparable to the cadence in G♭) establishes F as the second well-defined harmonic goal of the Prelude, ending the middle section.[25]

---

22. Cycles that divide the octave into major thirds are common in nineteenth-century music (as are cycles of minor thirds and major seconds). They are feasible, however, only under the assumption that different **enharmonic** versions of any pitch are **equivalent** (see n. 16).

23. The next chord is actually a cadential $^6_4$ chord, which, as always, is the beginning of a large-scale dominant harmony; it resolves to an explicit V[7] in m. 54.

24. In the first pair of deceptions (D to B♭, and B♭ to G♭), the two progressions are essentially transpositions of one another. The second pair of progressions (F, V of B♭, to the dominant of A, and the dominant of A back to F), in contrast, is more like a mirror image.

25. The first deceptive move of each pair (to B♭ and A, respectively) sets up a cadence that is itself deflected by a further deceptive move. The second of each (to G♭ and F) continues to a strong section-defining cadence.

The keys of A and F are also a major third apart, though not part of the major-third–cycle that contains D, B♭, and G♭. That D, B♭, and G♭ so clearly move through a cycle of major thirds suggests that A and F might constitute part of their own, separate major-third–cycle. After the deceptive progression from A to F, another deceptive move to ♭VI of F would have produced a D♭ chord, but, just as the dominant of G♭ does not move on deceptively to E♭♭ (i.e., D), the dominant of F resolves to its own tonic. D♭ is, however, enharmonically equivalent to C♯, which is the key of the entire Prelude—and the key of the reprise, which does follow hard upon the heels of the F major cadence. In other words, a second major-third–cycle is lurking beneath the surface here; the approach to the reprise elaborates a pattern of A to F to C♯.

This C♯–A–F cycle is projected horizontally across the bottom of figure 20.3. It accounts for the overall shape of the Prelude's beginning (C♯ minor to A) and end (F back to C♯ minor); in contrast, the D–B♭–G♭ cycle is the source for the harmonic motion through the middle. This graphic representation reveals a remarkable parallelism: the first section's initial sequential move from C♯ minor to A is mimicked by an analogous move from F♯ minor to D (these patterns are aligned in score 20.2). Elements from the C♯–A–F cycle begin the piece, although there will be no trace of F until the end of the second section. The latter opens up the F♯–D–B♭ cycle, although the tonic of D is avoided by the deception of m. 27.

Figure 20.4 presents these two cycles as a symmetrical array of major-third–related keys and thus defines the harmonic space through which the Prelude moves.[26] Because of the parallels between the two sequential openings in the first section, C♯ minor and F♯ minor are displayed as the symmetrical anchors of this array.

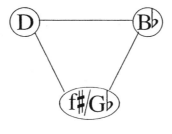

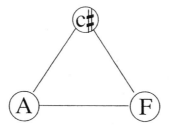

Figure 20.4. Symmetrical major-third–cycles

---

26. Only one key in the Prelude appears clearly both in minor mode and major mode versions, namely F♯ minor/G♭ major.

Figure 20.5 represents the harmonic narrative of the Prelude as a succession of moves through the space of figure 20.4, one for each of its five distinct sections. The first array shows how the introduction lays out chords of A major, F♯ minor, and (obliquely) D major, which serve to project two of the three members of both cycles; both B♭ (soon to be supplied by the first deceptive progression) and F are absent. The remaining arrays display the keys associated with those chords and tell the story of how the two interlocked cycles—or rather two interlocking subnarratives—are worked out.

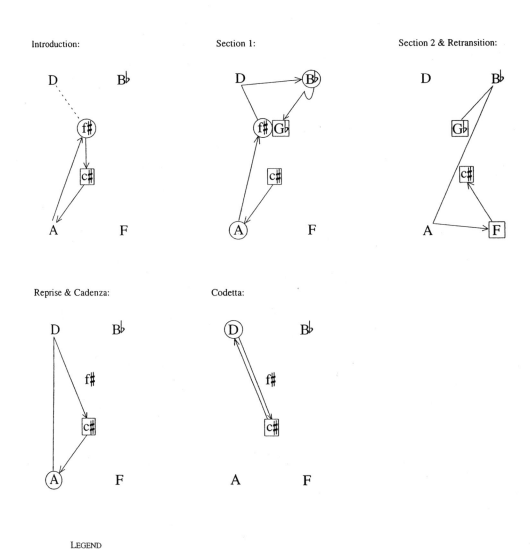

Figure 20.5. Narrative of major-third–cycles

The Frame-Up: F and the Retransition

The last member of the C♯–A–F cycle appears decisively only when F appears as the strongly defined key in which the second section ends. Three other F chords have already appeared in the Prelude; each of the four has a different harmonic role.

- The first is the dominant of B♭ in mm. 29–30 (score 20.3).
- The next (score 20.4, mm. 47–50) is approached as if another V of B♭, but it is abruptly reinterpreted as ♭VI of A minor.
- The third again involves a reinterpretation of F as ♭VI of A minor, but as an abrupt cadential deflection away from the key of A (score 20.5, m. 55).
- Finally F is firmly established as tonic in m. 59 ff. (score 20.5), leading to the retransition.

At that point, this cycle is fully represented but has not yet returned to the home key of C♯ minor. Given all the deceptive progressions that precede it, the F major cadence could easily have been followed by another deceptive cadence back to D♭/C♯. Likewise, as the climax of the film approaches, the viewer has been conditioned to expect that Dean Keaton, the cleverest of the crooks, will soon be unmasked as Keyser Soze.

Unfortunately, all of Keaton's plans go wrong when the smugglers' boat is stormed . . . and we find out that Keaton is not Keyser Soze after all. Likewise, the actual retransition to C♯ minor (score 20.6) avoids the expected deception in favor of a different kind of misdirection.[27] The move from F major to the dominant of C♯ minor takes just four chords (mm. 63–67), over a bass that descends chromatically, from F through E to D♯—under a V^7 of V in C♯. Despite this chromatic bass line, functional connections between the constituent chords of this retransition are difficult to discover . . . but look more carefully.

Figure 20.6 juxtaposes the score of the retransition with an outline of the chords of mm. 30–47 and reveals the following coincidences.

- Just as the key of G♭ is approached from F in m. 31, so F leads to an $F\sharp^7$ chord over E in m. 64.
- Just as $E\flat^7$, the dominant of A♭, is approached (sequentially, by ascending seconds) from G♭ in m. 39, so the $F\sharp^7$ chord leads to a $D\sharp^7$ chord in m. 65.
- Just as A♭ is approached from E♭ (its dominant) in m. 43, so the $D\sharp^7$ chord leads to V^7 of C♯ minor in m. 66.[28]
- In the earlier passage, A♭ is followed by F (V of B♭), so that the whole passage begins and ends with F chords; in the retransition, G♯ is V of C♯ minor, the goal of the whole progression.

In other words, the retransition embodies a disguised version of something already heard; mm. 63–67 may sound strange and eerily abrupt, but that progression is actually

---

27. Curiously, no dominants of the three principal keys of the Prelude (C♯, G♭, and F) ever move deceptively; these dominants are thus the dependable harmonic foundation on which the piece is built. Similarly, the few events actually witnessed by the police in the narration of *The Usual Suspects* are the foundation on which the story is based; the accuracy of everything else we are told or shown is up for grabs.

28. In retrospect, this comparison clears up a small mystery about the earlier progression. For in the midst of the sequence of score 20.4, both of the tonicized G♭ and A♭ chords appeared with embellishing sevenths (mm. 37–38 and 45–46, in both cases anticipating part of the following augmented-sixth chords)—not usual in tonics that are never reinterpreted as dominants. But if these chords are due to be transformed into a retransition progression back to C♯ minor, these sevenths can be heard as harbingers of their later roles.

Figure 20.6. Mm. 63–67 of the retransition, compared with mm. 30–47

lifted from mm. 30–47. In its earlier incarnation, surrounded by Fs (as V of B♭, soon to become ♭VI of A and then tonic), the progression is relatively straightforward. In the retransition, the same chords are given a new context, to become part of a major-third–traversal of the space between F and C♯ minor—which is why the progression sounds so obscure in its later incarnation.[29]

THE WRAP-UP: D AND THE CODETTA

The investigator in *The Usual Suspects* reconstructs the events of the story with brilliance and insight . . . and comes up with the wrong answer. We might likewise conclude from the neatness of the closing of the C♯–A–F cycle and the self-referential intricacy of the final move from F back to C♯ that the Prelude is now essentially over—that the reprise, in returning to the opening key and the opening material, and in persuasively linking the missing key F to its cyclical neighbors, has rounded off the narrative.

Wrong! Just as in the film, the central protagonist, a shadowy participant for most of the story, suddenly steps out of the shadows and reveals himself to have been in full view

---

29. This narrative strategy is essentially that of unmasking a distinctively unfamiliar character as an old friend in disguise. The comparable final climax of *The Usual Suspects* is the revelation that what had appeared to be two distinct characters is actually the same person.

(if disguised) all along. The end of the Prelude completes the second cycle, F♯–D–B♭, by revealing the hidden key of D, unmasked only at the last possible moment.

Though D has been set up several times as the next member of a cycle-based pattern, that key is the only member of either major-third–cycle not clearly tonicized before the reprise.[30] Each of these set-ups is deflected somehow. The story of D proceeds as follows.

- The introduction (score 20.1) lays out a pattern of first-inversion triads, which essentially move down in diatonic thirds, C♯ to A to F♯.[31] A natural next step in this pattern would be to a D-major triad, and indeed a first-inversion D chord does occur at the end of m. 3, but the sequence breaks off before an accented ♭II⁶ chord can appear.

- After the sequential move from C♯ minor to A (score 20.2), the sequence ends, F♯ minor is tonicized, and a D-major chord follows (in a progression based loosely on the introduction). No dominant of D appears to confirm that key, however, and the passage ends amorphously, without any clear tonal affiliation—until the second major-third–cycle begins in F♯ minor in mm. 19–20. In retrospect, D major does not sound much like a tonic here—nor is it clear exactly what it *does* sound like. Its effect is simply . . . shadowy.

- After those nebulous D chords, F♯ minor is established; the sequences in that key are exactly analogous to those in C♯ minor. As the goal of the C♯-minor sequence was to A (m. 13), so the goal of the F♯-minor sequence should be D major in mm. 20 ff. (score 20.2). The dominant of D, however, resolves deceptively.

- After cycling from this avoided D through B♭ to G♭ (score 20.3), the next cyclic step would be to continue to D, that is, to return to where the cycle started. Instead, one of the Prelude's few ascending sequences appears and reverses the direction of the process, back to B♭ (score 20.4).

- Three of the four appearances of the middle section's melody, in its four different keys, harmonize the second measure with a IV chord. When this tune appears in A major, however (mm. 51–55, score 20.5), what should be a D-major chord (IV of A) is replaced with a secondary dominant of V in A (m. 52).

The central narrative of the C-sharp Minor Prelude, therefore, is a story of setting up, alluding to, but never revealing D. The cadenza (score 20.8) continues this story; it begins with a Ger⁺⁶ in C♯ minor, which is, of course, enharmonically equivalent to a dominant seventh on A—that is, a dominant of D (cf. mm. 26–27!). The first of the cadenza's two parts slides down through a long series of dominant-seventh chords, the last of which is a dominant seventh on D—so that the whole process can be heard as an elaboration of a progression from V⁷ of D to a D chord. The second part is a pattern of diminished-seventh chords moving up by major seconds, toward a secondary dominant of V of C♯.

30. Three different keys are left hanging by the Prelude's deceptive maneuvers. In two cases, the relevant tonic has already been heard but fails to appear after its dominant(s). B♭ is jettisoned twice, in mm. 30–31 (score 20.3) and in mm. 47–50 (score 20.4)—but it has already appeared as the deceptive resolution of the dominant of D in m. 27. The tonic of A, abandoned in mm. 51–54 (score 20.5), has been convincingly tonicized in the first section (m. 13, score 20.2) and will be again in the reprise (score 20.7).

31. This descending-third pattern can be thought of as the diatonic template from which the C♯ to A to F major-third–cycle is derived.

The cadenza is so fast and so chromatic, however, that it is difficult to single out these boundary chords; its job is more to set up the codetta than to definitively reveal D as a protagonist. The actual appearance of D as a tonicized key is reserved until the last possible moments of the piece. The last phrase of the Prelude (score 20.9) *finally* allows D to be tonicized and to proceed (as a ♭II chord) to V of C♯ minor. Only thus is the second major-third–cycle completed.

The cadenza revisits many of the early elements of the Prelude, moving by at bewildering speed—something like the penultimate scene in the film, when the detective scans the clippings on the bulletin board, all in plain sight the whole time, and suddenly realizes how completely he has been fooled. Then the codetta unveils the manipulator— the central character in the story, heard clearly only now.

In light of this final revelation, "codetta" is a misleading label for the final measures of this piece; that word suggests an afterthought, something essentially dispensable. The codetta of Chopin's C-sharp Minor Prelude is anything but an afterthought—certainly no less indispensable than are the last five minutes of *The Usual Suspects*, when Keyser Soze's identity is revealed, our false assumptions are exposed, and the rug is pulled out from under a good portion of what has preceded it. Not until virtually the last harmonic event of the Prelude are all of its narrative threads pulled together. Not until the very last measures is the central figure of D allowed its long-postponed appearance, which transforms and reshapes everything that has led up to it. Not until the last possible moment do we find out what's really been going on.

And then, like that . . . it's over.

~21~

Texture and Timbre in Barbara Kolb's *Millefoglie* for Chamber Orchestra and Computer-Generated Tape

Judith Lochhead

Judith Lochhead (Stony Brook University) teaches courses on recent music practices in the Western concert tradition and on the philosophical and intellectual implications of music theoretical concepts and analytical practices. She is the coeditor with Joseph Auner of *Postmodern Music/Postmodern Thought* (Routledge, 2001) and is currently finishing a study of the possibilities of music analysis for recent music, *Reconceiving Structure: Recent Music / Music Analysis*. Lochhead is also an active clarinetist and has written about performance and analysis, especially of twentieth-century music.

Barbara Kolb (1939–) studied at Hartt College of Music of the University of Hartford. Winner of numerous awards, she has received MacDowell Fellowships, two Gugenheim Fellowships, and a Fulbright Scholarship. Kolb was the first woman to receive the American Prix de Rome (1969–71) for composition. In her nine-month residency at IRCAM she completed *Millefoglie,* which is frequently performed around the world and which received the Kennedy Center Friedheim Award in 1987. Lochhead's analysis of Millefoglie demonstrates the focus upon nonpitch elements that have been so critical to much later twentieth-century music. In addition, the study demonstrates the challenges of analyzing electronic music, a medium for which there is not yet precise, technical language for describing the wealth of possible sounds.

Millefoglie was composed by Barbara Kolb in 1985 and revised in 1987. The work is scored for a computer-generated tape and chamber ensemble of two oboes (or flute and oboe), clarinet, bass clarinet, trombone, vibraphone, marimba, harp, and violoncello. The computer-generated tape was made or "realized" at the Institute de Recherche et Coordination Acoustique/Musique (IRCAM), a music research and technology center in France conceived and run by the composer Pierre Boulez. Kolb, an American composer, was

---

Some reminders: (1) all words in **bold** are defined in the glossary; (2) full citations for incomplete references are found in the selected bibliography; (3) the authors use their preferred notational system (e.g., Roman numeral, form label, and register notation). Most of the essays denote register by middle C as C^4.—Ed.

commissioned by IRCAM to work at the center and to write the piece. *Millefoglie,* meaning in Italian "a million folds," is published in score format by Boosey and Hawkes.[1] The score includes a staff system above the traditional orchestral layout for the computer.

The presence of this computer part within the score reveals one of the issues confronting those who would analyze works utilizing late-twentieth-century technologies of sound generation. For instance, example 21.1 cites mm. 108–11, the passage during which the electronically generated sound begins. The notation dedicated to this "electronic part" does not represent fully the sounds occurring on the tape but rather sketches out some of the sounds in order to provide cues for the conductor and players. This "cueing" role of the notated computer part draws attention to the performance function of scores in general and suggests some of their limitations for music analysis. The score is not intended as a representation of the piece for purposes of analysis; rather, it represents those aspects of compositional intention that are sufficient to a successful performance of the work. Nonetheless, most music analysis is dependent on scores that provide visual access to compositional design. While a notated score is often useful for the purposes of music analysis, it is not sufficient in those instances when the notation does not represent musical sound in ways adequate to analysis. This is especially true in the case of electronically generated sound whose visual representation does not serve as a set of performance instructions but rather as a schematic depiction of sound.[2]

Another issue arising from recently composed music utilizing electronically generated sound involves a change of focus from pitch-based toward texture- and timbre-based structures. That issue is raised most obviously in works solely for electronically generated sounds such as Bulent Arel's *Stereo Electronic Study no. 2* or Paul Lansky's *Idle Chatter,* but it is present in pieces such as *Millefoglie* that combine acoustic and electronic sound sources and also in acoustic pieces exploring the structural domains of texture, timbre, and other such qualitative aspects of sound.[3]

By texture I mean an overall effect made by the combination of the different sounds in a particular passage. We borrow the term "texture" from the visual and tactile domain of textiles, where it refers to the effect made by the nature of the strands and their interaction through the weaving process. Such concepts as "homophonic," "contrapuntal," or "monophonic" are some very general textural characteristics.[4] By "timbre" I mean an overall effect made by the quality of sound of a given sound source (acoustic or electronic) or a combination of sound sources. We often identify and name timbral quality with the sound-producing medium—"clarinet" sound or a "metallic" timbre. Other kinds

---

1. The Boosey and Hawkes score was published in 1989 and the copyright is from 1985. Performance parts and the computer-generated tape are also available from the publisher. An excerpt of the piece occurs in *Contemporary Anthology of Music by Women,* ed. James R. Briscoe (Bloomington: Indiana University Press, 1997), 74–90.

2. Some other recent works utilize extended performance techniques whose notational representation is often not suitable for the goals of analysis. This is not the case for *Millefoglie,* however.

3. Arel's *Stereo Electronic Music no. 2* (1970) has been rereleased in CD format: *Pioneers of Electronic Music,* CRI (CD611). It was composed on magnetic tape using "classical studio technique." Paul Lansky's *Idle Chatter* (1985) was created on an IBM 3081 mainframe. It is available on *More Than* Idle Chatter, Bridge (BCD 9050).

4. Here are some brief definitions of these textural types.
Homophonic. *A texture in which there is a prominent melody line and a subordinate accompaniment part. Also, a multipart passage in which all of the parts move together rhythmically.*
Contrapuntal. *A texture in which two or more parts or lines have a relative independence from one another. The individual parts together but as separate entities.*
Monophonic. *A single melodic line. Multiple players or singers may produce that single line.*

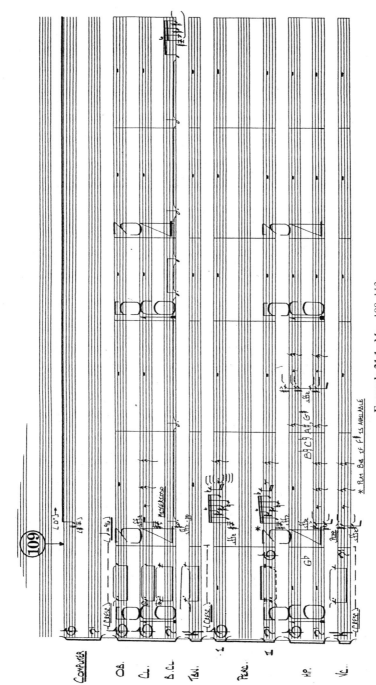

Example 21.1. Mm. 108–113

of terms are often used to describe the qualitative aspects of more-complex sound combinations—a "bright" sonority or a cluster. While texture and timbre are distinguishable characteristics of musical sound, they are inextricably intertwined. Such an interdependence often makes their separation difficult when one is dealing analytically with the overall effect made by a particular passage. For instance, consider these two types of textural and timbral situations: (1) a passage played by a string quartet in which the sounds are closely spaced and played with an identical rhythm, and (2) a passage played by piccolo, oboe, French horn, and contrabass in which the spacing covers four octaves and the sounds are played with an identical rhythm. In such a situation, the timbre and register of the sounds affects the overall sense of the texture. Thus, my focus here is not on texture or timbre as absolutely distinct features of musical sound, but rather on the two together. My discussion will sometimes conflate the two into a hybrid—as in the textural/timbral aspect of musical design; but sometimes I will invoke the general distinctions between texture and timbre as defined above when the musical context makes such differentiations useful.

Since there are no standardized procedures, I must preface my analysis of Kolb's *Millefoglie* by defining a methodology that reveals these aspects of aesthetic design. Three fundamental issues of analysis arise in this context: (1) the relation of analytic observation to preexisting theoretical concepts, (2) the role of visual representations of sound for analytic process (either in the score or in scorelike transcription), and (3) the nature of the processes of analytic observation.

1. Much analysis occurs in a context in which the analyst works with existing general types of theoretical concepts that address particular aspects of musical organization. For instance, tonal harmonic analysis typically assumes a fixed number of chord types, distinctions between chord and nonchord tones, and definitions for chordal succession and connection. These concepts of tonal harmonic structure serve as the tools for harmonic analysis that guide and determine the types of analytic observations about a particular work that can be made. By contrast, there are few preexisting concepts for textural/timbral analysis.[5] The few general categories of textural types— homophonic, contrapuntal, monophonic, heterophonic—do not allow the analyst to make fine distinctions between musical occurrences, and there are no existing concepts for the succession of differing textures or how they might relate to one another over time. The analyst's task in such a situation entails more than applying existing concepts. Analysts must determine—that is, must theorize—the concepts that will guide analytic observation. Such determinations are often ad hoc and rely on a mix of existing concepts about music and the world in general. The analytic language I use below often relies not on technical terms but on metaphorical descriptions that refer to sound qualities. This metaphorical descriptive terminology then becomes the information on which an analysis is built. Such metaphorical terminology has a function like that of preexisting concepts: articulation of structural distinctions that have musical relevance. Thus, the analyst who would address the textural/timbral aspects of a particular piece must take as part of the analytic process the delineation of metaphorical terminology and concepts that will guide the analysis itself.

2. As I have suggested earlier, some pieces composed more recently, such as *Millefoglie,* employ electronically generated sound and have an aesthetic design more

---

5. See Robert Cogan and Pozzi Escot, *Sonic Design: The Nature of Sound and Music* (Englewood Cliffs, N.J.: Prentice-Hall, 1976); Robert Cogan, *New Images of Musical Sound* (Cambridge: Harvard University Press, 1984); and Wayne Slawson, *Sound Color* (Berkeley and Los Angeles: University of California Press, 1985).

fully focused on textural and timbral features of sound. Additionally, neither electronically generated sounds nor overall features of texture and timbre have visual representation in a score, if one even exists.

The visual representations of the score have been fundamental to the practice of analysis for at least two reasons. First, the score depicts an unperformed version of the work and relieves the analyst from assessing performance accuracy and other issues of interpretation. Second, visual access to a piece through the score bypasses the "real time" of performance, allowing the analyst to ponder relationships and structural features without the constraints of "time's arrow." Recognizing here the value of a visual, scorelike representation of the piece, the analyst of textural/timbral features that are not directly represented in a score must "transcribe" those features into a visual format that allows them to be accessed by the analyst and by others as well.

Such transcription of timbral and textural features is not like the dictation occurring in musicianship classes; rather, it is a representational practice that attempts to depict overall characteristics and depends essentially on distinctions that are already analytic in nature. In other words, the process of transcription is itself part of the analytic process. Determining how to capture a particular textural or timbral configuration in words or symbols requires the analyst to make decisions about, for instance, what characterizes a texture and how it is similar or distinct from other textures. These determinations engage the analyst in questions of structure and relationship that are part of the analytic process itself.

3. While it is impossible to define a standard analytic process at the turn of the millennium, there has been a tendency within English-language practices to focus on issues of compositional technique and to understand how a piece works with respect to such technique. Analyses so focused have tended to be score based and directed toward design with respect to compositional intent, in an effort to retrace aspects of the compositional process. In the case of analyses addressing texture and timbre, the need to create analytic transcriptions and to rely on recorded performances orients the analytic process more toward the analyst as listener. Thus, analytic observation so oriented refocuses the analytic process toward issues of aesthetic design rather than of compositional technique.[6]

DOING ANALYSIS AND WRITING AN ANALYSIS

There are two distinct stages comprising the process of analysis: the first is an active investigation of a particular piece that entails the development of theoretical categories of textural and timbral organization relevant to the piece; second is the organized presentation of the analyst's particular understanding of the work's design in terms of the relevant categories. While the details of the investigative stage are not typically present in the written analysis, that first stage is intrinsic to the second stage. Thus it is important to attend carefully to both the process of doing and its outcome in the analysis.

While my primary concern here is to present "an analysis" of *Millefoglie,* some sense of how I forged that analysis should foster an understanding of its significance. I began with the assumption that textural/timbral distinctions play a role in defining formal processes of the piece. The first investigative stage of the analytic process entailed repeated

---

6. It is not possible to disentangle the compositional techniques a composer employs from issues of aesthetic design. Here however I want to focus on the aesthetic results of compositional choice, not on the technical aspects of that choice.

listening to the recorded performance with the goal of making an analytic transcription that would show the formal articulations of the piece.[7] The repeated listenings were accompanied by study of the score when specific questions of instrumentation occurred. The particular analytic distinctions and concepts that arose during the process were ones defined by existing concepts of texture and timbre, by other musical concepts, and by perceptual experience generally that could be metaphorically mapped onto musical understanding. The conceptual categories that arose during the process and which shaped the analysis itself resulted from a process of investigative engagement that had as its goal the creation of an analytic transcription: the musical distinctions that are reflected in such a visual representation are induced by the analytic process.

As a consequence of such a listening-based investigation, the analytic transcription articulates formal distinctions that are not neutral descriptions but rather are analytic in the sense that they reflect theoretical categories of textural and timbral types. Additionally, the analytical transcriptions can themselves be the basis for further analytical observations about the piece, acting much like a score would in more traditional sorts of analyses.

MILLEFOGLIE

My analysis begins with an account of how textural and timbral features articulate overall formal design and then focuses in more detail on particular details of this design. The composer herself, writing in a program note, defines four sections.[8] As figure 21.1 indicates, my analysis confirms those sections. The figure shows the timings of work across the horizontal axis, and the sections are shown as Ia and b, IIa and b, III, and IV. Reading down the page, the rows show overall timings for each section in two ways. First, "Time: Formal" shows the total length of each section, and second, "Time: Internal" shows the timings of the subsections. Figure 21.2 excerpts those timings; from which we may make two kinds of observations. Section IV is the longest, Section II the shortest, and the subsections articulate the first two sections into unequal parts. These relations suggest that temporal symmetry is not a factor in the formal rhythm of the piece. Rather the piece suggests a flexible, nonmetrical rhythm that might be schematized as in figure 21.3, which uses a proportional graph to suggest duration.

Row 3 of figure 21.1 displays a theoretical category I call "Textural/Timbral Type" (abbreviated as T/T Type). These are generalized types of textural/timbral relations that recur in variation over the course of the piece. Before I define in detail each of those T/T Types within the discussion of sections, a few general observations may be made here. First, I have analyzed the piece as having three distinct T/T Types/Types—Types A, B, and C—and each as having variations within those types, each variation indicated by a superscript. Second, the T/T Types occur at various times throughout the piece and are not clustered in any one particular section. The recurrence of these textural types generates a series of referential associations over the course of the piece, pulling the diverse sections together.

Rows 4 and 5 display in a general way the timbral character of the sections, showing which instruments or what types of electronic sounds occur with respect to the major sectional divisions. These rows show when instrumental and electronic components are

---

7. *Millefoglie* is recorded on *New World Records*, (80422-2) 1992. The work is performed by Nouvel Ensemble Moderne, conducted by Lorraine Vaillancourt.

8. Readers of this analysis should ideally listen to a recording of the piece as I discuss its various sections. Contrary to a score-based analysis, in which one can peruse the score for the relationships noted, the sort of analysis I offer here must be studied by listening to the recorded performance of the piece.

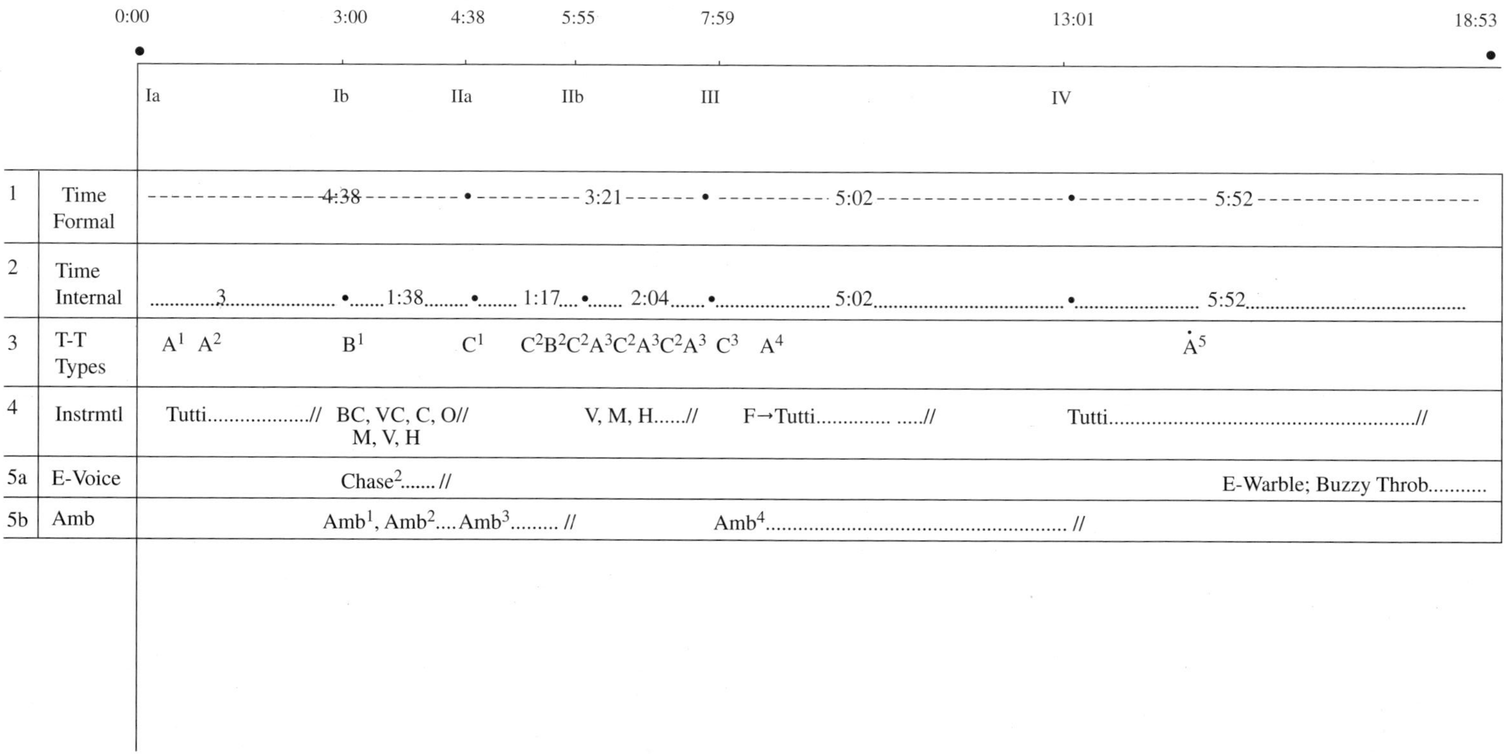

Overall formal design — timeline markers: 0:00, 3:00, 4:38, 5:55, 7:59, 13:01, 18:53

#	Row	Ia	Ib	IIa	IIb	III	IV
1	Time Formal		----4:38----	----3:21----		----5:02----	----5:52----
2	Time Internal		...3...	...1:38...	...1:17...	...2:04... ...5:02...	...5:52...
3	T-T Types	A^1 A^2	B^1	C^1	$C^2B^2C^2A^3C^2A^3$ C^3 A^3	A^4	$\grave{A}^5$
4	Instrmtl	Tutti........//	BC, VC, C, O// M, V, H	V, M, H....//		F→Tutti.........//	Tutti.............//
5a	E-Voice		Chase^2.......//				
5b	Amb		Amb^1, Amb^2.....Amb^3.........//			Amb^4	E-Warble; Buzzy Throb.......//

Figure 21.1. Overall formal design

Section	I		II	III	IV
	4:38		3:21	5:02	5:52

Sub-	Ia	Ib	IIa	IIb
Sections	3:00	1:38	1:17	2:04

Figure 21.2. Timings of the four sections and two subsections

segregated and when combined. Such timbral distinctions sometimes, but not always, serve as sectional markers. For instance, the entrance of electronic sounds marks the beginning of subsection Ib, and the formal distinction between IIa and IIb is also marked by a change from an electronic to an acoustic timbral quality. Row 5 itself contains a distinction between what I call an "E-Voice" and an "ambient" layer. The "E-Voice" refers to the presence of a single timbral electronic part or "voice" that has an identity as a "line." The "ambient" layer refers to a timbrally complex sound texture that often is constantly changing and active.

We will return to figure 21.1 and a consideration of overall formal design after considering in more detail each of the sections, their sub-sectional divisions, and their internal designs. We will then examine how each part contributes to overall aesthetic design of the work.

Section I

Example 21.2 cites mm. 1–11 of the score. Figure 21.4 organizes the musical occurrences of section I using a "train schedule" model, that is, reading time down rather than across as in a "score" model. Reading across the page from the left, the columns show time, with a sub-column for major formal articulations and another for internal articulations within those divisions. The second shows T/T Types, and the third gives descriptive names of the elements constituting those types. Two sub-columns within the constitutive elements distinguish those that have a primary presence in the musical texture and those having a secondary presence.[9] The terms "primary" and "secondary" are meant to suggest a distinc-

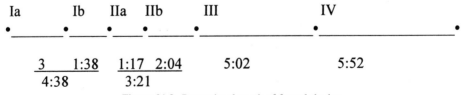

Figure 21.3. Proportional graph of formal rhythm

---

9. I might have used the terms "foreground" and "background" here, as in the sense of pictorial space that implies something closer and focal versus something set back and providing context. While I do want to imply the general characteristics of foreground and background, I want also to avoid the connotations these terms have in the context of linear and specifically Schenkerian analysis. The use of the terms "background" and "foreground" in these types of music analyses differs from their use in a visual and pictorial context.

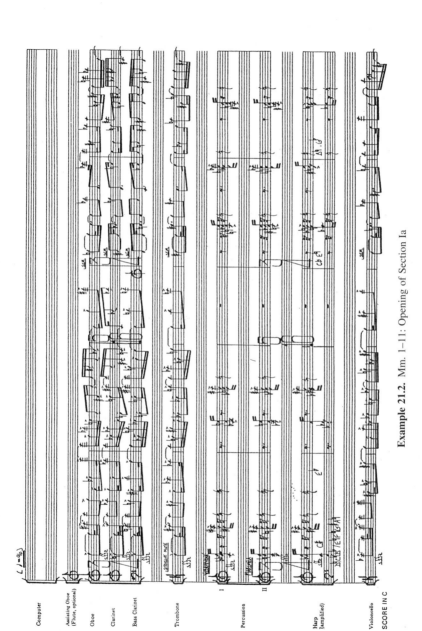

Example 21.2. Mm. 1–11: Opening of Section Ia

Time		T-T Type	Constitutive Elements: Descriptive Names			Dyn.	Details	
frml.	intnl		Primary	Secondary			Instrumental Component	Electronic Component
Ia :00		A¹	A & F	Punctuations		f	Angular and Fast; coordinated; tutti: punctuations by V,M, H	
:47		A²	A & S	Punctuations		p	Angular and Sparse; coordinated; tutti; punctuations by various insts.	
	1:17			Interruptions A&F				
	1:23							
	1:29							
	1:38							
	1:47							
	1:57							
	2:22							
	2:38			Tb. Solo emerging; M trill		cresc.		
Ib 3:00			Rising Articulation; Electronic presence	Ambient¹		$f\!f$		Ambient¹-- continuous background presence of an electric sound
	3:08	B¹	Chase Voice 1 Chase Voice 2	Punct.	Amb¹	mf	Chase¹-BC; punctuations by V,M, H	Chase²-- electric voice growing from Amb¹
	3:29		Chase¹ Chase² Punct		Amb²		Chase¹-BC and VC; Add E-Voice of Chase² to Punctuations	Ambient² buzzy, electric sound
	3:36		Chase¹ leading voice				Chase¹-BC, VC, and C	
						cresc.	Chase¹-BC, VC, C, and O	
	3:49				——	cresc.		buzzy, electric sound stops
	3:51				Amb² recurs	cresc.		Buzzy sound re-starts
	3:57				——	cresc.		Buzzy sound stops
	4:09				Amb² recurs	cresc.		Buzzy sound re-starts
	4:28		stop	stop	Amb²	$f\!f$		Buzzy sound tops
	4:29		fadeout	stop	Amb²	subito pp		

Figure 21.4. Section I

tion between music that is focally present in the musical texture and music that provides an aural setting for other music. Column 4 shows dynamics over the course of the section, and column 5 provides commentary that gives a bit more detail on occurrences, separating out the acoustical instrumental sonic component from the electronic component.

The major internal division of Section I occurs at 3:00 when the electronic timbral component enters with Ambient¹. This sound type provides a continuous background that includes a sonority, which I associate with a kind of "electric" quality. This articulation is also marked by the beginning eight seconds later of a new T/T Type, B^1, which has a contrapuntal component in the melodic "chasing" between, at first, the bass clarinet (BC) and an E-Voice that grows out of and retains features of the "electric" timbral quality of ambient.[1] The chase voices, as the primary textural layer, are punctuated in the secondary layer by recurring short, accented gestures in the vibraphone, marimba, and harp, retaining this aspect of T/T Type A in subsection Ia.

The beginning of subsection Ib is articulated by the occurrences of a T/T type different from that at the beginning of the piece. The articulation of the second subsection, beginning with B^1, relies on its timbral and textural distinction from the subsection beginning the piece. The initial music is characterized by T/T Type A, which occurs in two variations. The first, A^1, consists of a musical idea that is Angular and Fast (A and F) and involves virtually all of the instrumentalists except for the vibraphone, Marimba, and Harp, which punctuate the texture as a secondary component. The change to A^2 at :47 entails a dynamic change to *piano* and a slower, more sparse presentation, but it is still angular, hence the designation "A & S" (Angular and Sparse). The temporally sparse texture after :47 is continually interrupted by the louder and more vigorous idea of A^1.

After the timbral articulation at 3:00, the trajectory of subsection Ib is toward a more active temporal texture involving both an increasingly persistent presentation of the Chase[1] voice with more and more instruments, a louder dynamic, and the increasing presence of a "buzzy, electric" timbral quality in Ambient[2] [which first appears at 3:29]. The trajectory toward a more intense presentation peaks at 4:28 when the chase[1] voices cease and a quiet version of Ambient[2] remains and fades out. The formal trajectory characterizing subsection Ib, that of a slowly increasing level of textural intensity, is picked up and enhanced in Section III, as we will see shortly. But first we consider Section II.

SECTION II

Like Section I, the second section has two parts whose differentiation relies on a timbral distinction (see figure 21.5). Subsection IIa (4:38) includes only computer-generated sounds, and IIb (5:55), only instrumental sounds. The constitutive elements presented in each subsection have similarities that establish associative relations within the section. This association is reflected in the recurrence of T-T Type C in two variations: C^1 and C^2. The electronic version of this type includes Ambient[3], which entails (1) a broad pitch band and a "throbbing, active" sonic surface and (2) punctuating gestures I have labeled as "E-Swish" and "soft-siren." The C^2 version (at 5:55) includes a "murmur" that is an instrumental version of the earlier "throbbing, active" sonic surface and a punctuating "Swish" that follows the "Murmur."

Example 21.3 cites m. 163 and the beginning of section IIb. In addition to establishing an associative relation with IIa, the second subsection also presents a textural type reminiscent of the first section and another that serves as a premonition of the dominating idea of Section III. At 6:16, ideas growing out of the punctuating "Swishes" of the immediately preceding music create a kind of "Dialogue" between two voices, the Harp and the Vibraphone/Marimba paired. This Dialogue texture, labeled B^2, reminds us of the "Chasing" texture occurring at 3:08 in Section I. The premonition occurs in subsection IIb within a reference to the opening T/T Type of the piece. At 6:53 the A T-T Type recurs as A3 with the angular movement in the Vibraphone and Marimba. At the same time,

Time		T-T Type	Constitutive Elements: Descriptive Names		Dyn.	Details	
frml	intnl		Primary	Secondary		Instrmntl Comp.	Elect. Comp.
IIa 4:38		C¹	Ambient³		p		Broad pitch band, Throb
	4:57			E-Swh; soft-siren			electric , rising swish; high, soft, siren-like sound
	5:11			E-Throb, E-Swh			
	5:20			E-Swhs			
	5:34			E-Throb			
	5:42			E-Swhs, soft-siren	dim. al niente		
IIb 5:55		C²	Murmur Swish		p f	V,M,H; throb-like tremolo to rising swish; transitional	
	6:05		Murmur Swh Swh		p f		
	6:16	B²	Dialogue		f	V+M and H	
	6:31	C²	Murmur		p		
6:53		A³	R&A		mf	Repeated idea in H; Angular movement in V, M	
	7:03	C²	Murmur		p		
	7:27	A³	R&A		mf		
	7:49	C²	Murmur		p		
	7:53	A³	R&A		mp		

Figure 21.5. Section II

the Harp presents a "Repeated" idea, a version of which will be the basis of a formal strategy I call a "textural *crescendo*" (defined in the following discussion) that dominates Section III. We may also note about sub-section IIb a quick alternation between differing T/T Types. Such an alternation **accelerates** what we might think of as the textural rhythm of the piece and creates a kind of textural accent when Section III occurs at 7:59. Figure 21.6 schematizes the accelerating alternation. Unlike the consistent presentation of T-T type C¹ in the first part of Section II, the second part entails a relatively quick change between three distinct types.

SECTION III

Example 21.4 cites mm. 164–73, the beginning of section III. The dominating trajectory of Section III is the gradual and persistent "textural *crescendo*" that begins with the "Repeated" idea—which I describe as a "Morse code–like" presentation—and continues through a series of transformations over the course of the section (see figure 21.7).

Both "textural *crescendo*" and "transformation" are terms referring to processes of musical form. In this section, "textural *crescendo*" refers to the effect made by the over-

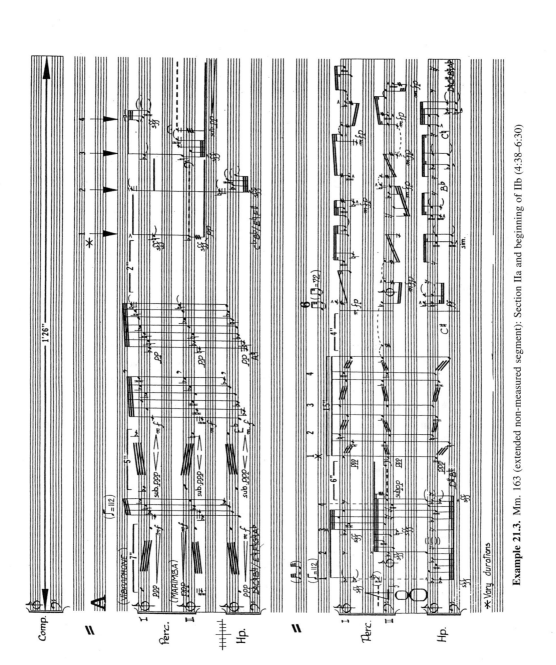

Example 21.3. Mm. 163 (extended non-measured segment): Section IIa and beginning of IIb (4:38–6:30)

Time	5:55	6:05	6:16	6:31	6:53	7:03	7:27	7:49	7:53
T-T Type	C^2	C^2	B^2	C^2	A^3	C^2	A^3	C^2	A^3
Duration		→ 10"	→ 11 "	→ 15"	→ 22"	→ 10"	→ 24"	→ 22"	→ 4 "

Figure 21.6. Accelerating alternation of T-T Types during Section IIb

time alterations of the timbral/textural configuration of the "Repeated" idea and to the continuously increasing dynamic from 8:27 through 12:18. Together, the combined effect of textural and dynamic increase provides a trajectory to the formal process of the Section. The term "transformation" refers to the step-by-step nature of the changes that occur over the course of the Section. In this context, it refers to the process by which the identity of the "Repeated" idea remains while it is being altered by differing timbral and textural configurations. In other words, an identifying element remains while other aspects change. Let us now chart the course of this formal process.

The "Repeated" idea is first transformed by instrumental additions and changes and by an increasingly louder dynamic. This process continues until the Marimba and Vibraphone play a series of soloistic "Flourishes" that take on the primary textural role and provide culmination of the process in the instruments. At 11:49 the "Repeated" idea is represented in an electronic version, and the process of textural crescendo is renewed. The idea culminates with a *forte* that then dissolves into a fadeout and a trill in the clarinet that continues in an instrumental version preceding the electronic throbbing.

Section III begins with a C T/T Type that is projected primarily by an electronic timbre. The Ambient[4] presents sustained octaves that are punctuated by "trombone-like blops" and higher, "electric blips." This C^3 T/T Type takes on a secondary role upon the entrance of the "Repeated" idea at 8:27, but it never fully disappears throughout most of the section but rather helps to enhance the overall *crescendo* effect of the passage.

Section IV

Example 21.5 cites mm. 284–93, the beginning of Section IV. In many ways the culminating passage of *Millefoglie* in terms of loud dynamics and increased rhythmic activity occurs within the *crescendo* effect of Section III (see figure 21.8). The concluding section is the longest of the whole work and provides a kind of calming response to that culmination. This section consists of a lengthy textural *decrescendo* that consists of several presentations of a "Swaying" idea over the nearly six minutes of this section. The "Swaying" idea becomes curtailed at 15:41, and the "Long" idea—a held-out tone in the instruments—that follows the "Swaying" idea is replaced by an "E-Warble" and "Buzzy Throb" after 15:31. The repetition of the "Swaying" idea together with its lulling quality dissipate the energy built up in the prior section. The coordination of the instrumental parts at the beginning of Section IV and the addition of electronic punctuations define the passage as a version of the T/T Type A. Further, the "Buzzy Throb" timbre refers to the "buzzy" timbres of Section I, associating earlier music with the closing textural *decrescendo*.

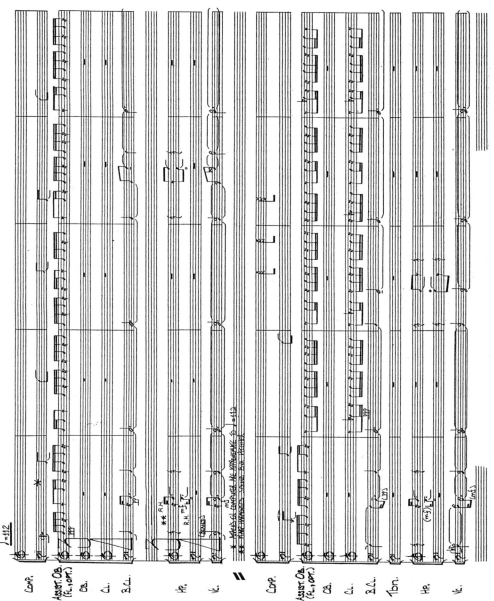

Example 21.4. Mm. 164–73: Section III, beginning

Time		T-T type	Const. Elements Descriptive Names		Dyn.	Details	
frml	intl		Primary	Secondary		Instrumental Comp.	Electronic Comp.
III 7:59		C^3	Ambient⁴		p	BC	Sustained octaves
	8:06			Blops;E-Blips	mp		low, trombone-like blops; high, electric blips
	8:20			; R&A (from IIb)	mp	R&A in V,M,H	
	8:27	A^4	R	Amb⁴; Blops, E-Blips	cresc.	Repeated, Morse-Code-like idea in F; add VC to Amb⁴	
	8:38		R+			add C; rising pitch	
	8:47		R+/-			add O; delete F	
	9:07		R+/-	–		add F; delete O	
	9:17		R+			add T, then VC	
	9:38		R+/-			add O; delete F	
	9:47		R+/-			add BC, H; delete T	
	10:17		R+			add V, T; then BC	
	10:47		Flourishes	R+	fff	add M; solo Flourishes in M, V; all insts.	
	11:49		R-Trans-formed				R instrumental idea transformed by electronic sounds; pulsing and throbbing
	12:18		, Throbbing	E-Punc			Electric punctuations
	12:49		, Throbbing		fadeout		
12:54				Trill-Throb	p	clarinet trill	

Figure 21.7. Section III

OVERALL FORMAL DESIGN

We have now traced the use of texture and timbre throughout the work. Considering the overall aesthetic design of *Millefoglie*, we note three different types of musical processes (refer again to figure 21.1).

First, *Millefoglie* delineates three broadly defined T/T Types that serve as a basis for association across the broad span of the piece. The five differing versions of the A Type occur in all of the sections, playing dominant roles in subsection Ia and in Sections III and IV. The framing of the piece with A^1 and A^5 creates referential connections while at the same time assuring a process of renewal. T/T Type B dominates most of subsection Ib and occurs briefly in subsection IIb, thus occurring only in the first third of the piece. T/T Type C occurs in Section II and the first part of Section III. Its first two versions, C^1 and C^2, alternate with versions of T/T Types A and B and participate in the textural intensification occurring in Section II. The third version, C^3, provides the "ambient" timbral context out of which the dominating textural *crescendo* builds during Section III. In

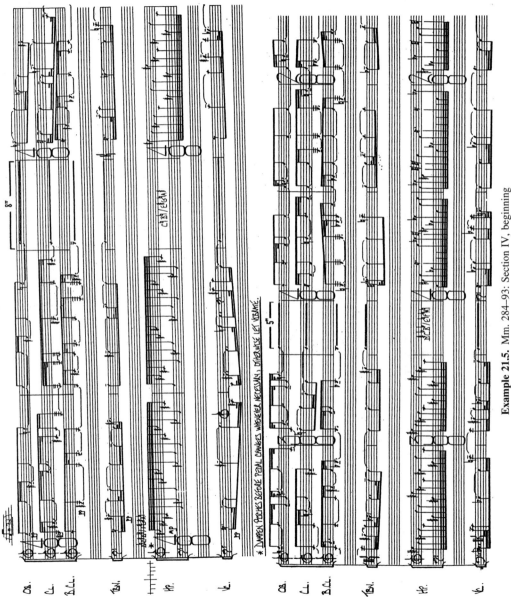

Example 21.5. Mm. 284–93: Section IV, beginning

Time		T-T Type	Descriptive Names		Dyn.	Details	
formal	internal		Primary	Secondary		Instrmt. Comp.	Elect. Comp.
IV 13:01		A^5	Swaying-Long		p	H, O, C, BC, T, VC	
	13:17		Swaying-Long				
	13:32		Swaying-Long				
	13:49		Swaying-Long				
	14:07		Swaying-Long				
	14:29		Swaying-Long				
	14:41		Swaying-Long				
	14:53		Long				
	14:58			Punctuations E-Warble, Buzzy Throb			Punctuations with E-Warbles and Buzzy throbs
	15:12		Swaying-Long				
	15:25						
	15:31		Swaying-Long				
	15:36						
	15:41		Sway'				E-Warble and buzzy throbs take over role of "Long"
	15:49		Sway'				
	16:00		Sway'				
	16:22		Sway'				
	16:38		Sway'				
	16:52		Sway'				
	17:07		Sway'				
	17:19		Sway'				
	17:37		Sway'				
	17:54		Sway'				
	18:53						

Figure 21.8. Section IV

general, the recurrences of the T/T types and the variations that occur within them create a rich web of referential associations and play a cohesive role over the course of the piece.

Second, there are several places in which a T/T Type initially realized by either the instrumental or electronic component is transformed and recreated in the other component. For instance, this kind of transformative process occurs in the change from subsection IIa to IIb: T/T Type C^1 is realized at 4:38–5:55 by the timbral features of ambient^3 and its punctuation with "E-Swishes" and the "soft-siren." That version is transformed into a C^2 version in the instruments that recreates Ambient^3 as the "Murmur" idea and

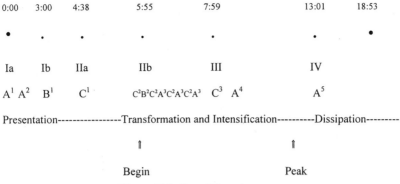

Figure 21.9. Overall formal strategy

the "E-Swishes" into instrumental "Swishes." Another such timbral transformation occurs in Section III during the textural *crescendo*. The A^4 texture occurring at 8:27 begins the buildup that is articulated and renewed at 11:49 when the electronic component transforms the texture. These two timbral transformations play a role in the aesthetic design of the form. In Section II, the transformation articulates the change from subsection IIa to IIb, and in Section III, the transformation serves to articulate and renew the process of the textural *crescendo*.

Third and finally, the formal strategy of *Millefoglie* depends centrally on the associations and transformations between textural/timbral types. As schematized in figure 21.9 below, the piece begins in a presentational mode, revealing the three types (A, B, C) through the first three sub-sections. Subsection IIb initiates a new formal process, that of timbral transformation and textural intensification. Section III builds further upon this process and brings it to a peak at roughly two-thirds of the entire piece. The long ending section of *Millefoglie* dissipates the energy created through that peak, enacting a textural *decrescendo* ending the entire work.

Analysis of the textural and timbral organization of Kolb's *Millefoglie* has revealed aspects of formal and aesthetic design. My analysis has shown how textural/timbral types serve functions of both association and variation, linking sections across the duration of the work while at the same time providing renewal that creates dynamic formal direction. It has also demonstrated how the timbral distinctions between acoustic instruments and electronically generated sounds play a role in the formal processes of the work, in particular through the timbral transformation of T/T Types. And finally, the analysis has clarified how the rhythms of the textural and timbral processes of association, variation, and transformation define the formal strategy of the piece and play a role in its overall aesthetic design.

While there are no preexisting conceptual categories that can guide and define analysis of the textural/timbral domain of music, an original investigative methodology that leads to an analytic transcription can reveal a great deal about aesthetic design, especially for works such as Kolb's *Millefoglie* that combine acoustic instruments with electronically generated sound. Furthermore, the processes of understanding the analyst must engage in order to develop relevant categories of textural and timbral distinction lead to a better comprehension of the aesthetic appeal of particular works and to a better understanding of what makes a piece "work."

FURTHER READING

Boulez, Pierre. "Timbre and composition—timbre and language," *Contemporary Music Review* 2, no. 1 (1987): 161–72.

Chou, Wen-Chung. "Ionisation: The Function of Timbre in its Formal and Temporal Organization." *New Worlds of Edgard Varèse: A Symposium*, I.S.A.M. Monographs 11 (1979): 17–74.

Cogan, Robert. "Tone Color: The New Understanding." *Sonus* 1 (1980): 3–24.

———. "Toward a Theory of Timbre: Verbal Timbre and Musical Line in Purcell, Sessions, and Stravinsky." *Perspectives of New Music* 8, no. 1 (1969): 75–81.

De Vale, Sue Carole. "Prolegomena to a Study of Harp and Voice Sounds in Uganda: A Graphic System for the Notation of Textures." In *Selected Reports in Ethnomusicology*, edited by J. C. DjeDje, 5:284–315. Berkeley and Los Angeles: University of California, 1985.

Fennelly, Brian. "A Descriptive Language for the Analysis of Electronic Music," *Perspectives of New Music* 6 (1967): 79–95.

Slawson, Wayne. "The Color of Sound: A Theoretical Study in Musical Timbre." *Music Theory Spectrum* 3 (1981): 132–41.

Scores

Several essays include the music scores; the rest are offered here.

Chapter 1 (Burkhart): Chopin, Mazurka in A-flat Major, op. 59, no. 2

Chapter 3 (Forte): Schumann, "Aus meinen Thränen spriessen," from *Dichterliebe*

Chapter 8 (Cone): Brahms, Intermezzo, op. 116, no. 4

Chapter 9 (Lewin): Mozart, *Marriage of Figaro,* act 1, scene 1

Chapter 10 (Schachter): Schubert songs

    Der Jüngling an der Quelle

    Daß sie hier gewesen!

    Der Tod und das Mädchen

    Nacht und Träume

Chapter 11 (McCreless): Wagner, Isolde's Transfiguration

Chapter 12 (Burns): McLachlan, "Ice"

Chapter 14 (Lester): Bach, Presto from G-Minor Violin Partita

Chapter 15 (Guck): Haydn, Piano Sonata no. 46 in A-flat

Chapter 17 (Rothstein): Mozart, Rondo, K. 485

Chapter 19 (Cohn): Beethoven, *Tempest* Sonata, op. 31, no. 2, movement 1

Chapter 1: Chopin, Mazurka in A-flat Major, op. 59, no. 2

CHAPTER 3: SCHUMANN, "AUS MEINEN THRÄNEN SPRIESSEN," FROM *DICHTERLIEBE*

CHAPTER 8: BRAHMS, INTERMEZZO, OP. 116, NO. 4

4. Intermezzo

J.B. 64

CHAPTER 9: MOZART, *MARRIAGE OF FIGARO*, ACT 1, SCENE 1

Chapter 10: Der Jüngling an der Quelle
Daß sie hier gewesen!
Der Tod und das Mädchen
Nacht und Träume

98

op. 59,2 Daß sie hier gewesen!

Friedrich Rückert
D 775

Sehr langsam

1823 (?)

Daß der Ost-wind Düf-te hau - chet in die Lüf - te,

da-durch tut er kund___, daß du hier ge - we - sen_, daß du hier ge - we - sen.

Daß hier Trä-nen rin-nen, da - durch wirst du

in - nen, wär's dir sonst nicht kund___, daß ich hier ge - we - sen_,

op.7,3 Der Tod und das Mädchen

Matthias Claudius
D 531

*) Takt 1, Klavierstimme: In A. Stadlers Abschrift findet sich hier der Zusatz „sempre con pedale e sordino".

CHAPTER 11: WAGNER, ISOLDE'S TRANSFIGURATION

259

CHAPTER 12: McLACHLAN, "ICE"

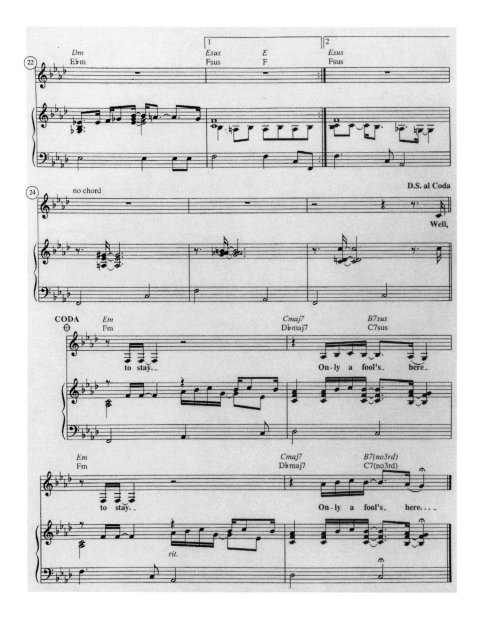

Chapter 14: Bach, Presto from G-Minor Violin Partita

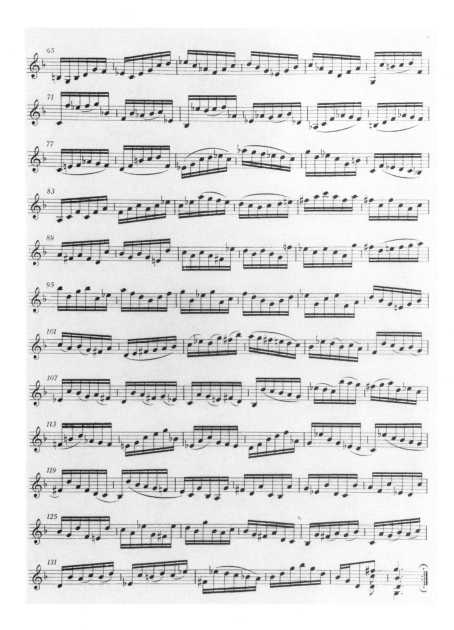

Chapter 15: Haydn, Piano Sonata no. 46 in A-flat

a) Original: ♩♪ ♩ b) 𝅘𝅥𝅮𝅘𝅥𝅮 c) Original: pf

CHAPTER 17: MOZART, RONDO, K. 485

CHAPTER 19: BEETHOVEN, *TEMPEST* SONATA, OP. 31, NO. 2, MOVEMENT 1

82

GLOSSARY

Acceleration A quickening of musical activity. (For a detailed explanation, see Edward Lowinsky, "On Mozart's Rhythm," in the selected bibliography.)

Aggregate The collection of all twelve chromatic notes (**pitch-classes**). In atonal music, the aggregate is the collection of all twelve chromatic pitches; in twelve-tone music, aggregate completion occurs in various ways, often through the combination of two or more row forms. This systematic row usage may function like harmonic progression. (For a more complete discussion of this and other twentieth-century issues, see the Mead essay.)

Agogic Accent, often on normally weak beats, that is created by long duration.

Ametrical Music having no perceptible metric organization.

Anacrusis A note (or notes in a group; for example, a phrase) that precede the first downbeat in the group. "Anacrusis" is synonymous with "upbeat."

Antecedent The first phrase or unit of a **period**; an antecedent phrase closes with a relatively weak cadence (either a half-cadence or an imperfect authentic cadence), thus inviting a varied repetition that leads to a stronger cadence (perfect authentic cadence). The repetition is called a **consequent** (see below).

Appoggiatura The conventional definition of the appoggiatura is an accented nonchord tone that is approached by leap and resolved by step. This definition considers the appoggiatura as distinct from suspensions and accented neighbor or passing tones. Another use of the term by William Rothstein "is to denote any embellishing note that precedes the main note, is not tied, and is played 'on the beat,' regardless of how the embellishing note is approached and whether it is consonant or dissonant. The term thus includes notes that might also be called rearticulated suspensions or accented passing tones. It even includes some chord tones." (See the Rothstein essay, Note 6.)

Asymmetrical meters Meters without the traditional duple or triple groupings. Traditional tonal meters include duples (2/4, 4/4) and triples (3/4, 6/8, 9/8). Twentieth-century composers used meters not easily divided into two or three such as 5/4 and 7/8. Subdivision of such meters results in nonequal parts such as 3 + 2 or 4 + 3.

Atonal pitch notation The notation of pitches distinguishing between pitches in a certain order (as in a melodic line) and those having no particular order, as in a nontonal chord. Angle brackets, $<\ >$, denote *ordered* pitches, while curly brackets, { }, indicate an *unordered* collection of pitches. These conventions were designed by John Rahn and Robert Morris. (See Mead essay.)

Background See **Schenkerian analysis**.

Note: A more detailed glossary of many terms used in analysis can be found in Ian Bent, *Analysis*, with glossary by William Drabkin.

Bimodal The combination of two different modes in one piece, usually—but not always—at the same time.

Bridge In classical music, a bridge is a transition or modulating section. In popular music, a bridge connotes a section that contrasts with the **verses** and **chorus**. It frequently begins with a tonicized subdominant and often leads to a tonicized dominant, ending with a dissonant, retransitional dominant seventh to prepare the return of the following verse.

Chorus The section of a popular song that is heard several times, repeating the same lyrics; this is in alternation with the **verse**, where the lyrics constantly change. The chorus is often very stable harmonically and usually expresses the song's lyrical message in a succinct manner.

Closure The process by which a musical grouping (phrase, section, whole piece) comes to an end. In tonal music, closure involves common harmonic cadences, particularly the authentic cadence; in addition, such aspects as rhythm, melody, and texture contribute to a group's ending as well. In nontonal music, closure occurs through nonharmonic means, including thinning of texture, slowing down of rhythmic activity, and returning to a stable pitch or chord.

Coda (*Ital.*, tail) A concluding passage that follows after the large-scale form of a piece has fulfilled its essential requirements for completion. In **sonata-form** movements, the term "coda" is applied to the section that follows the **recapitulation**. Codas, especially by Beethoven and his successors, often contain the climax of the entire movement, thus becoming an essential, fourth section of the form.

Codetta (*Ital.*, little tail) A postcadential, tonic-prolonging unit following a perfect authentic cadence; the codetta usually prolongs the tonic and ranges in length from a single chord to a four-measure phrase. Whereas a **coda** serves as the final section of a complete movement, a codetta can occur after any perfect authentic cadence within the form.

Consequent The second phrase or unit within a **period**; a consequent repeats the **antecedent** (often in a modified way) but ends with a stronger cadence (a perfect authentic cadence).

Contour The shape of a line, whether it rises, falls, or some combination of the two. Line contour is very audible and plays an important role in motivic development, closure, and expressivity.

Cycle of thirds Third cycles occur as chromatic harmonic progressions or modulations where the chord roots move systematically by either major or minor thirds. (This kind of cycle is also called "equal divisions of the octave," where other cycles can move by second or tritone.) A major-third–cycle completes the octave in three moves, from, say, C major to E major to G♯ (or Ab) major back to C major; a minor-third–cycle takes four moves, from C to Eb to F♯ (or Gb) to A to C. (See Smith essay, Note 22.)

Denouement A term borrowed from form in drama that denotes the gradual deceleration of musical events and intensity following the acceleration to the climax and the climax itself.

Development section See **sonata form**.

Dorian mode The second of six church modes revived in early-twentieth-century music and subsequently used in much rock and jazz. The Dorian mode is minor in quality, having both ♭$\hat{3}$ and ♭$\hat{7}$. It differs from the natural minor scale in that it has the raised scale degree $\hat{6}$. One can remember the Dorian mode by playing from D to D on the white notes of the piano. See the twentieth-century texts in the selected bibliography.

Dyad A pair of notes that occurs simultaneously or sequentially.

Elision An overlapping of phrases where the goal (the last chord) of a harmonic progression occurs simultaneously with the beginning of the next phrase. Because of the elision, a phrase ending and beginning occur within a single moment in time, creating an **acceleration** of phrase structure. (See Schmalfeldt essay.) Elision is synonymous with the term "overlap."

Enharmonic equivalence Two pitches having the same sound but different spellings and different functions, as in C♯ and D♭. The C♯ spelling suggests a resolution up to D, while the D♭ spelling implies a resolution down to C♮.

Expansion An internal lengthening of a phrase or section. This enlargement of a unit occurs somewhere in the middle, in contrast to **extension**, where lengthening occurs at the end of a section or phrase.

Exposition See **sonata form**.

Extension The addition of extra measures of similar material that lengthens the end of a phrase or section. The effect is to delay phrase completion. This lengthening contrasts with expansion, where the additional measures occur in the middle of the phrase.

Foreground See **Schenkerian analysis**.

Fragmentation A breaking down of a musical idea into shorter units. This technique often occurs in development and cadential sections. (See Stein essay and William Caplin, *Classical Form*, in the selected bibliography.)

Grouping Combining elements into a perceivable unit. A group of notes can be perceived as a specific rhythmic idea; a group of phrases can be perceived as a phrase group, and so forth. For more discussion of grouping, see the books by Lerdahl and Jackendoff, Cooper and Meyer and Jonathan Kramer in the selected bibliography.

Harmonic rhythm The rate of chord change. In classical music, changes in harmonic rhythm (**acceleration** or deceleration) affect the pacing of the music (the level of activity). Changes in harmonic rhythm influence the shape of a phrase or the larger unit of a section.

Harmonic sequence See **sequence**.

Head motive A segment of a larger motive that recurs in development and modified reprise sections. (See essays by Stein and Graybill.)

Hexachord A group of six notes. They may occur melodically, harmonically, or some combination of the two. In twelve-tone theory, row forms are often divided into hexachords for various musical effects, such as when two or more row forms are combined.

Hypermeasure A term coined by Edward T. Cone denoting a group of measures in which each measure constitutes one beat in a larger-scale meter. The measure is to hypermeasure what the traditional beat is to measure. Since the term applies only to a unit of *time*, it is not synonymous with "phrase"; some phrases are commensurate with hypermeasures, while others are not. (See essays by Burkhart and Krebs.)

Hyperbeat One unit of **hypermeter**; usually one measure equals one hyperbeat. (See Krebs essay.)

Hypermeter Large-scale meter (see **hypermeasure**, also essays by Burkhart and Krebs).

Intervallic cell A group of notes with a distinctive intervallic identity. The term "intervallic cell" is synonymous with **pitch-class set**. It also can represent a small collection of pitch-classes that, when considered in an abstract sense, generate a significant amount of harmonic and melodic material by virtue of the intervals contained between and among them.

Inversion The repetition of a musical idea or a series of intervals by maintaining the order and exact interval size but reversing the contour. Pitches going *up* a major 2nd invert to going *down* a major 2nd. (See Mead essay.)

Microtonal inflection Also called pitch bending, microtonal inflection is the use of ornamental pitches other than those of the equal-tempered scale (intervals smaller than a half-step) in classical music and many popular styles, including blues, country, rock, gospel, and jazz. Such expressive microtones can appear as sliding glissandi before, after, and between principal tones. (See Satyendra essay.)

Middleground See **Schenkerian analysis**.

Mixolydian One of six church modes revived in early-twentieth-century classical music and subsequently used in much rock and jazz. The Mixolydian mode is major in that it has both a major-mode $\hat{3}$ and $\hat{6}$. The only difference between the major scale and Mixolydian mode is scale degree $\hat{7}$: in major mode, $\hat{7}$ is the leading tone; in the Mixolydian mode, $\hat{7}$ is lowered. Thus Mixolydian has no leading tone. The mode can be remembered as the scale from G to G on only white notes. (See essay by Stein and the twentieth-century textbooks in the selected bibliography.)

Motto A specific type of motive that either (1) embodies an important reference (as in a composer's name: "DSCH" for Dmitri Shostakovitch and "EsCHBEG" for Schoenberg) or (2) denotes a lengthier thematic statement. (See essays by Graybill and Stein and the article by Allen Forte, "Schoenberg's Creative Evolution," in the selected bibliography.)

Octatonic A symmetrical, nontonal scale comprised of alternating whole and half-steps. Used in music by late-nineteenth-century composers (including Liszt and Rimsky-Korsakov) and twentieth-century composers (including Bartok, Debussy, Messiaen, Ravel, and Stravinsky). (See Graybill essay.)

Ostinato From the Italian word meaning "obstinate," this term refers to a significant repetition of a motive or phrase. In seventeenth- and eighteenth-century music, the ostinato often presented a recurring theme, as in a chaconne or passacaglia (see Schmalfeldt essay). In the twentieth century, the ostinato created musical motion in the absence of harmonic progression and developed melodic and rhythmic material (see Stein essay).

Pentatonic A five-note scale built of major seconds and minor thirds. The black notes of the piano comprise one version of this scale (see Stein essay).

Period A phrase group (two or more phrases) that combine to form a unit. The opening phrase or unit (called **antecedent**, or "question") ends on a weaker cadence (such as a half-cadence, or imperfect authentic cadence), while an ensuing phrase or unit (called **consequent**, or "answer") concludes with a stronger cadence (such as a perfect authentic cadence). Theorists disagree about other characteristics of the period structure. By far the most common feature of a period is that each uses the same or similar thematic material.

Phenomenal accent An accent created not by rhythm or meter but rather by other factors, such as notated accents, changes in register, texture, timbre, dynamics, and so forth. The term is defined by Lerdahl and Jackendoff, in *A Generative Theory of Tonal Music,* thus: "by phenomenal accent we mean any event at the musical surface that gives emphasis or stress to a moment in the musical flow" (17); it is also discussed by Jonathan Kramer in *The Time of Music,* 86–87. Kramer and others prefer the word "stress" to "phenomenal accent."

Pitch-class A note without reference to the octave or register in which it occurs. "Middle C" is a pitch, but "C" is a pitch-class, representing all possible Cs.

Pitch-class set An unordered collection of **pitch-classes**, that is, a bunch of notes whose order and register is unspecified (see Mead and Straus essays).

Polymeter The simultaneous use of two or more time signatures; the two (or more) meters may be distinguishable, or the meter may be ambiguous. (See Stein essay.)

Prolongation See **Schenkerian analysis**.

Recapitulation See **sonata form**.

Refrain Lines of poetry or phrases of music that recur throughout a poem or a piece of music.

Reinterpretation A special type of phrase overlap in which **hypermeasures** overlap, e.g., bar 4 of a four-bar hypermeasure is "reinterpreted" as the next bar 1. (See Burkhart essay.)

Reprise There are at least two common meanings of this term: (1) in the eighteenth century, a repeated section, such as the music enclosed by repeat signs; (2) the repetition of opening material later in the piece. In **sonata form**, the **recapitulation** is a reprise.

Retransition A passage that modulates from a secondary key to the home key. In **sonata form**, a retransition serves as the final stage of the **development**; it prepares for the return of the main theme at the beginning of the **recapitulation**, and its harmonic goal is usually the home dominant. The retransition is often prolonged via a pedal.

Retrograde The statement of a musical idea in reverse order (last becomes first, etc.). (See Mead essay.)

Rhetoric Language used for particular effect, whether to influence or persuade or to express something more vividly through imagery. In music analysis, the term "rhetoric" also refers to the sense in which music is akin to speech (laying out ideas, developing those ideas, exploring a single subject, etc.).

Rounded binary form Like the small ternary, the rounded binary consists of an **exposition** (A), a contrasting middle (B), and a **reprise** (A'). The rounded binary repeats the opening section and then repeats both the contrasting middle and the reprise. The opening A section may or may not modulate, and the return of A (as A') may include modifications or a transformation of the opening. Rounded binary and small ternary forms can serve as themes within larger compositions or as self-contained movements—for example, as classical minuets and trios or scherzos.

Rubato (*Ital.*, robbed, as of time) In metered music, rubato refers to changes in tempo by a performer: stretching and compressing the beat by slowing down and hurrying the tempo. Two basic types are recognized, each characteristic of different historical periods and genres: (1) against a strictly maintained beat (probably in the accompaniment), the melody is performed with slight **accelerations** and retards; thus the time "robbed" is "paid back"; (2) the beat itself is subjected to **accelerations** and retards, with no maintenance of regularity.

Schenkerian analysis A method of analysis of tonal music developed by the Austrian theorist Heinrich Schenker (1868–1935) that sees a given composition as an elaboration of an underlying structure that is conceived as a series of ever simpler levels discovered through a process of reduction. Schenker's theory of **structural levels** demonstrates that just beneath the surface of the music are several elaborate levels called the "**foreground**." By "reducing out," or looking beyond the embellishing pitches, several "middleground" levels emerge that convey the work's underlying structure. Further reduction results in several "background levels," which serve as a voice-leading paradigm for a given work. The principal means of creating a rich and complex work from a simple background structure is **prolongation**, both harmonic and melodic. (See Forte essay.)

Sentence First identified by Arnold Schoenberg, this is a type of theme that consists of a "presentation" followed by a "continuation." The presentation is a tonic-prolonging unit that features a "basic idea" and its immediate, often varied repetition. The continuation mobilizes the theme—by means of **fragmentation**, harmonic **acceleration**, faster **harmonic rhythm**, and/or **sequence**—and it closes with a cadence. (See William Caplin, *Classical Form,* cited in the selected bibliography.)

Sequence A repetition of a melodic, harmonic, or both melodic and harmonic (or contrapuntal) musical idea on different pitches (in tonal music, different scale degrees). This repetition (or transposition) often includes repeated rhythms.

Simultaneity The collection of notes sounding at some point in time (also called "verticality" or "chord").

Sonata form A tripartite, full-movement form that became a hallmark of the classical style. This form contains (1) an **exposition** (consisting of a main theme or theme-group, a transition, a new-key secondary theme or theme-group, and a closing theme or **codetta**; (2) a **development** (usually featuring unstable, sequential repetitions and then a **retransition** leading to the dominant of the home key); and (3) a **recapitulation** (a modified version of the **exposition**, in which the secondary-theme materials now return in the original key, thus resolving tonal conflict). Sonata-form movements can begin with a slow introduction and end with a **coda**. For fuller accounts of **sonata form**, see the works by Douglass M. Green and William Caplin in the selected bibliography.

Strophic A song is referred to as "strophic" when it features a series of verses that each employ the same music but different lyrics. In the folk and country traditions, such strophic songs can sometimes narrate a complicated story or series of events.

Structural levels See **Schenkerian analysis**.

Syncopation A musical accent occurring on a normally weak beat that obscures the customary accent on the subsequent strong beat.

Syntax The placement of chords within a musical phrase, similar to placing words within a sentence in language.

Tetrachord A group of four notes. They may occur melodically, harmonically, or some combination of the two.

Transition A section that may have its own theme or may develop motives from expository themes. Often a transition is modulatory in nature, frequently moving from the home tonic to the dominant of the new key.

Transposition The repetition of a musical idea or a series of intervals by starting on a different pitch.

Trichord A group of three notes. They may occur melodically, harmonically, or some combination of the two.

Tritone substitution In jazz theory, a tritone substitution is the substitution of a dominant chord, say D^7 with a chord whose root is a half-octave distant from the dominant pitch: $A\flat^7$. (See Satyendra essay.)

Verse In rock music, a verse is the passage that is repeated numerous times, often in alternation with the **chorus**. In contrast with the repeated lyrics of the chorus, those in the verse sections often change, unfolding aspects of the story or the idea a song is meant to express.

Wholetone A symmetrical nontonal scale that is comprised solely of six whole tones. The collection includes a limited number of other intervals: major thirds (minor sixths) and tritones.

SELECTED BIBLIOGRAPHY

Part I is a list of a few publications by each author in the book; Part II cites other readings of particular importance that are suitable for our readers; and Part III offers selected textbooks.

PART I: SELECTED READINGS BY THE CONTRIBUTORS

Charles Burkhart

"Chopin's 'Concluding Expansions.'" In *Nineteenth-Century Piano Music: Essays in Performance and Analysis*, edited by David Witten, 95–114. New York: Garland Press, 1997.

"Departure from the Norm in Two Songs from Schumann's *Liederkreis, Op. 39.*" In *Schenker Studies*, edited by Hedi Siegel, 146–64. Cambridge: Cambridge University Press, 1990.

"Mid-Bar Downbeat in Bach's Keyboard Music." *Journal of Music Theory Pedagogy* 8 (1994): 3–26.

"Schenker's Theory of Levels and Musical Performance." In *Aspects of Schenkerian Theory*, edited by David Beach, 95–112. New Haven: Yale University Press, 1983.

"Schoenberg's Farben: An Analysis of Op. 16, No. 3." *Perspectives of New Music* 12, nos. 1 and 2 (1973–74): 141–72.

Lori Burns

"Analytic Methodologies for Rock Music: Harmonic and Voice-Leading Strategies in Tori Amos's 'Crucify.'" In *Expression in Pop-Rock Music: A Collection of Critical and Analytical Essays*, edited by Walter Everett, 213–46. Charlottesville: Garland, 2000.

Bach's Modal Chorales. Stuyvesant, N.Y.: Pendragon Press, 1995.

Disruptive Divas: Feminism, Identity and Popular Music (co-authored with Mélisse Lafrance). New York and London: Routledge Press, 2002.

"Genre, Gender, and Convention Revisited: k. d. lang's Cover of Cole Porter's 'So in Love.'" *Repercussions* 7–8 (1999–200): 299–325.

"'Joanie' Get Angry: k.d. lang's Feminist Revision." In *Understanding Rock: Essays in Music Analysis*, edited by John Covach and Graeme Boone, 93–112. New York: Oxford Press, 1997.

Richard Cohn

"As Wonderful as Star Clusters: Instruments for Gazing at Tonality in Schubert." *Nineteenth Century Music* 22, no. 3 (1999): 213–32.

"Bartók's Octatonic Strategies: A Motivic Approach." *Journal of the American Musicological Society* 44 (1991): 262–300.

"Dramatization of Hypermetric Conflicts in the Scherzo of Beethoven's Ninth Symphony." *Nineteenth Century Music* 15, no. 3 (1992): 22–40.

"Maximally Smooth Cycles, Hexatonic Systems, and the Analysis of Late-Romantic Triadic Progressions." *Music Analysis* 15, no. 1 (1996): 9–40.

Edward T. Cone

Note: Most articles are reprinted in *Music: A View from Delft* (see below).

"Analysis Today." *The Musical Quarterly* 46, no. 2 (1960): 172–88; reprinted in *Problems of Modern Music*, edited by Paul Henry Lang, 34–50. New York: W. W. Norton, 1960.

The Composer's Voice. Berkeley and Los Angeles: University of California Press, 1974.

Music: A View from Delft. Edited by Robert P. Morgan. Chicago: University of Chicago Press, 1989.

Musical Form and Musical Performance. New York: W. W. Norton, 1968.

"Three Ways of Reading a Detective Story—or a Brahms Intermezzo." *The Georgia Review* 31, no. 3 (fall 1977): 554–74.

John Covach

"Echolyn and American Progressive Rock." In *American Rock and the Classical Music Tradition*, edited by John Covach and Walter Everett, 13–61. London: Harwood Academic Publishers, 2000.

"Jazz-Rock? Rock-Jazz? Stylistic Crossover in Late-1970s American Progressive Rock." In *Expression in Pop-Rock Music.* edited by Walter Everett, 113–34. New York: Garland Publishing, 1999.

"Popular Music, Unpopular Musicology." In *Rethinking Music*, edited by Nicholas Cook and Mark Everist, 452–70. New York: Oxford University Press, 1999.

"Stylistic Competencies, Musical Humor, and 'This is Spinal Tap.'" In *Concert Music, Rock and Jazz since 1945: Essays and Analytical Studies,* edited by Elizabeth Marvin and Richard Hermann, 402–24. Rochester, N.Y.: University of Rochester Press, 1995.

"We Won't Get Fooled Again: Rock Music and Musical Analysis." *In Theory Only* 13, nos. 1–4 (1997): 119–41; reprinted in *Keeping Score: Music, Disciplinarity, Culture,* edited by David Schwarz, Anahid Kassabian, and Lawrence Siegel, 75–89. Charlottesville: University Press of Virginia, 1997.

Allen Forte

The American Popular Ballad of the Golden Era, 1924–1950. Princeton: Princeton University Press, 1995.

The Atonal Music of Anton Webern. New Haven: Yale University Press, 1998.

Introduction to Schenkerian Analysis (with Steven E. Gilbert). New York: W. W. Norton, 1982.

The Structure of Atonal Music. New Haven: Yale University Press, 1973.

"Schoenberg's Creative Evolution: The Path to Atonality." *Musical Quarterly* XLV/2 (April 1978): 133–76.

Roger Graybill

"Brahms's Integration of Traditional and Progressive Tendencies: A Look at Three Sonata Expositions." *Journal of Musicological Research* 8, nos. 1–2 (1988): 141–68.

"Harmonic Circularity in Brahms's Op. 99 Cello Sonata: An Alternative to Schenker's Reading in *Free Composition.*" *Music Theory Spectrum* 10 (1988): 43–55.

"Pedagogically Speaking: Consonance and Dissonance in the Freshman Theory Class." *In Theory Only* 9, nos. 5–6 (January 1987): 51–56.

"Prolongation, Gesture, and Musical Motion." In *Musical Transformation and Musical Intuition: Essays in Honor of David Lewin*, edited by Raphael Atlas and Michael Cherlin, 199–224. Roxbury, Mass.: Ovenbird Press, 1994.

"Towards a Pedagogy of Gestural Rhythm." *Journal of Music Theory Pedagogy* 4, no. 1 (spring 1990): 1–50.

Marion Guck

"Analytical Fictions." In *Music/Ideology: Resisting the Aesthetic*, edited by Adam Krims and Henry Klumpenhouwer, 157–77. Amsterdam: Gordon and Breach, 1998; reprinted from *Music Theory Spectrum* 16, no. 2 (1994): 217–30.

"Beethoven As Dramatist." *College Music Symposium* 29 (1989). 8–18.

"Musical Images as Musical Thoughts: The Contribution of Metaphor to Analysis." *In Theory Only* 5, no. 5 (1981): 29–43.

"Taking Notice: A Response to Kendall Walton." *Journal of Musicology* 11, no. 1 (1993): 45–51.

"Two Types of Metaphoric Transference." *Music and Meaning*, edited by Jenefer Robinson, 201–12. Ithaca, N.Y., and London: Cornell University Press, 1997.

Harald Krebs

"Alternatives to Monotonality in Early 19th-Century Music." *Journal of Music Theory* 25, no. 1 (spring 1981): 1–16.

Fantasy Pieces: Metrical Dissonance in the Music of Robert Schumann. New York: Oxford University Press, 1999.

"Some Extensions of the Concepts of Metrical Consonance and Dissonance." *Journal of Music Theory* 31, no. 1 (spring 1987): 99–120.

"Tonal and Formal Dualism in Chopin's Scherzo, Op. 31." *Music Theory Spectrum* 13, no. 1 (spring 1991): 48–60.

"Tonal Structure in Nielsen's Symphonies." In *The Nielsen Companion,* edited by Mina Miller, 208–49. New York: Faber and Faber, 1995.

Joel Lester

"Analysis and Performance in Schoenberg's Phantasy, Op. 47." In *Pianist, Scholar, Connoisseur: Essays in Honor of Jacob Lateiner,* edited by Bruce Brubaker and Jane Gottlieb, 151–74. Stuyvesant, NY: Pendragon, 2000.

Analytic Approaches to Twentieth-Century Music. New York: W. W. Norton, 1989.

Bach's Works for Solo Violin: Style, Structure, Performance. New York: Oxford University Press, 1999.

Compositional Theory in the Eighteenth Century. Cambridge: Harvard University Press, 1992.

"Performance and Analysis: Interaction and Interpretation." In *Performance Studies,* edited by John Rink. Cambridge: Cambridge University Press, 1995; reprinted in Spanish translation in *Quodlibet* 15 (October 1999): 106–29.

David B. Lewin

"Amfortas's Prayer to Titurel and the Role of D in *Parsifal*: The Tonal Spaces of the Drama and the Enharmonic C♭/B," *Nineteenth Century Music* 7, no. 3 (April 1985): 336–49.

"Auf dem Flusse: Image and Background in a Schubert Song." In *Schubert: Critical and Analytical Studies,* edited by Walter Frisch, 126–52. Lincoln and London: University of Nebraska Press, 1986.

"Brahms, his Past, and Modes of Music Theory." In *Brahms Studies,* edited by George Bozarth, 13–17. Oxford: Oxford University Press, 1990.

"Parallel Voice-Leading in Debussy." In *Music at the Turn of Century,* edited by Joseph Kerman, 57–70. Berkeley and Los Angeles: University of California Press, 1990.

"Some Notes on *Pierrot Lunaire*." In *Music Theory in Concept and Practice,* edited by James Baker, David Beach, and Jonathan Bernard, 433–57. Rochester, N.Y.: University of Rochester Press, 1997.

Judith Lochhead

"Analysis, Hearing, and Performance" (with George Fisher). *Indiana Theory Review* 14, no. 1 (1993): 1–36.

"Joan Tower's 'Wings' and 'Breakfast Rhythms I and II': Some Thoughts on Form and Repetition." *Perspectives of New Music* 30, no. 1 (1992): 132–57.

Postmodern Music/Postmodern Thought. Co-edited with Joseph Auner. New York and London: Routledge, 2001.

"Retooling the Technique." *Music Theory Online* 4, no. 2 (March 1998): http://www.ucsb.edu/mto-home.html.

"Temporal Processes of Form: Roger Sessions's Third Piano Sonata/I." *Contemporary Music Review* 7, no. 2 (1993): 163–84.

William Marvin

"The Function of 'Rules' in Die Meistersinger von Nürnberg." *Journal of Musicology* 20/3 (2004): 414–460.

"Review of Daniel Kazez, 'Rhythm Reading: Elementary through Advanced Training.' " *Music Theory Online*, 3, no. 4 (1997).

"Tonality in Selected Set-Pieces from Richard Wagner's Die Meistersinger von Nürnberg: A Schenkerian Approach." Ph.D. dissertation, Eastman School of Music/University of Rochester, 2002.

Patrick McCreless

"The Cycle of Structure and the Cycle of Meaning: Shostakovich's Piano Trio in E Minor, Op. 67." In *Shostakovich Studies,* edited by David Fanning, 113–36. Cambridge: Cambridge University Press, 1995).

"An Evolutionary Perspective on Semitone Relations in the Nineteenth Century." In *The Second Practice of Nineteenth-Century Tonality,* edited by William Kinderman and Harald Krebs, 87–113. Lincoln: University of Nebraska Press, 1996.

"Music and Rhetoric." In *The Cambridge History of Western Music Theory,* edited by Thomas Christensen. Cambridge: Cambridge University Press, forthcoming.

"Rethinking Contemporary Music Theory." In *Keeping Score: Music, Disciplinarity, Culture,* edited by David Schwarz and Anahid Kassabian, 13–53. Charlottesvile: University of Virginia Press, 1997.

"Schenker and the Norns." In *Analyzing Opera,* edited by Carolyn Abbate and Roger Parker, 276–97. Berkeley and Los Angeles: University of California Press, 1989.

Wagner's Siegfried: Its Drama, History, and Music. Ann Arbor: UMI Research Press, 1982.

Andrew Mead

"Bodily Hearing: Physiological Metaphors and Musical Understanding." *Journal of Music Theory* 43, no. 1 (1999): 1–20.

An Introduction to the Music of Milton Babbitt. Princeton: Princeton University Press, 1994.

"'Tonal' Forms in Arnold Schoenberg's Twelve-Tone Music." *Music Theory Spectrum* 9 (1987): 67–92.

"Twelve-Tone Organizational Strategies: An Analytical Sampler." *Intégral* 3 (1990): 93–169.

"Webern, Tradition, and 'Composing with Twelve Tones . . .' " *Music Theory Spectrum* 15, no. 2 (1994): 173–204.

William Rothstein

"Ambiguity in the Themes of Chopin's First, Second, and Fourth Ballades." *Intégral* 8 (1995): 1–50.

"Analysis and the Act of Performance." In *The Practice of Performance: Studies in Musical Interpretation,* edited by John Rink, 217–40. Cambridge: Cambridge University Press, 1995.

"Heinrich Schenker As an Interpreter of Beethoven's Piano Sonatas." *Nineteenth Century Music* 8, no. 1 (summer 1984): 3–28.

"Phrase Rhythm in Chopin's Nocturnes and Mazurkas." In *Chopin Studies*, edited by Jim Samson, 115–41. Cambridge: Cambridge University Press, 1988.

Phrase Rhythm in Tonal Music. New York: Schirmer Books, 1989.

Ramon Satyendra

"Aesthetics of a Tabla Solo: Rule and Application in Theme and Variation Forms," *Perspectives of New Music* (forthcoming).

"Chromatic Tonality and Semitonal Relationships in Liszt's Late Style." PhD diss., University of Chicago, 1992.

"Conceptualizing Expressive Chromaticism in Liszt's Music." *Music Analysis* 16, no. 2 (1997): 219–52.

"An Informal Introduction to Some Formal Concepts from Lewin's Transformational Theory." *Journal of Music Theory* (forthcoming).

"Liszt's Open Structures and the Romantic Fragment." *Music Theory Spectrum* 19, no. 1 (1997). 184–205.

Carl Schachter

Note: All of the articles cited here are found in *Unfoldings: Essays in Schenkerian Theory and Analysis* (see below).

"The Adventure of an F♯: Tonal Narration and Exhortation in Donna Anna's First-Act Recitative and Aria." *Theory and Practice* 16 (1991): 5–20.

"Chopin's Fantasy, Op. 49: The Two-Key Scheme." In *Chopin Studies*, edited by Jim Samson, 221–53. Cambridge: Cambridge University Press, 1988.

Counterpoint in Composition: The Study of Voice Leading (co-authored with Felix Salzer). 1969; New York: Columbia University Press, 1989.

"The Triad As Place and Action." *Music Theory Spectrum* 17, no. 2 (1995) 149–169.

Unfoldings: Essays in Schenkerian Theory and Analysis. Edited by Joseph Straus. New York: Oxford University Press, 1999.

Janet Schmalfeldt

Berg's Wozzeck: *Harmonic Language and Dramatic Design.* New Haven: Yale University Press, 1983.

"Cadential Processes: The Evaded Cadence and the 'One More Time' Technique." *Journal of Musicological Research* 12 (1992): 1–52.

"Form As the Process of Becoming: The Beethoven-Hegelian Tradition and the *Tempest* Sonata." *Beethoven Forum* 4 (1995): 37–71.

"On the Relation of Analysis to Performance: Beethoven's Bagatelles, Op. 126, Nos. 2 and 5." *Journal of Music Theory* 29, no. 1 (1985): 1–31; reissued in Spanish in *Orpheotron*, a journal published by the State Conservatory Alberto Ginastera, Buenos Aires, Argentina, 2001.

"Towards a Reconciliation of Schenkerian Concepts with Traditional and Recent Theories of Form." *Music Analysis* 10, no. 3 (1991): 233–87.

Deborah Stein

"The Expansion of the Subdominant in the Late 19th Century." *Journal of Music Theory* 27, no. 2 (1983): 153–80.

Hugo Wolf's Lieder and Extensions of Tonality. Ann Arbor: UMI Research Press, 1985.

Poetry into Song: Performance and Analysis of Lieder (in collaboration with Robert Spillman). New York: Oxford University Press, 1996.

"Schubert's 'Die Liebe hat gelogen': The Deception of Mode and Mixture." *Journal of Musicological Research* 9 (1989): 109–31.

"Schubert's 'Erlkönig': Motivic Parallelism and Motivic Transformation." *Nineteenth Century Music* XIII/2 (fall 1989): 145–58.

Joseph N. Straus

Collected Writings of Milton Babbitt (co-edited with Stephen Dembski, Andrew Mead, and Stephen Peles). Princeton: Princeton University Press, 2003.

The Music of Ruth Crawford Seeger. Cambridge: Cambridge University Press, 1995.

Remaking the Past: Musical Modernism and the Influence of the Tonal Tradition. Cambridge: Harvard University Press, 1990.

Stravinsky's Late Music. Cambridge: Cambridge University Press, 2001.

"Uniformity, Balance, and Smoothness in Atonal Voice Leading." *Music Theory Spectrum* 25, no. 2 (2003): 305–52.

PART II: SELECTED BOOKS FOR STUDENT READERS

Bent, Ian with William Drabkin. *Analysis* from *The Norton/Grove Handbooks in Music.* New York: W. W. Norton & Co., 1987.

Caplin, William. *Classical Form: A Theory of Formal Functions for the Instrumental Music of Haydn, Mozart, and Beethoven.* New York and Oxford: Oxford University Press, 1998.

Cook, Nicholas. *A Guide to Musical Analysis.* New York: G. Brazilier 1987.

Cooper, Grosvenor, and Leonard B. Meyer. *The Rhythmic Structure of Music.* Chicago, Ill: University of Chicago Press, 1960.

Epstein, David. *Beyond Orpheus: Studies in Musical Structure.* Cambridge: MIT Press, 1979.

Frisch, Walter. *Brahms and the Principle of Developing Variation.* Berkeley and Los Angeles: University of California Press, 1984.

Kramer, Jonathan. *The Time of Music: New Meanings, New Temporalities, New Listening Strategies.* New York: Schirmer Books, 1988.

Lerdahl, Fred, and Ray Jackendoff. *A Generative Theory of Tonal Music.* Cambridge: MIT Press, 1983.

Lowinsky, Edward. "On Mozart's Rhythm." In *The Creative World of Mozart*, edited by Paul Henry Lang. New York: W. W. Norton, 1963.

Meyer, Leonard B. *Emotion and Meaning in Music.* Chicago: University of Chicago Press, 1956.

Oswald, Jonas. "The Relation of Word and Tone." In *Introduction to the Theory of Heinrich Schenker*, translated and edited by John Rothgeb. New York: Longman, 1982. 149–161.

Rosen, Charles. *Classical Style: Haydn, Mozart, Beethoven.* New York: W. W. Norton, 1972.

———. *The Romantic Generation.* Cambridge: Harvard University Press, 1995.

———. *Sonata Forms.* New York: W. W. Norton, 1980.

Schoenberg, Arnold. *Style and Idea: Selected Writings.* Edited by Leonard Stein, translated by Leo Black. Berkeley and Los Angeles: University of California Press, 1975.

Tovey, Donald. *A Companion to Beethoven's Pianoforte Sonatas.* London: Royal Schools of Music, 1931.

———. *Essays in Musical Analysis.* London: Oxford University Press, 1935–44.

———. "Tonality in Schubert." In *The Main Stream of Music and Other Essays.* London: Oxford University Press, 1949. 134–159.

Zuckerkandl, Victor. *The Sense of Music.* Princeton: Princeton University Press, 1959.

PART III: TEXTS

Aldwell, Edward, and Carl Schachter. *Harmony and Voice Leading.* 3d ed. New York: Schirmer, 2003.

Berry, Wallace T. *Form in Music.* Englewood Cliffs, N.J.: Prentice-Hall, 1966.

Cadwallader, Allen, and David Gagné. *Analysis of Tonal Music: A Schenkerian Approach.* New York: Oxford University Press, 1998.

Clendinning, Jane Piper, and Elizabeth West Marvin. *The Musician's Guide to Theory and Analysis.* New York: W. W. Norton, 2005.

Forte, Allen. *The Structure of Atonal Music.* New Haven: Yale University Press, 1973.

Gauldin, Robert. *Harmonic Practice in Tonal Music.* New York: W. W. Norton, 1997.

Green, Douglass M. *Form in Tonal Music.* 2d ed. New York: Holt, Rinehart and Winston, 1979.

Kostka, Stefan. *Materials and Techniques of Twentieth-Century Music.* Englewood Cliffs, N.J.: Prentice-Hall, 1999.

Kostka, Stefan, and Dorothy Payne. *Tonal Harmony, with an Introduction to Twentieth-Century Music,* Fourth ed. New York, NY: McGraw-Hill, 2000.

Laitz, Steven. *The Complete Musician.* New York: Oxford University Press, 2003.

Lester, Joel. *Analytic Approaches to Twentieth-Century Music.* New York: W. W. Norton, 1989.

Morgan, Robert. *Twentieth-Century Music.* New York: W. W. Norton, 1991.

Perle, George. *Serial Composition and Atonality.* 6th ed. Berkeley and Los Angeles: University of California Press, 1981.

Phillips, Joel, Jane Piper Clendinning, and Elizabeth West Marvin. *The Musician's Guide to Aural Skills.* New York: W. W. Norton, 2005.

Rahn, John. *Basic Atonal Theory.* New York: Longman, 1980.

Simms, Bryan R. *Music of the Twentieth Century: Style and Structure.* New York: Schirmer Books, 1986.

Straus, Joseph N. *Introduction to Post-Tonal Theory,* Third ed. Upper Saddle River, NJ: Prentice Hall, 2005.

Whittall, Arnold. *Musical Composition in the Twentieth Century.* New York: Oxford University Press, 1999.

CREDITS

Reprints

Edward T. Cone, "Attacking a Brahms Puzzle." This essay was first published in *The Musical Times.* February 1995, Volume cxxxvi, Number 1824, pp. 72–79.

Allen Forte, "Schenker's Conception of Musical Structure," was first published in *Journal of Music Theory* III/1 (April 1959): 7–14, 23–24. Reprinted by permission of the *Journal of Music Theory,* © 1959.

Carl Schachter, "Motive and Text in Four Schubert Songs," was first published in *Aspects of Schenkerian Theory* (1983), pp. 61–76, David Beach, ed. Reprinted by permission of Yale University Press, © 1983.

Joseph Straus, "Two Post-tonal Analyses" from *Introduction to Post-Tonal Theory,* 2nd Edition, Prentice Hall, 2000, pp. 20–29. Permission granted by the author.

David B. Lewin, "Figaro's Mistakes" was first published in *Current Musicology #*57 (© 1995). Permission to reprint has been kindly granted by *Current Musicology.*

Music

Sarah McLachlan, "Ice." Words and Music by Sarah McLachlan

Copyright © 1993 Sony/ATV Songs LLC and Tyde Music

All Rights Administered by Song/ATV Music Publishing, 8 Music Square West, Nashville, TN 37203

International Copyright Secured

All Rights Reserved

Barbara Kolb, *Millefoglie*

© Copyright 1985 by Boosey & Hawkes, Inc.

Reprinted by permission.

INDEX

Acceleration, 127, 182, 196, 199, 206–08, 229, 264, 294, 327

Aeneid, 152, 153

Aeolian, 142, 146

Aggregate. *See* Total chromatic

Agogic accent, 83, 87, 327

Aldwell, Edward, 30

Ambiguity, 77–87, 89–90, 149, 151, 169, 171

  Ambiguity Principle, 78n

  formal ambiguity, 90

  metric ambiguity, 83–87, 169–174

  modal ambiguity, 82–83

  musical ambiguity, 77–87

  tonal ambiguity, 78–80, 90, 92, 113, 115, 132

Ametrical, 327

Anacrusis, 83, 327

Anapestic meter, 124

Antecedent, 91, 207, 327

Appoggiatura, 204–206, 327

Arel, Bulent, 254

Asymmetrical meters, 327

Atonal pitch motion, 40, 81, 327

Augmentation, 132, 228

Babbitt, Milton, 36, 48, 49

Bach, Johann Sebastian, 203, 205

  D-minor Partita (Chaconne), 179

  Violin Sonata in G minor/Presto, 167–179, 293, 307–08

Background, 31–35, 120

Bailey, Robert, 132, 134

Bartky, Sandra Lee, 137

Bartok, Bela, 77–88

  "Boating" (*Mikrokosmos*), 80–87

Bassbrechung, 32

Basso ostinato. See Ground bass

Beaumarchais, 101

Beethoven, Ludwig van, 226–35

  "Tempest" Sonata, op. 31/2, 226–35, 273, 320–26

Bellini, Vincenzo, 168

Benjamin, Jessica, 138

Bent, Ian, 56

Bimodal, 83, 86, 87, 328

Binary, 177, 179

Blues, 67, 73, 136

  Blues pentatonic scale, 53

  Blues scale, 53–54, 60

Boulez, Pierre, 253

Brahms, Johannes, 89–90

  Intermezzo, op. 76, no. 4, 34

  Intermezzo, op. 76, no. 2, 78–79, 81

  Intermezzo, op. 116, no. 4, 90–96, 273, 279–81

Bridge, 69, 70, 71, 74, 75, 141, 146, 207, 212, 328

Burkhart, Charles, 3–12, 13

Burns, Lori, 136–48

Busch, Adolf, 179

Cadwallader, Allen, 30

Carter, Elliott, 36

Chopin, Frederick, 236–52

  Mazurka in A-flat Major, op. 59/2, 3–12, 273, 274–77

  Prelude in C-sharp minor, op. 45, 236–52

Chorus, 67, 69, 71–3, 138, 140, 145, 146, 147, 328

Clarke, Eric, 138

Claudius, Mathias, 115

Closure, 19, 28, 32, 53–4, 61, 68, 86, 87, 142, 162, 182, 191, 192, 194, 198–99, 213, 328

Coda, 11, 12, 55, 61–62, 92, 102, 107, 109, 111, 120, 157, 162, 182, 189, 208–09, 211–12, 214, 328

Codetta, 104, 188, 208–09, 211, 213–14, 242, 244, 250–52, 328

Cohn, Richard, 13

Collin, Matthäus von, 118

Computer-generated tape, 253–72

Cone, Edward T., 13, 18, 63, 177–78

Consequent, 92, 207, 212–13, 328

Contour, 83, 87, 93, 173, 175, 220, 223, 224, 328

Contrapuntal texture, 256

Corea, Chick, 50–64

Covach, John, 65–76

Cycle of thirds, 246–47, 251, 252, 328

Da Ponte, Lorenzo, 101
Dénouement, 86, 96, 328
Der Freie Satz, 30
Development, 186, 193, 201, 211, 213, 227, 230, 232, 235, 328
Dichterliebe, 78
Donizetti, Gaetano, 168
Dorian mode, 73, 82, 87, 328
Double-tonic complex, 132
Dunsby, Jonathan, 89–90, 96
Dyad, 45, 48, 328

Elision, 10, 11n, 41, 124, 136, 157, 161, 162, 186, 328
Epstein, David, 89
Equivalence, 11, 53, 216
    durational equivalence, 15, 17, 18, 20
    enharmonic equivalence, 12, 120, 121, 127, 134, 242, 246n, 247, 251, 329
    interval equivalence, 220
Expansion, 5, 10–12, 20, 21, 27–29, 91–3, 95, 106, 329
Exposition, 182, 188–89, 193–196, 210–12, 228, 230–31, 234, 329
Extension, 5–12, 90–92, 103, 106, 227, 329

Feminism, 137–38, 148
Foreground, 31–35, 118, 120
Forte, Allen, 30–35
Fragmentation, 87, 329
Freud, Sigmund, 52, 99
    Interpretation of Dreams, 52
Fundamental line, 31–35
Fundamental structure, 31–35

Gagne, David, 30
Graybill, Roger, 191–201
Ground bass (*basso ostinato*), 154, 157–58, 161–63, 224
Grouping, 8, 14, 15, 83–4, 198, 329
Guck, Marion, 180–90

Harmonic rhythm, 27, 206, 329
Haydn, Joseph, 180–89
    Sonata no. 46 in A-flat, *Adagio,* 180–189, 273, 309–11
Head motive, 154, 329
Heifetz, Jascha, 78
Heine, Heinrich, 78
Hexachord, 44–45, 329
Hierarchy, 4
    metric hierarchy, 168–71
Homophonic, 256

Hypermeter, 13–29, 329
    hyperbeat, 18, 329
    hypermeasure, 10n, 18, 19, 329
    hypermetric irregularity, 20–29

Interpolation, 93–95, 117
Interruption, 32, 35
Interval class, 49, 216, 221–22
Intervallic cell, 196–198, 329
Introduction, 55, 57, 59, 69–71, 74, 240, 244, 248, 251
Inversion, 41, 47–8, 120, 228, 329
IRCAM, 254

Joachim, Joseph, 179
Jonas, Oswald, 111

Keller, Hans, 51, 52, 55, 60, 61
Koch, Heinrich Christoph, 204, 207
    Musikalisches Lexikon, 204
Kolb, Barbara, 253–72
    Millefoglie, 253–72
Kramer, Lawrence, 132, 133
Kremer, Gidon, 178
Krebs, Harald, 3, 13–29

Lang, Josephine, 13–29
    "Mignons Klage", 5–21, 26, 28
    "Nur den Abschied schnell genommen", 21–28
Lansky, Paul, 254
Leitmotif, 124
Lester, Joel, 167–79
Lewin, David B., v, 39, 99–109
Linear progression, 144–47
Lochhead, Judith, 253–72
Lowinsky, Edward, 208

Major-third–cycle. *See* Cycle of thirds.
Marvin, William, xi–xiv
Mattheson, Johann, 176
    Der vollkommene Capellmeister, 176
McCreless, Patrick, 122–35
McLachlan, Sarah, 136–48
    "Ice", 136–48, 273, 303–06
Mead, Andrew, 36–49
Menuhin, Yehudi, 178
Messaien, Olivier, 30
Microtonal inflection, 54, 329
Middleground, 31–35
Mixolydian, 82, 330
Monophonic texture, 256
Monteverdi, 155

Motto, 86, 87, 192, 194–200, 330
Mozart, Wolfgang Amadeus, 202–14
    Don Giovanni, 109
    La clemenza di Tito, 205
    Marriage of Figaro, 99–109, 273, 282–86
    Piano Sonata in B-flat, K. 333, 8n
    Rondo in D Major, K. 485, 202–214, 273, 312–19

Octatonic, 82, 330
Onomatopoetic, 113
Ordered pitch class, 216–218
Ordered pitch class intervals, 220–21, 223
Ordered pitch intervals, 216, 218, 220–21
Oster, Ernst, 111
Ostinato, 82–83, 86–87, 223, 330

Paganini, Niccolo, 167–169
Passacaglia, 223
Pentatonic, 53, 60, 82, 83, 86, 87, 330
Period, 330
    double period, 91
Perpetual motion, 167–169, 179
Phenomenal accent, 83, 330
Phrase rhythm, 3–12
Phrygian cadence, 154
Pitch center, 82, 83, 192–95
Pitch class, 39, 41–2, 44, 45, 196, 215–25, 330
Pitch-class intervals, 216
Pitch-class set, 330
Pitch intervals, 216
Poetic meter, 124
Polymeter, 86, 330
Polyphonic melody, 34
Prolongation, 11, 20, 32–35, 67, 92, 146
Purcell, Henry, 149–63
    Dido and Aeneas, 149–63

Rahn, John, 49
Rameau, Jean-Philippe, 174, 203
    Treatise on Harmony, 175
Reaching over, 161, 162
Recapitulation, 162, 187–189, 193–96, 210–13, 227, 231, 234
Recitative, 116
Refrain, 70, 124, 126, 129, 204, 207–08, 212, 331
Reinterpretation, 331
Reprise, 10, 70, 71, 87, 92, 177, 230, 241, 247, 250, 251, 331
Reti, Rudolph, 93
Retransition, 10, 87, 210–12, 233, 241, 249–50
Retrograde (also retrogression), 47, 48, 331
Rhetoric, 92, 96, 149, 176, 177, 331
Rhythm and blues, 66

Rondo, 202–214
Rounded binary form, 242, 331
Rothstein, William, 3, 13, 19, 26, 202–214
Rubato, 7, 40, 179, 331
Rückert, Friedrich, 113

Salis-Seewis, Johann, 111
Sarasatae, Pablo de, 179
Satyendra, Ramon, 50–64
Schachter, Carl, 3, 13, 110–21
Schenker, Heinrich, 3, 6, 9, 30–35
    Schenkerian analysis, 6, 30–35, 109, 141–42n, 331
Schmalfeldt, Janet, 149–163
Schoenberg, Arnold, 30, 36, 40, 45–47, 52, 222–25
    "Nacht," (*Pierrot Lunaire,* op. 21), 222–25
    Piano Piece, op. 19/2, 40
    String Quartet No. 4, 45–47
Schröder, Jaap, 178
Schubert, Franz, 110–121
    "Dass sie hier gewesen", 111, 113–15, 273, 289–90
    "Der Jüngling an der Quelle", 111–13, 273, 287–88
    "Der Tod und das Mädchen", 111, 115–18, 273, 291–92
    "Nacht und Träume", 111, 118–21, 273, 293–94
Schumann, Robert, 13
    "Aus meinen Tränen spriessen" *(Dichterliebe),* 30–35, 273, 278
    "Im wunderschönen Monat Mai" *(Dichterliebe),* 78–80
Sentence, 206, 331
Shakespeare, William, 226, 234
Shostakovitch, Dmitri, 191–200
    String Quartet No. 8, 191–200
Smith, Charles J., 236–252
Sonata form, 32, 182, 187, 193–96, 204–214, 332
Sprechstimme, 223
"Starlight", 50–64
Stein, Deborah, 77–88
Straus, Joseph, 49, 215–225
Stravinsky, Igor, 30
Strophic, 332
Structural levels, 31–35
Stufen, 33
Subset, 197–98
Symmetry, 258
Syncopation, 130, 131, 143, 170, 171, 189, 217, 332
Syntax, 332
Szigeti, Joseph, 178–79

Tate, Nahum, 149–63
Tetrachord, 86, 87, 157–58, 162, 332
Textural analysis, 253–71

Third relations, 128
Timbral analysis, 253–71
Tin Pan Alley, 69–71
Total chromatic (aggregate), 40, 44, 47, 48, 327
Tovey, Donald F., 207
Transition, 91, 188, 195, 198, 232–33, 332
Transposition, 41, 47, 48, 53, 157, 175, 187,
    195–97, 223, 225, 228, 230–31, 234, 240–41,
    332
Trichord, 37, 40, 83, 87, 196, 332
Tritone substitution, 55, 332
Trochaic meter, 124
Twelve-bar blues, 66–69
Twelve-tone music, 36–49

Unordered pitch class intervals, 216, 220, 224
Unordered pitch intervals, 216, 219, 220

Urlinie, 32, 109
Ursatz, 32, 109

Verse, 67, 69–73, 140, 146, 332
Verse-chorus, 71–75, 138
Virgil, 150–53, 163
Voice exchange, 117, 154, 161

Wagner, Richard, 122–35
    Isolde's Transfiguration, 122–35, 273, 295–302
    Tristan und Isolde, 122–35
Webern, Anton, 30, 37–40, 48
    Variations for Piano, op. 27, 37–40
    "Wie bin ich froh!" (Three Songs, op. 25),
Wedge, 129, 130
Wholetone, 82, 332